Praise for *In Sam We Trust*

"A page turner that demystifies the nearly folk-hero status of Walton."
USA Today

"Every person who wants to get anywhere in the retail field should read it."
Red Slater, in the St. Joseph News-Press (St. Joseph, Missouri)

"Lands some real blows. Wal-Mart's attempts to cover up the fact that it was importing clothes made in third-world sweatshops in the midst of a 'Buy American' campaign shows the group could play as dirty as anyone when its image is under threat."
The Economist

"It's fun when a talented reporter tries to cut someone he doesn't care for down to size, and that's exactly what Bob Ortega does here ... Ortega does an excellent job of providing a context for Wal-Mart's remarkable rise."
Publishers Weekly

"Ortega provides a vivid analysis ... Here is well-researched, high-end business reportage, readable and informative."
Kirkus Reviews

"Ortega has written an insightful, judicious and immensely illuminating book, one of the best on retailing I have ever read."
Worth

"If the managers at Wal-Mart have learned anything from Sam, they won't angrily ignore Ortega's critical book. Instead, they'll be pouring over the Kmart chapters for an inside look at how arrogance can kill a giant."
Business Week

"Ortega ... describes the company as 'an implacable, driven and manipulative business that uses cut-throat tactics while operating behind a disarmingly folksy façade.' Strong words, strong case, strong author, strong book."
American City Business Journals

"A hard-hitting, thoroughly researched look inside a huge corporation and a social history of discount retailing in America ...
"Ortega keeps the story skimming along, spinning lively anecdotes ... he lets his stories envelop us, gracefully allowing their meaning to emerge.
"The rhythm and verve of Ortega's storytelling so sweeps us up that only after we have turned the last page do we reflect on how many tough tangles and contradictions he's led us to consider."
The Princeton Alumni Weekly

"Provocative title, eh? You'll find the book just as provocative. Ortega ... has managed that impressive journalistic feat, the pretty-damned-close-to-objective piece of investigative journalism. Incredibly well researched."
The Sunday Camera (Boulder, Colorado)

"This is a doggedly researched and coolly told tale of how Walton became one of the most influential retail geniuses of the 20th century.
"Ortega poses this beguiling question: Why did avowedly moral, religious men at the top of the Wal-Mart empire close their eyes to the costs in human terms of delivering inexpensive goods to consumers?"
St. Louis Post-Dispatch

"Makes for great reading ... *In Sam We Trust* gives you a look into the darker side of the retail empire that Walton built."
The Labor Beacon

"Almost like a guide to how to do business in very clever, shrewd ways, but also how to cut corners and do some things that are not quite so ethical."
Daniel Zwerdling, All Things Considered, National Public Radio

"Ortega keeps the issues and story line fresh through crisp writing and well-organized chapters that each read like short stories in themselves.
"For the student of marketing and retail, the book holds several textbook cases of how Walton unrelentingly built his retailing empire under the guise of 'Made in America' rhetoric and family values.
"Ortega's book ... brims with juicy titbits, at the same time bringing to light many heroes and may small hands making big money."
Denver Rocky Mountain News

"Ortega ... tells Wal-Mart's inside story in this thoroughly researched book. And the story he tells, informed by a clear, sharply delineated point of view, is a darker one than the discount merchant would like to have told.

"Ortega places on Sam Walton's shoulders a sweeping responsibility for helping to transmogrify American consumer culture ...

"In the end, this book isn't only a piece of incisive journalism. For better or worse, it's a call to action."
Milwaukee Journal Sentinel (Wisconsin)

"*In Sam We Trust* is an important work about a man who changed the face of retailing, for better and worse ... investigative journalist Bob Ortega exposes the underside of Wal-Mart and defrocks Sam Walton, the founder of the retailing mammoth."
Dan Ring, Amazon.com

"A fine business history."
The Baltimore Sun

"He proves it's possible to write a bona fide page-turner about the department-store business ...extensively researched, well rounded.

"Ortega builds a strong case for ... ceasing to buy blindly into the myth of low prices at whatever the cost. Walton left a legacy of thousands of domestic jobs lost offshore, the destruction of numerous downtown business districts, overconsumption of natural resources, accelerated and uncontrolled sprawl, nonunion retail jobs with benefits and wages so skimpy some Wal-Mart workers qualify for welfare, and overseas and domestic sweatshops, including those using child laborers."
Anchorage Daily News

"Ortega's extensive research and journalistic narrative makes this comprehensive study of how Walton built an empire by selling at the cheapest price. A fascinating read."
The Star-Ledger (Newark, New Jersey)

"A well-rounded story that provides a multidimensional characterization of the one-time dime-store retailer whose success made him the richest man in America ...

"Ortega skillfully sets Walton's legend against some of his business practices that could detract from the carefully crafted image of a homespun, grandfatherly-style retailer. Pulls no punches."
Fort Worth Star Telegram (Texas)

"Reveals a different side of the Wal-Mart phenomenon ... Ortega documents how Sam Walton – perhaps the most driven corporate executive ever to walk the face of the planet – built his empire. Walton used Asian child labor to make blouses for sale under 'Made in America' signs in his Wal-Mart stores. When he began his operation ... he hired a union-busting lawyer to keep workers from organizing.

"Ortega documents how communities around the country have revolted against Wal-Mart's plans to create giant superstores in their communities, ripping apart the fabric of small-town life."
San Francisco Bay Guardian

"Every once in a while, someone recognizes that good reporters are full of good stories and advances enough money to give tem the time to tell them. That's what this book is all about: a very good reporter's pursuit of a change in the way America shops. If it were only about the departed Sam Walton, that would surely be enough, because he was a most interesting man. But Ortega has constructed the Wal-Mart story on a solid foundation built of an understanding of American culture, American business, and the nation's perpetual lust to fill its life with an abundant collection of things at decent prices."
Across the Board

"It should be read by anyone concerned with the future of our small towns and cities because that great sucking sound you hear may be the Big Box on the edge of town draining the last ounce of blood from the remaining downtown merchants."
The Register-Herald

"Students of retailing history, labor-management strife, empire-builders' psyches and political activism will find food for thought in this book ... Ortega argues convincingly that there were two Sam Waltons: the 'aw-shucks' entrepreneur who built a multi-billion-dollar empire with pathbreaking ideas and hard work; and the ruthless, union-busting destroyer of small-town commercial life who promoted a myth of caring for his customers and employees."
Upside

"This engagingly written American success story ... contains stories of Third World child and prison labor making products for Wal-Mart, as well as union busting and strong-arm tactics used to muscle into small-town commerce. Bob Ortega graphically shows how Wal-Mart's single-minded pursuit of profit has shaped life around the world in ways that might make anyone who buys Milton Friedman squeamish."
The News & Observer (Raleigh, North Carolina)

"Know thine enemy, goes the saying, and we become very familiar indeed with this company, thanks to Ortega's insightful reporting. He all but gives us the opposing team's play book, and whether you think Wal-Mart is the best thing since sliced bread or the worst thing since Robert Moses, you'll find this book an irresistible read."
Coffee Cup Publishing

In SAM we TRUST

the untold story of
SAM WALTON
and how
WAL-MART
is DEVOURING THE WORLD

BOB ORTEGA

KOGAN
PAGE

First published in the USA by Times Books, a division of Random House, Inc., New York, and simultaneously in Canada by Random House of Canada Limited, Toronto in 1998

This UK edition published by Kogan Page in 1999

Kogan Page Limited
120 Pentonville Road
London N1 9JN

British Library Cataloguing in Publication Data

A CIP record for this book is available from the British Library.

ISBN 0 7494 3177 6

Printed and bound in Great Britain by Biddles Ltd, Guildford and King's Lynn

For Dalyn

Contents

Preface to the 1999 Paperback: Cents and Sensibility

In June, 1999, to general adulation, Wal-Mart announced that it was bringing its brand of discounting to Britain. Rarely has a Trojan horse been greeted so eagerly. But then, it's easy to understand why many Britons would be keen with anticipation.

Starting in the fall of 1998, the rumor had bubbled up again and again for months that Wal-Mart was about to dive into the United Kingdom. Pick a source, pick a day, and it was circling Asda, or Sainsbury, or Safeway, or some other retail chain to snatch up.

As with most rumors, the kernel of truth in this one was surrounded by a fat dollop of wishful thinking. The very idea of this giant, aggressive cost-cutter charging into the British market sent the media into a tizzy. Everyone knew that British retailers saw their customers as a bunch of mugs to be overcharged at will. After all, didn't nearly everything cost less on the Continent? Indeed, Tony Blair's consumer affairs minister, Kim Howells, would tell Parliament that car makers had dubbed the U.K. "Treasure Island", because prices and profit margins were so piratical. And it was the same for most other goods. Even as the government's consumer-watchdog Competition Commission moved to wrap up one investigation of alleged price-gouging by the auto industry, it was launching another one focusing on supermarkets. This, after a 1998 report commissioned by Britain's Office of Fair Trading said supermarket margins in the U.K. were triple those in the U.S. and the Continent.

As for Wal-Mart, the average Briton might not know much about the world's largest retailer, but what could be better than a hungry and powerful new rival slashing prices and forcing every other merchant to do the same? The prime minister himself hinted as much in April, 1999, when he eagerly confirmed that a few weeks earlier he had met privately at Downing Street with a Wal-Mart delegation led by Bob Martin, the head of the company's international division. To be sure, a Blair spokesman denied pro forma that the men discussed any concrete business—claiming, rather, that they had merely exchanged views on the economic situation. But Blair had repeatedly said before this how keenly he wanted to see lower prices in British shops, and the very fact of the meeting spoke volumes about his zeal to bring in a discounting Savonarola that could light a fire under existing retailers.

It also stoked media speculation: Would Wal-Mart swoop down and tear apart the proposed acquisition of Asda by the Kingfisher retail chain? Had Blair promised to loosen planning policies so Wal-Mart could build stores far larger than anything yet seen in the U.K.? Was Wal-Mart trying to steal a march on other foreign retailers eyeing the British market, such as France's Carrefour or the Dutch supermarket chain Ahold?

Within days, the giant discounter categorically denied it had any plans to invade the U.K. Speaking at a retail conference in London, senior vice president and treasurer Jay Fitzsimmons offered various well-reasoned explanations of why such a move would make no sense. British retailers' profit margins and prices already were coming under pressure, he said. Why pay a premium to buy into a retailing market that could expect shrinking profit margins for the foreseeable future? There were better opportunities elsewhere. Besides, land was expensive, and the U.K.'s strict planning laws would make it tough for Wal-Mart to follow its usual model of building huge stores on the edges of towns and suburbs. The biggest store yet built in the British isles occupied barely 90,000 square-feet, less than half the size Wal-Mart preferred for its new supercenters. Then, too, he noted, Wal-Mart didn't like getting into competitive bidding situations.

All these points were quite reasonable. But anybody who believed Fitzsimmons's denial wasn't paying close enough attention.

Just after 7 a.m. on June 14, Sir Geoffrey Mulcahy, Kingfisher's Chief Executive, got an unexpected phone call at his office from his counterpart at Asda, Allan Leighton. Mulcahy greeted him pleasantly. A few days earlier, the two men had jointly made the latest of several presentations to big investors on how the proposed merger of their companies would work—presentations that all agreed had gone rather well.

But now Leighton apologetically said he had a bit of a problem. In a few minutes, he told Mulcahy, Asda would announce that it was rejecting Kingfisher's bid to acquire Asda for £5.6 billion in stock, in favor of Wal-Mart's offer of £6.7 billion in cash.

Mulcahy was stunned. They'd already shaken hands with him on his offer. That should mean something, though obviously it didn't. But what could he do? He wasn't about to get involved in a bidding war with a far larger and wealthier company. Within hours after Wal-Mart and Asda astonished the City with their announcement, Kingfisher tersely said it wouldn't make a counter-offer. Even as the news sent shares of Sainsbury, Kingfisher, Boots and other retailers tumbling, commentators rhapsodized about the Wal-Mart deal. *The Times* of London captured the general sentiment, crowing that shoppers could soon celebrate the end of what it called "Rip-off Britain".

It's understandable that Mulcahy felt pole-axed. Leighton and the other Asda executives had taken enormous pains to keep secret their efforts to woo Wal-Mart even as they met with their Kingfisher counterparts.

But then, Leighton and Asda's chairman, Archie Norman, had long been enamoured of Wal-Mart, which they had used as Asda's model from early on. Most fundamentally, they'd decided to imitate Wal-Mart's obsessive focus on beating rivals' prices. They had also aped Wal-Mart's policy of "Every Day Low Prices," eschewing having frequent sales; Wal-Mart's practice of parking "people greeters" at store entrances (both to welcome shoppers and to discourage shoplifters); and had gone Wal-Mart one better on its groundbreaking employee stock-ownership plan by adopting one of the U.K.'s widest-ranging options schemes, granting share options to all workers who stayed a year or more and put in more than 15 hours a week.

Since Norman's first friendly visit to Wal-Mart's Bentonville, Arkansas headquarters in 1994, he and Leighton had sent a steady runnel of Asda managers there to meet with and learn from their opposite numbers. Top executives at the two companies had kept in regular contact. In 1998, a few months after Wal-Mart made its first move into Europe by acquiring the 21-store Wertkauf hypermart chain in Germany, a group of Wal-Mart executives met with Norman, Leighton and Asda finance director Phil Cox in London. The Asda men all but wore 'For Sale' signs to the meeting. But the Wal-Mart camp was divided, with some Wal-Mart executives arguing against buying Asda, or going into the U.K. at all, insisting that there were riper fruit to pluck on the Continent; and David Glass, Wal-Mart's taciturn chief executive, was frustratingly noncommittal.

Asda might have been a rather plain girl trying to attract the attention of a far too popular boy. Bat her eyes as she might, she seemed to be getting nowhere.

And, indeed, all through 1998, like shoppers scouring a flea market for the biggest bargain, Bob Martin and his minions hopped around the Continent, from Scandinavia to France, perusing the prospects. But, in effect, Wal-Mart soon got swept up in the very shock-wave that caused its own arrival.

That December, Wal-Mart added Germany's 74-store Interspar hyper-mart chain to its cart, lopped prices on thousands of goods, and panicked rival retailers throughout Europe. With stock analysts and store owners alike predicting that retail chains would have to merge and get bigger to survive, a wave of consolidation began that soon spread beyond Germany's borders.

In Great Britain, Kingfisher's Mulcahy sounded out Norman and Leighton at Asda. Before Mulcahy led a buyout and renamed the company in 1982, Kingfisher had been owned by the U.S. retail chain Woolworth. Under Mulcahy, Kingfisher had become a conglomerate, owning the U.K. Woolworth stores; the Superdrug, Comet (consumer electronics), and B&Q (do-it-yourself) chains, and two chains in France. But Mulcahy, too, was well aware of and keenly interested in Wal-Mart's way of business. By combining Asda's expertise in discount-food operations with Kingfisher's strength in general merchandising, Mulcahy told the Asda men, they could launch their own Wal-Mart-like supercenter operations in Britain and beyond. A year earlier, talks between Asda and Kingfisher had gone nowhere. But now, seemingly spurned by Wal-Mart, Norman and Leighton were receptive.

In April, 1999, the two companies announced their proposed merger. It was immediately pegged in the British press as a pre-emptive defensive move against Wal-Mart.

But the move had another effect. As Wal-Mart's senior vice chairman, Don Soderquist, later conceded, the Kingfisher offer convinced Wal-Mart's leaders to reconsider their own coy attitude towards Asda. Almost as soon as the offer was announced, Geoffrey Cohen, a New York-based retail analyst for the investment banking firm Wasserstein Perella, started lobbying Wal-Mart to make a counter-offer. He didn't have to lobby hard. Within a few weeks, after one more internal debate, Glass agreed they should jump in with a cash bid.

As surprising as this abrupt reversal might seem, there were several good reasons to move quickly. After all, Britain offered a reasonably large and healthy market, and one where language was no barrier. And if Wal-Mart were to go into the U.K. at all, where could they find a more suitable partner than Asda, its most fervent acolyte?

When Wasserstein Perella's London office called Asda to gauge its interest, Norman and Leighton were keen, but apprehensive. How serious was Wal-Mart? What if word leaked to Kingfisher or the press? Norman had Leighton call his counterparts at Wal-Mart to sound them out directly. It quickly became obvious Wal-Mart was very serious, and both sides agreed to meet in person. Glass zipped a team on a company jet to Leeds, Asda's base, taking time there to visit not only Asda stores but those of rivals such as Sainsbury and Tesco.

Fitzsimmons, who just weeks earlier had so emphatically denied that Wal-Mart had any intention of investing in the U.K., was dispatched to London, both to discuss Wal-Mart's bid with Wasserstein Perella, its financial advisors, and to have them check whether his earlier comments posed any legal problems. They didn't.

Meanwhile, Asda's Leighton, between talks with Wal-Mart and Wasserstein Perella, continued making his joint presentations to investors with Mulcahy, keeping up the pretense of commitment to the Kingfisher merger. Once the terms with Wal-Mart were agreed on after a marathon weekend negotiating session, the American company's habitually secretive leaders insisted that Mulcahy not be told anything until minutes before the general public announcement.

For Asda, it was a tremendous deal. Wal-Mart agreed, at least for the time being, to keep the Asda name, and to keep Asda's management in place. Asda shareholders—including many employees—would get a windfall. Norman himself, because of the shares he held, would gain about £4.6 million, with Leighton raking in about £3.3 million.

The more important question, of course, was what Wal-Mart's invasion of Great Britain would mean for everybody else.

To start with the obvious, would it drive down prices? That one was easy. Yes—though perhaps not as dramatically or as quickly as Blair and many others might hope. Even Don Soderquist, Wal-Mart's zealously affable senior vice chairman, told *The Times* that price cuts "will be evolutionary rather than revolutionary."[1] Wal-Mart almost certainly would take as much advantage as possible of the porcine profit margins in Britain: It could use its buying clout

---

[1] Sarah Cunningham and Fraser Nelson, "Wal-Mart beats Kingfisher with £6.7bn bid for Asda," *The Times* of London, June 15, 1999, p. 39.

and operating efficiencies to cut Asda's costs; but instead of passing along all
the savings to shoppers, it would likely drop prices just enough to gain an edge
on rivals. That's what Wal-Mart did in Canada, for example. Average retail
profit margins there hovered at about 34 percent when Wal-Mart arrived. It
clipped prices enough to take a 32 percent margin, rather than slashing to get
to the 27.5 percent margins it aimed for in the U.S.[2]

But the spread of Wal-Mart and its way of doing business would have
other, less obvious impacts, from making life more difficult for high street
merchants, to potentially driving down wage scales and benefits across an
entire industry, to perhaps changing the very shape of British towns and
suburbs—and not for the better.

At the time of this writing, the Asda deal was still pending, though it
seemed all but certain to be completed. But even if that acquisition were
unexpectedly to fall through, Wal-Mart already had set in motion changes
likely to have a profound impact across the entire U.K., as other retailers
scrambled to remold themselves in Wal-Mart's image. Perhaps the easiest
way to see what to expect is to look at what changes Wal-Mart has wrought
elsewhere, for good and for ill.

Retail analysts are fond of noting Wal-Mart's aggressive use of the
very latest computer and satellite technology to constantly improve the
way it tracks shipments and sales of its goods. The company's expertise
with such systems lets it get goods on its shelves more quickly and
cheaply than any rival—and has pushed retailers on four continents to
improve their own use of technology so they can operate efficiently
enough to stay competitive.

This is all to the good, from a price standpoint.

Then there's customer service. Take Germany, where not long past
customer service was, well, let's say service isn't quite the word we're looking for. Even before Wal-Mart's arrival, increasing retail competition and
the presence of service-oriented chains such as Marks & Spencer were
putting pressure on German retailers to improve. Still, it was widely predicted that Germans would be put off by Wal-Mart's glad-handing
approach to customer service, which goes so far as to requite every worker
to greet any customer who comes within ten feet of them, and to offer help
without waiting to be asked. And, in fact, Wal-Mart belayed its 10-foot rule
in Germany, at least initially. But still, it turned out that—once they got
over the initial shock—Germans liked Wal-Mart's relentlessly friendly

---

[2] The figures come from an analysis by Stephen Arnold, a retailing professor at Queen's University, as
reported in the *Sunday Times*.

service. Now, as has happened elsewhere, rivals are rushing to get their clerks to be friendlier and more helpful, too.

But Wal-Mart's success with less appetizing strategies has driven other retailers to emulate it in those areas, as well.

As you'll see in the chapters that follow, in the United States, over more than three decades, Wal-Mart has been a prime mover in making the norm retail practices that rely on and encourage suburban sprawl. That's one reason why scores of communities across North America have fought tooth and nail to keep Wal-Mart out: They see it as the harbinger of a pattern of exclusively automobile-based development that ultimately depersonalizes neighborhoods and erodes a sense of community.

Wal-Mart has led the way in eliminating factory jobs in the U.S., mercilessly pushing its suppliers to cut costs by moving their production of apparel, toys and other goods to the developing world, where wages are lower, labor laws are weaker, and sweatshops and child labor are the rule rather than the exception. As recently as August, 1999, the New York-based National Labor Committee, a human-rights watchdog group, reported that a Wal-Mart contractor in Bangladesh was paying teenage seamstresses less than half that country's legal minimum wage, and illegally forcing them to work overtime, with 80-hour, seven-day work weeks. (Wal-Mart executives wouldn't respond to the charges.)

Implacably anti-union, Wal-Mart has helped transform the American workplace, in retailing and beyond, by showing how profitable it can be to rely heavily on part-time and temporary workers who don't have to be paid benefits. Many Wal-Mart workers are poor enough to qualify for public assistance; as the *Wall Street Journal* noted: in early 1999, 38 percent weren't covered by the company's health-insurance plan. In effect, for such workers, taxpayers subsidize Wal-Mart's low wages, which in the spring of 1999 often started at under $6 an hour, and averaged $7.50 an hour, 14 percent below the retail industry's average wage of $8.71 an hour.

Wal-Mart has kept unions out of its U.S. stores by tactics that—as later chapters discuss—are sometimes illegal. When it moved into Canada by buying the Woolco chain, the company rejected the few of the chain's stores that had any unions in them; and when workers at one Canadian Wal-Mart store subsequently organized, the company mounted an intimidation campaign that was only halted under court order.

To be sure, one could argue that British laws and regulations should rein in any company's excesses; but, in fact, labor laws in the U.K. have been as thoroughly emasculated as those in the U.S., offering unionists or the average worker little protection from unfair employers.

And while British land-use planning regulations are far tougher, laws can always be changed; in contrast to Ireland and Norway, which have recently tightened restrictions on the size of supercenter and mall developments, the Blair Government has already hinted at its willingness to accommodate the needs of this Brobdingnagian investor.[3]

Even before its acquisition by Wal-Mart, Asda was moving to open larger supercenter-style stores; but you could tuck five average Asda stores (at 42,000 square-feet each) inside a single Wal-Mart supercenter.[4] The Blair Government "may well decide that the most effective way to lower the nation's grocery bill is to ease up on planning restrictions and allow some of these megastores to be built," said Clive Vaughan, of the London-based consulting group Retail Intelligence. Any other large retailer could take advantage of looser laws, too, of course, though with Wal-Mart's muscle and money, Asda is likely to snap up the prime sites fastest, he noted. But any loosening also would further speed a tendency toward a shrinking number of ever-larger chains controlling the retail market.

Then too, Wal-Mart's executives have demonstrated an often breathtaking contempt for laws and regulations. In the U.S., courts again and again have found the company to have lied, to have illegally falsified, destroyed and withheld documents, to have committed civil fraud, to have willfully sold counterfeit goods, to have deliberately discriminated against disabled job applicants, to have illegally fired workers for interracial dating, to have discriminated against black and Mexican employees in other ways, to have allowed managers to sexually harass women workers—and to have fired women who had the temerity to complain.

In April, 1999, an exasperated judge in Texas slapped Wal-Mart with an $18 million fine for hiding evidence against them in one case—making it 15 times in three years Wal-Mart had been found to have done so; in August, Wal-Mart agreed to pay $6.4 million to settle a case in which company executives twice flatly ignored court orders to stop selling fake Tommy Hilfiger brand clothing.

These aren't isolated cases, but recurring instances showing a pattern of corporate behavior that essentially amounts to obeying the law only when it

[3] Blair's planning minister, Richard Caborn, told the Commons a few weeks after the Asda deal that Blair had made Wal-Mart no assurances, and that Wal-Mart, Asda and other developers would have to demonstrate that there was "need" for any plans involving out-of-town superstores, according to *The Times*. Just how Blair's government planners intended to define "need" remains to be explained.
[4] Before its acquisition by Wal-Mart, Asda had received approval to build its first "Asda Supercenter" outside Havant, Hampshire, a store that would be over 100,000 square-feet, roughly the size of a football pitch.

doesn't get in the way of the bottom line. Corporate critics may say such an attitude is depressingly frequent these days, but rarely is it found to this degree. A judge in one case in Alabama asked, "What do they teach in Arkansas? Is there something in the drinking water in Arkansas that says perjury is all right?" Another judge, in a Texas sexual harassment case, said of Wal-Mart, "rarely has this court seen such a pattern of deliberate obfuscation, delay, misrepresentation and downright lying to another party and to a Court."[5]

Of course, you could reasonably point out that, in buying Asda, Wal-Mart is merely taking over the number-three supermarket chain—one that is far from dominating the grocery industry, let alone the broader retail market. So what is the big deal?

Keep in mind that Wal-Mart started small in Canada and Mexico, too, and that despite stumbling early on, in less than seven years it had become the largest retailer in both countries. Germany's Wertkauf was merely the 15th largest food retailer in that nation when it was acquired by Wal-Mart at the end of 1997, with almost all of its stores in the southwest corner of the country, in the Baden-Wurttemberg region. But German retailers—quite rightly—saw this move as the camel's nose poking into the tent.

When Wal-Mart immediately cut prices on thousands of items by between 10 percent and 17 percent, reportedly selling some goods for under its own cost, other German retailers started discounting too. Wal-Mart quickly ran afoul of "unfair-competition" laws, meant to protect small shopkeepers, that bar certain discounts or customer benefits such as frequent-buyer programs; but other big chains soon began pressuring the government to abolish the laws, potentially setting up a major political battle against small shopkeepers, unions and Greens.

More importantly, Wal-Mart's entry set off a furor of consolidation, as other retailers decided that only the largest, strongest companies could survive. Within two years of Wal-Mart's entry, retailers accounting for one-fourth of the country's hypermart and discount sales had changed hands. According to a recent survey in the German grocery-industry publication Lebenmittel Zeitung, discount stores now dominate retailing in that country. By early 1999, Wal-Mart was the fourth-largest retailer in Germany, with 15 percent of the market, and was planning by the end of the year to put its own name on all its Wertkauf and Spar stores. Many German retail analysts predict that, within a few years, thousands of smaller retailers will

---

[5] Bob Van Voris, "Wal Mart Cited for Discovery Abuse," National Law Journal, May 3, 1999, p. A01.

fail, and that a handful of huge pan-European chains will dominate the industry. In other words, they expect retailing in their country and across Europe to go the way of the United States, where huge chains along the Wal-Mart model dominate every single sector of retailing.

In Great Britain, an Asda controlled by Wal-Mart can be expected to operate increasingly as Wal-Mart does, and to expand far more rapidly. Where 75 percent of Asda's offerings are food items, and 25 percent general merchandise, Wal-Mart favors a 40 percent food/60 percent general merchandise mix. As Asda moves increasingly to building larger stores at the edges of towns and suburbs, it will likely also carry a wider array of general merchandise: clothing, electronics, housewares, drugs, shoes, books, music and so on. That means Asda will compete with a broader range of retailers, big and small. And with Wal-Mart's bargaining power with suppliers, and its skill at shipping goods cheaply and efficiently from factories to stores, Asda likely will be able to cut prices without hurting its margins.

That will put pressure on rivals to cut their costs. Some may seek to become more efficient on their own; many more will eat or be eaten in a frenzy of consolidation. Many can be expected to jump at the quick fix of trying to chop labor costs, by cutting wages or benefits to their workers. And, as has happened elsewhere, many smaller companies can be expected to close their doors.

Wal-Mart may well make other acquisitions in the U.K., to ramp up quickly to a size that will give it the maximum efficiencies of scale. Steve Davies, at Retail Intelligence, predicts that Kingfisher will race to find a new merger partner, such as Tesco or Sainsbury. Other large European retailers such as France's Carrefour and the Netherlands's Ahold may buy their way into the British market too, to establish a foothold while they still can. All of these players can be expected to follow Wal-Mart's lead in seeking to build bigger stores outside of town centers.

Indeed, Wal-Mart's acquisition of Asda is but one harbinger of the changes that may be coming to retailing in Britain. Already, between 1994 and 1999, government planners allowed the number of factory-outlet malls, which follow the same model of a massive structure outside a town center surrounded by acres of parking, to increase to 25 from five. Costo, an American warehouse-club chain that came to the U.K. in 1993, had seven stores by mid-1999, but said (just after the Asda acquisition was announced) that it plans to open 40 more. Tesco, Asda and Sainsbury all have raced in recent years to open larger stores more or less on the hypermart model, as has Makro, a "cash and carry shed" chain first set up by a

Dutch firm, and bought in 1997 by Metro, a German retailer surpassed in size only by Wal-Mart.

Except where they're stymied by strong local land-use laws and aggressive preservationists, Wal-Mart and its imitators prefer to build on previously undeveloped land, sparking further low-density retail and residential development that eats up countryside. Wal-Mart, eyes firmly fixed on the bottom line, treat their buildings and employees alike as disposable. They design and construct their stores as cheaply as possible, on the assumption that any particular store may likely be replaced (that is, cast aside for a new building in a new location) within three to five years. In Bentonville, where Wal-Mart is headquartered, the landscape is littered with the carapaces of abandoned buildings that once housed Wal-Mart stores. The same is true across North America.

Ellen Dunham, an architecture professor at the Massachusetts Institute of Technology who studied the causes and effects of sprawl, said, "it is a pattern of development that consumes the environment as though it too was disposable".

With that in mind, this book describes in detail not only how Wal-Mart became what it is, but also how it works today—and what, in effect, Britons can look forward to.

As has been the case in the U.S. and elsewhere, it will be up to British consumers and activists—up to you—to decide to what extent Wal-Mart's approach to retailing will be allowed to reshape their workplaces and neighborhoods.

INTRODUCTION:
Sam's World

When he died in 1992, he had amassed what was then the greatest fortune in American history. The company he founded had grown out of one tiny variety store on the main square of a backwater town in Arkansas to become the world's largest merchant empire.

Within a few years of Sam Walton's death, his company, Wal-Mart, expanded to become bigger than the three next-largest retailers combined, with sales of more than $138 billion a year—which is to say, more than $510 a year from every man, woman, and child in the United States. Wal-Mart is one of the world's largest corporations of any kind, with more workers than General Motors, a buying network that reaches into every corner of the world and a long-range plan to more than triple in size yet again.

In the United States, it is the biggest seller of underwear, soap, toothpaste, children's clothes, and scores of other goods, and among the biggest sellers of books, videos, and compact discs. Such men as David Glass, its imperturbable chief executive, and Rob Walton, Sam's son and the company chairman, hope to make Wal-Mart, within a few years, the country's biggest grocer as well. It dominates retailing in Canada. It has invaded Mexico, Argentina, Brazil, China, Indonesia, South Korea, Germany and, now, the United Kingdom; and a host of other countries are still on the menu.

But, really, all of this is secondary.

What is more significant about Sam Walton, and the retailing juggernaut he created, lies beyond the triumphs of his company: It is the spread of his way of thinking, the way of seeing the world that Wal-Mart has come to embody. It's a way of thinking that underpins Wal-Mart's astonishing success; but more than that, it's a way that has become the norm both in retailing and across most other fields of American business, and thus of global business.

How many times have TV broadcasters and newspaper or magazine writers dubbed some fast-rising company "the Wal-Mart of" its industry? How often have hucksterish entrepreneurs declared their intent of turning their outfit into "the Wal-Mart of" whatever it may be?

Sometimes this is just hype, a convenient way of pointing out some industry's 900-pound gorilla or gorilla wannabe. But many of these "Wal-Marts of" are applying to their business, to their industry, the principles that Sam Walton made his own: Offer the lowest possible price. Be bigger. Keep your costs lower. Make any other considerations secondary. Seem pretty basic? Sure. But applied with the unswerving single-mindedness of which Walton and his acolytes were capable, these principles have taken on a power to transform business practices, to transmogrify whole communities, and to mold the average person's life, in ways both obvious and subtle.

Wal-Mart represents the pinnacle, the uppermost branch of a particular evolutionary limb of retailing. Back in the primordial swamps of merchandising, 200 years ago, there were no such things as "consumers." There were no chain stores, no advertising industry, no "satisfaction guaranteed." In the United States, one did not shop for pleasure; the very idea of coveting goods ran counter to a broad Puritanical streak in American society, and to its proclaimed values of living simply, working hard (the famous "work ethic"), being thrifty, and seeking salvation through faith.

But starting in the early nineteenth century, such notions gradually but steadily lost ground to a new ethos. When the industrial revolution reached the United States, the ability of factories to churn out goods—fabrics, ironware, watches, clothing—suddenly and drastically outstripped the demand. This cornucopia of new goods demanded new ways of selling them. In New York, Philadelphia, and Chicago, the first department stores opened their doors. Railroads and telegraph wires snaked across the country, giving storekeepers a new way to order goods and get them on the shelves faster than ever before. A whole new industry sprang up to persuade people, through advertisements with enticing pictures and clever slogans, to buy things they'd never known they needed, to turn America, in the phrase of department-store pioneer John Wanamaker, into the Land of Desire.

As advertisers stoked ever-higher the fires of this desire for material goods, the marketplace of ideas, too, was overhauled. Customers became consumers; acquisitiveness became a virtue; in a uniquely American twist, desire was democratized. Retailing and social values co-evolved. Sears Roebuck & Co.'s mail-order catalog became the bible of a new consumer culture, proselytizing the notion of happiness through buying more.

Hand in glove with this came the rise of the large corporation as the dominant form of business. Heavy industry had its Standard Oil and U.S. Steel; consumer goods had Swift in meat-packing, R.J. Reynolds in tobacco, Procter & Gamble in soap. On the selling end, one retailing mutation after another evolved, devoured its smaller rivals, and then faded before a still newer, fiercer model. Woolworth, Penney, Sears, A&P, Kroger—each had its day in the sun.

The first small discount stores—no-frills shops with all the ambiance of bus stations, but with dirt-cheap prices—began scuttling around the fringes of the retailing scene in the 1930s, like the first tiny mammals in the age of dinosaurs. In the boom years after World War II, with Americans spending as never before, they too evolved. By the 1960s, the rise of the giant discount chains began—still no frills, but now in huge stores packed with name brands. The fastest out of the blocks—Kmart, for example—built rings of stores around big cities, reacting to the spread of cookie-cutter suburbia even as their stores helped to propel it. It was in these days that a forty-four-year-old, moderately successful businessman from the boondocks had a great notion: Why not try the same discount approach in towns everybody else ignored as too small? Sam Walton knew from the decades he'd spent in the rural depths of Arkansas, Oklahoma, and Missouri that small-town folks craved all the wonderful goods promised by the consumer culture just as much as did any suburbanite. He knew there was far more business in rural small towns than most folks suspected, and a lot less competition.

NB

This was the great insight that set him on his path to fortune—though, somehow, with Walton, one had a sense that even if he'd missed that brass ring, he'd have grabbed another. He was a man who confounded his friends and competitors with the combination of his powerful driving ego and his utter humility. He never seemed seduced by his success—he delighted, in fact, in ignoring the trappings of wealth and power, in picking up some visiting corporate mogul or social lion in a trashed-out old truck, with seats that stank of wet dog. He could turn on an ingenuous, folksy charm—or he could be implacable, with eyes as piercing as steel gimlets. Even as a college boy, he had seemed destined for big things, though nobody, not even Walton himself, was quite sure what big things. Law maybe, or politics? Insurance? He began his career as a small-town shopkeeper only at his wife,

Helen's, insistence; Sam had wanted to run a department store in St. Louis. Even after he was successful enough to open his third store, he tried to become a shopping-mall developer, only giving up on that idea after taking a two-year bath in red ink.

But once he settled on discount retailing, he never took his foot off the gas. Hailed as the greatest entrepreneur of his age, Walton disclaimed having any genius or unique ability and freely admitted he borrowed ideas from anywhere he could. If he did have a genius, it was in his ability to know what he didn't know, to recognize his own shortcomings as a businessman and to assume, even after his enormous success, that he still could learn something from almost anybody. He never stopped looking for cheaper, better ways to do business. He was as likely to interrogate a store clerk as a captain of industry—and to take away something useful. He had a restless, probing curiosity that he focused very, very narrowly. Walton rarely made small talk. He was a man for whom the cliché "he was all business" might have been coined.

He was a man who unrelentingly remolded himself into a merchant first and last. Selling eventually would squeeze almost everything else out of his life. The man who had led Bible classes in college ultimately would write an autobiography with no mention of God and only the most passing reference to any kind of faith—except his faith in free enterprise and the market economy. He might sit in church every Sunday—but he worshipped six days a week (and often seven) at the altar of commerce.

He wasn't alone in doing so, of course. But in his unwavering dedication, his setting of an example through words and even more through deeds, it isn't too much to say that he was to the faith of consumerism what the Mahatma Gandhi was to nonviolence. Not for nothing do Wal-Mart employees, even today, swear to serve the customer, "So help me Sam."

Within Wal-Mart he was revered. His arrival always electrified a store, workers fluttering breathlessly to shake his hand and say hello, as flustered and thrilled as if meeting the queen of England or the pope. Workers loved "Mr. Sam's" down-home manner. They loved that he drove a rattletrap pickup truck and might show up at a store with his hunting dogs in tow. They loved his firm handshake, his friendly smile—and most of all, they loved that he looked them in the eyes and really listened to what they had to say.

He was well aware of the power of his persona, as were those around him, and he cultivated it. Never—not even after *Forbes* and other magazines touted his status as the richest man in America, inundating him with unwanted attention—did he adopt an unlisted telephone number. It was part of the catechism at Wal-Mart that the lowliest clerk could call the founder at home, and many did. Even six years after his death, Sam Walton was still listed in the Bentonville phone book. And still, Helen Walton continued to get his calls.

His enormous personal magnetism masked his many seeming contradictions, as it masked those aspects of the Wal-Mart mythology that are more hype than reality. Sam Walton could wrap Wal-Mart in the Stars and Stripes and vaunt his Buy American program even as his stores' shelves carried an ever-greater share of goods imported from Third World sweatshops. (In fact, it was only after his Buy American ad campaign was in full swing that Wal-Mart became the United States's biggest importer of Chinese goods in any industry.[*])

He could motivate his near-minimum-wage workers with promises they too could grow rich through a generous stock-ownership plan that was ahead of its time. And some workers did retire with fat nest eggs, as the company endlessly reminded those still toiling in the vines. Never mind that most low-level workers left too soon or worked too few hours to cash in big, so that not one in fifty workers amassed as much as $50,000 through Wal-Mart's stock-ownership pension plan. Never mind that from the viewpoint of the boardroom, the pension plan's best feature was that it kept 28 million more shares in firm control of company executives. Most workers *perceived* that they could cash in, so the cost of the plan paid off in spades by helping keep the unions out and the wages low.

But that was the way at Wal-Mart: Beneath the warm and fuzzy facade, everything, absolutely everything, came down to the bottom line. People chuckled at stories of how Sam Walton often bummed dimes and quarters if he had to make a phone call or buy a soda on the road, and of how he shunned first-class to fly economy. These were taken as reflections of how little importance the billionaire attached to money. But they were more a reflection of what might have been called one of Sam's unstated commandments: Don't spend a penny you don't have to.

Walton liked to pontificate about his rules for business. He would talk sincerely about sharing your profits with your "associates," as he called workers; he would talk about talking to your associates, making sure they know what's going on; he would talk about making sure to serve your customers, to give them what they expect and a little more. And he did do all these things.

---

[*] Based on both direct and indirect imports, as reflected in a review of 1994 import manifests for all U.S. ports compiled in the *Journal of Commerce* Piers database.

But really, the fundamental credo was simpler: Offer the lowest price. Cut your costs to the bone, and keep cutting, so you can offer the lowest price. Make your profit by selling more goods, instead of selling goods for more.

That was it. Nothing else was to stand before this commandment in the name of satisfying the customer: Thou shalt offer the lowest price.

Everything else grew out of that. Why are Wal-Mart stores so huge? Why do they grow bigger and bigger? Why are they on the edge of town instead of on Main Street? Why does Wal-Mart sell goods made by children? Why is it so adamantly anti-union? Why have so many of its suppliers moved their factories overseas? Why is it the most widely imitated company in business today? Almost any question you can ask about Wal-Mart ultimately can be answered by going back to that credo, which was itself Walton's answer to the only question that really mattered to him: How do you sell more?

Now that Walton is dead, that answer still animates his creation. Walton had looked around him and seen that the annals of business were littered with the bleached bones of companies that never found the answer, or that lost their way, that forgot what they had once known, that forgot who they were selling to—that withered when a visionary founder passed on, without passing on that vision to a successor.

So, now, almost every aspect of the corporate mindset at Wal-Mart, of the company culture, reflects Walton's determination to make sure his vision for the company outlasted him. And just as Walton, who started as an amiable small-town merchant, lending a hand at Boy Scouts and Little League, transformed himself into the world's greatest merchant by shedding other concerns one after another, refocusing his efforts in one direction with a laserlike intensity, so too did he transform his enterprise bit by bit into the incomparable selling machine that is Wal-Mart today. Behind the eagerness to please that he tried to inculcate in workers, there operates the most technologically sophisticated and efficient system in the world for getting goods from factories to store shelves. It's a system operated by men (and they were all men, as recently as 1999, at the top) for whom, like Walton, the end of selling more obliterated all other concerns.

It's not hard to picture Sam Walton as a Victor Frankenstein, snatching ideas from other businesses as if they were body parts, stitching here, inserting a bolt there, applying a judicious blast of electric current, and setting into lurching motion a creation that would enthrall his business counterparts, but that many others would come to regard as a monster.

There's a terrific irony—if one not much appreciated by Wal-Mart executives—in the fact that hundreds of towns and suburbs across North

America will fight mightily to keep the dreaded Wal-Mart at bay, even as many of these communities let in scores of other superstore retailers that try to ape Wal-Mart in every way they can: Kmart, Target, Toys "R" Us, Home Depot, OfficeMax, Staples, CompUSA, Circuit City, Food Lion, Price Chopper, Barnes & Noble, Borders, Blockbuster Video, Rite-Aid, Petsmart, and many, many more. To the extent that Wal-Mart's critics blast it for wiping out Main Street businesses, for homogenizing communities, for trying to crush any and all rivals, for selling goods made in sweatshops here and abroad, for busting unions, and for a multitude of other sins, they are missing the forest for its biggest tree.

Walton and Wal-Mart have transformed retailing the way Henry Ford revolutionized transportation. It's easy to forget, nowadays, that Ford invented neither the car nor the assembly line. What he did was to make them the new paradigms, to make life without cars, or industrial production without assembly lines, unthinkable.

Of course, making cars affordable to the masses carried trade-offs: The freedom to drive anywhere brought with it pollution, traffic jams, and sprawling suburbs. We became highly mobile—and our sense of community atrophied. Assembly lines spit out goods with far greater speed and efficiency; but they replaced highly skilled crafts jobs with simple, mind-numbingly repetitive tasks.

So, too, have cheaper underwear, deodorant, and toys sent their own ripples across our society. Wal-Mart's way of doing business is the new paradigm, and the company embodies both the shining success and the dark underbelly of modern American business. With its enormous size, more than 3,600 stores, all huge windowless boxes surrounded by seas of asphalt, it has the clout and buying power to sell goods for less money than smaller outfits can buy them wholesale; and so, in town after town, downtown storefronts go dark as local shopkeepers give up or move out next to the big box, where all the traffic goes anyway. Pressure from Wal-Mart and its competitors to make goods at the lowest cost has helped drive manufacturers out of the United States to countries where they can pay a fraction of their U.S. wages. Maybe you've driven past one of these shuttered factories and read of its move overseas. But, unless you're an eleven-year-old Guatemalan girl or a Bangladeshi boy of twelve, you probably haven't seen the inside of that manufacturer's new factory, where illiterate children may work 16-hour days behind barbed-wire fences, to take home less in four or five days than the American worker they replaced made in an hour. Yes, of course executives at Wal-Mart and Nike and many other businesses promise that they won't knowingly sell goods made by children—and every

time they get caught, over and over and over again, they shed a few croco-
dile tears and insist that they're shocked—shocked!—that such things
could have happened under their noses.

In the United States, service industries—including chain retailers and
restaurants—now dominate the job market, offering what are sneeringly
but appropriately dubbed "McJobs": high-turnover, near-minimum-wage,
often temporary or part-time, and inevitably nonunion positions. In this
new blue-collar world, a Wal-Mart job looks good: At least some workers
there *have* grown rich and retired with hundreds of thousands of dollars.
Scores of other companies—Home Depot, Federal Express, MCI
Telecommunications, among others—have taken Wal-Mart's route of
rewarding even low-level workers partly with shares of company stock and
have adopted to some degree Walton's call to make workers feel they have
a stake in the business. Of course, those stock incentives don't look quite so
enticing when the company's shares lie dead in the water for years on end,
as Wal-Mart's did through most of the 1990s.* But at least they're something.

Wal-Mart executives like to talk, as Walton did, about how their more
than 950,000 workers are all members of the "Wal-Mart family." And
through video satellite linkups to the stores, endless visits, and huge annual
meetings-cum-pep-rallies, company leaders such as Chief Executive David
Glass and Senior Vice Chairman Don Soderquist try devotedly to instill a
sense of community in their workers. Often they invoke the spirit of Sam,
telling workers that he's looking down on them from heaven. Of course, any
worker who tries to organize, or who engages in such heresies as discussing
his or her pay, finds, as have the thousands of workers who are part of a
floating slush pile of temporaries, that you can be booted out of this "family" in the blink of any eye.

Many workers really do want to feel as though they're part of a family.
Since Walton's death, though, the happy face he gave Wal-Mart has begun
to crumble bit by bit. And the contradictions he glossed over so easily have
become more apparent as his memory recedes. More than 575,000 workers have been added since he died. Still growing, Wal-Mart is so immense
that when it fires employees for dating other employees, or for trying to or-

---

*Shortly after a 2-for-1 split in February 1993, Wal-Mart common stock peaked at $34.125 a share, and
then sank over the next few years to as low as $20 a share. It took four years and five months for the
stock to climb back above that post-split price. This, during one of the greatest bull markets in American history. For comparison, the Dow Jones Industrial Average, over those years, rose more than 4,700
points to break the 8,000-point barrier.

By the summer of 1999, as the Dow Jones average topped 10,000, Wal-Mart stock took off again,
flirting with the $50 a share level after a two-for-one stock split in March of that year.

ganize, or for accusing their manager of sexual harassment, any worker who reads a newspaper or watches TV can't help but hear about it. So, too, when towns vote to keep Wal-Mart out. When a news show such as *Dateline NBC* broadcasts footage of twelve-year-old girls making Wal-Mart clothes in Bangladesh, and David Glass, with all the empathy of a stuffed frog, feebly responds on camera that "you and I might define children differently," how can workers help but wonder what is going on?

Of course, Wal-Mart's way of doing business is America's way. Other giant retailing chains differ only in that they aren't quite as fast, as tough, as successful. Strictly in business terms, Wal-Mart and its imitators thrive because the Wal-Mart formula *works*. That's why there are dozens of such superstore chains for everything from books to baby toys stalking through the globe. The fact that Walton's credo ignores other ethical and moral concerns—whether one should profit from child labor, for example—doesn't enter into it. In that sense, Wal-Mart and hundreds of other businesses are only following the maxim of economist and corporate apologist Milton Friedman, who famously argued that a corporation's only social responsibility is to increase its profits.

For his part, Sam Walton once said that his company's greatest contribution to society is that its low prices have saved people billions of dollars over the years and so have, in effect, helped raise people's standard of living.

Sometimes, though, the low price tag carries others costs. Sometimes there are hidden premiums. You may have seen glimpses of these.

Now it's time for a deeper look.

In Sam
We Trust

1

129 Billion
Reasons to Live

Imminent death has a way of clarifying one's thoughts.

So it was with Sam Walton, who discovered how short his thread was running thanks to a seemingly minor screwup on a fine November day in 1989, on a remote stretch of the Rio Grande Valley, in Texas.

Walton had come back from a full day of tromping through the prairie grass and mesquite, hunting for quail, only to find that he'd locked himself out of the ice house at one end of his hunting camp.

Walton's Campo Chapote was not the sort of place likely to be featured on *Lifestyles of the Rich and Famous*—just several battered trailers ringing a barbecue pit, with a few water wells, a dog kennel, a barn where he kept his truck and supplies, and the ice house, which was more of a shed, really. The camp moldered away on a 31-square-mile tract of land about 80 miles southwest of Corpus Christi. One indication of how crazy Walton was about the place was the fact that this otherwise frugal billionaire had happily dished out about $120,000 a year to lease the tract from a local rancher since 1983, when he'd hunted in Texas for the first time. It was the hunting he cared about, not the ambiance. By contrast, his brother Bud's digs, on another nearby ranch, included a stone mansion with a swimming pool.

The land in that part of Texas is wide open and flat enough that, usually, the hunters would climb up onto a bench mounted on the bed of a four-wheel-drive pickup truck and roll slowly along the prairie, watching for the dogs to point quail. Walton would walk for stretches too. At seventy-one—even after having fought leukemia into remission a few years earlier—he was still athletic, fit, able to set a strong pace, though in recent months he'd felt some odd aches and pains.

A slender, balding man with white hair, a sharp nose, and a sun-beaten, wrinkled face, Walton loved to hunt quail. He had, ever since his father-in-law had introduced him to the sport more than forty years earlier, around the time Walton opened his first business, a little five-and-dime store in Newport, Arkansas. Hunting was the one passion that could tear him away from work, though, typically, he found ways to combine the two. It would have been inconceivable for him to go hunting without stopping off at a Wal-Mart store or two along the way.

These days, he often used the camp for business. A few times a year, he'd fly down Wal-Mart managers, two dozen at a time, for a weekend. He'd say he wanted to let his managers get to know each other outside of the usual business setting—though some of his executives suspected it was just an excuse to squeeze in a few more weekends of working and hunting, for the talk around the campfire at dusk revolved around Wal-Mart business as invariably as if the men were sitting in a boardroom back at headquarters in Bentonville, Arkansas. Even after a day of hunting, Walton just didn't make idle chatter.

Often, though, he would fly down with just a friend or two for company, or hunt on his own. Walton could be surprisingly absent-minded. One of the chores of Walter Schiel, a former rodeo cowboy from Waller, Texas, who now worked as the ranch's hunting guide and dog handler, was to retrieve shotguns Walton left behind. After seeing Walton get lost or run out of gas a few times on the vast prairie, Dick Jones, the ranch owner, had talked him into putting in a two-way radio; and it had proved its worth time and again.

On this late November afternoon, Walton stood outside the ice shed with Schiel. Noticing a small window was open, the slim Walton clambered up onto the cowboy's shoulders and tried to squeeze through. He made it, but the dog whistle around his neck caught on the window and jammed painfully into his sternum.

The next morning, he still felt sore, but shrugged it off to go hunting anyway. By the end of the day, though, he was still in pain, and the ache had spread to his upper arm. This was worse than any of the other inexplicable aches he'd felt in recent months. Reluctantly, Walton decided he'd better check in with his doctors. He hopped in the twin-engine Cessna he'd picked up a few years earlier (used, of course) and flew to Houston.[1]

•　　•　　•

Walton had been commuting to Houston for medical care regularly since 1982, when he was diagnosed with hairy cell leukemia, a type of blood cancer that destroys the body's white blood cells. Walton had always been an active and energetic man, usually up and working long before dawn, but that year he had been feeling increasingly tired and run down. At first, he had thought that maybe, as his wife Helen kept claiming, he was just working too hard; so, though it cut against his grain, he began delegating more work, cutting back on his busy travel schedule, and trying to relax more by hunting and playing tennis.

But that hadn't helped. So, reluctantly—Walton had always hated seeing doctors—he'd gone in for an extensive physical checkup. His doctors in Arkansas discovered he had a disturbingly low white-cell count. They told him that he had a chronic type of leukemia that had been developing for at least six or seven years. What caused it? They didn't know. Could it be cured? They couldn't say. But Walton, of course, could afford the best treatment money could buy, so they referred him to Houston's M.D. Anderson Hospital, one of the country's leading cancer research centers. There, an oncologist named Jorge Quesada was testing an experimental treatment for hairy cell leukemia using interferon, an astonishingly expensive substance painstakingly extracted from white blood cells. At the time, it took 300 donors to provide enough interferon to treat one patient for three months, at a cost of about $10,000 a month.

Quesada wasn't the type to sugarcoat matters. The standard treatment, he said, would be removal of Walton's spleen, followed by chemotherapy. But, he told his unhappy patient, this procedure only had about a 25 percent success rate (with "success" meaning the patient was still alive five years down the road). Walton had loathed the idea of going under the knife, and he had been almost combative. Surgery, he said flatly, was absolutely out of the question. Any other options?

There was really only one alternative, Quesada said: He could become an interferon research patient. There would be risks, such as the possibility of hemorrhage and of opportunistic infections; there were potential side effects, including flulike symptoms and fatigue. But even though Quesada had given interferon to fewer than ten hairy cell leukemia patients up until then, he was obviously very enthusiastic about the initial results. It seemed to help these patients maintain their white-cell counts, and to bolster their immune systems, he told Walton. Still, he added, it was an experimental treatment, and the results so far, while encouraging, had to be considered preliminary. Anyhow, he shrugged, at worst, if it didn't work, they could fall back on surgery and chemotherapy.

Become an experimental subject? Walton didn't care much for that idea either. He'd need to think about it, he said. "Predominantly, he wanted to be sure the treatment wouldn't interfere with his extraordinarily busy schedule," Quesada recalled. Walton had flown home to Bentonville, discussed the situation with Helen, and, in October 1982, even published a letter in his company's internal newsletter, *Wal-Mart World,* telling all 41,000 company employees, or associates, about the diagnosis. With his usual mix of businesslike purpose and folksy manner, he tried to downplay the significance of the illness. Noting that he was otherwise in good health, he had written:

> I've got lots of odds going to have successful treatment.
>
> So, my friends, I hope you'll excuse my referring to a personal matter of this type, but we've always believed in communicating with one another for better or for worse, and in being up front and open about everything that affects our Company and our Wal-Mart family.
>
> If I'm to have a health problem, I'm really fortunate to have this type of disorder. I'm completely confident, too, that with the right treatment I'll be able to continue doing the things I enjoy most for at least another 20 or 25 years. I'll be coming around—maybe more infrequently—but I'll be trying and wanting to see you. You know how much I love to visit with you all on how you're doing and how we can further improve our Wal-Mart Company, so I'll be stopping by. Let's put this subject to rest.
>
> I am, and have been, so blessed to have enjoyed the support, affection and loyalty of you wonderful Wal-Mart associates through the years. Together, we can be more than a little proud of our accomplishments. You know we are, and will continue to be, partners. I've just been lucky in so many ways, and feel that this is certainly the case now. The last thing I need or want would be undue sympathy or undue conversation concerning my health. I just wanted to clear the air and not let there be a lot of untrue rumors floating around as many of you knew of the recent tests I have been undergoing.

He closed the letter by talking about a couple of puppies he planned to train.

The offhand manner he adopted in his letter didn't come close to reflecting Walton's real feelings. In business, he could snap out decisions on the fly, relying on instincts keenly honed by decades of experience. But this was different. He was utterly at sea. His mother had died of cancer when she was fifty-two, far younger than he was now. He spent an entire month mulling over what to do, then winged down to Houston to ask more questions about the treatment. Quesada greeted him with the news that doctors now had discovered how to make synthetic interferon using genetic engineering, making the substance more readily available—not that, for Walton, this would have been an issue anyway. Walton grilled Quesada and other doctors about the risks and benefits. Again, Quesada bluntly told him that because the drug was so new, much about it remained unknown. Walton went back home and thought about the treatment for another long month, and finally decided he would try it.

He learned how to give himself injections and how to have someone else give them to him. His regimen called for interferon injections daily for six months, then three times a week for another six months. Less than halfway through the treatment, the disease's progression stopped; the leukemia went into partial remission and stayed there. It turned out, after all, to be that easy.

That had been almost seven years ago, and the leukemia hadn't really troubled him since, though he continued to visit Quesada for checkups several times a year. He'd last seen the doctor about three months before this hunting trip; Quesada had fretted about a slight change in Walton's blood count, but he hadn't been able to pin down the cause because Walton wouldn't stick around for the three days Quesada needed to run the tests he had in mind.

Now, when Walton showed up with this odd pain in his sternum and arm, doctors removed and analyzed some bone marrow from his hip—and discovered he had a malignant cancer of the bone marrow, multiple myeloma.

This time, Quesada's prognosis was bleaker. There was no cure. This, he said, was a much more aggressive disease. Chemotherapy and radiation treatments might put it into remission, he said, but keeping it in remission would be difficult.

The treatments, too, would be harder. Walton hadn't suffered any serious side effects from the interferon; but he should expect the radiation and chemotherapy to be draining, Quesada warned. The disease itself, unless they were very lucky, would be painful, at times severely so. His bones were already laced with lesions, and were soft; and he could expect to become more frail and to tire more easily.

Walton trusted Quesada more than he had the first time around, but he still interrogated him closely. Wasn't there some other treatment, something more natural they could try? On top of everything else, chemotherapy and radiation sounded so time-consuming. With the help of his family, particularly his son John, whose daughter had had cancer, he researched alternatives, peppering his doctors with questions about natural treatments, unconventional therapies, vitamins, anything that might replace or reduce the need for chemotherapy and radiation.

He contacted People Against Cancer, a nonprofit group in Iowa that acts as a clearinghouse to give cancer patients information about cancer research and therapies, including treatments outside the medical mainstream. Walton was nothing if not methodical. But it was soon clear to him that the myeloma almost certainly would prove fatal.[2] In the end, Walton reluctantly decided to accept the conventional chemotherapy and radiation.

How did Walton react to the prospect that he might be dead soon? It's hard to say. For all his glad-handing, for the evident delight he took in rousing up his workers, at turning his store visits into pep rallies, Walton was an exceptionally private man. He just never talked about himself, except perhaps with Helen, who was as closemouthed as he was. "I'm probably as close to Helen, as an individual, and probably was as close to Sam as anybody around here," said William H. Enfield, a friend of the Waltons for more than forty years, "but a lot about them I've never known and I've never tried to."

It would be tempting to assume that Walton felt driven to reexamine his life, to wonder whether, say, he should have slowed down sooner and spent more time with Helen and their children and grandchildren, or whether he should have been gentler with the many men he'd burned out in building his retailing empire.

It would be tempting—but probably wrong. Walton did admit—eventually, as death drew even closer—to having flickerings of late-night existential doubt, though, in the end, they seem to have been just that: flickerings, quickly extinguished.

But that was later. Just after his diagnosis, he had bigger quail to bag.

As one might expect, Walton had long since arranged both who would succeed him at the company and what would become of his fortune, which is to say, how he would keep it out of the clutches of Uncle Sam. The succession he'd taken care of a year and a half earlier. In March 1988, the Wal-Mart chairman had made things official by handing his post as chief executive to David Glass, Wal-Mart's president. In some ways, the fifty-four-year-old Glass seemed out of place at Wal-Mart; he was, as would be pointed out abundantly to him in his first years at the helm, no Sam Walton. Poker-faced, soft-spoken, and deliberate in manner, he gave the impression of being game but vaguely ill at ease carrying out the kinds of crowd-pleasing stunts that Walton had put at the heart of the corporate culture. Take the time Glass, decked out in leis and a grass skirt, had to dance the hula in front of howling employees at company headquarters to celebrate Wal-Mart's stock price hitting a record high. It was a performance memorable enough that Walton himself promised to hula on Wall Street if the company hit his aggressive earnings goal for the year.

But Walton had spotted Glass as someone with his own rare predatory instinct for retailing. He had spent a dozen years trying to land him before hauling Glass on board as an executive vice president back in 1976. By the time he had outflanked or outlasted his rivals to become chief executive, Glass had put in another dozen years at Wal-Mart, spearheading the creation of much of what would become the most sophisticated and efficient system in retailing for getting goods from factories to store shelves.

The annals of Wal-Mart are filled with stories of frazzled executives who quit, retired young, or were canned after burning out under the strain of the enormous workloads, endless road trips, and relentless pressure to perform that came with working for Sam Walton. The stress almost certainly contributed to the heart attack that struck Glass one evening after an all-day meeting in February 1985, when he was fifty. But it barely seemed to faze him. He dived back into his work after the briefest possible rest. By then, there had really been no doubt that he would one day run the show.

As for Walton's then $20-billion fortune, he had set up trusts and mechanisms to leave it in his wife's and children's hands long before the fortune—or Wal-Mart itself—had even existed. He had taken care of that little matter more than thirty-five years earlier, under the prodding and guidance of his father-in-law, Leland Stanford Robson, a banker, lawyer, and rancher in tiny Claremore, Oklahoma.

Robson may have been the most important of Walton's early mentors: He put up the money to get his son-in-law started in business—and, later, he in effect determined what would become of Walton's fortune.

Robson had made his own bundle. Raised in Georgia, he first made his way to Oklahoma in 1909, as a twenty-five-year-old itinerant peddler of pots, pans, Bibles, and picture frames. He raised enough money to put himself through law school back in Georgia; then he headed again to Oklahoma, planning to hang out his shingle in the booming oil town of Tulsa.

But he soon moved about 20 miles northwest to a smaller pond, the more sedate town of Claremore. There, in 1916, he married a local girl, Hazel Corrine Carr, who bore three sons and a daughter—Helen—in less than four years.

He was what folks called "country"—a man who loved to hunt and fish and train dogs. He wasn't refined or effete, but a horse trader, smart, clever, always with his ear to the ground. Robson's law practice had flourished, and as prominent citizens often do in small towns, he soon had his fingers in a passel of pies. He served as city attorney for twelve years. During the Great Depression, he snapped up 18,500 acres of land on the cheap and began ranching. In 1936 he became a founder of the Rogers County Bank in Claremore, which he ran as a director, president, and chairman over the following three decades. During World War II, he angled successfully for a seat on the Oklahoma Highway Commission. He wound up with interests in coal-mining, farming, and other industries, as well.

But it's what Robson did with all these holdings that would become important for Sam Walton. Early on, Robson organized his ranch and family businesses as a partnership, with Helen and her brothers as equal partners. From the day his daughter married Walton in 1943, Robson actively involved himself in their financial affairs. By 1952, when Walton's five-and-dime store in Bentonville had done well enough to allow him to open a second store in Fayetteville, 24 miles away, Robson convinced his ambitious young son-in-law that he should organize his own business as a family partnership, too. So, in early 1953, under Robson's watchful eye, Bentonville attorney William H. Enfield drew up legal documents establishing Walton Enterprises, in which Sam, Helen, and their four children—Rob, then eight years old; John, six; Jim, four; and Alice, three—were all partners.

"Over the years," Walton wrote in his memoirs, "our Wal-Mart stock has gone into that partnership. Then the board of Walton Enterprises, which is us, the family, makes decisions on a consensus basis. Sometimes we argue, and sometimes we don't. But we control the amount we pay out to each of us, and everybody gets the same. The kids got as much over the years as Helen and I did, except that I got a salary, which my son, Jim, now draws as head of Walton Enterprises. That way, we accumulated funds in Enterprises rather than throwing it all over the place to live high."[3]

By 1989, besides holding 218 million Wal-Mart common shares, the partnership also had acquired extensive real estate holdings, four banks and half of a fifth bank, and other assorted businesses. As it was organized, Sam and Helen Walton together owned a 20 percent stake in the partnership, and each of the children owned 20 percent.

When Sam Walton died, in 1992, Helen Walton immediately had his will sealed in state chancery court. But, from comments he made earlier, he seems to have arranged to have his interest in the partnership pass to a marital trust for Helen. That way, he deferred any estate tax. On her death, it apparently was to pass to various family charities, resulting in no estate tax for either the Walton children or the family businesses. The charities would get a minority interest in the family partnership, so that the vote of the bloc of stock would stay under the control of the family.[4]

By turning over ownership of 80 percent of his holdings to his children so early on, Walton avoided any substantial gift or inheritance taxes. He put it the way his father-in-law probably had put it to him: "The best way to reduce paying estate taxes is to give your assets away before they appreciate."[5]

Another benefit Robson had pointed out was that creating a family partnership established, early on, the children's responsibilities to the family business and to each other.

Sam and Helen Walton involved their children in family decisions—large and small—from very early on. On one vacation to the Grand Tetons, recalled Rob, the oldest boy, "We had an opportunity to take what was a very expensive—for that time—pack trip up into the mountains to a fishing camp and stay there for a few days. But that was going to use up all our money, and we had to take a family vote to decide whether to do that or not. We decided to do it, and it was fun. But after we had spent all of our money on the big trip, we made a quick stop in the Black Hills and hiked it on home in a hurry."[6]

After the kids had grown up and moved away, Sam Walton would arrange family meetings several times a year to discuss Walton Enterprises business, in such places as the Ritz-Carlton in Naples, Florida, and the Del Coronado in San Diego. The family agreed to his decision to make his third son, Jim, the president of Walton Enterprises. Why Jim? He was, Walton thought approvingly, nearly as tight-fisted as his father.

Rob Walton would take over the chairmanship of the company. That was a given. As the oldest son, he had long understood that eventually it would fall to him to oversee the family's company. Bright but quiet, he looked a bit like Sam Walton—he had his father's sharp features—but he sure didn't act like him. He would dutifully come along to Campo Chapote for some of Sam's hunting trips with managers or folks from vendors such as Procter & Gamble. But Rob wasn't a hunter. While the other men drove off to hunt, he'd slip on his running shoes and jog away on his own. At Wal-Mart meetings and visits to stores, Rob Walton could be even more diffident in public, more reserved around the workers, than David Glass.

But he had been well prepared to assume the throne. In one form or another, he had been involved in company business most of his life. Like his brothers and sister, Rob, as a child, had worked in the five-and-dime on the Bentonville town square. Sam had hauled him along on visits to other stores. Like Sam, he had been a high school football star; he made the All-State team as a senior. Helen had talked him into enrolling at a small Presbyterian college in Ohio, Wooster College; though, after two years, he transferred to the University of Arkansas, from which he graduated in 1966.

Sam Walton had appointed him Wal-Mart's corporate secretary and general counsel as soon as Rob had received his law degree from Columbia University in New York, in 1969. But, to Sam's chagrin, Rob hadn't come back to Bentonville. Instead, he had joined a law firm in Tulsa, Oklahoma. Still, he had done much of the legal work for the company's initial public offering while juggling his role in Tulsa with his duties as Wal-Mart's general counsel. While in Tulsa, he left his first wife and their three children to marry his secretary, Carolyn Funk. After years of continuous pressure from Sam, Rob Walton reluctantly agreed to move back to Bentonville with his new bride and work for Wal-Mart full-time.

Sam Walton had promoted him to senior vice president and put him on Wal-Mart's board of directors in 1978. In 1982, he appointed Rob Walton vice chairman. He had held that post ever since—even while taking a long leave of absence to train for and compete in the 1985 and 1986 Ironman Triathalons in Hawaii. (That race begins with a 2.4-mile swim, followed by a 112-mile bicycle ride, and ends with a 26-mile marathon.) He completed both races, finishing in the middle of the field each time. If one took the sabbatical as a sign that the heir presumptive was a reluctant draftee to head the company—and many did—one wouldn't be far off. Rob Walton, though, later explained himself by saying "what I saw happening was that I was going to work really, really hard for 20 years with Dad still around and then sometime he would be gone and then I'd really have the responsibility. So I decided that I would get a little bit different orientation for a while."[7]

Reluctant or not, Rob Walton was ready, his father knew, to assume the mantle.

In all, then, at the time he got the bad news from Dr. Quesada, Sam Walton had no real worries about what to do with his fortune or his company. Helen and the children were taken care of and could manage their affairs. He felt confident—having drilled this into them—that the children would conserve the partnership's holdings in Wal-Mart rather than sell off stock and spend the money. He was confident, too, in Rob's ability to represent the family in Wal-Mart's dealings and felt certain that Glass, and the management team he had spent decades building around him, could come as close as anyone could to running Wal-Mart the Sam Walton way.

Walton had never been a particularly introspective man, as he readily admitted. His immediate inclination, as he brooded over the diagnosis of bone cancer, then, almost certainly was not to review his life, nor to wonder whether his time might have been better spent in other ways. What he does seem to have done—based on comments he made a few months later at a Wal-Mart gathering—was to contemplate what lay ahead for the enterprise that gave his life whatever meaning it had and to reassure himself that this most important of his progeny—Wal-Mart—could achieve what he had in mind.

For several months he had been working, reluctantly and with extreme discomfort, with a reporter from the *Wall Street Journal*, Eric Morgenthaler, who was ghostwriting Walton's autobiography. Sam Walton had agreed to the project only grudgingly, under constant prodding from Helen, Rob, and Alice Walton, along with David Glass and several other senior Wal-Mart officers. They had set Morgenthaler up in an office down the hall, giving him the run of the officers. With that advantage, and the collusion of Walton's secretary, Becky Elliott, Morgenthaler even had managed to pin down the notoriously elusive Walton himself for several interviews.

As an interview subject, Walton inevitably turned any question about his own life into a discussion about Wal-Mart. So much did he loathe having to talk about himself that several times he had threatened to kill the book. Now, on returning from Houston, Walton called Morgenthaler into his office.

He matter-of-factly told him about the cancer and then said, "I have to simplify my life . . . so I have to get rid of things I don't want to do." In a manner that was friendly but brooked no argument, he added, simply, "I never wanted to do this book. I'm getting rid of it."*

By "simplifying," Walton evidently meant focusing even more than before on his one overriding ambition—the one that had led him to head to his office so many mornings at 4 A.M.; to spend so many Saturdays in meetings; to visit more stores across the country and around the world than, he was sure, any other person ever had; to leave his wife and children at campgrounds or resorts while he checked out competitors' businesses; and to

---

* Walton paid Morgenthaler to turn over his notes and interview transcripts to the family. Later, having that material on hand helped persuade Walton to change his mind again. The next time, Walton hired *Fortune* editor John Huey, a writer he liked, but who had been unavailable the first time around.

keep at his grinding schedule for years beyond the age at which anyone else might have retired. It was to create the biggest and most successful company he could—to be, as one of his early managers, Charlie Baum, had put it, the top of the heap.

Walton had long said that the money, beyond a certain point, was incidental. Certainly, his personal habits—bragging about the cheap shoes he bought at Wal-Mart, borrowing change from other executives—sustained an image of sometimes comical frugality.

His public image of nonchalance toward his wealth had been cemented for good by his widely reported response to the great stock market crash of October 19, 1987, when the Dow Jones Industrial Average plummeted 508 points in a day and Wal-Mart shares fell 23 percent from their price of a week earlier, wiping out $1.7 billion of Walton's net worth. Walton had gone to Little Rock to join other Arkansas corporate leaders for a press conference on higher education. As he arrived at Governor Bill Clinton's office, reporters asked for his reaction to the crash.

"It's paper anyway," he had said, seemingly untroubled. "It was paper when we started and it's paper afterward."[8]

It wasn't the money. It was the scale of his business. His goals had always been audacious. In 1976, when Wal-Mart reported $340.3 million in sales for the year from its 125 stores, all within a day's drive of Bentonville, Walton had been confident enough to promise publicly that he would triple its size within five years. "Write it on the wall now if you want to," he told Jeannette Reddish, a writer profiling him for *Financial World*. "By January 31, 1981, we'll be a billion-dollar company."[9] As it turned out, Wal-Mart's sales had reached $1.25 billion a year ahead of his schedule.

By 1985, when Wal-Mart posted $6.4 billion in sales, still leagues behind Kmart's $22 billion and Sears's $25.3 billion, Walton and Glass were already talking openly about becoming the biggest retailer in the country—and that same year Herbert Fisher, the chairman of the New Jersey–based Jamesway Corp., another regional discount chain, said he too could foresee the day when Wal-Mart would pass Kmart to become the number-one discounter.

Now, in 1990, in the weeks after dismissing Morgenthaler, Walton began calculating and recalculating, on the yellow pad he always carried, his projections for Wal-Mart over the next decade. Catching Sears and Kmart he took as a given. That would happen within the next two years, he felt certain, so he might live to see that. He was more interested as to Wal-Mart's potential further out.

This was the calculation he confidently announced to cheering shareholders at the next annual meeting: With or without him, by the year 2000, Wal-Mart would boost its sales more than five-fold, to $129 billion a year—blowing far beyond Sears and Kmart to become the most dominant retailer the world had ever seen.

There was, to Sam Walton, no doubt about it.

2

The Storekeeper
on the Square

Before Sam Walton came along, Bentonville, Arkansas, might charitably have been described as a sedate Southern backwater, the kind of place where a Confederate statue watches over the shady town square, a place with so little traffic there wasn't even a stoplight in town. All in all, an improbable Eldorado.

But an Eldorado is exactly what it would turn out to be for Sam Walton, bringing to a close four generations of Walton wanderings in search of a better life.

The Walton family traces its roots back to Virginia, which one William P. Walton left in 1838 to try his luck farming near the tiny town of La Mine, in central Missouri. Of more interest is one of his sons, Samuel W. Walton, born on the family farm in 1848. Like his far more famous namesake and grandson, this Sam Walton started his career as a storekeeper, in his case running a small general store in La Mine. At the time, outside of cities, small country stores were where people shopped. Often run by men who were farmers themselves, such stores carried cloth and clothing, tools and cutlery, drugs, fruit, tobacco, and other goods. And often they doubled as the local post office; Sam Walton, in fact, was La Mine's postmaster.

It wasn't an easy business. The farm families who made up the clientele were short of cash much of the year, and a storekeeper had to be willing to take eggs, vegetables, or other barter for his goods as often as cash. Twice a year, typically, the storekeeper would have to trek to some big town, such as

16

St. Louis, to buy the inventory of goods he would sell over the coming six months.

Walton had married a local farmer's daughter when he was twenty; but in 1880 she died after giving birth to their sixth child. Maybe it was her death that soured him on La Mine. Maybe there was some other reason. But he soon packed up the family and left, moving twice over the next few years before joining relatives who'd settled in the small southwestern Missouri town of Diggins, in Webster County. There, Walton opened another small general store and again became the local postmaster. He also bought a fruit farm and soon began selling and shipping lumber.

Photos of Samuel Walton from those days show a cheerful man with a broad forehead and an extravagant walrus moustache. He remarried on Christmas Day in 1883, less than two years after arriving in Webster County. His new wife, Clara, bore three sons. But when the youngest, Thomas, was just over a year old, in the fall of 1894, Clara and then Samuel Walton died within a few months of each other. The details—how and why they died, what arrangements, if any, they had made for the children and the businesses—are maddeningly sketchy. Charles Walton, his oldest son from his first marriage, shows up in records as his partner; but for reasons lost to history, Charles seems essentially to have disowned his younger brothers and sisters, and his half-brothers, all of whom were parceled out among various relatives.

Samuel's youngest daughter, Mollie, moved west to join her uncle, J. W. Walton. Once the sheriff of Webster County, J. W. Walton had decided to gamble that he would find greater prospects in the undeveloped and windswept plains to the west. So he had left five years earlier to take part in what later became known as the great Oklahoma land rush. He was one of the more than 50,000 settlers who were allowed, on April 22, 1889, to race onto, and stake claims for, up to 160 acres apiece on what had been Indian territory. J. W. Walton had staked out his land not far from where government surveyors laid out the proposed town of Kingfisher, 7 miles south of the Cimarron River.

He may have arrived as a homesteader, but Walton soon found a less backbreaking way to make a living. Watching many of his fellow homesteaders fall into debt and find themselves forced to sell their stakes for a pittance, he decided to get in on the lending end of things and became a farm loan agent.* Business was terrific. He was successful enough for the

---

* Most likely, he was acting as the local representative of a larger insurance company or state bank.

new *Kingfisher Times* newspaper to refer to him, in 1901, as "a safe man with whom to deal" adding, "he treats everybody fairly and honestly, and we are safe in saying his record is without blemish in a field which admits of much peculation."[1]

Soon after joining him in Kingfisher, his teenage niece Mollie finished her schooling there and found work as a schoolteacher, for $35 a month. Then she sent for her three half-brothers and took charge of raising them herself. Once the youngest, Thomas, finished high school, he joined his uncle J.W.'s farm mortgage business.

But he didn't care for it. So in 1917, when he was twenty-five, Thomas did what any self-respecting young Oklahoman might do: He married a local farmer's daughter and got himself a farm. His wife, eighteen-year-old Nannia Lee Lawrence, was then in her first year of college. She dropped out, soon became pregnant, and the two settled on some acreage Thomas Walton had acquired a few miles out of town.

His timing seemed perfect—not to mention patriotic: The U.S. government was begging farmers to plant more crops, so the surplus could be shipped to war-torn Europe. World War I was now in its third year. The profits for the farmers were intoxicating. Meanwhile, Nannia gave birth at the farmhouse to their first son on March 29, 1918, a Friday. They decided to name him after the father Thomas had never really known and christened him Samuel Moore Walton. He would be followed three years later by a second son, James L. Walton, nicknamed Bud.

But suddenly, Thomas Walton had to struggle to keep his head above water. Once the war ended, in late 1918, European farmers began producing again with surprising speed; and American farmers were stuck with huge surpluses. Prices for cotton, wheat, corn, and other crops plummeted. A postwar recession plunged huge numbers of farmers deeply into debt.

After several tough years, Thomas Walton gave up on farming. He would have to go back to the one other business he knew, appraising farm loans. He moved the family to Springfield, Missouri, where he went to work for a mortgage company, run by his older half-brother Jesse Walton, that represented Metropolitan Life Insurance Co. Shortly, though, at Jesse Walton's orders, he moved the family again to the smaller town of Marshall, in the center of the state. There, Thomas Walton soon quit to strike out with his own insurance and mortgage business.

And strike out he did. His business failed within a few years, at the start of the Great Depression. Fortunately, Jesse Walton welcomed him back into his mortgage business, which proved more robust. Thomas Walton became a repo man. It wasn't cheery work; but it was all too steady. Over the next few years he would repossess hundreds of farms from people who were unable to repay their loans, people whose families, in some cases, had owned and lived on those farms for generations. To expand the family business into a new corner of the state, Walton agreed in 1931 to move his family to Shelbina, an even smaller town 75 miles northeast of Marshall.

Throughout these years, Thomas Walton's earnings, while adequate, weren't extravagant. Sam Walton later claimed that on one occasion his father had swapped his wristwatch (evidently a rather nice one) for a hog "so we'd have meat on the table."[2] Sam tagged along with his father on some of the farm repossessions; and if his later behavior is any indication, these experiences must have seared frugality into his soul even more than with most children of the Depression. He downplayed it, saying that seeing families turned out of their land "must have made an impression on me as a kid, although I don't ever remember saying anything to myself like, 'I'll never be poor.' " It certainly made an impression on his parents. "One thing my mother and dad shared completely was their approach to money: They just didn't spend it," he said.[3]

Sam Walton was thirteen when the family arrived in Shelbina; Bud was ten. They were very close. Both, like most children their ages, already had been working before and after school for years. Sam Walton milked the family cows every morning; his mother would bottle the milk while he was at school, and after football practice he would deliver the bottles. He also delivered newspapers, sold magazine subscriptions, and raised and sold rabbits and pigeons. He still found time to be a Boy Scout and managed—with only limited help from his father, who had to spend a lot of time traveling throughout his region—to become an Eagle Scout shortly after arriving in Shelbina. That made him, at the time, the youngest Eagle Scout in Missouri history.

With Thomas Walton so much on the road, Nan Walton took on most of the work of raising, disciplining, and motivating the two boys. She had high ambitions for them. "She read a lot and loved education," Sam Walton recalled. Maybe because she keenly regretted not having finished college herself, "she just ordained from the beginning that I would go to college and make something of myself," he said.[4]

Not finishing college wasn't her only regret. Over the years, Thomas and Nan Walton, for reasons that neither of their sons discussed publicly, grew farther and farther apart. Sam Walton avoided talking about his parents, just as he avoided talking about anything personal. But, prodded by his wife Helen's insistence that his parents' antagonism toward each other had shaped the way he handled his own family relationships, Sam Walton did say in his autobiography that "Mother and Dad were two of the most quarrelsome people who ever lived together. . . . They were always at odds, and they really only stayed together because of Bud and me."

"As the oldest child, I felt like I took a lot of the brunt of this domestic discord," he added. "I'm not sure exactly how this affected my personality—unless it was partly a motivation to stay so busy all the time—but I swore early on that if I ever had a family, I would never expose it to that kind of squabbling."[5]

This is as close to baring his soul as Sam Walton gets. And in its own elliptical way, this comment may reveal quite a bit about the man Walton became. Certainly, by all accounts, he did avoid squabbling with Helen. ("That was a part of our agreement when we got married, that we would not do that," Helen Walton said once on a TV interview.[6]) But he clearly implies that his own workaholic tendencies sprang from a childhood need to escape his parents' bickering.

None of their close friends express any doubt that Sam Walton loved and cared for Helen Walton—and the children—devotedly. But at the same time, many can relate, with some puzzlement, how Sam would go out quail hunting while Helen sat at home on her birthday, or similar stories. Time after time, in their marriage, Helen would push him to spend more time with her and with the children; and time after time he would opt to immerse himself in work instead—or in his hunting. Indeed, late in their marriage Helen Walton took up quail hunting herself, not because she enjoyed it (by all accounts, she didn't) but because at least it let her spend a little more time with Sam.

"His idea of coming home was to have dinner, and come in to sit down, and read and read and read," Helen Walton said. "It was difficult. I tried to make it so the children wouldn't miss their dad."[7]

He wound up becoming, like his father and grandfather, a man who, when it came to home life, mostly wasn't there. Sam's grandfather Samuel Walton, of course, had no choice in the matter, having died when his son Thomas was an infant. Thomas Walton, for his part, had to be thankful during the Depression that he had a job at all, even if it did force him to be away from home much of the time. Sam Walton, though, increasingly absented himself from home by choice—and would do so to his final days. His memoirs make a point of quoting several of the children as saying they didn't resent his absences, that they didn't feel neglected. But it is clear, from his friends and workers, and from Helen's guarded comments, that he was mostly absent. (Helen mentions, for example, how Sam agreed to take turns with her getting the kids to Sunday school, but that she always wound up doing it because he would be in the office, even after working until ten on Saturday night.) Work was his security. Even when he was in the hospital, dying of cancer, friends recall that nothing cheered him up so much as when they arranged for a Wal-Mart store manager to drop by Walton's hospital bed, to chat about how sales were going in his store.

Largely at Nan Walton's urging, Thomas Walton agreed to uproot the family again in 1933, at the start of Sam's sophomore year in high school. This time they moved to Columbia, Missouri, which, with nearly 30,000 people, was the largest town between Kansas City and St. Louis, and home to several colleges, including the University of Missouri. Nan Walton felt the move would improve the boys' chances of going to college. The family moved into a large, two-story brick house near the university; to help pay for it, they rented three of the four upstairs bedrooms to university students.

Over the summer, Sam Walton broke a leg sliding into home plate during a baseball game. But the accident didn't seem to hobble him much when school started that fall at Columbia's Hickman High School. The friendly, outgoing boy proved popular with classmates. He became vice president of his junior class and president of the student body his senior year. Like his father, Sam was slight of build and not very tall—5 feet 9 inches—but he also played football and basketball and was intensely competitive. In 1935, as quarterback, he helped lead the Kewpies (named after a carnival-prize doll) to an undefeated season and the state championship. He joined every school club in sight, worked part-time in a five-and-dime store, and delivered newspapers for the *Columbia Missourian*, the university newspaper.

Naturally, he went to college at the University of Missouri. He established himself as a campus leader quickly, helped by connections he'd made with his family's boarders and with college students he'd met delivering newspapers to the fraternities. He waited tables and worked as a lifeguard. He also expanded his newspaper delivery business, hiring helpers and eventually making, as he recalled, more than $4,000 a year.° Those earnings paid for his clothing, tuition, food, and other expenses, including a car he bought his sophomore year. The joke on campus was that there wasn't a club he wouldn't join just to run for office. He became an officer of the fraternity he joined; president of an ROTC club; president of the senior

---

° The equivalent, in 1998 dollars, of $48,750 a year.

men's honor society; a member of the governing board of the college year-book; president of his Bible class; and president of his senior class.

Nan Walton wanted him to be a lawyer. He daydreamed about becoming president of the United States, he said later. In his more pragmatic moments, he talked about becoming an insurance agent. In high school, he had dated a girl whose father was an insurance salesman; he said, "it appeared to me that he was making all the money in the world. Insurance seemed like a natural to me because I thought I could sell."[8]

Walton also looked into going to business school—specifically the Wharton School at the University of Pennsylvania, in Philadelphia—but he decided it would be too expensive. Shortly before the end of his senior year, he had interviews with recruiters from Sears Roebuck & Co. and from J.C. Penney Co. Both offered him jobs.

He opted to go with Penney and was told to report to the Penney store in Des Moines, Iowa, three days after his graduation. On June 3, 1940, he began work as a management trainee for $75 a week, plus commissions.°

Within weeks of his graduation, his parents separated. Nan Walton moved to California and found a job working in a defense plant.

Sam Walton later said it was his stint at Penney that convinced him to make his career in retailing. Selling—and especially trying to sell more than the other trainees—was fun. He was good at it. He'd get chewed out for his tendency to let paperwork slip, being too eager to move on to the next sale, but he got along well with his manager, who liked his gung-ho attitude. On his lunch hour, Walton would cruise the aisles of competing stores, such as the nearby Sears. And he began reading books on retailing. He quickly decided that he liked the way Penney operated—so much so that he phoned his brother Bud and talked him into becoming a Penney trainee too (in his case, at a store in nearby Cedar Rapids).

It was at Penney that Walton first came across many of the management ideas that, decades later, would popularly be thought of as his own: One such idea was calling workers "associates," as a way of making them feel more like partners in the business. Another was letting store managers buy small stakes in their stores, to give them more of a personal investment in the store's success. Another was "management by walking around," as some would label Walton's habit of incessantly visiting his own stores. These visits let him see firsthand how local managers were doing, pass on tips to them about how to do this or that better, pick up on anything new they might have come up with, and, of course, meet all the workers.

° The equivalent, in 1998 dollars, of $920 a week.

All of these were ideas that James Cash Penney had adopted first, and that Penney considered fundamental to his success. (Walton met Penney once, when the founder, then sixty-five, visited the Des Moines store; Walton said Penney showed him how to wrap packages using less string and paper.) Penney and two partners had opened their first store in Kemmerer, Wyoming, in 1902. By 1917, Penney ran 17 stores with $3.6 million a year in sales, by 1923, he had 475 stores; and by the time Walton came on board as a trainee, the Penney chain consisted of just under 1,600 stores. Only Sears Roebuck and Montgomery Ward were larger retailers of general merchandise.

Walton quit his job at Penney after about eighteen months. As he explained it in his memoirs, he left because he figured he'd be called up for military service soon anyway. What he didn't mention was that he also wanted to escape a romantic entanglement.

He had begun dating a woman, Beth Hamquist, who worked as a cashier at the store. He'd had to carry out the romance on the sly, because Penney policy strictly forbade associates from dating one another (another rule Walton would later adopt for his business, perhaps because of his own experience). As the relationship developed, she wanted to marry him—and though Walton had decided he didn't want to marry her, he apparently left her with a very different impression at the time he left Des Moines for Oklahoma, in January 1942.[9]

At his Army physical, shortly before he quit Penney, Walton had been classified as unfit for combat duty because of a heart irregularity. But he remained eligible for limited duty. In Oklahoma, still waiting to be called up, he found work at a Du Pont gunpowder plant in the town of Pryor, northeast of Tulsa. Like many towns with war work, Pryor was overrun with workers; the nearest housing Walton could find was a room in a house in Claremore, 19 miles away. It was there, one evening at a bowling alley, that he met twenty-two-year-old Helen Robson. "My date had gone to bowl," Helen Walton recalled, when a young man sitting at the next lane chatted her up. "This fellow with his right foot hung over the seat said, 'Haven't I met you someplace before?' "[10]

The two soon began dating. But early on, the courtship was interrupted by a surprise visitor: Beth Hamquist, who came by train to visit the man she apparently still considered her fiancé. Walton's landlady graciously allowed her to stay in a vacant room at the house. As the landlady recalled, after some days Walton finally made it clear the engagement was off; the two had "a big row," and Hamquist left by the next train.[11]

None of this escaped Helen Robson. But it didn't derail her relationship with Walton, whom she clearly saw as a suitable spouse—as he did her. Robson wasn't the typical small-town girl. By the time she was a teenager, her father—a lawyer, rancher, and banker—was one of the wealthiest men in the region. Friends in Claremore still talk about how, as a way of training his children to manage money, he had given her and her three older brothers generous checking accounts they were allowed to use to pay for whatever they considered necessary. And, of course, he'd made the children partners holding equal shares in the family's 18,500-acre ranch.

She had been a quiet but intelligent child, outdoorsy, athletic, and, like her mother, very religious. She was valedictorian of her class at Claremore High School. She, too, had gone to college in Columbia, Missouri, enrolling at Christian College in the fall of 1937; but she and Walton hadn't crossed paths. After two years, she had transferred to the University of Oklahoma at Norman, from which she graduated in 1941 with a degree in economics. She, of course, hadn't had to support herself in college. She had been very active in sports—including swimming, fencing, and field hockey—and in music, playing the piano and the bassoon, an instrument on which she'd won a state competition in high school.

After college, she went to work for her father in his law office; one of her jobs was to keep the books for the family ranch. She was still working there when Walton began courting her. When he finally was called up for Army service, he asked her to marry him. Though the two had known each other only a few months, both sets of parents gave their eager approval, and Helen Robson set the date: Valentine's Day 1943. Walton flew back to Oklahoma from Los Angeles on a three-day pass for the ceremony. Bud Walton, who was in training to be a Navy pilot, came down on leave from St. Paul, Minnesota, to serve as best man. The newly married couple returned to California together.

Because of his ROTC training, Walton was commissioned as a second lieutenant. His war was utterly uneventful, spent directing security at various prisoner-of-war camps and aircraft plants in California and Utah. Off duty, he read books on retailing and prowled the Mormon Church's department store, ZCMI, studying its business. Helen Walton became pregnant and traveled back home to Oklahoma to give birth, on October 28, 1944, to a son they christened Samuel Robson Walton and nicknamed Rob.

Two days after Japan's unconditional surrender ended the war the following August, Walton was discharged as a captain. Even before the discharge, Helen's father, L. S. Robson, lobbied the young couple to come to Claremore. But Helen Walton vetoed the move, saying she felt they should set out on their own. So instead, they moved to St. Louis, where Sam Walton looked up a college roommate, Tom Bates, whose father had owned a store in Shelbina.

Bates worked in the shoe department of Butler Brothers, a company that franchised the Federated Stores department store chain and the Ben Franklin five-and-dime chain. He proposed that he and Walton join forces, putting up $20,000 each to buy a Federated Store franchise in St. Louis.

It would be a good franchise, Walton knew. Butler Brothers had a long and solid history. It had been founded in Chicago in 1877 as a wholesaler, supplying goods to small department stores and variety stores around the country. When many of the small independent stores it served had been pushed out of business in the 1920s and 1930s by big variety store chains such as Woolworth and S.S. Kresge, Butler Brothers had struck back by franchising its own stores.

The Federated Stores franchises were quite successful. Walton knew he could borrow the money from his rich father-in-law, and he was quite excited about the idea of running a big downtown department store. In all likelihood, Walton and his partner would have done well. But here Helen Walton made a decision that would have an impact far beyond anything she could have dreamed. She exercised her veto, saying she would not settle in any city of more than 10,000 people. She also told Sam she frowned on the idea of a partnership, saying her family had seen some "go sour."

Now Sam Walton talked further with Butler Brothers. There was still their other franchise; many of their Ben Franklin stores were in the kind of small town Helen wanted to live in. In fact, the company soon told him of a Ben Franklin franchise in Newport, Arkansas, that was for sale. Still in his Army uniform, Walton hopped on a train and went down to inspect the store. It would do, for now. L. S. Robson readily agreed to lend him $20,000; with that and $5,000 of his and Helen's money,° he bought the store, and the family moved to Newport.

A fat and happy town of 5,000 on the White River, about 80 miles northeast of Little Rock, Newport was surrounded by cotton and pecan farms. There were several industries in town, including a shoe factory and a metal mill. And, as the seat and market center of Jackson County, it was a railroad center for that part of the state.

Walton's store sat next to a J.C. Penney on Front Street, the main down-

---

° The total price would be the equivalent, in 1998 dollars, of $245,000.

town thoroughfare. It was a typical Ben Franklin of about 5,000 square feet, with a 50-foot frontage and counters ringing the walls, behind which clerks waited on customers and rang up sales on several cash registers. After two weeks of training at a Ben Franklin franchise in Arkadelphia, Arkansas, Walton, at age twenty-seven, took over his first store on September 1, 1945.

It was a perfect setup for a neophyte. Like other franchisees, Walton was handed accounting manuals that explained how to keep accounts payable and profit-and-loss sheets. He was told what merchandise to buy, how to display it, how much he could buy it for, and how much he could charge. He didn't have to buy all his merchandise from Butler Brothers, but he could expect a hefty rebate if he bought at least 80 percent of his goods from them. Retailing specialists in the company's Chicago headquarters advised him on how much help to hire and how much advertising to run, how the store should look if it was remodeled, and so forth. His hand would be held every step of the way.

All this support was intended both to help franchise owners like Walton compete successfully with other chains and to make sure that one Ben Franklin looked like the next and carried mostly the same goods. Most Ben Franklins were in country towns, and they were smaller than the Woolworth or Kresge variety stores. They carried everything from underwear to cleaning supplies, cookware, toys, cosmetics, and notions. Many items cost less than a dollar. A typical store would be open six days a week, from 9 A.M. to 5 P.M., often closing later on Saturdays.

In those days, as business historian Sandra Vance has noted, "competing" small-town merchants often informally colluded to keep prices fairly uniform, and higher than in cities, where there was more competition. It was a cozy, lazy setup—and one Walton immediately decided not to follow, in large part because for him it would have been a losing proposition. He quickly discovered that while the store he'd taken over had been averaging $72,000 a year in sales, a competing variety store across the street, a Sterling Store, run by John Dunham, was averaging more than $150,000 a year, even though it was slightly smaller.

Just as he had once used his lunch hour as a Penney trainee to cruise through the nearby Sears and other stores to see how they did things, now Walton began to discomfit Dunham by wandering over and spending a great deal of time overtly inspecting his rival's displays, checking his prices, and unabashedly studying his business as closely as he could. It would become his habit. On family trips, too, he'd habitually wander off to visit Woolworths, or Kresges, or whatever other stores he might find of interest.

The more he tried to compete with Dunham, the more Walton found it irksome to have to buy his goods from Butler Brothers. Their markups were just far too steep. So he started calling on manufacturers himself, though most refused to sell to him directly, fearing it would anger Butler Brothers. Walton soon was driving as far as Tennessee and Missouri to find whatever he could get at wholesale prices; then he'd turn around and sell the goods for less than the usual price. He hooked up with a fellow named Harry Weiner, a manufacturer's agent in New York who would buy goods directly from factories and ship them for only a 5 percent markup, instead of the 25 percent Butler Brothers took.

He was beginning to develop the idea of aiming for a high volume of sales, with a small profit on each sale, instead of taking a fat markup on fewer sales. Walton—who could talk about this kind of stuff until one's eyes glazed over—later described what he would do with the lower markup, using the example of women's panties. Butler Brothers sold him panties for $2.50 a dozen, and he was supposed to sell them at three pairs for $1.00. This gave him a gross profit of $1.50 for each dozen he sold. Weiner would sell him similar panties for $2.00 a dozen. Instead of pocketing the extra 50 cents, Walton began offering the panties at *four* pairs for $1.00. This actually cut his gross profit to $1.00 a dozen—that is, 50 cents *less* than before. But at the cheaper price, he sold so many more pairs that his overall profit from the panties soared.

He did the same thing with anything on which he could get a good deal. His business did so well he was able to repay his father-in-law's loan after two and a half years, and catch up in sales with Dunham. Walton was deadly serious about the rivalry. One day he heard that Dunham was going to expand his Sterling Store by buying out the lease of the Kroger grocery store next door. Walton dived into his car and raced 140 miles to the owner's home in Hot Springs, Arkansas, to buy the lease ahead of Dunham. "I didn't have any idea what I was going to do with it, but I sure knew I didn't want Sterling to have it," he said.[12]

In the end, Walton opened a tiny department store, called the Eagle Store, which, in its 2,500-square-foot space, never proved very profitable. It didn't have to; it did what he wanted it to, namely, to keep his rival from expanding.

Needing help as he juggled the two stores, Walton talked his brother Bud into moving to Newport to join him. The brothers had been close as children, and Sam Walton had long tried to steer Bud's progress. Bright and capable, Bud had a very different personality. He wasn't as outgoing as Sam; but at the same time he adopted a far more carefree attitude. He, too, had been president of his class in high school. But he didn't seem driven to achieve the way his older brother did. Where Sam was abstemious, never smoking and rarely drinking, Bud thoroughly enjoyed both vices.

Just as Bud had followed Sam in becoming a Penney's trainee, when Sam quit and wound up working in the gunpowder plant in Pryor, Bud too quit Penney and joined him there. During the war, Bud, a Navy lieutenant, became the leader of a torpedo bomber squadron aboard the carrier Manila Bay. He took part in the attack on Okinawa. Now he came to Newport, with his bride Audrey, whom he had met during his pilot training.

Bud became his brother's assistant manager, with the idea that he would learn enough about the business to open his own store. He paid his dues by doing, along with Sam and the clerks, a lot of grunt work: stocking, washing windows, helping trim windows, and one odious chore his sibling had lovingly reserved for him. Sam Walton had bought a popcorn-making machine and parked it on the sidewalk in front of the store to draw in business. It worked so well he borrowed $1,800 from a local bank to buy a soft-ice-cream machine, which proved an even better draw and highly profitable. But the messy machine had to be cleaned religiously. "I never forgave him for making me clean out that damned ice cream machine," Bud complained, not entirely in jest. "He knew I'd hated milk and dairy products ever since we were kids."[13]

But Bud soon moved on. In 1948, he snagged a Ben Franklin franchise in the town of Versailles, near the Lake of the Ozarks, in central Missouri.

In these early days, Sam Walton, though he put in the long hours any small-town shopkeeper was familiar with, found time for a slew of local activities. He would sneak away from the store for a few hours to fish or to hunt—as now, under the tutelage of his father-in-law, who visited frequently, he was learning to hunt for quail. He became president of the chamber of commerce and worked to try to attract more manufacturing businesses to the town, which had lost some of its workers to defense jobs elsewhere during the war. He joined the Rotary Club and served on the county levee board.

Helen, meanwhile, gave birth on October 8, 1946, to a second son, whom they named John Thomas. He was followed just twenty months later by James Carr, born June 7, 1948, and then by the couple's sole daughter, Alice, born October 7, 1949. Helen Walton told writer Vance Trimble of those days, "It was difficult because he worked so much at night. . . . I became accustomed to putting the babies to bed at night alone."[14]

In five years, Walton hiked his store's sales to $250,000 a year, making his store the top Ben Franklin franchise in a six-state region. Unfortunately, one of the people most impressed by this success was his landlord, P. K. Holmes. When Walton's five-year lease came up, Holmes refused to renew it, saying he wanted to buy the franchise to give to his son. Walton was flummoxed, then furious. He stormed off to a lawyer, who took one look at the lease and gave him the bad news: Walton had bumbled by failing to demand a set option to renew the lease when he first signed it. Legally, there was nothing he could do.

Holmes gave him a fair price. But though he walked away with more than $50,000 for the franchise, fixtures, and inventory, Walton was angry and embarrassed at being forced out. He immediately sold the Eagle Store lease to his erstwhile rival, Dunham, so he could expand his Sterling Store. Then Walton began looking for another store he could buy somewhere in northwest Arkansas—so the family could be closer to the Robsons in Claremore, and so he could be close enough to take advantage of the quail-hunting seasons in Oklahoma, Missouri, and Kansas, as well.

Robson, too, had been shocked by Walton's mistake in Newport; so this time, he took a hands-on approach to helping his son-in-law set up his business. He drove around with Walton, searching for a suitable store. After a few false starts, the two discovered that a small variety store was available on the main square in the tiny burg of Bentonville. Neither the town nor the store was ideal. The town, near the Ozark Mountains and surrounded by farms, apple orchards, and wooded hills, was half the size of Newport, with a population of about 3,000. "I worried about coming to this town because it was so small—it was smaller than what I'd grown up in," Helen Walton said.[15] Founded in 1837, it was the seat of Benton County; but as a trading center, it lagged behind the nearby town of Rogers, which had the advantage of being on the main rail line.

The store itself, Robson and Walton agreed, was too small. They would have to buy out the barbershop next door to expand. When Walton couldn't get the owners to come to terms, Robson personally took charge of negotiating the lease—making a point of signing one for ninety-nine years.

Tearing out the wall to the barbershop gave Walton a 4,000-square-foot store in a prime location. The square, guarded by a statue of a Confederate soldier, was shaded by oak and elm trees in a small park. It was then the heart of the city. Walton hauled over the fixtures from his Eagle Store in Newport, hung new lights, and reopened for business with a "remodeling sale" in July 1950. He called the store, which he'd paid $55,000 to buy and remodel, Walton's 5 & 10, though it was again a Ben Franklin franchise.

Here, as in Newport, Walton plunged into local activities, becoming president of the Rotary Club and of the chamber of commerce, running successfully for a seat on the city council, serving on the board of the local hospital, working on a committee that launched a Little League baseball program, teaching Sunday school at the Presbyterian church, joining the PTA.

And still he kept driving his car and a makeshift trailer to Tennessee and Missouri searching for manufacturers who would cut deals with him. He quickly repeated his Newport success. By October of 1952 he decided to open a second store on the town square in Fayetteville, 24 miles south, and home to the University of Arkansas. He felt confident enough not to make this one a Ben Franklin franchise. That would free him to sell whatever stuff he could find good deals on without having to worry about making sure 80 percent of his goods came from Butler Brothers.

He poached the store manager from a TG&Y variety store in Tulsa, after wandering in one day and being impressed with what he saw. "I had to move myself there, work half days for free until the store opened, and I remember sleeping on a cot in the storeroom," said Willard Walker, the manager. "But he said I would get a percentage of the profits, and that appealed to me."[16]

Before the opening, Walton ran across an article mentioning two Ben Franklin stores in rural Minnesota that had gone to "self-service." This was a new concept, to him anyway. Under self-service, instead of having clerks stationed at cash registers on counters throughout the store, all the check-out registers sat at the front of the store. Instead of waiting for a clerk to attend them, customers could retrieve items themselves, then take them up front and pay for all their goods at once. This was supposed to boost sales because customers didn't have to wait to be waited on; and it cut costs because a storekeeper needed fewer clerks. Walton hopped on an overnight bus to check out the Minnesota stores. Liking what he saw, he opened the Fayetteville store as a self-service outlet and converted his Bentonville store to the same format the following year.

He advertised the change heavily. Prices, the huge ads promised, would be clearly marked; clerks would be ready to help; and the store would have "lightweight shopping baskets in which to gather your choices as you go from counter to counter."[17]

With both stores thriving under the new format, now Walton grew bolder. On a trip 220 miles north to the Butler Brothers warehouse in Kansas City, he heard about a new subdivision being built at the edge of the city that would have something called a "shopping center" in the middle, a 100,000-square-foot cluster of stores, with parking all around, that would include a grocery, a drugstore—and a Ben Franklin franchise. This, to Walton, was another new concept he wanted in on.

But he didn't have the cash to do it alone. He called his brother Bud, who met him in the new suburb, Ruskin Heights, and looked over the development. He, too, liked the idea, so the two borrowed enough money to split the franchise 50-50. The store opened in 1954 and immediately took off, ringing up $250,000 in sales and $30,000 in profit its first year.

Dazzled by this success, Walton began dreaming—not about opening more stores, but about the fortune he could make as a mall developer. The fact that he was short of capital and treading on unfamiliar turf didn't dent his optimism. Walton plunked down $10,000 for an option on a 40-acre site in Little Rock. Walton's instincts about shopping malls were right, of course, but malls were too new to be an easy sell to the fellow investors he needed. Even his father-in-law wouldn't bite. After sinking two years and $25,000 into trying to develop a mall—at one point carrying petitions door to door to get the road to his site paved—he realized that it was time, as he put it, to take his whipping and walk away from the loss.

Focusing again on his retail business, Walton now decided he was getting mighty tired of spending so many hours driving on the narrow, winding two-lane blacktops that snaked through that part of the country. He phoned Bud and asked him to meet in Kansas City again, this time to help him buy an airplane. Bud, who considered his brother a reckless leadfoot—an opinion widely shared by family and friends—tried to talk him out of it, convinced he'd be even more of a menace in a plane. Sam Walton, never one to be easily discouraged, bought a plane anyway, an old single-engine two-seater Air Coupe that could cruise at 100 miles an hour.* Bud, who had as many misgivings about the rust-bucket plane as he did about his brother's piloting, refused to ride in it for nearly two years. Eventually, one day, the engine blew an exhaust stack just after take-off from an airstrip at Fort Smith, Arkansas; but Sam Walton, who led a charmed life when it came to airplanes, managed to circle around and land with a dead engine.

Now that he had wings, Walton began using his profits to open more variety stores, some of them Ben Franklin franchises, some not, in towns all around the region, such as Little Rock, Springdale, and Siloam Springs, in Arkansas, and Neodesha and Coffeyville, in Kansas. Some were partnerships with Bud, others with Robson or with Helen Walton's two brothers. He offered each new manager he hired the option to invest up to $1,000 in his store and become a limited partner.

---

* This was a plane once sold through Macy's and advertised as stall-proof.

In 1962, he decided to experiment with a larger Ben Franklin format, opening a 13,000-square-foot store he called Walton's Family Center in St. Robert, Missouri. The town itself was teensy, with a mere 1,500 people, but it was next to the Fort Leonard Wood military base. The store roared off to such a fast start that Sam would quickly decide to open two more Family Centers—one of them in Bentonville—and the next year he would expand the St. Robert store to 20,000 square feet. It would rack up $2 million in sales that year, second-highest of the more than 2,500 Ben Franklins across the country. By the end of 1962, Walton's fiefdom, in partnership with Bud Walton and the Robsons, encompassed 16 variety stores, making him the biggest single Ben Franklin franchisee and the biggest independent variety store operator in the country.

His abortive shopping center venture aside, Walton was riding high. For one thing, he had hit on some of the basic strategies that would become his hallmarks: locating in small towns, where he faced less competition from larger, more established chains; going straight to the manufacturers whenever possible so he could wangle goods at lower cost; selling those goods for less, shrinking his markup on each item to boost overall sales; scoping out competitors for any good ideas he could adopt; and offering managers a stake in their store, to attract better talent and keep them happy.

But, as Walton knew from reading trade journals and from his travels to talk to manufacturers and suppliers, there was a grave threat beginning to materialize, back east, to exactly the kind of variety store retailing Walton had now mastered.

How to face that threat would be his next great challenge.

3

Making the Turns

For one to understand the nature of the revolution that was about to hit retailing, it's important to have a clear picture of why and how Walton, in the early 1960s, was hitting pay dirt in all these small towns. To begin with, he was part of a retailing gold rush that followed World War II, when the huge economic expansion of the war years flooded over into the consumer economy. Americans were making and spending money like never before, and manufacturers and retailers could barely keep pace with the demand. In small towns, the sought-after consumer goods floated in on a wave of new variety stores. The Ben Franklin chain alone, for example, grew from 1,277 stores in 1947 to more than 2,500 by 1960.

These new stores brought with them new ways of doing business—new, at least, in the context of the remote small towns now being targeted by Walton and others. For in a broader sense, these hinterlands were only now catching up with a series of sweeping changes in retailing that, in some cases, dated from before Walton was born.

Take self-service. More than forty years earlier, in 1916, a Memphis entrepreneur named Clarence Saunders had founded a whole grocery chain based on that novel concept. In those days, if you shopped at a typical grocery store, you had to ask a clerk (once your turn came) to get most items for you from behind a counter. They would wrap your goods and then send someone along to deliver them to your home. Saunders's grocery, Piggly-Wiggly, was shockingly different. There, customers who wanted to look over a can of beans could actually pick the can off the shelf themselves.

They would carry their goods in handbaskets (another innovation) to checkout counters at the front of the store and then . . . they would have to *carry the groceries home themselves.* It was, in the South, utterly novel. The trade-off, of course, was that Saunders's prices, all clearly marked, were a lot lower (because his expenses were lower, since he needed fewer clerks).

Even earlier, in the Northeast, the Great Atlantic & Pacific Tea Co., or A&P, became the country's largest retailer through a strategy of dropping some of the usual services (such as home delivery) so it could cut costs and offer rock-bottom prices. But the evolutionary path of retailing that eventually would lead to Sam Walton and his gigantic discount-store chain actually began earlier still, in the mid–eighteenth century, with the spread of the railroad and the telegraph.

Rural merchants—men like Walton's grandfather—had always had to trek twice a year to the major market cities to buy a six-month supply of goods they would haul back home themselves. Together, though, these new technologies for the first time gave these merchants a practical alternative. The telegraph let them place orders within minutes and have them swiftly confirmed; and the railroad offered a speedy, reliable, and consistent way of shipping goods, giving merchants more confidence that what they ordered would arrive reasonably promptly.

Now the Samuel Waltons of that time, if they were on a rail line, could spend more time tending to business at the store. And they didn't have to keep enough inventory of each item to last six months; so they could now sell a broader variety of goods, and more of them. That boosted their profits and let them sell goods for less than before.

The railroad also brought them that staple of vaudeville jokes the traveling salesman. Wholesale houses in Chicago and other cities would pack salesmen out to the merchants to show them samples of the new goods and to take orders. Chicago, as the great rail center for points west, became home to the greatest wholesale companies—companies far bigger than any retailer had been before. Marshall Field & Co., which had its own retail store and sold wholesale to merchants elsewhere, saw its sales climb from $9.1 million in 1865 to $36.4 million in 1900 (two-thirds of which was wholesale). This was nearly 100 times as much as the sales that the country's largest retailers or wholesalers had made in a typical year in the 1840s. And the reason was simple: Now the reach of a Marshall Field was far greater.

The traveling salesmen didn't just drum up business; they acted as scouts, sending word back to their companies about economic conditions, the creditworthiness of merchants, and so forth. Credit was important because, under this system, the merchants didn't pay for the goods in advance or on delivery. Typically, they would be given twenty days to pay, with a discount if they paid in ten days or less. Knowing when and how much credit to grant was vital, because the wholesalers needed to know how much cash was coming in so they could pay the manufacturers promptly and keep their own costs down.

The salesmen also took on helping individual storekeepers with such things as knowing how much inventory to keep on hand, how to display goods, even how to keep the books—the sort of help the Ben Franklin chain would give to the young Sam Walton.

Each wholesaler set up far-flung buying arms to find new goods and manufacturers. By the 1870s, Marshall Field, for example, had buying offices not only in New York and other eastern cities, but across the Atlantic in Manchester and Paris. One buyer would take charge of each major line of products—shirts, say—and would work closely with manufacturers, sometimes giving exact specifications on how each item was to be made.

At the wholesale house, the goods would be unpacked, repacked, labeled, and shipped out. By the 1890s, bigger firms carried assortments of up to 6,000 products, made by as many as 1,000 manufacturers. They created traffic departments, to take orders, arrange shipments, and bargain with the railroads. And they came up with a new concept, called the "stock turn." This described how many times the stock on hand was sold and replaced within a certain time period, usually a year. The higher your stock turn with a given number of workers and the same facilities, the lower your cost per unit. It was a way to measure efficiency. As historian Alfred D. Chandler Jr. noted, Marshall Field's most frequent demand to his managers, and to the retailers his company sold to, was to "keep one's stocks 'turning' rapidly."[1] In the 1880s, Marshall Field averaged about five turns a year.

The success of the wholesalers soon gave rise in turn, in major cities, to department stores. Some began, as with Marshall Field, as sidelines to wholesale businesses; others, such as Bloomingdale's and Macy's, grew out of small dry goods or retail clothing stores that expanded into other lines. Their rough equivalent, for rural customers, was the next innovation, the great mail-order houses such as Montgomery Ward and Sears Roebuck & Co. It was also in these years that the first "chain stores" sprang up, stores that would begin moving into smaller cities, towns, and suburbs in the twentieth century.

All of these concerns followed the early wholesalers in carrying ever-broader assortments of goods: furniture, books, kitchenware, jewelry—whatever people might want to buy or could be convinced they wanted to buy. And all of them aimed at making profit by hiking not their prices, but the volume of their sales. In the old days, goods that didn't sell just sat on the shelves, gathering dust. Now, under the new commandment to turn stock, retailers began regularly clearing out goods that didn't move by marking down their prices and advertising the markdowns as sales. Ever-fiercer competition forced a whole new approach to selling: When someone like Richard Sears offered customers a money-back guarantee as a way of gaining their trust, other businesses had to offer guarantees too.

Ever-higher turnover became the key goal. By 1887, Macy's turned its stock an unheard-of twelve times in one year. The phenomenal flow of goods let Macy's take a smaller margin, sell for lower prices, and *still* make more money than the smaller, more specialized retailers it competed with, such as men's and women's clothing stores.

The competition was devastating to the small urban retailers and to the wholesalers that supplied them—so they howled for new laws to protect them from the department stores' lower prices. Their protests were soon echoed by country storekeepers, who by the 1880s and 1890s saw their trade being swiped by mail-order houses.

Wholesalers and some other merchants had printed catalogs and sold some goods by mail—usually to country stores—even before the Civil War, but it was only in the 1870s that Aaron Montgomery Ward founded the first company to sell a wide variety of goods exclusively by mail. Working out of a tiny office above a horse stable in Chicago, he put out his first mail-order catalog in 1874. "Cheapest Cash House in America" the cover blared. By 1887, his 540-page catalog listed more than 24,000 items for sale.

That same year a former railroad worker and P. T. Barnum–like huckster named Richard Sears joined with a watch repairman, Alvah Roebuck, to peddle watches by mail. They quickly added jewelry, then bicycles, medicines, clothing, and by the turn of the century, everything from horse buggies to gramophones. Early on, Sears wrote nearly all the copy, and he would hype anything from bust-enhancing creams ("unrivaled for . . . making a plump, full, rounded bosom") to electric "Heidelberg" belts (meant to stimulate one's, um, juices). But, beyond the hyperbolic prose with which he crammed his catalogs, Sears knew the other key to success. "Our very life Demands Volume," he wrote, in his usual understated way, "and if one hot fire doesn't get it I would build more fires."[2]

Sears knew that the best way of getting volume was, of course, to offer the lowest possible price. At one point, he jawboned one manufacturer into dropping the price it charged him for sewing machines, and he chopped his lowest price from $15.55 down to $12.50. Sales exploded, with 19,000 orders in one month, and profits from the line soared. He adopted the same tactic in every line he could. The covers of his catalogs, echoing bitter rival Montgomery Ward, trumpeted Sears as the "Cheapest Supply House On Earth."

Sales skyrocketed from $138,000 in 1891 to $10.6 million in 1900, and then more than tripled by 1905 to $37.8 million.

Sears grew to have 24 departments buying, setting prices for, and writing the advertising copy for each line of goods. To handle the cataract of goods thundering through its Chicago headquarters, the company created a distribution system that was the technological marvel of its time. It could handle 100,000 orders a day—more transactions than a traditional merchant fifty years earlier might have dealt with in a lifetime. The 1905 catalog breathlessly described it: "Miles of railroad tracks run lengthwise through, in and around this building for the receiving, moving and forwarding of merchandise; elevators, mechanical conveyors, endless chains, moving sidewalks, gravity chutes, apparatus and conveyors, pneumatic tubes and every known mechanical appliance for reducing labor, for the working out of economy and dispatch is to be utilized here in our great Works."[3]

A young Henry Ford (in the days before he popularized the assembly line) was reported to be among the visitors who traveled to Chicago to study this paragon of efficiency.

As Sears and Montgomery Ward kept accelerating their turnover, and lowering their margins and prices, the squeals of protest from country merchants and wholesalers could be heard nationwide. Playing off racism, local merchants often spread rumors that Richard Sears and Montgomery Ward were black. Some held public burnings of Sears and Ward catalogs. Sears, for his part, responded with unctuous sarcasm. In his 1902 catalog, he penned an editorial titled "Our Compliments to the Retail Merchant." It read, in part, "If a certain article in our catalog is quoted at $1.00 and your hardware merchant asks you $1.50 for the same article, we wish to say in behalf of your hardware dealer that this difference of 50 cents does not represent an excessive profit he is charging you" because, Sears noted, the local merchants could not buy in lots as large as the huge Sears.[4] He didn't have to spell out his obvious point, that Sears would always be cheaper.

The furor peaked in 1912, when merchants and wholesalers lobbied Congress to kill a bill that would extend the parcel post service on which the mail-order firms relied. They predicted (pretty accurately, too) that the bill would bring ruin to country stores, traveling salesmen, and wholesalers. Sears and Montgomery Ward lay low during the bitter fight, quietly funneling money through farm and labor groups that supported more parcel post; and they won the day.

Even then, though, another major retail rival was on the rise: the chain store. The earliest chains staked out turf that the bigger mass retailers largely had passed over, such as groceries, drugs, or furniture. But as the chains grew bigger, and as more of them sprung up, they began to take on the department stores and mail-order houses more directly.

A&P, the grocery outfit, was the first major chain store. It was founded in New York in 1859 by George F. Gilman as the Great American Tea Co. Gilman started out in the leather trade, but then was struck by the insight that people wanted cheaper tea. Most grocers priced tea as a luxury item, taking a fat profit on it to make up for the slimmer margins they took on other staples. Gilman, who sold *only* tea at first, aimed for volume instead, charging less and taking a lower margin. In seven years, he built a chain of 26 small tea stores, all in lower Manhattan. He also sold tea by mail. Within a few more years, Gilman and his partner George Hartford renamed their company the Great Atlantic & Pacific Tea Co., and began pushing outward. By 1880 they ran 100 stores as far south as Norfolk, Virginia, and as far west as St. Paul, Minnesota. Gradually adding coffee, cocoa, spices, extracts, sugar, and baking powder, A&P reached $5.6 million in sales by 1900. It moved into general groceries, began doing its own wholesaling, and in 1913 pioneered the "economy store," with the idea of offering food for as low a price as possible.

At these economy stores, A&P cut its costs by dropping home delivery, trading stamps, and other usual frills. It passed much of the savings along by cutting prices—sparking fights with its suppliers. At one point, executives at the Cream of Wheat Co. refused to sell to A&P, enraged that it was charging 12 cents per box instead of the 14 cents other grocers charged. Naturally, such fights—gleefully covered by the press—encouraged shoppers to think of A&P as the place to save money. This was no small feat at a time when the average family spent about 28 percent of its income on food (compared with about 16 percent in the 1990s), according to census figures.

With its new format, A&P expanded at an astonishing rate. George and John Hartford, who now ran the company (Gilman had retired), opened 7,500 stores in three years, though they closed half of those within a short time, following a strategy of saturating major markets and then weeding out the weak stores. By 1929, A&P had more than 15,000 stores and rang up sales for the year of $173 million, more than Sears, Montgomery Ward, and J.C. Penney combined. Imitators quickly followed.

Another pioneering chain was founded by Frank W. Woolworth, who in 1879 in Lancaster, Pennsylvania, opened a store where nothing cost more than a dime. His chain grew to 59 stores by 1900, with $5 million in sales—and, mostly by swallowing up rival chains, soared to 596 stores with $50 million in sales by 1912, the year it became a publicly owned company. As A&P was followed by the companies that became Kroger and Grand Union, among others, Woolworth sparked such imitators as Kresge and McCrory.

When it came to buying, the chains operated much like the other mass retailers. The biggest difference was that, because they were so spread out, they needed more management. Typically, chains divided their fast-growing territories into regions, each run by a manager whose assistants would ride regular circuits to check up on store managers at each location.

Compared to independent, mom-and-pop retailers, though, chains were far easier to run. If you owned an independent store, you had to train yourself to be a bookkeeper, buyer, seller, advertiser, and (often) janitor rolled into one. But big chains such as A&P and Woolworth, and franchise operations such as Ben Franklin, compiled manuals culled from the experiences of hundreds of store managers, giving newcomers to the chains an immense advantage. And higher up, the chains split up bookkeeping, advertising, buying, and other duties among their managers, giving each one a job that, while big, was pretty straightforward. (Indeed, in a critical article on management in *Fortune* in 1978, Theodore Levitt argued that it was easier to be the head of Kmart than to be the owner-manager of a small variety store, for just these reasons.)

But, of course, America was changing in other ways too that helped the chains. For one thing, more and more people were migrating from farms to towns, and as they did, they came within easier reach of the stores. In 1800, according to the U.S. census, only 6 percent of the population lived in towns of 2,500 or more, areas then deemed urban. By 1900, it was 40 percent; and by 1920, more than 51 percent lived in urban areas, now defined as cities of 8,000 people or more. That shift hurt the mail-order houses, which adapted by organizing their own chains of retail outlets. From a base of zero in 1924, Sears, for example, opened 324 retail stores by 1929.

The visionary who led Sears into opening stores was Robert Wood, a former Army man forever known as "the General." He became one of the most influential figures in American retailing history—and one of the strangest. In his later life a reactionary crank and McCarthyite, a lifelong

anti-Semite who was given his greatest opportunity by a Jew, Wood controlled Sears for more than 40 years. He kept a viselike grip on the company while maintaining it was less a corporation than a "cooperative
democracy." He would end his days shuffling aimlessly through the corri-
dors of Sears's headquarters, drooling and disheveled. But he also would
mold Sears into the world's largest retailer, and irrevocably change the
American landscape.

Intriguingly, Wood had first tried to steer arch rival Montgomery Ward
into becoming a chain. In 1921, while at Ward, Wood wrote a long memo
pointing out the strengths and weaknesses of chain stores and proposing
Ward open its own stores. Wood noted that small towns and cities, where
the only chains in operation were groceries, offered great promise. His
memo was ignored, and three years later, at odds with a higher-up, he was
fired. This was one of the greatest blunders in retailing. It was the decision
by Sears chairman Julius Rosenwald to hire Wood immediately and adopt
his strategy that gave Sears an insurmountable lead by the time Ward, belatedly, began opening its own stores years after it might have.

Wood would claim he devoured census reports the way other people
flipped through dime novels. He spotted not only the migration from farms
to cities, but the coming growth in the South and the West. And he recognized early on the implications of these shifts, and of booming car sales,
highway construction, and the growth of suburbs.

Cars needed parking, so Wood led Sears into buying large parcels of
land near highways, well outside the central cities, where land was cheap
and the stores could be surrounded by huge parking lots. He said later that
"as time went on, as the number of cars increased, as the lack of parking in
the downtown shopping sections grew more pronounced, as the congestion
in the streets and highways became more overwhelming, the importance of
this one basic factor became greater and greater. It largely nullified our initial mistakes, the superior cleverness of many of our competitors, and enabled us to grow at an astounding rate and to make very large profits."[5] By
the early 1930s, traditional downtown department stores followed his lead;
they too began to build branches in the new suburbs already beginning to
ring cities.

A&P, Woolworth, Sears—the chains that grew to dominate retailing did so
mainly because they could distribute goods for so much less than the retailers they displaced. The high volume of sales—the fast turnover of
stock—created a steady river of cash that gave the chains tremendous flex-

ibility to build stores, negotiate with manufacturers, and otherwise carry out business. They could grow by adding new lines of goods, opening new stores, or finding ways to boost the sales of existing lines. They could sell goods for less and still make more profit than smaller, independent retailers.

The department stores, mail-order houses, and chains created some of the largest fortunes in the land for the families that controlled them: the Gimbels, the Wanamakers, the Woolworths, and others. And in many cases the entrepreneurs who founded the companies, and their families, were able to keep their grip on the reins of the businesses because the enormous cash flow limited their need to raise money through selling stock.

But just as they had opposed department stores and mail-order houses, small merchants now banded together to battle the even greater threat they saw in chain stores. Their fears are captured perfectly by the ominous tone of the 1922 book *Meeting Chain Store Competition.* It begins: "Every retailer who has to meet chain store competition thinks he needs no one to tell him what a chain store is. To him it is a cut rate competitor managed from the outside by a soul-less corporation. What the principles behind it may be he neither knows nor cares. He is confronted with conditions, not theories, with the necessity for keeping trade which shows a persistent tendency to drift over to the chain store which shouts loudly and continually for business with colored window banners and multitudinous price cards."[6]

The book implored merchants to organize their friends, bankers, landlords, suppliers, and other connections to oppose the chain-store menace. And that's exactly what happened. The next year, in 1923, friendly representatives in the Missouri legislature introduced a tax on chain stores, meant to level the playing field. That bill was beaten back, but by 1927, 15 states were considering similar taxes; and two states—Georgia and North Carolina—adopted them. Another—Maryland—outlawed the expansion of chain stores within its borders.

The fight sparked a public relations war. For a flavor of the bombast one could hear at the time, on the radio, here's William K. Henderson, known as "Old Man Henderson," whose Shreveport, Louisiana, radio show was carried on stations across half the country: "American people, wake up! We can whip these chain stores. We can whip the whole cockeyed world when we're right. . . . I'll be your leader. I'll whip hell out of them if you will support me. We can drive them out in 30 days if you people will stay out of their stores."[7]

Henderson organized a "Merchant's Minute Men," which citizens could join for $12, to fight the chains. But, of course, even as the $12 checks and money orders poured in, people didn't stay out of "their stores." The lower prices were too seductive a draw.

Local merchants and their associations fought even more desperately with the arrival of the Great Depression. By 1939, 27 states had adopted chain taxes (though some of the earliest had been repealed by then). Business historians still debate just how much the taxes actually slowed the spread of the chains; ironically, it *is* clear that these taxes encouraged chains to build bigger stores (rather than more stores), which gave nearby independents even tougher competition.

Another favorite weapon was the "fair-trade" law, adopted by many states, that let manufacturers control the markup by setting a minimum retail price for their products. Chains couldn't legally charge less than that price. (A series of court decisions in the 1950s gradually diluted or voided these laws, though some survived into the '90s.)

A&P, as the largest retail chain in the country, bore the brunt of the anti-chain attacks. One broadside—meant to be a death blow—came in 1936, when associations of grocers and merchants, labor unions, and other groups joined together to push through the Robinson-Patman Act. Representative Wright Patman said quite baldly that the act, intended to help protect small local merchants, was aimed squarely at A&P. Dressed in the robes of antitrust law, the act essentially tried to make it next to impossible for chains to use their greater size and efficiency to get goods for less from manufacturers and to charge customers less for them. But the act, while it made things somewhat tougher for the chains, turned out to be a confusing legal morass, laced with loopholes.

Patman was back two years later, with a proposed national chain tax; but that measure died in the House Ways and Means Committee, after A&P alone spent about $500,000 to defeat it.

By then A&P had learned how to fight back more effectively. The Hartford brothers commissioned the public relations firm they had hired to fight the first Patman bill, Carl Byoir & Associates, to mount a series of ads touting the benefits to shoppers of lower prices and to farmers of having a chain on their side. One ad described how a promotional drive by A&P had helped triple sales of grapefruit in 1936, during a market glut, saving farmers from taking losses on their bumper crop.

Their backs against the wall, the Hartfords also wooed the unions, one of A&P's enemies in the 1936 fight. Where they once had closed stores rather than allow unions in, in 1938 and 1939 they signed a series of union contracts—and many unions turned around and lobbied actively against the Patman tax bill.

But the defeat of the tax bill didn't end the attacks. In 1939, the Justice Department brought criminal antitrust charges against A&P, based on a petition from the National Association of Retail Grocers. The company spent seven years fighting the charges. After losing the case in 1946, and paying $175,000 in fines, A&P was hit with a civil suit that would have forced it to break up. But the company managed to drag out this court battle for five years, until the Eisenhower administration came to power. Under Eisenhower, who was very friendly to big business, the Justice Department meekly settled out of court, leaving A&P essentially unchanged.

Eventually, the company fell for far different reasons: It couldn't keep up with even fiercer competition, in the form of the modern supermarket.

The father of the modern supermarket was one Michael Cullen, a man who very nearly became the Sam Walton of his day. In 1930, Cullen, then a forty-six-year-old grocer and warehouse man working for the Kroger grocery chain, wrote an audacious, red-hot letter to Kroger's president asking for an interview and proposing a radically new approach to the business. He wanted to build what he called "monstrous" stores, three to four times the size of standard grocery stores. These bigger stores, he said, would offer a huge assortment of name-brand foods and goods. To keep costs down, he wouldn't offer delivery or credit, and the stores would be built in low-rent areas, such as warehouse districts, where it would be cheap to provide ample parking. He would buy directly from suppliers to cut costs. And he would sell about one-fourth of the goods at his cost, to draw in customers who would then buy other goods.

Here's how he put it in his letter: "When I come out with a two-page ad and advertise 300 items at cost and 200 items at practically cost, which would probably be all the advertising I would ever have to do, the public, regardless of their feelings towards chain stores . . . would break my front doors down to get in. It would be a riot. I would have to call out the police and let the public in so many at a time. I would lead the public out of the high-priced houses of bondage into the low prices of the house of the promised land."[8]

Cullen also championed self-service. Despite Piggly-Wiggly's example in the South, at that time Kroger and most other grocery stores (as with other retailers) still kept the bulk of their goods behind counters staffed by clerks. Cullen proposed saving money by eliminating most of the clerks and putting the goods on shelves within reach of the customers.

Cullen helpfully included estimates of his costs and projected sales. He projected his stores would enjoy 10 times the sales volume of a typical A&P (then the industry leader) and 10 times the profit. He bragged that he had already tried this approach with one store in the small mining town of West Frankfort, Illinois (population 14,000) and had made a profit of $15,000 in one year, despite competing with an A&P store.

He closed the letter with lines Sam Walton might have taken for his own, decades later: "The one thought always uppermost in mind—How can I undersell the other fellow? How can I make my company more money? The answer is very simple: by keeping my overhead down, and only by keeping this overhead down can I beat the other fellow."[9]

Perhaps it shouldn't be surprising that Kroger's executives weren't the least bit interested and wouldn't even meet with Cullen. Nowadays, of course, Americans are so used to the kind of store he described, the kind of shopping he envisioned, that it's easy to forget how new and strange his ideas must have seemed—so much pie in the sky to the conservative Kroger men. Cullen immediately resigned from Kroger and, with another backer, opened his first King Kullen grocery store in Queens, in New York City, later that year. By 1933, *Business Week* reported that he had 8 stores averaging more than $1 million a year in sales. He increased that to 15 stores by 1936—and then, quite suddenly, he died, reportedly of overwork.

He didn't have a strong successor. Without Cullen and his cocksure energy, his budding chain wilted. But by the time of his death, the appeal to customers of his approach was obvious. And this time, it stuck. Though Saunders, at Piggly-Wiggly, had tried self-service earlier, he had lost control of his company to Wall Street raiders who split it up and sold it off. There are other, isolated examples of self-service grocery stores as early as 1896; but the historian Richard Tedlow concludes (as have others) that it was Cullen's success that sparked the spread of the modern supermarket across the country.*

There is one other pioneer concept worth mentioning, one that looks very much like a direct precursor of the modern discount supercenter. This was the Big Bear supermarket, which opened in a vacant automobile plant in Elizabeth, New Jersey, in 1932. This store—a then-unheard-of 50,000 square feet, more than 20 times the size of a typical grocery store—offered not only groceries, but general merchandise such as hardware, drugs, auto

---

* By 1937 William H. Albers, the Kroger president who had dismissed Cullen's proposal, was sounding a different tune. That year, in a speech at the founding meeting of the Supermarket Institute, Albers called Cullen the "one man who had the vision and the confidence to back up and build what is today, ladies and gentlemen, the supermarket industry."

accessories, radios, and paints. It had a soda fountain and a lunch counter. Opened on an investment of $10,000, it earned more than $166,000 its first year.

The Big Bear approach of combining food and general merchandise wouldn't catch on as a major form of retailing for decades; but the spread of the supermarket was immediate. It arrived at a time when more and more shoppers could hop behind the wheel of an automobile, which made them willing to travel a little farther to lower-rent areas, if it would save them money. By the time A&P itself jumped on board in 1938, the supermarket was coming to dominate the industry. Over the following decades, A&P and other grocery chains closed thousands of their older, smaller stores; supermarkets continued to grow larger; and the chains added more and more goods that traditional grocers hadn't carried. Thousands of smaller, independent grocers closed too; many of their owners wound up working for the supermarket chains they had been unable to compete with.

In the late 1950s and early '60s, competitors such as Safeway invested heavily to build new, even bigger supermarkets in the newest suburbs. These rivals increasingly carried other merchandise besides food—school supplies, seasonal goods, cosmetics, over-the-counter drugs, paper products, and other goods that offered higher profit margins than did food. A&P failed to keep pace. Instead of investing heavily in new stores, its president, Ralph W. Burger (who controlled 60 percent of the company stock), opted to pay out 90 percent of his company's profits in dividends to shareholders. They, of course, didn't complain. But this meant that while A&P did build some new supermarkets, it did so at a creakingly slow pace. It stayed with too many older, smaller stores; it moved too slowly into nonfood merchandise; and Burger and other company leaders made a host of other strategic blunders. Sales and profits gradually slipped. In 1965, A&P was surpassed by Sears, which with $6.4 billion in sales (versus A&P's $5.1 billion) now became the country's largest merchant. After a series of losses and missteps, a new chief executive, in 1975, closed one-third of A&P's stores; and as one retrenchment followed another, the company continued to flounder through the following decades.

Just as the development of supermarkets grew out of the same idea as some of the original A&P innovations, namely focusing on low prices and high volume, the strategies of Cullen and the other low-cost food merchants would be lifted wholesale by people such as Sam Walton and, at Kresge (later Kmart), Harry Cunningham, to create the great discount chains that would dominate retailing by the 1980s.

In natural history, sweeping changes in climate often have set the stage for new species to flourish while others, not adapted to the new conditions, wither away—as with the rise of large mammals and the demise of dinosaurs due to global cooling after several massive meteorite impacts.

Just so did a sweeping change in the U.S. economic climate, with the beginning of World War II, reorder the retail scene. During those years, deficit spending to fuel the war effort led to an enormous expansion. The gross national product climbed from $91 billion in 1939 to $166 billion by 1945; 17 million new jobs were created. And, despite war shortages, Americans who had scrimped and saved through the Depression began spending like never before. The average department store sale, $2 before the war, leaped to $10 by 1943.

To the surprise of many merchants, the end of the war didn't end the economic boom. Continued high employment, rising pay, and government policies that loosened consumer credit all helped rev up retail spending. And the rising prices that accompanied the boom set the stage for the new low-cost operators, the discount merchandisers.

In the late '30s and early '40s, various entrepreneurs borrowed from facets of the supermarket approach to open "discount houses" that offered national brand-name goods, such as watches, cameras, jewelry, radios, appliances, or what have you, at prices far lower than those of department or variety stores. Two brothers, Stephen and Phillip Masters, offer a typical example. In 1937, they founded their discount house, Masters Inc., as a flyspeck store selling radios and appliances in a low-rent section of New York City. Like most early discounters, the Masters bought their goods directly from manufacturers, sold only for cash, and offered no delivery or other services. They ran a tiny, no-frills operations far outside of the usual shopping districts. This was typical; discount houses might be opened in older office buildings, in warehouses—anyplace rent was cheap.

After World War II, discount stores really began to spread. By 1953, as the production of consumer goods, crimped by the war, finally caught up with demand, makers of name-brand goods began looking for ways to keep their output at full bore—and many turned to discounters, who could push through higher volume because they were willing to take dramatically lower markups. Business historian Sandra Vance estimates that discounters in these years took, on average, a 15 percent markup, compared with 38.8 percent for department stores. Discounters also found it increasingly easy to circumvent what tattered fair-trade laws still remained. They began building chains. By 1958, the Masters, for instance, had eight stores, offering a broad range of goods.

E.J. Korvette, another pioneer discounter, sold stock, becoming publicly held, in 1958. Founded by Eugene Ferkauf, whose father had been a luggage merchant in New York, Korvette had opened its doors ten years earlier as a 1,000-square-foot store in a second-story loft in New York City, selling luggage for about two-thirds the price of traditional retailers. After moving to the ground floor and adding apparel and household goods, Ferkauf opened four more stores by 1953. In 1954 he opened a 29,000-square-foot store in New York, and less than a year later, he opened a *162,000-square-foot* leviathan on Long Island. To grasp an idea of the scale, imagine putting a roof over four football fields side-by-side. By 1960, Korvette had 12 stores in four states. And it turned over its inventory up to 12 times a year, about par for a discounter, compared with 4 to 5 turns a year at the average department store.*

By 1962, discounting was a $2-billion-a-year industry, and many of the country's biggest retailers, especially the variety store chains, were wheeling their guns around to take aim. Had you sat in that year on an executive committee meeting at practically any big variety store chain, you would have heard elaborate campaigns laid out worthy of D day. Harry Cunningham, chief executive of the Kresge dime-store chain, looked to the obvious success of chains such as Korvette in committing Kresge to charge headlong into discounting. He announced a plan to open 38 discount stores, called Kmarts, within two years. Kresge's traditional variety store rival, Woolworth, wasn't far behind. Three months after the opening of Kresge's first Kmart store in a Detroit suburb, in March 1962, Woolworth opened its first Woolco discount store in Columbus, Ohio. The early Woolco stores were huge, 115,000 to 180,000 square feet, usually located in or near shopping centers.

Dayton Corporation, a regional department store chain based in Minneapolis, opened four Target discount stores, also in 1962. Many other big retailers began rumbling into discounting. Nearly all of them, as with Korvette, Kresge, Woolworth, and Dayton, targeted suburbs of large cities as their first markets, looking for strong customer bases that would give them the high turnover their operations would need to succeed.

Back in Bentonville, meanwhile, Sam Walton had been reading with

---

* In 1887, when Macy's had 12 turns a year, department stores were the low-cost operators. Over the years, their stock turns had slowed as they offered ever more upscale, expensive goods, focusing more on high margin than high volume.

avid apprehension about the growth of discount chains. By 1960, he'd made a point of traveling east to look over several Korvette stores and to talk to Ferkauf; in his ingenuous, aw-shucks manner, he grilled the founders of any other discount chain who'd agree to meet with him, including the heads of Spartan's, Zayre, and Mammoth Mart, among others. He devoted an increasing amount of time to studying their operations.

In part, Walton was worried that his variety stores wouldn't be able to compete with discount merchandisers—a competition that already was underway. A Texas-based wholesaler, Gibson Products Co., had begun converting its wholesale houses into discount outlets in 1958 and selling franchises. Herbert R. Gibson, the founder, had decided to open his stores in small cities—including Fayetteville, Arkansas, where the Gibson's Discount Center was pulling customers right out of one of Walton's stores. Gibson's credo was "buy it low, stack it high, sell it cheap."[10]

But then, too, discounting fit in with Walton's own impulse to aim for high sales volume instead of a fat profit margin. He was convinced that if he didn't go into discounting, his variety store chain would be doomed. The unexpectedly strong sales at his new Walton's Family Center in St. Robert, Missouri, a town of only 1,500, convinced him that he had an ace up his sleeve: There was much more business in those small rural towns than anyone else suspected. Since his visit east, Walton had been considering getting into discounting himself and contemplating how best to make it work in the small towns he knew so well. In early 1962, he came to a decision. He would go to Chicago and make a proposal to Butler Brothers.

4

We Sell for Less

Sam Walton had set his mind on opening a discount store as soon as he'd seen the crowds snatching up bargains at one discounter after another on his swing through the East Coast in 1960.

He couldn't get over those crowds. Back home, while flying his plane or driving his car he would find himself scouting locations, looking over towns with an eye to where he might put up not another Ben Franklin but a huge discount store, with plenty of parking, of course. He began sowing the seeds with his banker, talking about how quickly discounters were springing up around the country, how fast the new chains were spreading, and how so many seemed to be turning huge profits. It was a wide-open market.

But however badly Walton wanted in on the action, however convinced he was that he could make it work, he didn't want to do it on his own. Look at all the time and energy he'd incinerated trying to become a shopping-mall developer when he'd been, he knew, so dreadfully undercapitalized. To do discounting right—to grab as big a market *now* as he could—would take more cash than he could easily lay his hands on. This time, he wanted some deeper pockets behind him.

That was the point of his trip to Chicago, to the headquarters of the Butler Brothers. Arranging the meeting was easy; Walton was, after all, the biggest franchiser of Ben Franklin stores in the country. Selling them on what he had in mind was another matter. Walton may well have suspected that this would merely be the first stop on a frustrating quest to find a well-heeled partner or backer.

Let's set the scene: several Butler Brothers executives on one side, Walton on the other. Glancing down at the note-filled yellow legal pad he invariably carries with him, Walton touches on the terrific sales he's seeing at his big new Ben Franklin in St. Robert. He makes the case that there's a lot more business in these small rural towns than most retailers suspect, and that, especially in Arkansas and the neighboring states, this is a market so far almost untouched by the booming discount industry. How long it will stay that way, who's to say? Already, some discounters are edging into smaller markets, as Walton knows from the Gibson's Discount Center store that's giving him a tough time in Fayetteville.

Now he gets to the meat: He wants to build a discount chain, to open dozens of stores in small towns that could rack up sales dwarfing what he's doing in St. Robert. If Butler Brothers would be his discounting arm, selling him goods and giving him merchandising support just as it now does for his Ben Franklin stores, he could roll out a chain that would rake in tremendous profits for them and him. There's just one catch: To make this work, he tells them, you'll have to agree to cut the usual 20 to 25 percent markup on your goods to half that amount, or less.

You'll more than make up the difference on increased volume, he adds hurriedly; but even in the instant before any Butler Brothers men speak, it's clear what they're going to say. They look as if he's just asked them to hand over their wallets.

They can't say no fast enough, or with enough vigor. His logic may be impeccable, but his pitch falls as flat as Michael Cullen's proposal to Kroger did three decades earlier.

As it happens—even aside from the usual bureaucratic inertia and resistance to new ideas that afflicts most companies—this wasn't the best of times to make such a radical approach. Butler Brothers was now a division of City Products Corp., an Ohio-based conglomerate that paid $53 million to buy the retail concern two years earlier. The new owners had immediately ordered a major overhaul of the Ben Franklin chain—and now, as they met with Walton, the chain's executives were still busily trying to breathe new life into the business. They either didn't see or weren't willing to see, as Walton did, how great a threat discounters posed to variety stores. To create some special program for Walton that would doubtless lead other franchisees to demand lower markups just wasn't going to be on the agenda.

• • •

Walton's next stop was Dallas, where he approached his much larger competitor, Herb Gibson, to ask about buying some franchises. As he so often did, Walton had just flown down without bothering to make an appointment. So Gibson let him cool his heels for several hours in a waiting room. When he finally agreed to see Walton, Gibson was far more brusque than the men from Butler Brothers had been. He asked a few curt questions about Walton's financial resources, said he wasn't impressed, and showed him the door.[1]

Walton's options were shrinking. Now, on returning from Dallas, he drove down to Rogers, a town neighboring Bentonville. Rogers was one place Walton had scoped out as a promising spot for his new concept. Maybe Max Russell, who owned the local Ben Franklin franchise, would go in with him as a partner in opening a big discount store there.

Nope. Russell, who had a thriving real estate business to keep him busy, said he wasn't interested either.

Looking back, it might seem surprising that Russell and the others approached by Walton could have passed up such an opportunity. But, to these people, Walton's own resources seemed stretched thin and what he was selling sounded risky. His optimism aside, most people didn't believe stores in the small towns Walton wanted to shoot for could draw the vast volume of business a discounter would need to make up for the slim margins. And, this early on, discounting wasn't at all the obvious winner as a retailing concept that it would later be seen as. Aside from a few standouts—Korvette, say—most of the early discounters were undercapitalized; their stores looked shoddy; their merchandise was larded with irregulars, seconds, and discontinued lines, and they had trouble getting name-brand goods. Discounting had been around for decades without taking off. To many retailers, the appeal of the concept seemed limited.

One reason Walton was so keen to find a partner was that he was hamstrung by a bank deal he'd gotten roped into. A year earlier, Walton had let himself be talked into buying the Bank of Bentonville. He'd had to borrow the money from a Texas bank to pay for it, and now, not only was he mortgaged to the hilt, but as one condition of the loan, he couldn't open any new stores without his banker's permission.

His banker was James H. Jones, a thirty-one-year-old vice president at

Republic National Bank of Dallas and, like Walton, a man of ambition. Born in the tiny village of Alpena, in northwest Arkansas, Jones had graduated from the University of Arkansas and then studied banking management at Southern Methodist University and Harvard Business School. He had joined Republic straight out of Harvard, in 1954. After spending several years handling his bank's business with other banks and companies in Arkansas and Missouri, Jones had decided he'd like to buy a bank of his own.

He settled on the struggling Bank of Bentonville and lined up as partners two men who controlled First National Bank of Fayetteville, the largest bank in northwest Arkansas. But after rival bankers raised a ruckus about First National getting even bigger, his partners had backed out, saying the deal might hurt their business with other local banks. At that point, one of them suggested Jones talk to Walton.

"They said, 'This guy, Walton, he's ambitious as hell. Got a couple of Ben Franklin stores,' " recalled Jones. "I'd never heard of him."

As it happened, Walton himself had recently become a director of the Bentonville bank. His friend, the attorney William Enfield, had begged Walton to come on board to help do something—anything—about the bank's new majority owner, Cornell Smith. Smith, a native New Yorker who'd moved to Bentonville to run the bank, understood the local ways of doing things about as well as if he'd moved from the moon.

"We had one old boy who was running cattle on several hundred acres north of Bentonville," Enfield remembers. "He was a substantial depositor, and very impetuous. One day, he's out in the pasture and it occurs to him he has some bank business; so he jumps in his pickup, drives into town, and charges into Smith's office. Smith took one look at the guy's dung-covered boots and snapped 'Get off my rug!' " The indignant rancher yanked his deposits and moved to another bank.

In six months, Enfield said, the bank's deposits, once $3.5 million, shrank by nearly a third. Walton, who relied on the bank for some of his own business needs, readily agreed to buy a few hundred dollars worth of stock and join the board.

It wasn't long afterward that Jones made a cold call to Walton from Dallas and tried to talk him into buying a majority stake in the bank outright. It could help Walton's other businesses, he said, and Republic National could loan him the money in full, at 3.5 percent interest. Walton heard him out, but "he said, 'I don't know anything about banking. . . . I don't think I'm interested,' " Jones said. But then, after talking it over with Helen, Sam changed his mind.

Jones drove up to Bentonville with his wife to meet the Waltons in person. As they sat outside of the Walton's home and discussed the deal, Jones asked to see Walton's financial statements. "He said, 'I don't have one.' . . . He got out a brown paper bag and a pencil and began putting numbers down. He basically had very little money. He had three stores, in debt, and the house. I said, 'This isn't going to work.' "

Walton didn't have enough collateral. Then Helen Walton mentioned the trust her father had set up for her and her share in the 20,000 acres of land in Oklahoma owned by the Robson family partnership. With Helen Walton signing for it (and with the approval of her father), Jones loaned the couple $350,000. Smith, by now only too happy to leave the wilds of Arkansas, readily sold them his majority interest in the fall of 1961.

Because, as part of the deal, Jones now had to sign off before Walton could open any new stores (since Republic National Bank would finance them), Walton almost immediately began selling him on the profits to be made from discounting. Jones liked the concept, and his own research convinced him Walton was right. But he had his own ideas. Even before Walton was spurned by Butler Brothers, Gibson, and Russell, he and Jones had spent months arguing over where in Rogers they should build the first store. Finally, after Walton got back from his round of rejections, they agreed to put up a 16,000-square-foot store a few blocks from downtown.

Bud Walton agreed to put up 3 percent of the money; another 2 percent was put up by Don Whitaker, a gruff, one-eyed fellow who would be the store's manager and whom Walton had lured away from a TG&Y variety store he managed in Abilene, Texas, by promising him a stake in the business and a share in the profits. Walton—with Helen again co-signing—pledged the family home as collateral and put up the other 95 percent.

The man who came up with the name for Walton's new venture was Bob Bogle, who managed Walton's Ben Franklin store on the Bentonville town square. How Bogle wound up with that job illustrates just how creatively Walton went about finding managers in the early days. Bogle and Walton had met in the early 1950s, at the Bentonville Rotary Club. Both of them loved quail hunting, and Bogle, who worked as a health inspector for the state, often invited Walton to hunt with him at his brother's farm in Kansas and his father's farm in Missouri.

When Walton decided in 1955 to hire a manager for his Bentonville store, he approached Bogle in a roundabout way, casually asking him if he knew of anybody who'd make a suitable manager. "I said I'd look around," Bogle recalled. A few months later, "as we were going into a Rotary meeting, he asked me if I had found somebody, and I said I'd get on it," Bogle said. "He said, 'I don't guess you'd be interested?' I said, 'I don't think so, but I'll sure listen to your proposal.' So that night we went over to their house, and he brought books home to show me the store's volume, and net profit.

"He said he needed somebody because he'd like to open a dozen stores. Helen about fell out of her chair. She hadn't heard that yet. She said she thought three stores was ample."

Helen's objection fell on deaf ears. After a little more discussion, Walton offered Bogle the same salary he made as a health inspector, plus 25 percent of the store's net profits. He also said Bogle could buy an interest in the store, if he liked, and in any of the new stores he planned to open. The fact that Bogle's only retail experience had been a brief stint during his college days working at a Rexall Drug Store in Tallequah, Oklahoma, didn't faze Walton in the least.

Company lore has it that Walton hired this way because he relied more on his instincts about people than on their résumés. But, really, he had little choice. It wasn't easy to attract experienced managers to his modest operation so far from any big city.

In this case, his instincts panned out. Bogle worked out well enough that Walton sent all the Walton children, as they got old enough, to work at the store, his sons as stock boys and Alice running the popcorn machine. Bogle, for his part, invested every penny he could in each store as they opened.

Now, as the construction crew was putting the finishing touches on the new building in Rogers, Walton and Bogle were flying together to Fort Smith, Arkansas, to scout out another store location. As Walton piloted his single-engine Tri-Pacer airplane (a replacement for the defunct Air Coupe), he reached into a pocket and pulled out an index card on which he'd jotted several notes. Handing it to Bogle, he said, "This building being built in Rogers has got an address, but we haven't got a name for it. We got to call it something."

Bogle looked over the several names Walton was toying with, each of them three or four words long. "As Scottish as I am," he said, "I'd call it something short, but keep the Walton name." Bogle lettered WALMART on the card and handed it back. Buying just seven letters to make up the sign would keep the cost down, he pointed out. Walton glanced at the card, stuck it back in his pocket, and moved on to another subject.

A few days later, Bogle stopped by the store to see how the construction was coming along. "Rayburn Jacobs, our sign maker at the time, was out there with a ladder and already had the *W, A*, and *L* up and was going up the ladder with the *M*," he recalls.

Walton didn't pick the name to save on letter costs, though. Completed, the store's sign read, "Wal-Mart Discount City." It was flanked by smaller signs that spelled out the new store's selling points: "We Sell for Less" and "Satisfaction Guaranteed."

In ads for the store's July 2, 1962, grand opening, Whitaker promised, in what would become another defining policy, that the new store would offer "everyday low prices."

As with many epochal moments in business history, it was decades before the significance of this date became clear—decades before Wal-Mart would celebrate the opening of this store as the beginning of its own rise, before Wal-Mart would be recognized as the standard-bearer for a revolution in retailing. It would be a revolution that would change not only how the entire country shops, but how and where the goods we buy are made; that would speed the country's shift from a manufacturing to a service economy; that would reorder the economies of thousands of small towns; and that would alter even the suburban landscape in which so many Americans live.

None of this was the least bit apparent then, of course. The store itself was nothing to set folks from bigger retailers quaking in their wing-tips. The ambiance was strictly bargain basement. Racks of clothes hung from metal pipes, and most of the goods, from automotive supplies to toys and sporting goods, were stacked on tables. There were three checkout stands. The store had a staff of twenty-five, mostly women, paid 50 to 60 cents an hour, well below the federal minimum wage of $1.15 an hour. Newspaper ads claimed the store sold only first-class merchandise—"No seconds or factory rejects in the store—our policy forbids it"—but that was, well, hooey. Many of the goods were junky.[2] Many manufacturers refused to sell to discounters, especially small ones with little clout. So Walton had been forced to scrounge for goods from any place he could, with low price taking precedence over quality.

But the prices—they drew in the shoppers. In those days, the manufacturer's suggested price was what most retailers actually charged. Opening ads for Wal-Mart offered a stark contrast: a Sunbeam iron for $11.88, versus the manufacturer's suggested price of $17.95; a Polaroid camera for $74.37, versus $100; a Wilson baseball glove for $5.97, versus $10.80. Customers were promised savings of 20 to 30 percent across the board, with nearly every item backed by a manufacturer's guarantee.

In its first year, the store's sales reached $700,000—roughly triple the sales from Walton's typical Ben Franklin store. But, at the same time, Walton's Family Center variety store in St. Robert was approaching $2 million in sales for a year. Then, too, in deciding whether to pursue this discount notion any further, Walton had another consideration to chew over: On the day of the Wal-Mart grand opening, grim-faced Butler Brothers executives from Chicago had trouped through the store, which offered direct competition to Max Russell's Ben Franklin franchise. They had issued Walton an ultimatum not to build any more of these stores, according to Walton's memoirs.

And for the next two years, in fact, Walton did not open another Wal-Mart. He opened two more Family Centers first—putting one in Berryville, Arkansas, and another in Bentonville. In 1964, though, he decided to try two more Wal-Marts, ultimatum or no, and opened stores in Harrison and Springdale, Arkansas.

The Harrison store was typical of the early Wal-Marts. It went into a vacant building on a site that had been a cattle-auction yard, just off the highway bypass leading into town. The store had a concrete floor, an 8-foot ceiling, goods stacked on wooden planks, and, at first, no rest rooms. And Walton, despite the way he'd been burned on the Newport lease, still had a tendency to skip the fine print. After agreeing on terms for a lease, Rex Younes, the owner of the Harrison site, asked Walton about drawing up a contract. Walton answered, "your word is good enough for me, Mr. Younes, if mine is good enough for you."[3] Younes agreed, and they wrapped up the deal with a handshake.

There was one thing about the Harrison store that would long be remembered and retold in company lore. And that was what happened when it opened.

Walton had been keen to make a big splash at the opening. He wanted the store to be a success, of course, but he also hoped to impress a particular guest he'd invited, a man Walton badly wanted to hire. He knew that to run and supply and keep control of a growing number of stores, that to expand the way he wanted to, he needed to bring on board more experienced retailers—especially people strong in areas he was weak in, such as distribution and finance.

A friend of Walton's who ran a regional discount drug chain, J. W. Crank Co., based in Springfield, Missouri, had bragged to him repeatedly about a young financial whiz they'd found who was doing great things at their company, a fellow named David Glass. Soon, Walton was wooing Glass; and he talked him into coming down to Harrison to see the kind of chain Walton was building.

The store opened on a witheringly steamy August day. In later years, when Glass would tell the story, he would remember it as 115 degrees. Walton had finagled a good deal on ripe watermelons, and had stacked truckloads of them outside the store's entrance. He'd also hired several donkeys to give children rides. But in the heat, the watermelons started popping. The sweet, sticky juices flowed across the lot, mixing in with donkey manure to form a disgusting, funky mess that customers tracked all over the store on their shoes. Glass was appalled. He turned Walton down flat. "He was a nice fellow, but I wrote him off," he said.[4]

As crude as the Harrison store—and Walton's efforts to promote it—seemed, it and the other early stores faced little enough competition to succeed. And under Walton's repeated visits, they steadily improved. Over the next couple of years, Walton would open a few more variety stores; but he turned his attention increasingly to the Wal-Marts. Sticking mostly to small rural towns and county seats, Walton opened another Wal-Mart store in 1965, four more over the next two years, then five more each year in 1968 and 1969. By the end of 1969, he had 14 variety stores (including nine Ben Franklin franchises), and 18 Wal-Marts: two in Oklahoma, five in Missouri, and the rest in Arkansas. All were a short flight from Bentonville or a few hours by road. The Wal-Marts ranged in size from an 11,000-square-foot store in tiny Morrilton, Arkansas, to a 44,000-square-foot mammoth on the outskirts of North Little Rock.

In almost every case, the Wal-Mart store was the biggest retailer in town. That was part of the reason that—with the exception of North Little Rock—Walton stuck to towns with fewer than 25,000 people. He figured that if he could offer goods in, say, Berryville, at prices people could match only by driving to a big city such as Fayetteville, they'd skip the drive and shop at his stores. And his discount competition really was minimal. Of the more than 900 other discount retailers operating by the end of 1969, few others targeted towns anywhere near as small. And of those few, such as Gibson's; Gamble-Skogmo, based in Minneapolis; Fed-Mart, based in San Diego; and Woolworth, which opened a few Woolco discount stores in towns as small as 25,000, only Gibson's overlapped Walton's territory. And even Gibson's only overlapped with a few of the very largest towns Walton would look at.

Walton's operations were not the most technically sophisticated around. He was too cheap to pay for market surveys. He preferred to scope out a town by counting the number of cars on the main square or on the main road through town. Walton's first office had been a cramped nook at the back of his Bentonville store, with orange crates for shelves and a plywood sheet for a desk. His upgrade consisted of moving to three small rooms with sagging floors, perched above the office of his attorney, Enfield, on the town square. He kept all his books and ledgers by hand.

The stores themselves were often, as Walton himself put it, truly ugly. Undercapitalized, mortgaged up to his keister, Walton was determined to keep his rents below a dollar a square foot, even if that meant going into buildings other retailers sneered at. He put the Morrilton store in an abandoned Coca-Cola bottling plant. When it opened, it had pipes sticking out of the floor and no air-conditioning. The fixtures were hung from the ceiling with baling wire. At some grand openings, when there weren't enough cash registers, clerks would stuff cash into and make change out of cigar boxes instead.

At a Ben Franklin franchise, keeping stock was a snap: Every store had the same basic assortment of goods, and each store had an inventory book out of which more of any item could be ordered as needed. Not so at the Wal-Marts. Their selection depended on Walton's catch of the day. "We really didn't have an assortment of merchandise, just whatever salesmen could offer us," said Claude Harris, one of Walton's early managers. Walton had few regular distributors—and hardly any that would give him credit. "A lot of companies wouldn't sell to us unless we paid them first," said Harris. Many big companies wouldn't sell to Walton at all; others, such as Procter & Gamble, "tried to tell us how much to buy and what to sell them for," said Harris.

Walton was determined to get products from the Procter & Gambles of the world. He knew, from his endless store visits, that the best discounters used the same key strategy: Take name-brand health and beauty aids—such as toothpastes, soaps, and shampoos—stack them high, and sell them at cost. Give them away for whatever you paid. Such bargains, advertised like crazy, pulled in customers who then loaded up on other goods that, while priced low, carried gross profit margins of up to 30 percent.

But for now, given his rural base and the relatively small size of his company, Walton had to take what goods he could get. Whatever he could buy cheaply was what he had to turn into his loss leaders.

"We didn't have systems," recalled Walton. "We didn't have ordering programs. We didn't have a basic merchandise assortment. We certainly didn't have any sort of computers. In fact, when I look at it today, I realize that so much of what we did in the beginning was really poorly done. But we managed to sell our merchandise as low as we possibly could, and that kept us right-side-up for the first ten years."

All that counted was one thing: "When customers thought of Wal-Mart, they should think of low prices, and satisfaction guaranteed. They could be pretty sure they wouldn't find it cheaper anywhere else, and if they didn't like it, they could bring it back."[5]

When he could get name brands, it was sweet. For example, when he opened the third Wal-Mart store, in Springdale, Walton scored bargains on several truckloads of Crest toothpaste and Prestone antifreeze, which he offered at 27 cents a tube and $1 a gallon, respectively. "We had people come from as far as Tulsa [more than 100 miles away] to buy toothpaste and antifreeze," remembers Clarence Leis, an early manager. "The crowd was so big that the fire department made us open the doors for five minutes, then lock them until shoppers left."[6]

On other goods, Walton stuck to a maximum markup of 30 percent, even when he could take a higher markup and still be well below a product's list price. If you got a good deal, pass the price on, he told his managers—because in the long run, planting the idea that Wal-Mart had the lowest prices would pay off in higher sales.

All through the '60s, finding good managers was just as tough as getting good merchandise. Not every unorthodox find worked out as well as Bogle, the health inspector. And, as his abortive effort to impress David Glass at the Harrison grand opening showed, it wasn't easy—even for someone as charming and forceful as Walton—to convince seasoned merchants to cast their lot with what, at the time, seemed an uncertain and haphazard venture.

Walton constantly trolled competing variety stores for veteran managers. Leis, for example, was running a McCrory variety store in Vinita, Oklahoma, when Walton wandered in one day and introduced himself. Leis soon agreed to visit Bentonville, where he stayed at the Waltons' home for several days while the two men negotiated.

But even variety store experience was no guarantee. Leis, who became the second manager of the Rogers Wal-Mart, got a call from Walton one day, telling him that his inventory was $20,000 too high and to stop buying goods until it was back in line. A few weeks later, visiting the store, Walton stopped in amazement before a shirt counter in the men's department that was utterly bare. When he demanded an explanation, Leis sheepishly said he was still overstocked on his overall inventory, so he hadn't ordered more shirts.

"Use your common sense," Walton told him. "Don't ever run out of shirts and things you need. What I meant was when you're long on inventory, don't load up with useless odds and ends."[7]

Claude Harris, who'd been trained in the Woolworth chain and was managing a store in Memphis for that company when Walton hired him away in 1960, said, "It was obvious to me a lot of the store managers didn't know how to run a store." Harris copied many of Woolworth's manuals to make many of Walton's earliest policy guidelines telling managers how to run stores, how to order goods, how to treat employees, and so on.

Most of Walton's early managers never went to college—and, in a pattern that would persist into the 1980s, they discouraged Walton from hiring college graduates, arguing that such men wouldn't be willing to work hard enough. So, in effect, working for Walton became these men's schooling; and Walton had to supervise his managers very closely. He made them turn in weekly and monthly reports. Each report had to include what Walton called a "Best Selling Item," to focus their attention on what merchandise was selling and why. Over and over again, he ordered them to check on the competition; when a Gibson's store opened in Rogers, Leis took to sending his assistant managers over at night to rummage through the dumpster behind Gibson's to collect price tags and anything else they could find.

Walton always asked a prospective manager to bring his wife to the interview. Helen Walton would be there too. Walton felt a man's choice of wife showed his character. Also, as Harris said, managing for Walton "was a demanding job—they knew the wife's support was very important." Often, too, the prospect's wife had to be sold on the idea, which was Helen Walton's job. The hiring of Ferold Arend in 1966 was typical.

Arend, who eventually became president of Wal-Mart, was a regional manager for the J.J. Newberry variety store chain when Walton approached him. Sam and Bud Walton flew to Omaha to meet with Arend and his wife and persuaded the couple to fly back with them to Bentonville, and then to Conway, Arkansas, where the fifth Wal-Mart store was under construction. But Arend had been unimpressed—the Bentonville store seemed disorganized and the location of the Conway store, next to a smelly stockyard, struck him as terrible. He turned Walton down. But Walton never took no as a final answer. He was soon back in touch, showing Arend the new Conway store's sales figures, which were as high for one day as some of Arend's Newberry stores made in a month. That popped open Arend's eyes; but then his wife said no, balking at moving to what seemed a hillbilly backwater. It took another visit by the Waltons for Helen to convince her that Bentonville would be a good place to live.

Walton spent more than a year reeling in his first financial officer, James Henry, an accountant in nearby Harrison. Ron Mayer, Henry's successor and a man who eventually became—briefly—Wal-Mart's chairman and chief executive, turned down Walton repeatedly before coming on board as a vice president in July 1969 for far higher pay than Walton initially had offered. And 12 years would pass before David Glass would change his mind and join the company.

Those who came on board quickly found that Walton set a brutal pace. He liked to start work over breakfast at a coffee shop downtown, always by 5 A.M. and often by 4 A.M. "That damn pickup truck of his had a hole in the muffler," said Enfield, who was Walton's neighbor as well as his attorney, "and I'd hear him every morning." On days he was out visiting stores and consulting with managers, Walton might stop back in the offices at six o'clock in the evening, just as his other executives were heading out the door, and collar them all, saying he had a few more things to go over.

It wasn't just a question of working long hours. Walton expected his managers to be available for work whenever he was. During the quail-hunting season, he regularly would disappear for a few hours in the afternoon with his dogs and shotgun. But when he would come back, he wanted to pick up wherever he had left off. Walton never had time to wait. When Jack Shewmaker—later briefly Wal-Mart's president—joined the company in 1970, he was overseeing the movers as they hauled furniture into his newly rented home in Bentonville when Walton called and sent him on the spot to St. Robert, Missouri, for two weeks to manage the opening of a new store.

By the late '60s, Walton had dropped off the city council and given up his presidencies of the chamber of commerce and the Rotary. While his boys were in their pre-teens and early teens, he had been active in the local Boy Scout troop; but as they got older, Walton set that and most of his other activities aside to concentrate on business. Other than sneaking away to hunt, his only diversion was to take an hour or so at lunchtime to play tennis. One of Walton's favorite tennis partners was George Billingsley, who handled sales for a family-owned real estate business. He claimed they played often because "I could play anytime, and Sam didn't want to pull anyone off the job at the office."

Walton gave his managers great leeway in running their stores and insisted that they show initiative when it came to selling goods. "You were never going to get fired for *trying* something," Harris said. "Sam used to say, 'I ain't gonna fire you for making a mistake—but if you make it twice, I will.' "

Another early manager said, "If you did your job for him, he'd pay you well." But for all his folksy demeanor and his willingness to give his managers scope, Walton "had no tolerance for ineptitude," he said. "He was very tough on people." Walton couldn't afford to be sentimental. He didn't hesitate to move aside those he didn't feel were up to the job. In 1966, he had practically begged Henry, the accountant, to become his financial officer. Three years later, when he felt Henry was getting swamped under his workload, he unblinkingly demoted him in favor of Ron Mayer. Henry left the company a few months later.

Up to this point Walton's distribution system for his new stores wasn't really any kind of system at all. Getting goods to the stores was a constant problem, and one that grew worse with every new store. Anybody might be drafted: Sam's son Rob barely had his license the first time he found himself hauling a truckload of goods down the highway to a Wal-Mart one night.

The process of distribution is one of the keys to understanding Wal-Mart. What is a retailer, after all, but a way for goods to get from factories into people's hands?

Walton's predicament was that most of his stores were too small to be able to take deliveries of merchandise in the pallet-loads manufacturers sent, so he had to do his own warehousing. Walton would have been delighted to use distributors, the middlemen who delivered scores of goods from manufacturers to most retailers. But he was in towns that were too small, too rural. Donald G. Soderquist, later vice chairman of Wal-Mart, put it this way: "The trucking companies did not have the delivery scheme for dependably sending shipments out to small markets, as opposed to the

Memphises and St. Louises; so [our] distribution system, in that sense, was born out of a necessity to get reasonable and dependable deliveries."[8]

As a makeshift measure, Walton rented a garage near his Bentonville store, where workers would repack shipments into smaller loads, then call delivery trucks to haul them to the stores. But even with just five or six stores, this system was often swamped. By the mid-'60s, Walton realized that he needed to build a real warehouse and find somebody who could figure out a better way of distributing goods to his stores.

At the same time, with the reports he had each store manager send him, he was already trying as best he could to track his inventory: how much merchandise he had in each store, what was selling and what wasn't, when to order more goods, and when to mark down prices on stuff that wasn't moving. But better record-keeping, he knew, could help refill empty shelves faster and boost sales. He needed somebody with expertise there, too. It was a problem he'd been mulling over for years.

Back in 1964, when he had decided to open his second and third Wal-Mart stores, Walton had flown back up to Chicago to try one last time to talk Butler Brothers into distributing to his discount stores. He was soundly rejected again, but he didn't seem to have been terribly dismayed. Just after the meeting, he collared one young executive, Soderquist, to talk not about his proposal, but about computers. Scribbling copiously on his yellow legal pad, Walton quizzed him about how and for what purpose the Ben Franklin division was using computers and what sort of future uses they might have.

The next morning, a Saturday, Soderquist went shopping at a new Kmart store that had recently opened in a Chicago suburb near his home. As he was wandering through the store, he noticed that a familiar figure had cornered one of the clerks and was scribbling furiously away in a notebook. It was Walton. As Soderquist walked up behind him, he could hear Walton peppering the clerk with questions: How frequently did they re-order goods? How big were their orders? How long did orders take to come in?

Walton got down on his hands and knees, yanked open a sliding cabinet door under a table stacked with folded garments, and asked the clerk how they tracked the amount of stock in the cabinet when they placed orders.

Finally, Soderquist interrupted them. "I said, 'Sam Walton, is that you?' And he looked up from the floor and said, 'Oh, Don! Hi! What are you doing here?' I said, 'I'm shopping. What are *you* doing?' And he said, 'Oh, this is just part of the education process. That's all.' "[9]

•   •   •

It was to learn more about computerized record-keeping—and maybe snag a good computer systems person—that Walton sat in on a program IBM sponsored in Poughkeepsie, New York, in 1966. In his usual, casually relentless way, Walton locked onto one executive at the program, Ron Mayer, who had introduced himself as the chief financial officer of the Kansas-based A.L. Duckwall Co. variety store chain. As Walton drew him out, it was clear Mayer knew his stuff. Walton immediately began trying to reel him in.

It took three years of courting, though, before Walton finally talked Mayer into coming down to Arkansas in May of 1969 to take a look for himself. Then Walton nearly killed them both in his airplane. Almost any of Wal-Mart's early executives can recount with relish some hair-raising misadventure flying with Walton, but Mayer may have come the closest to shuffling off his mortal coil. Walton was taking him on a tour of Wal-Mart stores in his newest plane, a speedy twin-engined Beech Baron. As they arrived over Carthage, a small town in southwest Missouri, Walton checked to see that the airstrip was clear—the field was too tiny to have a control tower—and then came in to land. But even as the Beech Baron touched down, Walton suddenly saw another plane, a Piper Cub, pull obliviously onto the strip directly ahead of them. He couldn't possibly stop in time. Slamming the throttles forward, he tried to regain speed to leap over the plane, yanking back on the yoke as they zoomed toward the Piper. At the last second, they skimmed over the top of the other plane by what seemed like inches.

Though the two men didn't let the incident halt their tour of stores, two more months passed before Mayer agreed to accept Walton's job offer.

By then, Walton had finally found himself a warehouse man. At Arend's recommendation, in 1968, Sam and Helen Walton flew up to Omaha to look over a 100,000-square-foot distribution center belonging to the Newberry chain. They introduced themselves to the center's manager and asked to look around. The manager, Bob Thornton, had never heard of Walton and said he didn't do tours. But Walton jawboned him for a while and soon not only got his tour, but talked Thornton into joining them for lunch. Then he took Thornton and his wife to dinner that night, where he persuaded them to come down to Bentonville, saying he'd like to talk to Thornton about a possible job.

His timing was impeccable. Thornton had just found out that Newberry wanted to transfer him to a larger distribution center in New York; and the prospect of moving east horrified both him and his wife.

A few days later, Thornton called and told Walton they could catch a Frontier Airlines flight down to Fayetteville on an upcoming weekend. "He said, 'That's fine, but that weekend's the Arkansas football game, and I don't miss any Arkansas games. I'll leave my car for you at the airport and give the keys to the agent at the gate. He can tell you how to find your way to Bentonville, and I'll get with you that evening,' " Thornton recalled.

"Well, my wife and I arrived in our best clothes, ready for a job interview, and got the key from the agent, expecting maybe he'd have a Cadillac out there. There were only about 15 cars in the lot . . . so I started trying the key in each car, and finally found a '64 Chevy Biscayne two-door that matched. It was filthy: the upholstery all torn up, a pile of rib bones on the floor, straw all over the back. I went back and double-checked with the agent, thinking this couldn't be the right car, and he said, 'I don't know what the car looks like; if the key fits, take it.' I found out later that was his hunting-dog car."

Wondering what they'd let themselves in for, the Thorntons drove to the home of Ferold Arend, whom they knew from his Newberry days. The next morning, when Walton showed him his offices on the square, Thornton thought to himself that his own office back in Omaha was nicer and larger. But Bentonville seemed preferable to New York, and Walton promised to build him a distribution center to run. "He asked me how much I was making," Thornton recalled, "and I lied—inflated it a bit—and he said he'd pay me $3,000 a year more than that."

Thornton spent most of his first year there visiting distribution centers around the country and drawing up plans for a new 100,000-square-foot warehouse and general office, the minimum size he thought would work. He had an extra motivation to get things rolling: The offices on the square were so cramped that to make space for Thornton, they'd knocked through the wall into a space next door, above a shoe store. He was stuck in an attic-like space with no heating or air-conditioning.

Then, six months along, Walton dropped a bomb on him, saying casually one day, "I don't think we're going to build a distribution center just yet—but don't worry, Bob, I've got a lot of jobs for you to do." Stunned, Thornton said that running a warehouse was the only thing he wanted to do. But Walton wasn't budging. Upset, but not sure what to do, Thornton kept working on his plans; and eventually, after he, Walton, Arend, and three others visited one of the first computerized distribution centers in the country, up in Wisconsin, Walton finally relented, and agreed to build one himself. He bought a 15-acre farm at the edge of town for about $25,000. But, to the end, he resisted spending a penny more than he thought he had to. Without telling Thornton, he ordered the architect to lop the size of the planned warehouse to 60,000 square feet. The general offices took up 12,000 more square feet.

Walton also balked at paying for a tow-line system, a track built into the floor that could pull detachable carts around the center, for loading and unloading goods. To Thornton, this was an essential system costing a mere $60,000. To Walton, it was $60,000 he couldn't see spending. "I just don't think we can afford it, Bob," he said. Thornton replied, "If we don't get one, then I don't belong here, because I don't know how to run a distribution center without one." Walton weighed that for a minute and then, reluctantly, agreed to pay for it.

Decades later, looking back, Walton said, "Everybody at Wal-Mart knows that I've fought all these technology expenditures as hard as I could. All these guys love to talk about how I never wanted any of this technology, and how they had to lay down their life to get it. The truth is . . . it was important to me to make them think that maybe the technology wasn't as good as they thought it was. . . . It seems to me they try just a little harder and check into things a little bit closer if they think they might have a chance to prove me wrong. If I really hadn't wanted the technology, I wouldn't have sprung the money loose to pay for it."[10]

What Walton didn't mention is that there was another reason he hated to loosen his purse strings: He was nervous about the nearly $2 million in personal debt he'd taken on, by then, to expand Wal-Mart.

In many ways, his early frugality created the mindset that came to permeate the corporate culture: Always strive to keep costs down. Walton was delighted, for example, when Thornton discovered that refrigerated trucks hauling frozen chicken from Arkansas to New York were driving back empty and arranged—at a bargain price—to have them load up clothing for Wal-Mart on their return trip.

But Walton might have done better not to be so unremittingly chintzy. His first warehouse, built for $525,000, proved too small almost from the day it opened in November 1969. Even though the center handled less than half the merchandise shipped to the stores (the rest was shipped directly by manufacturers), within less than a year, Walton had to shell out again to expand it to 120,000 square feet—and wound up spending more money than he would have spent to build it that big in the first place. All through the '70s, the distribution system would struggle constantly, and not quite successfully, to keep pace with the growth of Wal-Mart stores.

Walton's parsimony on technology and equipment helped spark organizing drives by truck drivers and loading-dock workers in Bentonville in 1976, and then twice over the following five years at the company's second distribution center, in Searcy, Arkansas. To stave off the union, Walton was forced to pay his truck drivers far above the going rate for years.

The distribution system was far enough behind the curve that workers at the Searcy center were unloading, repacking, and shipping out goods even before all four walls and the roof were up. "We had no heat, people were wading in mud around the building, we were getting trucks stuck," recalled Thornton. As for why workers tried to unionize, he said, "I don't believe it was the salaries—we were just pressing too hard, asking them to work 60 hours a week."

Walton's reluctance to fork out cash soon led to occasional clashes with Mayer, the newly hired computer and finance whiz. Personable and down to earth, Mayer knew where he wanted to go, and he was in a hurry to get there. Walton had hired him with the idea that he would spearhead the nuts-and-bolts underpinnings Wal-Mart needed to expand: sophisticated communications, distribution, and transportation systems. The thirty-four-year-old Mayer also was to help recruit other young, technology-savvy managers.

As Mayer charged into these tasks, it drove him to distraction that Walton didn't seem to share his sense of urgency, that he was constantly slamming on the brakes. Siding with Thornton, Mayer argued ardently for improving and expanding the distribution system. Mayer also pushed relentlessly to develop the company's first data processing computer systems, designed to track what merchandise each store needed and when. These systems would prove vital to keeping the growing empire under control.

By early 1969, looking at his huge personal debt and a seemingly endless series of cash crunches, Walton began contemplating another way of raising money: selling shares in the company to the public. The stores were hauling in solid profits. For the 1969 fiscal year,* the company's 27 Wal-

---

* The twelve months ending January 31, 1969.

Mart and variety stores generated $21.4 million in sales and $650,000 in net income. But the stores weren't spitting out anywhere near the cash Walton needed to pay off his debts and still hike the pace of construction to a dozen or more new stores a year, as he wanted to do. Each new store cost nearly $500,000 to build and stock.

And Walton wasn't too happy with his bankers, either. Jones had left Republic Bank to become president of the National Bank of Commerce in New Orleans, and with his departure, Republic's interest in Walton's needs evaporated. One day in August, an officer at Republic refused to let Walton draw on his $1.5-million line of credit. Walton, who had immediate debts to pay, was apoplectic. Upon realizing that arguing over the phone was getting him nowhere, he leaped into his Beech Baron, flew to Dallas, and marched into Republic's offices to plead in person. He still got nowhere. In a panic, he phoned Jones, who told him to hop back in the plane and come to his office in New Orleans; he promised to wait for him as long as necessary. Jones sent a limousine to meet him at the airport, and early that evening, at Jones's office, Walton signed a $1.5-million unsecured note and got his money.

But such Hail Mary financing had to stop, Walton knew. He already had begun sounding out, with Bud Walton, Mayer, and a few others, whether it might make sense to take the company public.

Helen Walton was dead set against the idea. She told family friends that she was worried about all the financial disclosures demanded by the Securities and Exchange Commission. It would reveal too much to prying eyes about the Waltons' own financial affairs. She questioned whether taking the company public might lead to the Waltons' losing control of the company. And she seems to have feared that it would leave her husband even less time for her.

It wasn't a question of the children. By early 1969, all four were out of the nest. Rob Walton was finishing law school at Columbia University, in New York City, and looking at joining a law firm in Tulsa. John Walton had returned safe and sound from serving as a medic with the Green Berets in Vietnam, where he was awarded a Purple Heart and a Silver Star. Like his older brother, John had been a football star at Bentonville High School, making the all-state team; and, like Rob, he had gone to Wooster College. But John had shocked his parents by dropping out after two years to join the Army. Once John had signed up and been accepted for Special Forces training, Sam Walton had tried to talk him into applying for officer candidate school; but, recalls family friend and neighbor Tom L. Harrison, John wanted to do things his own way. Not long after he made it back from the war, he took flying lessons and then agreed to work for his father as a company pilot. But he made it clear he wasn't interested in the executive track.

Jim Walton, after playing football and being elected president of his junior class at Bentonville High, had graduated in 1965, and now was studying business at the University of Arkansas. Alice, the youngest, had graduated from high school in 1967 as vice president of her class and was now a sophomore, studying business, at Trinity College in San Antonio. None of the children seemed to be champing at the bit to take a role at their father's company, though Sam Walton made it clear he would be pleased if they would.

If the kids were ambivalent about enlisting at Wal-Mart, Helen Walton felt the same way about Sam's deepening involvement. Helen had tried to put the brakes on before, but over the years, her veto power had crumbled. "I do remember Sam told Helen once that 18 stores would be all they would ever have," said Enfield. "That had to have been around 1960."

But, as before, Sam Walton was not to be dissuaded. On hunting trips together, he and Bud talked endlessly about their need for funds and what to do about it. Already, a lack of ready cash had forced them to give up five sites on which they had planned to build stores. Bud Walton, always more cautious than his older brother, was much less enthusiastic about the idea of going public, but he had to admit that the numbers made sense.

Among the few others by whom Walton floated the notion was an executive at a life insurance company that had loaned him the money to build the Bentonville warehouse. That company was owned by Stephens Inc., the powerful Little Rock investment banking concern; and the astute insurance executive had passed word of Walton's plans along to Jackson Stephens, the head of the firm. Stephens hadn't underwritten many public offerings—just one, in fact. But that one had whetted his appetite for the potential profits, so he shipped off to Bentonville the young bond salesman, Mike Smith, who had overseen that one previous offering.

Walton bundled Smith into his airplane and spent a day shuttling him to one Wal-Mart store after another—getting lost at least once along the way, a common happenstance when Walton was at the controls. It was while Smith and Stephens were drawing up the paperwork in Little Rock for the offering that Walton had been forced to clutch at Jones for an emergency loan.

Walton asked his son Rob, who had now finished law school and moved to Tulsa, to look at the company's options. Rob said the obvious first step should be consolidating all the company's debts. So Sam Walton and Mayer flew to the East Coast to seek a $5-million loan. Their first stop was at the New York offices of Prudential Life Insurance Co. A few years earlier, Prudential executives had turned down Walton for a $1-million loan; but he knew they'd loaned other retailers money since then. Walton, his usual yellow legal pad in hand, offered the loan officer his projections. These called for boosting sales, which had reached $21.4 million for fiscal 1969, by more than sevenfold over the next few years, to more than $150 million for fiscal 1974. As Walton recalled, "[I] talked about our strategy of going to the small towns where there was no competition and told the loan officer how much business we thought there was out there waiting to be plucked."[11]

As it would turn out, Walton's projection was rather too modest: Wal-Mart's sales for fiscal 1974 would reach $167.6 million. But to the loan officer, such a heady forecast must have seemed absurdly optimistic. He wouldn't agree to make the loan. Next, Walton and Mayer headed to Boston and the offices of Massachusetts Mutual Insurance Co. Officers there said they'd be delighted to loan him $2.5 million—if he would agree to give them 9.75 percent interest and 15-year options to buy 45,000 Wal-Mart shares at the initial offering price (which would turn out to be $16.50 a share). Walton considered it highway robbery. But what choice did he have? He agreed. It was a hell of a deal for Mass Mutual: At the offering price, 45,000 shares cost $742,500; 15 years later, after seven stock splits and appreciation, those same shares would be worth just under $300 million.

As plans for the offering moved forward, Walton decided, to Smith's and Stephens's dismay, to shop around at competing, and more experienced, investment firms. On a buying trip to New York—without bothering to make an appointment—he strolled into the offices of White, Weld & Co., an investment banking firm that recently had taken the Omaha-based Pamida discount-store chain public. He introduced himself to the receptionist and asked if he could talk to somebody about taking his company public. She alertly turned him over to Harmon "Buck" Remmell, an Arkansas native who'd moved to New York years earlier. Remmell and White, Weld quickly agreed to lead the underwriting and, at Walton's request, let Stephens underwrite one third of the offering.

Now there was one last step to take: Walton had to completely reorganize both the company and his family partnership. Originally, he had set up every store as a separate company, with stakes of various sizes held by him, his brother Bud, in-laws, relatives, and various company managers. Each interest in all 31 of these different companies had to be weighed and assigned so many shares in the new company.°

In February 1970, everybody swapped their stakes for part of 1.3 million Wal-Mart common shares. The Waltons wound up owning 69 percent of the shares; other relatives and managers held 8 percent; and 23 percent, or 300,000 shares, was set aside for the public offering. But that spring, as the stock market slumped, the offering was put off. Finally, on October 1, the company went public. Wall Street scarcely noticed. A small cadre of institutional investors snapped up most of the shares.

The offering netted the company about $4.6 million, picayune by Wall Street standards, but big money to Walton. Much of it went to repay debts and to finish paying for Thornton's new distribution center.

Walton's stake in Wal-Mart was now worth just under $15 million. He would never have to take on personal debt for the company again.

Best of all, now he could *really* start expanding.

°The new company was incorporated in Delaware as Wal-Mart Inc. on October 31, 1969. The name was changed to Wal-Mart Stores Inc. two months later.

5

The Organization Men

At the time it went public, Wal-Mart was barely a blip on the retail industry's radar screen—still too small to earn a spot on a list of the 71 largest discount chains in the country, published that year by the retail journal *Discount Merchandiser.* Topping the list: Kmart, which racked up $2 billion in sales that year, more than 45 times Wal-Mart's volume.

Just how unimportant the company seemed from the vantage point of Wall Street quickly became clear. Every publicly traded company is required to hold an annual shareholder's meeting. That first spring after Wal-Mart went public, Mike Smith, from Stephens Inc., talked a dubious Walton into holding Wal-Mart's meeting not in Bentonville, but at a motel in Little Rock, the Coachman's Inn. Smith argued that this would make it much easier for all the New York analysts and out-of-state shareholders to get to the meeting, since Little Rock, the state capital, was served by major airlines—unlike tiny Bentonville.

Unfortunately for Smith, Wall Street analysts avoided the meeting in droves—or perhaps, given how few analysts actually followed Wal-Mart that early on, one should say, in one rather modest drove. Big shareholders, too, stayed away. So, the next year, Walton moved the meeting back to Bentonville. But Smith had another brainstorm. To get analysts to make the trek from New York, he said, why not make it free and fun: Offer to fly them out and put them up, and not just for the night. Wal-Mart, he proposed, should host them for the weekend at Bella Vista, a resort and residential development just north of Bentonville with golf courses, tennis courts, lakes to paddle around on, and other attractions. Walton was skeptical and loath to have the company spring for the cost, but grudgingly agreed to give it a shot.

It worked. Each of the following years, the number of analysts and major shareholders coming down picked up bit by bit. Walton would assign managers to meet the analysts at the airport, take charge of them, show them around the company, and spend time with them. After each annual meeting, always held at the company's headquarters on a Friday, there would be a big picnic. Then the guests would be invited to sit in on the Saturday morning managers' meeting, after which they and the Wal-Mart managers would play golf, go fishing, or take part together in whatever other activities the company had planned for that year.

Of course, there was another reason the company drew steadily more attention: its growth. Walton's whole purpose in going public had been to expand more quickly. In 1970, the company had built eight new stores (seven of them Wal-Marts), including its first in Louisiana; and it had remodeled or expanded a third of its 18 other Wal-Mart stores. The number of employees reached 1,500. But now Walton redoubled his plans.

A few months after going public, in 1971, Sam and Bud Walton and the other executives created a real estate and construction division. Bud Walton, whom Sam considered a tough negotiator and who was of one mind with his brother when it came to what made a good store location, took control of the division, which was charged with finding sites for stores, arranging financing, and building some of them (others would be built by developers who would then lease the buildings to Wal-Mart). That year, Wal-Mart added 14 new stores; and the following year, 16 more. (Crews also rebuilt three stores that were destroyed, two of them by fires and one by a tornado.) By January of 1973, there were 55 Wal-Mart stores across five states: Arkansas, Missouri, Kansas, Oklahoma, and Louisiana.*

The Walton brothers agreed on two rules in deciding where to open most of their stores in those years. The first: Keep sticking to small towns, where Wal-Mart could avoid competing discounters. The second: Build all stores within a day's drive of Bentonville. That would keep stores close enough to the distribution center so goods could be shipped out quickly, and close enough so that Walton's five regional managers could drive out to stores readily and keep an eye on them.

---

* Wal-Mart, like many retailers, operates on a fiscal year that ends January 31. So, for example, its 1973 fiscal year included the last 11 months of 1972 and the first month of 1973. Besides the 55 Wal-Mart stores, the company also still operated nine variety stores (seven others having been sold off or converted into Wal-Marts over the years).

•   •   •

Thomas Jefferson was one of those regional managers. A retailer with twenty-one years' experience at Sterling Stores, he joined Wal-Mart in 1972. And as so often seemed to be the case with the company's early executives, it was as a result of having bumped into Sam Walton. Years earlier in Newport, as a divisional manager for Sterling, Jefferson often called on Walton's rival, John Dunham. On one of those visits, he met Walton, who was forever scoping out his rival's store. The two men had hit it off, and Jefferson took to meeting Walton for breakfast when he came to Newport. "I'd meet him at ten 'til six," Jefferson remembered. "He'd be sitting on the curb outside his store, reading the *Wall Street Journal*." They had stayed in touch, and two decades later, when Jefferson vented one day about his disenchantment with his prospects at Sterling, Walton jumped to offer him a job. As a bonus, when he defected, Jefferson brought with him a half-dozen other experienced Sterling managers.

As a regional manager, he was given a company car, a Plymouth; in those days, a manager "had to be lucky" to get to use one of Wal-Mart's two company planes, Jefferson said. Like the other managers, he would put 60,000 miles on his Plymouth in a year, heading out each week to visit his stores; each year the cars would be traded in for new models. Most executives on the operations side spent four, sometimes five days a week out in the field. Then they'd meet back in Bentonville on Fridays and Saturday mornings to share their findings. Walton himself would come in as early as 3 A.M. on Saturdays to go over the results store by store before that day's meetings got underway at 7:30.

Eventually, of course, Wal-Mart began planting stores far enough from Bentonville that the regional managers had to fly out to their territories instead of driving; but by then the idea of keeping stores within easy reach of a distribution center had been carved into stone. Early on, as we've seen, Walton had no choice but to have Wal-Mart do its own warehousing and distributing of goods to its stores in the small towns he targeted. Forced to create Wal-Mart's distribution system, Walton now settled on a strategy that would hold steady until there were Wal-Mart stores from sea to sea. "We would go as far as we could from a warehouse and put in a store," Walton said. "Then we would fill in the map of that territory, state by state, county seat by county seat, until we had saturated that market area."[1] And saturation meant just that: Within 100 miles of Springfield, Missouri, for example, Wal-Mart eventually built 40 stores.

"We saturated northwest Arkansas. We saturated Oklahoma. We saturated Missouri. . . . Sometimes we would jump over an area, like when we opened store number 23 in Ruston, Louisiana, and we didn't have a thing in south Arkansas, which is between us and Ruston. So then we started back-filling south Arkansas," Walton said.[2]

When the territory included larger cities, Walton adopted the strategy that had worked well with his Ben Franklin store in Kansas City's Ruskin Heights (and that Robert Wood had used decades earlier at Sears). He would build a Wal-Mart store well outside the city and wait for the growth of suburbs to bring out the shoppers. Eventually, Wal-Marts would ring the outskirts of dozens of cities.

Walton saw the saturation strategy as a money-saver in other ways, too. By opening stores near to one another, Wal-Mart would be familiar enough to people, Walton felt, that it wasn't necessary to do much advertising after the initial burst of grand-opening ads. Wal-Mart could save money by printing one advertising circular a month, versus the weekly circulars that bigger discounters such as Kmart put out.

The notion of trying to adapt cheap existing spaces—as with the store in Morrilton, built in the old Coca-Cola bottling plant—soon fell by the wayside. Instead, Bud Walton's division came up with five cookie cutter designs (as Sam Walton called them) for stores from 30,000 to 60,000 square feet, depending on the size of the town. Often, the two Walton brothers would fly out to a town and swoop over it in low circles, studying the roads, the patterns of development, and who and where the competitors were. As soon as they agreed on a likely spot, often they would land right then, try to find out who owned the property, and start wheeling and dealing.

When Jim Walton, Sam's third son, joined the company, Bud immediately began training him in handling real estate. After graduating from Bentonville High School in 1965, Jim Walton hadn't rushed through college; he took six years to finish his studies in business at the University of Arkansas. Once he graduated, in 1971, he spent a year relaxing, traveling, and getting a pilot's license before agreeing, to Sam Walton's delight, to join the company. (Sam and Helen Walton worried—needlessly, as it turned out—about whether any of the children would feel motivated to work.)

Jim Walton looked like anything but the prototypical conservative Wal-Mart executive. On campus, his long, shaggy hair and beard had been no more unusual than his blue jeans. But this was an era in which the length of one's hair seemed to declare one's social and even political beliefs; and among the Wal-Mart men, long sideburns and perhaps a neatly trimmed mustache were considered the height of daring. By their standards, Jim was a hippie.

But beneath that Haight-Ashbury exterior beat the heart of a business-man. Jim Walton used his looks to advantage, flying out to find store sites, landing, and hauling his bicycle out of the back of his plane to pedal around a town without attracting the attention of local businesses. He would ques-tion property owners without mentioning his corporate connection. And he quickly developed a reputation as a fearsome negotiator—tougher than Bud, Sam Walton liked to claim. But Jim Walton soon opted out of Wal-Mart. Instead, eventually he took over as president of Walton Enterprises, the family corporation that already, by 1972, owned a couple of banks and other businesses.

All but one of the Walton children put in the briefest possible stints at the company. John Walton explained one reason that he, at least, was reluctant to work for his father: "You never really know whether you're getting a job because of who you are, or whether you earned it. So you go out on your own, and you get a lot better feel for what's going on."[3] John, who had be-come a company pilot after returning from Vietnam, quit after less than a year to become an itinerant crop duster, spraying cotton fields for compa-nies in Louisiana, Mississippi, Texas, and Arizona. The most independent of the four children, he indulged in hobbies such as scuba diving and sky diving. In 1973, he married a woman he'd met several years earlier, Mary Ann Gunn, who joined him in his nomadic pursuits. They would get a di-vorce after three years.

Alice, who graduated from Trinity College in 1971, came home briefly and worked at Wal-Mart as a buyer, but she, too, soon decided she didn't care for the family business and went to New York City. After a year in Arkansas and New York, she talked James Jones, whom Sam Walton had appointed as a director of Wal-Mart, into offering her a job with his bank in New Orleans. She moved into the French Quarter and began a very active social life in New Orleans high society.

Only Rob Walton, the oldest, would be yoked to Wal-Mart for most of his adult life. Not that this was his first choice. But how could he say no when his father asked him to help with the legal work involved with the public offering? How could he refuse when Sam then asked him to become

Wal-Mart's corporate secretary and de facto legal counsel? At first, Rob insisted on handling his Wal-Mart duties from Tulsa, where he was on track to become a partner at the law firm that had recruited him while he was at Columbia University's law school. He became involved in an affair with a secretary at his law firm, Carolyn Funk, and left his wife Patti and their three young children to marry her. "When Rob broke up with Patti, that just broke Helen's heart," Jim Jones recalled.

Perhaps the remarriage made him more willing to leave Tulsa; perhaps it was the relentless pressure from Sam for him to come home and work for Wal-Mart full-time. But Rob Walton finally agreed to move back to Bentonville to stay.

As Wal-Mart expanded ever further, Sam Walton tried to inoculate his growing executive corps with his own sense of frugality. On buying trips to New York, he ordained that expenses should come to less than 1 percent of the amount spent for goods. So the Wal-Mart men would stay in cheap hotels near Madison Square Garden and walk, rather than take cabs. To keep the trips brief, on the occasions he went up, Walton always tried to pack in as much work as possible by trying to talk apparel makers into meeting far earlier in the morning or later at night than their normal hours.

When a new store was being completed, assistant managers often would be called in from existing stores to help set up for the grand opening. At least once, Walton, to avoid having to shell out for hotel rooms, convinced the assembled crew to snooze in sleeping bags at the not-yet-furnished home of the local manager.

He wasn't, however, absolutely unbending. For example: He had hated the idea of paying people to sit around; so after Wal-Mart began hiring company pilots, Walton soon decreed that instead of waiting at the airstrips for the executives they were shuttling around, pilots should go into stores and check what goods were in or out of stock in various departments. The pilots rebelled instantly. After several months of their incessant carping, he reluctantly dropped that policy. Then, too, when the company's new general offices and distribution center had opened, Walton had groused about the expense involved in putting in carpeting, which he considered an unnecessary luxury, but he allowed himself to be talked into allowing this extravagance in some parts of the building.

Meanwhile, the new senior managers Walton was hiring increasingly brought with them expertise that gradually transformed every area of operations. Jefferson, the regional manager, was one of several newcomers who helped design cleaner and more efficient store layouts. Ron Mayer and Royce Chambers, Mayer's data processing protégé, convinced Walton to buy more sophisticated cash registers, not to mention the computer system at the Bentonville headquarters dedicated to keeping track of merchandise sales and orders. By 1973, the computer system could collect some sales information from terminals at 22 stores. By later standards, the system was crude; the data couldn't be transmitted instantly, but had to be collected and then sent out each night. Still, the information helped Wal-Mart cut costs by keeping closer track of when goods needed to be reordered; and over the coming decades, as the system became ever faster and more powerful, it would give Wal-Mart a vital edge over less technologically adept rivals: keeping the flow of goods to the stores not too fast, not too slow, but just right.

At this point, though, Bob Thornton and his distribution workers were still struggling to keep their heads above water. They enlarged the Bentonville distribution center again in 1972 and opened an additional center just for apparel, also in Bentonville. Walton, again reluctantly, agreed the time had come for the company to begin developing its own fleet of trucks.

Meanwhile, Walton gradually sold off or closed the Ben Franklin variety stores and Walton's Family Centers, in some cases replacing them with Wal-Marts. From a high of 16 in 1968, that side of the business shrank to nine stores in 1973, and then just two stores in 1974.

By almost any measure, by early 1974 Wal-Mart was enjoying tremendous success. Kmart, the industry leader, was still leagues ahead, with $4.6 billion in sales for the year just ended; but Wal-Mart's sales of $167.6 million for the year were nearly eightfold its sales of five years earlier, and its stores dominated most of the towns they were in. Twice, Wal-Mart had declared two-for-one stock splits. A second stock offering in 1972 had raised more than $9 million and produced enough new shareholders to let Wal-Mart move onto the New York Stock Exchange. Sam Walton's empire now spanned 78 stores in six states, with 24 more stores on the drawing board for that year. And with seasoned executives such as Ferold Arend and talented comers such as Ron Mayer, Walton could feel confident about the road ahead.

Now Walton began to waver under pressure from his wife to hand the reins over to someone else. Helen Walton didn't give up easily. From as early on as when they owned three variety stores, she had tried repeatedly to talk Sam into stepping back a bit from the business, to take things easy.

Again and again, he had told her that maybe, after a few more stores, the time to do that would come—even as he jotted and calculated on his legal pads how much bigger his company could grow another five years out.

Even though he'd overridden her strong and deeply rooted objections to taking the company public, and though since then he had devoted more time than ever to the business, Helen Walton had never given up on trying to persuade him to retire.

Now, in 1974, her arguments seemed increasingly persuasive. Sam Walton was fifty-six years old, and Helen was fifty-four. He had put in twenty-nine years running his own business. After the stock splits and appreciation of their Wal-Mart stock, their net worth had increased nearly tenfold in the past four years. With the stock, Helen's share of the Robson properties, and other holdings, they were worth more than $130 million.

To add to the pressure, Ron Mayer began hinting, and then making it clear with increasing bluntness, that if he didn't get a chance to take over, he would leave. Mayer's main rival for the job was Walton's other lieutenant, Arend. Arend had been at Wal-Mart longer, of course, and with his twenty-one years at the Newberry chain he had far more retailing experience than Mayer. Walton thought highly of Arend, enough so to have appointed him to the board of directors in 1970. But then, he'd put Mayer on the board too, in 1972.

At forty-four, Arend was only five years older than Mayer, but to Walton, he represented the old guard. And that was the clincher. As Walton wrote in his memoirs, "I really felt at the time that Ron was absolutely essential to the company's future. . . . He made it pretty well known that his goal, which I respected, was to run a company, preferably Wal-Mart. He told me one day that if he couldn't run our company, he wanted to get out and run another one. So I thought about that a few days, and I really worried that we were going to lose Ron. Then I said to myself, 'Well, I'm getting pretty old, and we could probably work together. I'll let him be chairman and CEO [chief executive officer], and I'll just enjoy myself, step back a little, and, of course, continue to visit stores.' "4

So, that November, Walton gave in. He appointed Mayer chairman and chief executive, and promoted Arend to president and chief operating officer. Walton moved his photos, files, and other belongings from his own spartan office to Mayer's slightly smaller space.

But, of course, getting Sam Walton to put himself out to pasture wasn't quite that simple. Though nominally retired, Walton remained chairman of the board's executive committee—not to mention, of course, that he was the majority shareholder. That gave him reason enough, if he needed any, to keep his hand in. He said he planned to travel with Helen and to spend more time hunting. And for a time he did. But of course, he continued to visit stores wherever he went, and he couldn't help but come back to head-quarters with ideas that seemed more like orders than suggestions. On a 1975 trip to South Korea and Japan, for instance, Walton was deeply impressed by the atmosphere at a tennis ball factory he visited near Seoul. "It was the first place he ever saw a group of workers have a company cheer," among other things, said Helen Walton. "He couldn't wait to get home and try those ideas out in the stores and at the Saturday morning meeting."5 Soon, he was haunting the office far more than either Mayer or Helen Walton probably would have preferred.

From outside the company, the transition seemed seamless. For most discounters, 1974 was a rough year. The previous October, OPEC (the Organization of Petroleum Exporting Countries) had declared an oil embargo against the United States, and the price of oil had quadrupled in just two months. This had helped push the nation into a recession, accompanied by double-digit inflation.° For most discounters, the combination was brutal. Clustered in cities and suburbs, they were locked into a fierce price competition that kept them from raising their prices much, even as the wages, interest payments, shipping costs, and other expenses they had to pay soared. Here, Wal-Mart was the exception. With little competition in its rural small towns, Wal-Mart faced less pressure on its prices or the wages it paid workers. Not only did it weather the recession unscathed; its sales for the year jumped 41 percent to $236.2 million, as the chain grew to 104 stores.

With Mayer at the helm, Wal-Mart opened a new, more technologically advanced distribution center. As usual, it was desperately needed, and even with the new center the distribution men were struggling mightily to keep up with orders from ever more stores. But Mayer proudly told sharehold-ers in the 1975 annual report that much of the merchandise "goes directly from the incoming rail cars or trucks to outbound trucks without being stored in the Center."6 Following aggressively in Walton's footsteps, Mayer also promised that sales for the coming year would crack $300 million. "We will be," he wrote, "more promotional and more competitive, price-wise, than ever before in our thirty-year history."7

Inside company headquarters, though, rifts were growing. Sam Walton had long cultivated an all-for-one-and-one-for-all mentality to minimize the deference to hierarchy and to discourage cliquish behavior. He posted sales

---

° The consumer price index rose 12.3 percent that year.

and profit numbers in open view, including in store stockrooms, so all workers could see them. Everyone was on a first-name basis. Office doors were left open. One of the purposes of the Saturday morning meetings was to have the regional managers share any good ideas spotted out at their stores; after the meetings, they would call out to their districts to share those ideas, so that anything that worked well in one store could quickly get out to all the stores. Walton never hesitated to ask for input or ideas from employees at any level, from loading-dock workers to executives, and his managers were expected to share suggestions not only with him but with one another. And while he often forced his people to compete fiercely with one another, Walton had always been there as the final arbiter.

Now there were three men trying to play that role. In part because of their rivalry, Arend and Mayer had never been pals. Now, Arend wasn't about to defer to Mayer when they disagreed—which happened more and more often—and the two men increasingly disliked each other. Walton, meanwhile, still hovered around, trying—when he thought of it—not to be in charge, and watching grim-lipped as the other executives and managers, many of whom owed their jobs to either Mayer or Arend, formed ranks behind one or the other. Arend had helped Walton hire many of the store managers and regional managers, and they were nearly as loyal to him as to Walton. Meanwhile, many of the younger, technology-savvy executives at headquarters had been Mayer's protégés, and they sided with him. Walton's cherished lines of communication shriveled. The supposedly retired founder soon found himself having to settle one dispute after another. And, temperamentally unable to step away and let the two men battle things out, he also increasingly second-guessed and overruled decisions by both of them, and particularly by Mayer.

For the year ending January 31, 1976, Wal-Mart sales soared 44 percent to $340.3 million. The company declared another stock split. But at headquarters, few people were smiling. As Al Miles, later an executive vice president, remembered, because of the rift between Arend and Mayer "you almost felt committed to say, 'Well, I'm on this team or I'm on that team.'

"We started seeing a looseness in our organization that had never been there, and things none of us liked were starting to happen regularly. The seriousness of running our stores and taking care of our people wasn't happening. And most of us district managers would get together and talk on the phone on Saturday mornings, and, you know, we thought we were going to hell in a handbasket. I'm not exaggerating. I mean we really did. Also, I remember that when Sam started spending more time in the office, he was very, very intense."[8]

It seems all but certain, too, that after decades of eating, sleeping, and breathing retail, Walton felt a void that no amount of hunting, traveling, or relaxing with Helen could fill. Wal-Mart defined his life. He simply could not walk away.

By late June 1976, Walton had had enough. He told Mayer that he was reassuming his posts as chairman and chief executive. If Mayer wanted to stay, he could be vice chairman and chief financial officer. As Walton expected, Mayer refused the demotion and left.

For public consumption, Walton issued a mea culpa. He mentioned nothing about Mayer's clash with Arend, or any other problems, instead blaming himself, saying that he just hadn't really been ready to retire. "I wasn't able to assume a passive role," he told a reporter for the *Wall Street Journal,* adding, "I wasn't about to force myself to stay out" of running the company.[9]

Walton was in for a rude surprise, courtesy of one of Wal-Mart's directors. Jack Stephens was the younger of the two brothers who ran Stephens Inc., the Little Rock firm that had helped Walton take Wal-Mart public. He had sat on Wal-Mart's board ever since then. It had been an obvious appointment: Stephens Inc. was the largest investment banking and brokerage firm outside New York, and Jack Stephens was one of the most influential men in Arkansas.

His brother Witt—Wilton Robert Stephens—had founded the firm. The brothers weren't born blue bloods; Witt Stephens started out as a Bible and jewelry salesman. He made his fortune during the Depression by snapping up for a song municipal bonds on which the state of Arkansas had defaulted. When those bonds became redeemable for face value during World War II, he raked it in. As his bond-trading business flourished after the war, he brought Jack into the fold. The brothers became among the wealthiest and most powerful men in the state. Over the decades, they'd spread their investments into oil and gas, real estate, shopping malls, nursing homes, and seemingly every other nook and cranny of business in and out of Arkansas.

At about the time Walton had handed the reins to Mayer, Jack Stephens had begun looking at buying his own discount retail outfit, a 40-store chain based in Indianapolis, called Ayr-Way. Mayer had been the one who first heard that Ayr-Way was on the block. Eager to make what looked like a great acquisition for Wal-Mart, he'd flown up to Indianapolis to check it out. But—in one more disagreement—Walton had vetoed the idea, saying that leapfrogging Illinois to get to Indiana didn't fit his strategy of expanding outward only into areas adjacent to existing Wal-Mart markets and distribution lines. That was when Mayer, champing at the bit to buy the chain, had appealed to Stephens for support. When Stephens heard his pitch, though, he began thinking about buying Ayr-Way for himself.

Now, Stephens moved quickly, putting together a group of investors that bought Ayr-Way for $19.9 million. As soon as Mayer resigned from Wal-Mart, Stephens offered him the chairmanship of the company. Mayer then turned around and lured away a half-dozen senior Wal-Mart executives, most of them protégés he'd brought to Wal-Mart. The exodus included Wal-Mart's controller, its data processing manager, and a top distribution man, among others.

Wall Street analysts reeled at the defections, and Wal-Mart's stock dived—though the drop would prove to be only temporary.

In the immediate aftermath, Walton reached past other senior managers to tap a brash but talented young vice president, Jack Shewmaker, for the post of executive vice president for operations, effectively the number-three slot at the company, behind Walton and Arend. Several more senior managers, angry at being passed over, quit. "By the time it was over," Walton later said, "I'll bet one third of our entire senior management was gone."[10]

If Walton was bothered by Jack Stephens's role in all this, he never talked about it or showed it; Stephens (who even twenty years later refused to discuss the incident) stayed on the Wal-Mart board for nearly two more years before he resigned, belatedly saying that his control of a competing retailer might pose a conflict of interest.

Mayer, though he finally had real control of his own company, couldn't turn Ayr-Way into another Wal-Mart, even with his team of fellow émigrés. Grafting Walton's formula onto an existing company turned out not to be that easy. Less than four years later Stephens washed his hands of the chain, which Mayer hadn't managed to expand by even a single store. He sold it to Dayton-Hudson Corp., a Minneapolis-based retailer, which folded Ayr-Way into its Target discount store chain.

Mayer wasn't part of the deal. He settled down in Indianapolis, running a small assortment of gift shops, golf and tennis shops, and apparel stores. Instead of the next Sam Walton, he would live as a mere—if that's the word—multimillionaire, thanks in no small measure to the Wal-Mart stock he'd hung on to.

Stephens, at Walton's invitation, would rejoin Wal-Mart's board as soon as the sale of Ayr-Way went through.

6

The Men Who
Would Be King

For Sam Walton, losing a third of his senior executives at once wasn't nearly as devastating as one might expect. It was largely his own doing, he knew. And given how fast Wal-Mart was growing, the exodus that followed Ron Mayer's ouster just intensified what had become, for Walton, a perpetual scramble to find enough experienced retailers. Wal-Mart was metamorphosing into a major corporation. Between 1970 and 1976, the number of employees quadrupled, to 6,000; and now the ranks were swelling by an average of almost 100 more employees every week. By the end of the decade, there would be 21,000 Wal-Mart workers.

Such numbers couldn't help but transform the way Walton and his executives, new and old, related to the fast-growing ranks of low-level employees.

Walton had always kept his management lean, with relatively few layers from the bottom to the top. In the stores, employees worked under department managers, who were supervised in turn by several assistant managers and the store manager. Each dozen or so store managers reported to a district manager; groups of three or four district managers were overseen by regional vice presidents; and they in turn reported to Jack Shewmaker, the new number-three man.

But Walton also had set up shortcuts from top to bottom. In the early days, he had spent as much time as possible visiting his stores because he knew he needed to keep a close eye on the retailing tyros he hired as managers. Right through the Mayer interregnum, Walton had spent much of each week out in the territory as a way of keeping in direct touch with what was happening in the stores. A writer for *Forbes* who tagged along with Walton one day in 1977 captured the flavor of these visits:

"He [Walton] is chatting graciously with the salesladies in the employees' lounge, a tiny, shabby room in back. The women are impressed.

" 'This store is looking real fine out there,' he tells them sincerely in a gentlemanly Arkansas accent. He is silver-haired, tanned, animated and very distinguished. 'I'm really impressed with the way you've got things set up in those departments,' he says. 'You're the people who really make us a success.' He solicits suggestions, and the middle-aged lady in charge of yard goods volunteers that she sells more cloth by displaying it by the flat-folded piece instead of in bolts. Since the pieces are remnants, she also buys them at a good price.

" 'Make a note of that, Al,' the chairman tells the vice president of sales promotion standing in the doorway to the crowded room. The vice president scribbles rapidly on a yellow legal pad. 'Thank you very much, Nadine,' the chairman [Walton] tells the woman gratefully."[1]

The *Forbes* writer goes on to describe how Walton passed the suggestion along at the next store he visited; how he consulted with the store manager on problems keeping automotive supplies stocked and other such mundane details. Walton focused on such little things for two very good reasons. First, of course, whether a customer comes back to shop again depends on just such picayune matters as whether a particular oil filter is on the shelf, whether a clerk has time to help a shopper, or whether the bathrooms are clean. But also, as much as his visits kept managers and clerks on the ball, they were just as important for making the low-paid clerks feel that Walton and his executives cared about them and wanted to hear what they had to say.

Walton always made a point of asking every worker he met how things were going, what problems they saw, how their store could be better, and so on. He made a point of asking them personal questions as well, and of trying to commit each face and name to memory. He kept his home phone number listed; and it wasn't unusual for employees with problems to telephone him personally. One of the favorite bits of company lore has Walton, unable to sleep one night, bringing boxes of donuts to the loading dock at the distribution center at 2:30 in the morning, chatting with workers there, and promising to put in extra showers after asking them what he could do to make things better.

But Walton also knew that, soon, there would be too many stores for him to visit them all even as often as once a year. So he had institutionalized the store visits. Other executives, too, were sent out to tour stores. But it was the regional vice presidents who now became the linchpins of the system. In their four days a week out in the field, they were supposed to work not only with the manager of each store, but with the entire staff, ideally both to teach and to learn—and to troubleshoot.

Walton had taken a great deal of trouble to craft Wal-Mart's emerging corporate culture—to convince workers, for example, that the doors were open, that they could take their problems and concerns to higher-ups, even to Walton himself, without getting slapped down or fired. Part of the challenge now was to establish that mindset in the thousands of new workers being hired—to "Wal-Martize" them, as it came to be called.

To make workers feel that, despite their low wages, they had a stake in Wal-Mart, and that they would prosper as the company did, Walton offered benefits matched by few other retailers. He gave rank-and-file workers profit-sharing. He encouraged workers to buy Wal-Mart's high-flying stock and sold it to them at a discount. He offered all sorts of bonuses for workers if their store beat various goals.

It wasn't that Walton was magnanimous toward his workers by nature, that it was something ingrained in him. No, it was something he arrived at, as with so much else, out of pure pragmatism. Though he certainly didn't say so, this was his way of keeping out the unions.

Back in 1970, locals of the Retail Clerks Union tried to organize Wal-Mart stores in the small towns of Clinton and Mexico, Missouri. For the union locals, it was a matter of survival: The large new Wal-Marts threatened both the older, smaller stores, and the higher salaries of the union workers at those stores. At the time, Walton's 25-store chain seemed ripe for organizing. To his managers and executives, Walton was generous—as he knew he had to be, to entice and hang on to men with experience. He didn't hesitate to dangle relatively fat salaries, generous stock options, profit-sharing and bonuses for boosting sales and profits—but only for those on the higher rungs. Hourly workers, were, well, just another commodity.

"In the beginning, I was so chintzy I really didn't pay my employees very well," Walton later wrote in his autobiography. "We really didn't do much for the clerks except pay them an hourly wage, and I guess that wage was as little as we could get by with at the time."[2]

He wasn't exaggerating. In his earliest days, Walton took questionable advantage of an exemption that legally allowed small businesses to pay employees less than the federal minimum wage. In the 1950s, when the Department of Labor, noticing the size of his operation, ordered him to start paying his workers at least the minimum wage, he fought the order in federal court. Walton claimed, weakly, that each of his stores was an independent company and therefore small enough to be exempt. He lost, but his attitude toward wages hadn't evolved much by the time Wal-Mart opened the Clinton and Mexico stores.

Years later, Walton would explain his attitude by citing the bottom line. "No matter how you slice it in the retail business, payroll is one of the most important parts of overhead," he said, "and overhead is one of the most crucial things you have to fight to maintain your profit margin." He would say that it was his obsession with keeping down overhead that had blinded him to the idea that "the more you share profits with your associates—whether it's in salaries or incentives or bonuses or stock discounts—the more profit will accrue to the company . . . because the way management treats the associates is exactly how the associates will then treat the customers."[3]

Helen Walton, who was more sympathetic to the workers, had raised such ideas in trying to convince Sam to do more for them. But she couldn't seem to make a dent. Once, while driving in the car on a trip, they were chatting about his salary and the high pay and benefits he was paying his top officers, when she argued directly that he should share more of those profits and benefits with all the employees.

"He didn't really appreciate my point of view at the time," she said, in her usual understated way.[4] But then everything changed.

Shortly after Sam Walton opened a Wal-Mart store in the small town of Mexico, in eastern Missouri, he heard that there was trouble. The Retail Clerks Union was rallying support around a worker, Connie Kreyling, who had been fired for talking about a union at the store. Other workers seemed sympathetic, and they were angry, with many complaining bitterly about their store manager being heavy-handed and unfair.

The last thing Walton wanted was a union, but he wasn't sure how to handle the situation. Then a friend told him about a labor lawyer from Omaha, John E. Tate, who'd recently defeated a unionizing drive at a livestock-auction center in the same town. That was the guy to call, his friend said.

And so began a relationship that would profoundly influence the nature of Wal-Mart as a company.

Tate was a professional union-buster. He had defeated hundreds of organizing efforts around the country. For him, it wasn't just a job; he loathed unions with a passion. The defining experience of his life had come in the summer of 1936, before his senior year in high school in Winston-Salem, North Carolina. Tate had been offered a 25-cent-an-hour summer job at a plant owned by the Reynolds Tobacco Co., where his father worked as a supervisor. On his way to his first day on the job, he tried to cross a picket line set up by workers trying to organize and wound up in the hospital with head wounds that would leave lifelong scars, inside and out.

That fall, when a school counselor asked the young man what he planned to do with himself, he said he wanted to be "a union-fighter." He'd have to go to college to do that, she told him. Tate had never considered college before—hadn't even realized it took four years. No one in his family had ever been to college. But to college he went and then, prodded by the same counselor, to law school, still determined to fight unions. After serving in the Army Air Corps in World War II, he began his career in Omaha. Tate would prove to be an uncompromising foe of organized labor. If workers go on strike, he would advise clients, then replace them—permanently.

But as he fought one organizing drive after another, Tate became convinced that most businesses could avoid problems if only managers would make a habit of talking to their employees. Tate's first fee, as a lawyer, came from a foundry owner who'd heard him speak at the Omaha Chamber of Commerce about learning from one's workers, and hired him to canvass foundry workers about the business. The suggestions Tate compiled had saved the business more than $50,000 a year.

When Walton called him, Tate was delighted to do the job. He took aside the workers at the Mexico store a few at a time and gave them a fire-and-brimstone view of what they could expect if they voted the union in. A union would cause nothing but trouble, he told them. They had no idea what they were letting themselves in for. Walton, meanwhile, at Tate's behest, transferred the troublesome manager to another store; and the organizing effort—such as it was—fizzled.

In fact, there hadn't been much of a drive. A few unhappy workers had tried to put together a single meeting at one woman's house to talk about whether a union made sense. Connie Kreyling, the twenty-year-old worker who was fired, hadn't even been that meeting's organizer; her husband, who didn't work at Wal-Mart but considered himself a union man, had called a couple of workers on his own initiative. One clerk he'd called had ratted to the store manager, who fired Kreyling as soon as she walked in the door the next morning.

After a two-year fight, the National Labor Relations Board ruled that Kreyling had been fired unfairly. Wal-Mart argued that she'd been fired for cause, and at one hearing, produced three "reprimands" she'd supposedly been given. Kreyling's attorney said they'd been fabricated, pointing out that Kreyling hadn't signed any of them and that one reprimand was dated on the same day she'd been given a merit raise.

Meanwhile, Kreyling, labeled as an organizer, had a hard time finding other work. "I went through emotional hell for those two years," Kreyling said later. "I didn't deserve to be fired." The turmoil played a part in her eventual decision to divorce her husband. By the time she had won her job back, she'd found another one and opted not to return to Wal-Mart.

At the store, after Kreyling was axed, workers complained but didn't make any other moves to try to organize. By the time Tate came in, there wasn't really a revolt to quell anymore.

Still, Walton was suitably impressed—and within a few months, facing another union push, he called Tate again. This time the Retail Clerks Union was threatening to organize a store he was opening in the town of Clinton and demanding that Walton hire union members to set up the store's fixtures. Tate said he'd recently handled a similar situation in Utah. He proposed Walton adopt the tactics that had worked there. So Walton had his managers cover the store's windows with brown paper, then work through the night to get the fixtures set up for the opening the next day.

The union, caught off guard, scrambled to put pickets out front. But Tate was ready for that, too. "We had advertisements, big signs on the windows that said 'Strike Sale,' with just ridiculously low prices on things," he said. As he remembers it, shoppers practically trampled the pickets in their rush to snap up the bargains.

Even as Walton was basking in this victory, though, Tate told him he should rethink the way he treated his workers. "You can hire me or someone like me to hold these people down, and fight them the rest of your life," he said. "Or you can decide to get them on your side."

Walton asked what he meant. Tate's answer echoed the arguments Helen Walton had made: Prove to them you care, he said. Let them share in the profits. Let them know you'll listen to what they have to say. Tate proposed that he discuss these ideas with all of Walton's store managers at a seminar.

"I don't know," Walton said. "It sounds expensive. How much is this going to cost me?"

"My fee is $600 a day," Tate told him.

"Oh, I can't afford that," Walton said, and began jawboning him down. Tate finally agreed to take $300 a day—and to mimeograph any handouts at his own expense.

Walton soon called him to say they would hold the seminar at the Tan-Tar-A Resort, on a lake in southern Missouri, where he'd gotten a special deal. Tate, he said, would have to share a room, with him. Wal-Mart never splurged for individual rooms for its managers, and Walton himself was no exception, he explained. Tate didn't mind, did he?

The night before the seminar, Tate watched as his roommate assiduously studied photo books of Wal-Mart managers and assistant managers, many with family members. "The next day, he was walking around, saying, 'Hi Frank, how's that new baby?' " Tate recalled.

That meeting laid much of the foundation of what would become Wal-Mart's corporate culture. Here began, for example, what the company called its "We Care" program, essentially an open-door policy promising workers that they could take problems to their managers without fear of retribution. "Saying 'we care' isn't enough," Tate told the managers. "If we can prove we care, then our people will care," he said—adding that employees who feel a vested interest in the company won't be as likely to steal or lay down on the job.

To create that vested interest, Walton agreed to extend profit-sharing to all employees who'd worked at Wal-Mart at least two years. That was followed by programs giving all workers the option to buy company stock at a discount and, later, by another awarding bonuses for meeting different company goals. The bonuses were based on such things as boosting sales and lowering "shrinkage," a term retailers use to describe merchandise that's stolen, damaged, or lost. To make this bonus program work, Walton agreed to take the unheard-of step of sharing financial information with hourly workers. Every employee would be told such things as the sales figures at their stores, and the losses from shrinkage, figures that, at other companies, were for management's eyes only.

The first year under the new profit-sharing scheme, Wal-Mart put in $172,000, but only 128 of the company's more than 2,300 employees took part. As with most low-paid, low-skill jobs, turnover was high. The vast majority of hourly workers hadn't worked there the two years it took to qualify.

But then, that didn't really matter. It was the promise that counted: the promise of sharing in the profits, of having a stake in the company's future, of being able to get ahead. The opportunities for advancement were there for the taking; as fast as the company was growing, almost anyone showing promise could hope to get a shot at running a department, perhaps of becoming a manager, or of climbing even higher.

Ferold Arend, Walton's deputy, said that when he'd been at Newberry, "a guy had to have ten years' experience before we'd even consider him to be what we called a manager-in-training. Down here, Sam would take people with hardly any retail experience, give them six months with us, and if he thought they showed any real potential to merchandise a store and manage people, he'd give them a chance."[5]

Walton couldn't promote good people—or good men, anyway—fast enough. By the late '70s, over the grumbling of some old-timers, Walton and his deputies began, for the first time, recruiting graduating college seniors as management trainees. And Walton kept raiding the competition. At one point, when Kmart chief executive Robert Dewar ordered policy changes that angered many long-time managers at that company, Wal-Mart "hired away 75 Kmart store managers over about a year and a half," said Jefferson. But such efforts still left plenty of room for advancing from within the company, as workers were well aware.

Walton encouraged an egalitarian ambiance. At the headquarters, no one, not even the company founder, had an assigned parking space; it was first come, first served. Even the company's directors, at board meetings, had to pay their quarter if they wanted a coffee or a soda. In 1973, in the wake of the Tan-Tar-A meeting, Walton decided to adopt the same term J.C. Penney used for workers: "associates." He said the idea struck him on a visit to England, where he and Helen had gone to see Wimbledon. Walking through London's retail district, he was struck by a storefront sign that read "Lewis Company, J.M. Lewis Partnership," and then listed, by name, all the associates in the partnership. Walton later claimed that the idea of a business as a partnership helped lead him to treat his own workers more fairly.

Efforts to get the associates involved in Wal-Mart gradually expanded—especially after a trip Walton took in 1975 to South Korea and Japan, where he was deeply impressed by factory workers doing group calisthenics and company cheers. At Wal-Mart's store openings, which inevitably featured local high school bands and cheerleaders, and local beauty queens or dignitaries to cut the ribbon, Walton added the practice—bizarre to outsiders—of leading employees in his own company cheer. After his Far East trip, he made the cheer part of his weekly store visits, as well. Workers would be gathered at the front of the store. "Gimme a *W!*" he'd shout. "*W!*" the workers would shout back, and on through the Wal-Mart name. At the hyphen, Walton would shout "Gimme a squiggly!" and squat and twist his hips at the same time; the workers would squiggle right back. The cheer always ended with Walton shouting "Who's number one?" and the workers shouting back "The customer!"

Walton wasn't shy about shouting "I can't hear you!" if the cheers weren't enthusiastic enough—but that didn't happen often. He was the antithesis of aloofness, and most folks responded to that. "I thought it was queer as hell," said Austin Teutsch, an employee who took part in the cheer for the first time at the grand opening of the Magnolia, Arkansas, Wal-Mart, in 1974. "I was somewhat embarrassed by the whole thing, but I was also in the minority. This man was selling himself and his store to his employees just as he had done all his life in every situation. When I saw all the old ladies of the lingerie department up on their toes in a frenzy, I learned a little about sheer motivation."[6]

The company began a monthly employee magazine, *Wal-Mart World*, that gave another platform for heaping praise on stores and workers, and for passing on personal word from Walton that often touched an emotional chord—as in 1981, when Walton told workers about the death of his favorite hunting dog, Ol' Roy, who had often come along on store visits Walton made on his way to or from hunting trips. In later years, the magazine would lovingly detail the growth in profit-sharing and the hefty sums that retiring workers took with them. And it would recount workers' reminiscences, often about Walton, who was inevitably referred to as Mr. Sam. "There were two things he told us that I have never forgotten," said Jackie Lancaster, a store clerk in Walton's original Newport store and later at the Newport Wal-Mart, in one typical issue. "He would praise us for the good job we were doing but he told us never to think that we got so important that we couldn't be replaced. He also used to tell us to always put the dollar bills in our register so that the face of the dollar was always looking up at us. That way, we wouldn't be tempted to take it. Now, I'd never heard that one before or since, had you?"[7]

In 1975, under Mayer, Wal-Mart held its first annual employee picnic; for years, a highlight of the annual meetings, for workers, would be the picnic at the Walton's home and the chance to shake hands and have their pictures taken with Sam and Helen. That year, the company also launched its training department—or what might have been dubbed the Department of Wal-Martizing. Its job was to create programs district managers could show at the stores, to teach everything from how to check out customers and prevent shoplifting to how to use employee benefits. Other programs trained department heads, assistant managers, and managers for each rung on the corporate ladder. The programs were also meant to boost the associates' motivation and were slathered with slogans such as "Customers are the reason for our work!"

More important, in 1976, the company let workers qualify for profit-sharing after one year, instead of two, substantially boosting the rolls.

After Clinton and Mexico, it was years before any unions made serious efforts to organize at Wal-Mart. The occasional clashes almost always were instigated by unhappy workers. And though Walton had other union-busters, too, usually Tate was on hand to help quash these uprisings. In 1976, truck drivers and loading-dock workers at Wal-Mart's distribution center in Bentonville, boiling over at what they considered overcrowded and dangerous conditions, called in the Teamsters. Workers at the center would break down truckloads of merchandise shipped in from suppliers and reload a mix of goods onto trucks bound for Wal-Mart's stores. But Walton's tight-fisted attitude toward distribution left them perpetually swamped. At the time the Teamsters came in, the workers were handling double the capacity that the warehouse was originally designed for, one executive recalled.

Coached by Tate, Walton met with the workers and, using a mix of bluster and contrition, pleaded with them to keep the union out. "I know why you're mad," he told them. "I know you're crawling all over each other."

"I don't know how I could have been so stupid" as to let conditions deteriorate as they had, he said. But he would take care of it. "Can you imagine having some Teamster in here saying you can't talk to me, that you have to go to the union and make them talk to me?" he asked. "You think I'm gonna listen to them more?" He picked out a driver. "Pete—you ever had any trouble talking to me?" He reminded them of times he'd come to the dock with donuts early in the morning, just to talk.

One driver, reached years later, said Walton also put out the word, indirectly, that raises would be forthcoming—*if* the vote went the right way. Tate, of course, maintains that Walton made no threats or promises that would have broken the rules set for union elections. But he admits that after workers voted not to unionize, "we did set up a pattern there on wages; for years our drivers made far more money than other drivers did."

Walton doesn't seem to have taken much to heart from this episode; within a few years, disgruntled workers at another Wal-Mart distribution center would call in the Teamsters again, under nearly identical circumstances.

•   •   •

Wal-Mart's new number-three man, Jack Shewmaker, reminded some at headquarters of Mayer, in a lot of ways. Like Mayer, he was bright, tough, and aggressive. Confident, even cocky, he'd proven himself to have good instincts as a merchant; and his ambition was no secret.

Shewmaker was from the small town of Buffalo, in the hilly southwest of Missouri. His father sold cars there. As a college boy, he had planned to be an architect; but when his girlfriend was gravely injured in a car accident that killed five other people, he left Georgia Tech to be with her. They soon married, and he found a job at a manufacturing company in Springfield, Missouri.

But he didn't stay there long. Shewmaker could have been the poster boy for the new mobility of American society in the early '60s. Always searching for better opportunities, he ran through a succession of jobs, working as a sales supervisor for a lawn mower company in nearby Lamar, managing a Montgomery Ward store in Sikeston, Missouri, moving to Minneapolis to become training director of the Coast to Coast hardware chain, then joining Kroger, where he managed a large new supermarket in LaPorte, Indiana, for nine months, before deciding he didn't like the company and quitting to head home to Buffalo.

It was at that point, in 1970, that he trekked to Bentonville to interview for a job with Wal-Mart. Shewmaker had sent down a copy of the training manual he'd written for Coast to Coast, along with other work he'd done, and Walton had been impressed. But, with his oddly blithe approach to hiring, the day of the interview Walton took off to visit stores out of town before Shewmaker arrived. So instead, Ferold Arend interviewed him, and then offered him what was practically an entry-level job, as an assistant store manager. Swallowing his disappointment, Shewmaker said no and went home. When Walton heard what had happened, he told Arend they should have made him a better offer. Then he phoned Shewmaker in Buffalo and asked him to come back down.

But Shewmaker, who never minced words, bluntly told Walton he didn't have the money to do that. So Walton offered to meet him halfway. The next day, at a booth at the Howard Johnson's restaurant in Joplin, Missouri, Shewmaker agreed to take a job supervising store openings—and to write a training manual for store managers.

From there, he'd risen quickly, becoming a vice president by 1973 and then vaulting to executive vice president when Mayer left.[8] He was the kind of man Walton found easy to like. Tall, hearty, and outgoing, he clearly felt at ease mingling with workers in Wal-Mart's stores. He wasn't the least bit ostentatious. Like Walton, he drove a pickup truck. Like him, he was an avid quail hunter and an excellent shot; and he became a frequent companion of Walton's in the field. At the office, Shewmaker developed a reputation as a creative thinker, a man who was fast, confident, and sure at solving problems, and at spotting retailing trends ahead of the competition. He would score frequent merchandising coups, such as the time he led Wal-Mart into selling kitchen appliances that fit under cabinet shelves some two years before most other retailers caught on to their appeal—an eternity, in retail. It wouldn't be long before people in the industry were talking about when Shewmaker's turn would come.

But he wasn't the only young Turk in the line of succession.

In October of 1976, Walton finally landed another hot prospect he'd long coveted, David Glass—the man who'd written Walton off after witnessing the popping-watermelon-and-pooping-donkey mess at the opening of the Harrison Wal-Mart in 1964. Despite that fiasco, Walton never stopped making overtures to Glass. When he had turned over the reins to Mayer, Walton had urged him to try to lure Glass, saying he was a man of tremendous talent. But Mayer never did so—perhaps, suggested one executive privy to the discussion, because he wasn't keen to have a rival in the wings whom Walton so clearly admired.

But with Mayer ousted, Walton had immediately gotten in touch again with Glass, who was forty years old and working as the general manager of Consumers Markets, a grocery chain. He offered him a job as executive vice president for finance and distribution, the number-four slot at Wal-Mart. Consumers Markets tried to block Walton's raid by offering Glass more money, but Walton raised the stakes right back until he won the bidding war.

His prize was cast from the same mold as so many other Wal-Mart men: Glass was another small-town boy who'd made good. He, too, shared Walton's background of hard work, his conservative religious values, and his disdain for ostentation. But at the same time, like Shewmaker, Glass was a true believer in new technology; he was keenly alert to how the fast-evolving computer, electronics, and satellite communications industries could revolutionize retailing.

Like Walton, his manner could be deceptive. Much as Walton masked his steely determination and incisive mind under a disarmingly folksy, gregarious, aw-shucks demeanor, Glass veiled his driving ambition and his great confidence in his own abilities behind a cool, deliberative, and circumspect manner. There were, of course, endless differences between the two men, small and large. Glass, for instance, never considered himself much of an outdoorsman and didn't care for Walton's blood sport, hunting. And he preferred golf to tennis, Walton's favorite game.

The respective games perfectly suited each man's personality as a businessman. Tennis is directly confrontational, a zero-sum game: Every point I win, you lose. Even when he was comfortably ahead in a match, Walton wouldn't dream of giving away a point (except, very rarely, when playing mixed doubles); it just wasn't in his nature. In his sixties, he could still thrash men at the game who were thirty years younger.

Glass didn't care for tennis. Golf better suited his careful, analytical style. To play golf well with any consistency it helps enormously to be unflappable; to be able to stay calm and centered even after a bad shot—especially after a bad shot. These were exactly the qualities Glass demonstrated on and off the links. Walton had tried golf—but found it hopelessly infuriating. He'd given up on the game decades earlier, after one round so frustrating he broke one of his clubs against a tree.

The flip side of Glass's diffident demeanor was that he could seem a bit of a stiff. His dry, rather sly sense of humor rarely showed in public. A slim man of average height, with thick, straight black hair, long sideburns, and a pair of beetling, sharply peaked eyebrows, Glass would need years of practice to carry off even pretending to enjoy some of Walton's outlandish motivational ploys—such as the time Glass had to go back to the Harrison Wal-Mart, on its twenty-fifth anniversary, don overalls and a straw hat, and awkwardly ride a donkey around the store's parking lot. Fortunately, he didn't have to be the company cheerleader; that wasn't his role, and he knew himself better than to try to assume it.

Glass knew what role he wanted to play. Beyond the boost in pay Walton had offered, the big reason Glass agreed to make the leap was that he'd been watching, and he felt sure that Walton and his company were headed for retailing's major leagues. Even with Arend and Shewmaker clearly ahead of him, this, he knew, was his big chance.

The man who would become Sam Walton's successor was born in September 1935, in a farmhouse in southeastern Missouri's hardscrabble Oregon County. His father, Marvin Glass, was a widower with two young daughters, Regina and Marvalene, when he met Myrtle Van Winkle, who became his second wife. They christened their first son David Dayne Glass. When Dayne, as they called him, was two, the family moved to Mountain View, a nearby town of under a thousand people where Myrtle Glass's parents lived. They settled on a 20-acre farm at the edge of town, across a field from the Van Winkles, and Marvin found work with a feed store. The Glasses soon gave Dayne two younger brothers: Gerald and Richard, nicknamed Dick.

After a few years, Marvin Glass saved enough to open his own feed mill. He would maintain that business for five decades, but it never made more than a modest profit. Not that the Glasses considered themselves poor. "We didn't have a lot, but we had what most people had in those days," was how Myrtle Glass would put it. They supplemented store-bought food with milk from the family cow, squirrels and rabbits hunted or trapped by various family members, and vegetables from their own garden. For many years, as was common in rural areas then, the home had neither plumbing nor electricity. Water for washing was heated in a cast-iron pot outside. "We didn't get indoor plumbing until I was in high school," Gerald Glass remembers.

Dayne was thirteen when his mother, to help pay the bills, went to work as a supervisor at the apparel factory of the Angelica Uniform Co. in town. Marvalene had to take charge of the boys during the day. Myrtle Glass decided when she started working that she would amount to something, said Dick Glass, the youngest son, and she did, eventually becoming the factory's manager.

The boys and Marvalene recall their childhood as easygoing, their parents as calm and even-tempered. "They never did whip us," Dick Glass said. Marvin Glass, who'd never completed grade school, was hard-working and quiet, very even-tempered and too soft-hearted to be much of a disciplinarian. He was not religious, but Myrtle took the children every Sunday to the First Baptist Church, "though Dayne sometimes managed to get out of it," recalls Gerald Glass.

Like most local boys in those days, Dayne went to work at a young age. He started shining shoes in the afternoon for ten cents a pair at the barbershop when he was nine years old. As often happens with people who become rich and famous, friends remember stories about him that seem to presage his later success—in his case, as a retailer. Joe Duncan, owner of the local ambulance service and funeral home, tells of going into the barbershop after his discharge from the Army in 1945 "and there was Dayne taking care of the shoe shines, and boy, he was really working."

"I said, 'Got any bargains, Dayne?' And he said, 'I've got the lowest prices around.' Then he said, 'Joe, I'll give you a special deal. I'll do the first shoe for free.' I said, 'How about the second shoe?' " Glass grinned and told him "That one'll be a dime."

But, like most people, Glass was more complicated than such a story makes him seem. Of course, he worked—as he got older, he delivered newspapers, helped out at the feed store, picked blackberries in the summer, pumped gas at a filling station, and even occasionally drove an ambulance for Duncan—but he wasn't driven. He liked to have fun too much for that. In fact, he was what a later generation would call a slacker. In high school, he mainly worked evenings in a pool hall owned by the father of one of his buddies, Don Brotherton—a job that let him socialize and still get paid.

At Mountain View High School, he was an indifferent student. He was always very bright—Marvalene remembers him reading her second-grade schoolbooks when he was four—but he was not highly motivated academically. Math came to him easily; he rarely spent long over his homework. "A lot of times during study hall, we'd go to the pool hall instead," Brotherton recalls. Fifty years later, when Dayne was a multimillionaire, ran the world's biggest retailer, and had become Mountain View's most famous son, Myrtle Glass would still sigh, with a hint of maternal regret, that "he could have been valedictorian, if he'd worked harder."

He had better things to do than study. Glass, Brotherton, and another buddy, Dean Dirks, cruised around as the self-styled Three Royal Ds. Glass played baseball and basketball in high school, managed the football team, and became a fanatical follower of the St. Louis Cardinals baseball team. Radio reception in Mountain View wasn't great; and not everyone's set could pull in the baseball broadcasts. But the owner of a furniture store downtown not only had a powerful radio, but would set a speaker outside; so Glass (even though he could catch the games at home) would often be among the crowd that would gather on the sidewalk out front of the store to take in the games. Like most of the kids, on weekends he and his buddies would hang out at favored teen stomping grounds such as the Jack's Fork River, a summer swimming spot a few miles out of town. Glass also organized a lot of class parties. By his junior year, he'd saved enough to buy a 1928 Chevy that had once belonged to his buddy Brotherton.

Myrtle Glass was determined that, unlike her and Marvin, the boys would go to college. But when Dayne graduated at seventeen, he was in no hurry to matriculate. He decided to meander up to Idaho for a while, to stay with Marvalene. She had married three years earlier and moved there with her husband, Lee Gustafson; he worked construction at a local atomic power plant. He briefly wangled Dayne a job with his company—briefly, because both of them were fired as soon as the company discovered Dayne was underage. Next the two found jobs hauling grain and coal for a trucking company—but the pay was lousy. Before long, Gustafson quit, and he and Marvalene decided to go back to Mountain View.

Glass quit too. Now, facing the draft, he decided to volunteer for the Army. It was in the service—not having any choice in the matter—that he began using his first name, David. He was assigned to a base near Albuquerque, New Mexico. In town, at a drive-in restaurant one night, he met a cute fifteen-year-old, Ruth Roberts. He talked her into giving him her phone number, but she turned him down three weeks running before agreeing to a date. Three months after they met, she became Mrs. Ruth Glass.

Marriage or the Army or both seem to have transformed Glass's outlook. Discharged, he returned to Missouri with his pregnant bride and enrolled at Southern Missouri State University, in Springfield. He worked hard at his studies; and to support his family and put himself through school, he worked full-time, at night, as a dispatcher at a trucking company. His parents had little money to spare, but Myrtle Glass made clothes for Ruth, and on weekend visits home she would give the young couple fruits and vegetables from the garden to take with them.

In 1959, Glass got his bachelor's degree in business administration and went straight to work for J.W. Crank Co., a Springfield-based drugstore chain. He was still there in 1964, after several promotions, when he met Walton and watched the hopelessly inept opening in Harrison. After the Crank chain was sold twice, though, Glass decided to look for lusher pastures. He put in a brief stint in Austin, Texas, building a Howard Johnson's motel; then Glass, his wife, and their (now) three children moved back to Springfield, where he lined up work with Consumers Markets Inc. There, he rose to become the chain's general manager, before succumbing to Sam Walton's overtures, in 1976.

Glass and Shewmaker, though unavoidably rivals, were of one mind on certain subjects. They worked together to coax Walton into investing more for new computers and better distribution. In tandem, they found it easier to budge Walton than Mayer had, convincing him to spend several hundred million dollars to complete an expensive company-wide computer terminal network, and to improve and expand the distribution centers to catch up with the growth in stores.

In 1977, Wal-Mart completed its first true computer network. Not only did it link stores to headquarters, letting sales data flow back to Walton and his executives more quickly, it also linked the stores to the distribution centers, so that orders for goods could be sent and filled faster. From this point on, the upgrades never paused. By 1979, the company was able to collect more kinds of data about sales and orders and—more importantly—draw more useful conclusions from crunching that data than almost any of its far larger rivals. Computers in all the warehouses were connected to a pair of IBM mainframes housed in a 16,000-square-foot building at headquarters. The computers stored daily sales data from every department in every store, payroll records for every employee, warehouse inventory levels, and a great deal more.

Unfortunately, when it came to using that data to get the goods on the store shelves, there was still the old logjam in distribution. The pressure still hadn't let up. In 1977, Walton agreed to build Wal-Mart's first distribution center outside Bentonville, a 390,000-square-foot building in Searcy, Arkansas, 164 miles to the southeast. The center, to be packed full of the latest in high-speed automation, would extend the company's reach farther into Illinois, Tennessee, Kentucky, and Mississippi, and would slash delivery times to existing stores in eastern Arkansas.

That same year, though, Wal-Mart added 42 stores, including 14 stores in Missouri and Illinois that Walton picked up in August by buying the Mohr Value discount chain.° Struggling to cope, Bob Thornton saw no alternative but to start shipping goods through Searcy before the building was finished—before it even had a whole roof—and long before the bugs were worked out of the new automated systems. "It took me six months to get it up and running as it should," recalls Thornton, still shuddering at the memory. He adds, "Sam never opened a distribution center until we were about a hundred stores behind."

He exaggerates a little, of course, but it must have seemed as if they were always a hundred stores behind. Certainly the strain told on the workers and truck drivers. For all of Wal-Mart's new one-big-happy-family policies, overloaded workers routinely put in 60-hour weeks under crowded, muddy, miserable conditions.

Just as in Bentonville, workers asked the Teamsters for help organizing. But again, Walton, Tate, and the others were able to preempt the crusade. One worker, Dennis Fox, said managers threatened the jobs of anyone supporting the union, a charge Tate still denies.[9] Whatever was said or implied, workers voted against joining the union by a two-to-one margin. Not that

---

° The chain had 16 stores, but Walton opted to close two of them.

the problems disappeared. Within two years, in fact, the Searcy workers would try to unionize again. And this time, they would be better organized.

If Shewmaker and Glass needed any assurances as to their places in Walton's scheme of things, they got it in 1977, when Walton appointed both of them to Wal-Mart's board. Then, the following year, unexpectedly, the one man closer to the throne was gone. One evening in April, Ferold Arend was chatting with Bud Walton on a flight back to Bentonville, after a typical day spent visiting Wal-Mart stores across Kansas. Suddenly, their plane got caught in a fierce thunderstorm, a spring squall. A vicious downdraft slapped the plane, jerking the passengers violently in their seats. Arend felt a searing stab of pain in his back. Rushed to the hospital, he was told that the wrench to his back had damaged a vertebra. Early on in his long, painful convalescence, Arend, who had worked for Walton since 1966, decided to retire.

Walton named Shewmaker president. Shewmaker himself was jubilant; and it was a popular choice with both store managers and Wall Street analysts. At forty, Shewmaker now looked to have a lock on succeeding the sixty-year-old Walton, if and when he ever actually retired. But whether Shewmaker realized it or not, Glass was coming on fast. In retrospect, the first annual report after the promotion seems to augur what would happen next. Walton had both men sign his letter to the shareholders, just below his own signature. Curiously, in the photograph of the three men that graces the letter, it's Shewmaker whose smile seems stiff and forced and Glass who is grinning.

7

The Rivals

By early in the fall of 1979, the daily sales figures zipping to Sam Walton through the company's fancy new computer system added up to an inescapable conclusion: Wal-Mart was going to break a billion dollars in sales for the year. Easily.

Walton had long expected this, of course—he'd even been brash enough to predict it to a magazine reporter, several years earlier. Now he was reaching that mark a year ahead of schedule. When he thought about it, the figure still seemed staggering, even to him. A billion dollars. And Wal-Mart still had stores in only eleven states. Who knew how much bigger it could get?

As always with Walton, such thoughts merely made him itch to grow still faster. He'd been keeping a wary eye on rival discounters, especially those operating in neighboring territories—and most especially on an outfit called Kuhn's Big K Stores. A Nashville-based company that had started out almost seventy years earlier as a variety store chain, Kuhn's now had more than 100 discount stores in nine Southern states. Hardly any of them overlapped with Wal-Mart stores; Walton and his counterparts, Jack and Gus Kuhn, had informally avoided each other's territories, until the past few years.

But now the Kuhns were in trouble, their finances stretched taut as a violin string. Two years earlier, the Kuhns had paid $8.9 million to snap up Edwards Inc., a 34-store chain in South Carolina and Georgia. At the same time, they'd splurged on a huge and lavish new headquarters and distribu-

tion center in Nashville. But converting the Edwards stores into Big K outlets had cost more and taken longer than the Kuhns had counted on. They
had badly overextended themselves. Now they were losing money, and the
wolf was at the door.

These developments provoked a Pavlovian response in Walton. Barring
a miracle, Kuhn would have to sell out pretty soon, he knew. If he could
buy the chain, if he could add its 106 stores to Wal-Mart's 276, Wal-Mart
would become the country's second-largest discounter in one fell swoop,
trailing only massive Kmart.

But what if he did buy it? Would he just be repeating Jack and Gus
Kuhn's mistake? The money and work involved in taking over such a huge
operation would stretch Wal-Mart awfully thin. It could wind up like the
anaconda that slipped through the bars into a cage to swallow a pig whole,
only to find itself trapped by its own greed.

But then again, what if Kmart or some other rival snatched up Kuhn's
Big K instead? Walton all but writhed at the thought.

His brother Bud urged caution. Sam Walton talked it over with Shewmaker, with Glass, with everybody on the Wal-Mart board. He ran the idea
past Don Soderquist, a newly arrived senior vice president who'd been
president and chief executive of the Ben Franklin chain for six years before
joining Wal-Mart. Soderquist was the executive who, nearly two decades
earlier, had bumped into Walton poking around a Chicago Kmart the day
after his pitch to take Ben Franklin into discounting had been shot down.
Tall and avuncular, he had come to Wal-Mart the usual way: He'd turned
Walton down a half dozen times—at one point, saying no to the presidency—before finally agreeing to make the jump. Eventually, Soderquist
would step into Walton's shoes as Wal-Mart's chief cheerleader at store
openings and big company meetings. But he had no more luck helping
Walton decide on this deal than any of the rest of them.

Rob Walton—much to the astonishment of some of the other executives—volunteered that he might just move to Nashville to run those stores,
if the deal went through. It wasn't that Rob wanted a stepping stone toward
running the company down the road. He made that pretty clear. But since
he was going to represent the family's interests after Sam retired or passed
on, he probably ought to get some firsthand experience running stores, he
said.

Sam Walton himself flipped and flopped on the deal. He only had to
look at Jack Kuhn's troubles to see what could come from overreaching. It
scared him nearly as much as it tantalized him. For more than a year,
heated debates on whether to buy or not to buy dominated board meetings,

and on any given day one could offer even odds on which side Walton would take.

Finally, one morning in December of 1980, he called a meeting of his executive committee: Arend (retired, but still on the board), Glass, Shewmaker, Bud Walton, Rob Walton, and Soderquist. It was time to settle this, Walton said. One last time, the debate raged; one last time, the risks and rewards were assessed; and then Walton called for a vote. The committee split: three for, three against. The men looked at Walton, awaiting his ruling. "Let's do it," he said.

In his memoirs, Walton describes this moment as though it was that split that forced him to take the responsibility for making the final decision—as though, had the vote been four-to-two against, he would have quietly acceded to the majority. Nothing could be further from the truth. Walton always goaded his executives to argue over any important decision. It helped him think. If a proposal couldn't provoke some debate, some doubt, then it must not be any good, he would often say.

But when it came down to it, there were everybody else's votes, and then there was Sam Walton's. Around Wal-Mart, there's no shortage of people who can recall Walton, on the short end of some debate or another, shutting it off by booming out "I still own most of the stock in this company, and this is what we're gonna do."

Buying Kuhn's Big K, though, wasn't as simple as voting yes or no. As first worked out, the deal carried a price tag of $17 million in cash and Wal-Mart stock. But Walton, with an eye to Kuhn's woes, insisted on a clause scuttling the agreement if Kuhn's net worth fell below $19 million before the next July. As it turned out, Kuhn's mounting losses dragged its stock price so low that the company's net worth sank to $13.2 million by spring. So Walton backed out. Then he came back with a new offer: $7.5 million, all in Wal-Mart stock. Jack Kuhn had no choice; facing a firing squad of his bankers, he was forced to agree to Walton's terms, and in August, Wal-Mart acquired the chain.

It was a steal. Given what Wal-Mart was paying to build or lease stores on its own, it would have had to shell out about $75 million to open as many stores as it had now swallowed in one gulp. The deal also gave Wal-Mart a hefty tax write-off, from assuming $15 million in Kuhn's losses.

Now came the tricky part: digesting this massive meal. Walton briefly toyed with planting some of his executives in Kuhn's fancy new headquarters, but instead decided to keep running everything out of Bentonville, just like before. Rob Walton took a pass on running the stores. The company closed 14 Big K stores that were too near existing Wal-Marts, and executives decided to sell the Nashville headquarters as soon as they could figure out a cheaper way to distribute goods to the rest of the newly acquired stores.

The job of converting the stores was handed to Paul Carter, a senior vice president (and another small-town Arkansawyer), who'd joined Wal-Mart four years earlier. Over the next few months, yo-yoing back and forth between Bentonville and Nashville and wrestling endlessly with grafting the new stores onto the Wal-Mart system ran Carter so ragged he dropped 25 pounds from his once 190-pound frame. Just getting goods to the stores was an ordeal: With Wal-Mart opening 69 other stores during the year, on top of the Big K acquisition, its distribution system was nearly bursting at the seams. Walton approved hiring an outside company to get goods to the former Big K stores. But that just put more strain on the managers converting the stores, who now had one more unfamiliar element to contend with.

By December, with 16 of the Big K stores renovated, Wal-Mart had to sell $60 million in bonds to pay for fixing up its acquisitions.

Meanwhile, back at the Searcy distribution center, the burden of trying to keep up with ever more stores soon left workers as crowded and miserable as they had been two years earlier, when the Teamsters had made their abortive organizing effort. That first time, Walton had delivered a masterfully rueful version of the same speech he'd given to workers at the Bentonville distribution center in 1976, when they had tried to organize. "You'd think I'd learn, wouldn't you?" he had asked the Searcy workers, shaking his head and apologizing for letting conditions get so bad, according to people present. He had humbly asked them for another chance, and had even offered to pay for some of the workers to go talk to their counterparts at the Bentonville distribution center. "Ask the guys up there, when they did vote for me, what happened," Walton had said. "Ask them if I made things right. Ask them did I fire people or did I let bygones be bygones."

His contrite manner and his promise to make things better had deflated that earlier effort before it could even become a formal organizing campaign. But this time, far more workers were angry, and their patience was wearing thin. Workers were putting in enormous amounts of overtime— some men even slept in their cars in the parking lot between double shifts—and too many of the people working on too little rest were getting hurt. The Searcy workers had reported 198 accidents in four months, and to make things worse, their complaints about conditions at the center seemed to fall on deaf ears. When ringleaders of the organizing effort argued that a union could force Wal-Mart to comply better with federal work-safety laws, they found a receptive audience.

Managers found out about the organizing effort early on. "They had spies at the meetings we held to organize," recalls one union activist who was later laid off. But before managers could head them off, organizers got 200 of the 415 workers at the center to sign cards asking the union to represent them—easily topping the 30 percent rate the National Labor Relations Board required to call an election. At a press conference, Joe Bellino, one worker, said Wal-Mart was refusing to pay for some work-related injuries, wasn't providing safe conditions, and wasn't paying enough money.

Another worker, Randy Powell, told reporters, "all we're asking right now is the right to negotiate hours, wages, and working conditions. They claim we have that now on an individual basis, but when you're one of 38,000 [employees], they're not going to hear you."[1]

The Teamsters seemed close to having the critical mass they needed to win. But the NLRB rules gave the company at least six weeks to work with before a vote could be held, and there were ways to gain even more time. With John Tate and another union-busting attorney from Houston mapping out strategy, Wal-Mart's managers fought back. If it might be tougher this time to convince workers that Wal-Mart cared, there were other ways to turn them against the union.

Workers arrived at the center one morning to find a 90-foot-long bulletin board running along one wall, covered with newspaper clippings describing every Teamsters strike, every violent incident, and every allegation of criminal activity, going back forty years or more, that Tate's researchers had been able to dig up. "At the top, it said, 'Walk the 90-Foot Walk of Teamster Strikes,' " recalled Ron Heath, who ran the organizing campaign for the Teamsters' local in Little Rock.

It was a direct hit on the Teamsters' weak spot. The Teamsters had engaged in hundreds of strikes, of course, and some of them had been violent; this was, after all, the largest and most powerful union in the country. But it was also notoriously the most corrupt—so much so, in fact, that the Teamsters had been kicked out of the AFL-CIO back in 1957 for corruption. Back in the Teamsters' earliest days, big employers had often hired goons and gangsters to attack pickets and break up strikes. Union organizers were often beaten and killed. Some union locals had fought fire with fire, hooking up with gangsters too, as a way of protecting themselves; and over the years, organized crime had thoroughly infiltrated the union. Many locals had become mob fiefdoms. Back in the late '50s and early '60s, Robert F. Kennedy, first as counsel to a Senate committee, then as U.S. attorney general, had headed investigations that led to the criminal convictions of more than a hundred Teamsters leaders—including union president Jimmy Hoffa, who was sent to prison in 1967 for tampering with the jury in an earlier trial. Other investigations had continued into the '70s, focusing on how the mob had gained control of the Teamsters' pension funds. And then, of course, there was Hoffa's disappearance in 1975, after his release from prison; he was (and still is) presumed to have been murdered for getting in the way of the same mobsters who earlier helped him take control of the union.

Impugning the Teamsters, though, was just the start. Tate and Wal-Mart managers met with groups of workers, promising to try to take care of their concerns. Sam and Bud Walton flew down from Bentonville to meet with the workers, too. Heath and many workers recall one meeting days before the election, at which Sam Walton bluntly told them he'd take away their profit-sharing if they voted for the union. When one man asked why workers at a newer distribution center in Texas were being paid $1.50 an hour more than the $6.20 hourly wage at Searcy, Walton said he could hire workers in Searcy for less than he could in Texas. Then he told them that he had five hundred applications on file for their jobs.

Tate denies that Walton made any threats or promises that would have been illegal under federal labor laws. But workers who sat gathered around Walton on the concrete floor of the warehouse remember his threats with perfect clarity. "He told us that if the union got in, the warehouse would be closed," recalls Larry Havener, who still worked at the Searcy center sixteen years later. "He said people could vote any way they wanted, but he'd close her right up." Adds another worker, "When Sam said he'd just shut the doors rather than have a third party involved, that changed a lot of minds. People didn't want to lose their jobs."* By the time the election finally rolled around on February 5, 1982, nearly four months after workers had petitioned for it, support had melted away. Workers voted down the

---

* Walton was the original Teflon man. Even workers who heard his threats firsthand held him in such high esteem as tough, but a straight shooter, that few held his threats against him. Many workers echoed the comments of one man, still at Searcy in 1997, who, after complaining bitterly about conditions at the center, then and now, nevertheless said, "Sam cared about people. He knew the people in his company, and he always tried to make things right. The guys running the company nowadays don't care. They just care about the dollar." Of eight current and former Searcy workers there at the time of the campaign who agreed to be interviewed (including several who opposed the union), all eight confirmed Walton's threat to close the center and considered it the key reason workers voted not to unionize.

union, 215 to 67. Heath claims it was that wide margin that convinced the Teamsters not to bother to contest the results nor to file accusations of unfair labor practices against Walton or the company. But it seems as though the Teamsters, like the pro-union workers themselves, simply lost heart.

Most of the union activists were soon laid off—always for some other stated reason, of course. Others quit. "If the union vote had gone through, it could have made a big difference," says Lannie Lee Leavell, who left soon after the vote, "but people were too scared." Leavell, who had worked tagging goods and placing them on a conveyor belt, found himself a construction job. He says he never regretted leaving. "They overworked you," he says. "There was all this 'cheer, cheer, cheer, go go go' pep-rally stuff, but I didn't care for how they treated you on the job."

As the Teamsters were going down to defeat in Searcy, workers across the country were terrified of losing their jobs. A brutal recession had gripped the nation. Through the late '70s, soaring oil prices had helped drive inflation to double-digit levels. In the summer of 1979, after years of hapless efforts to tame the worst inflation in memory, President Jimmy Carter had appointed Paul Volcker chairman of the Federal Reserve Board. Volcker had immediately proposed attacking inflation the only way he could think of: by squeezing the money supply. Carter knew this was likely to provoke a recession that could doom his reelection campaign (as in fact happened); but nothing else he'd tried had worked, so he agreed.* Once Ronald Reagan took office in early 1981, Volcker had tightened the money supply even more, out of worry that Reagan's promised tax cuts might stoke further inflation. By the summer of '81, the result seemed to be the worst of both worlds: The country was mired in its most severe recession since the Depression; millions of people were out of work; and with inflation still raging, interest rates topped 20 percent, putting any business with substantial debts under terrible pressure.

There were industries far worse off than retailing, of course: Automobile makers, for instance, saw sales plummet 27 percent in '81 and laid off hundreds of thousands of workers. But retailers were hit hard, too—especially discounters, who were facing the toughest competition most of them

---

* During the 1980 presidential campaign, Ronald Reagan's stump speech inevitably said of Carter: "When he took office, inflation was 4.8 percent and he said he was going to do something about it. And he did. It's now averaging 16.4 percent." Joseph Nocera cites the line in *A Piece of the Action,* his 1994 book about the rise of the personal finance industry.

had ever seen. The days when a discounter could stake out unclaimed territory were over. Big national chains and small regional outfits alike had been trying to expand as fast as possible, often by swallowing smaller rivals and piling on debt. At the same time, as more and more once-regional firms invaded each other's territory, the growing competition made it harder to get away with raising prices, despite inflation. So profit margins shrank even as labor and energy costs, and the cost of borrowing money, spiraled higher.[*] What happened next wasn't very surprising. Dozens of chains slipped under the waves, including some of the earliest pioneers, such as E.J. Korvette, Mammoth Mart, and Vornado. Other chains, such as Caldor and Ayr-Way, were devoured by bigger, healthier outfits, just as Kuhn's Big K had been gulped down by Wal-Mart. Woolworth, which had gone into discounting back in 1962, would liquidate its struggling 336-store Woolco discount division in 1982.[†]

Even mighty Kmart was floundering. Its sales kept climbing, but its net profits fell throughout 1980 and 1981. Part of this could be blamed on the same inflationary and recessionary pressures that were hammering other retailers; but Kmart also was paying for some shockingly bad bets it made in the '70s.

Wal-Mart was facing more competition too, of course. Twelve of the former Big K stores, for example, were in Nashville, where they vied for customers with four other discount chains, including Kmart, which had 16 stores in town. And Kmart had begun moving into Wal-Mart territory— opening stores in some of Wal-Mart's bigger towns, including Rogers, Arkansas, just a 15-minute drive from Wal-Mart's headquarters. Price battles could become absurd: At one point, the Kmart and Wal-Mart stores in North Little Rock both were selling Crest toothpaste for 6 cents a tube, for example.

Even so, though, barely a fourth of Wal-Mart stores faced such direct discount competition. By far, most Wal-Mart stores were still in small towns where no other discounter had ventured. And that advantage showed up clearly on the bottom line. Just as Walton had expected, for the year ending on January 31, 1980, Wal-Mart's sales soared to $1.25 billion, up nearly 39

---

[*] Skyrocketing interest rates were killing any retailers with significant debt. One reason Kuhn's was drowning in red ink, for example, was that a $14.5-million bank loan it had taken out to buy a smaller chain and to build its new headquarters had carried an adjustable interest rate. The rate kept climbing higher and higher with inflation—reaching 24.6 percent in 1981. The interest payments devoured all the company's profits. When Wal-Mart bought Kuhn's, it renegotiated the loan, cutting the interest rate to a fixed 12 percent.

[†] In the United States, anyway. Woolco stores in Canada would keep operating for another decade.

percent from a year earlier.° And net income—the company's earnings—
jumped 40 percent to $41.2 million. The numbers offer a clear picture of
how scant the profit margins were. Wal-Mart made about 3.3 cents in net
income for every dollar of sales that year. But still, compared with almost
any other retailer, it was considered fat and happy.

And fat and happy perfectly describes how the company felt. One executive bragged to Maggie Gilliam, an analyst at First Boston Corp., that
within three weeks of Woolco's announced closing, Wal-Mart had hired 120
new managers from the company. (It also hired 650 hourly workers.) In fact,
he claimed, Wal-Mart couldn't have opened the 91 stores it added the following year without all those Woolco refugees. Wal-Mart also bought 32 of
the old Woolco stores in 1983. As rivals dropped left and right, Wal-Mart's
sales climbed by nearly a third during fiscal 1981; by 49 percent—*49 percent!*—the year after that; and by 38 percent the next year, to reach $3.38 bil-
lion by early 1983. Each of those years, earnings climbed even faster.

These kinds of results, coming as they did in middle of the worst economic conditions in more than fifty years, hit Wall Street analysts and rival
retailers alike like a two-by-four over the head. But many people who now
began studying the company noted all the small towns Wal-Mart was in and
became instant skeptics. Sure, Wal-Mart's numbers looked good. But to
keep growing, they would say, Wal-Mart increasingly would have to fight
for turf with the big boys, such as Kmart. The free ride was over, and Wal-
Mart was about to take its lumps.

This seemingly logical conclusion popped up in trade magazines and
analysts' reports; it could be heard at retailing conventions. And, as so often
seems to happen with the conventional wisdom, it was dead wrong. Some
Wall Street analysts who'd followed the company for a long time—Walter
Loeb at Morgan Stanley & Co. and Gilliam at First Boston, to pick two—
knew better. They recognized that Wal-Mart had more going for it than the
lack of competition in small towns. They recognized that Walton and his
men had created what was already, for all its growing pains, perhaps the
leanest and fastest distribution system in the country.†

By early '83, compared with three years earlier, Wal-Mart had roughly

---

° Reporting financial results by a fiscal year that ends on January 31 makes it easier to tally results for
the all-important Christmas season
† Gilliam noted in a June 10, 1982, report that 80 percent of Wal-Mart's merchandise went through its
own distribution centers, compared with 30 percent at Kmart and 50 percent at Target. She also noted
that half of Wal-Mart's merchandise was shipped out of its distribution centers in less than two days and
that the company was trying to shorten that time even further. This meant, generally, that Wal-Mart
could get goods on the shelf faster and at less expense than its rivals.

doubled its outlets, with 551 stores in 15 states. The stores themselves were bigger, too. In 1976, the average new Wal-Mart took up 46,400 square feet. By 1980, it was 50,200 square feet; by 1983 (partly because of the Woolco stores, which were as big as 80,000 square feet), the average new Wal-Mart was 63,900 square feet. Even ignoring the Woolco stores, Wal-Mart was building bigger stores only in part because more of them were in bigger communities. Mostly, it was building them bigger because it needed the space.

Thanks to Wal-Mart's greater size, makers of name-brand goods that had once snubbed Walton now came to Bentonville hat in hand. And as in every other area, Walton made sure his buyers used the company's growing clout to demand special discounts and the lowest possible price from manufacturers. Put that buying power together with Wal-Mart's ability to deliver goods to its stores faster and cheaper than anyone around, and the company had a price advantage in most burgs that quickly became obvious to anyone who shopped the stores. The typical small-town Wal-Mart could offer such attractive prices that it drew shoppers not just from the town itself, but from a surrounding area that Wal-Mart executives estimated to stretch 20 miles or more in each direction.

And what about Kmart, the mightiest discounter in the land, a retailer so big it was approaching the Olympian scale of number-one Sears? As a discounter, it wasn't much older than Wal-Mart; back in 1962, the first Kmart store had opened just four months before the first Wal-Mart. But there was no comparison in how the companies had grown. Now, in early 1983, Kmart had four times as many stores as Wal-Mart and took in more than five times the annual sales, with $18.6 billion in sales for the year just ended. It was the second-largest retailer in the world—and gaining on number one.

Of course, Kmart had started a bit ahead of the game, too. It had begun corporate life as the S.S. Kresge Co., a five-and-dime chain founded by Sebastian Kresge in 1899 in Detroit, and modeled on Woolworth. By 1912, Kresge had 85 stores with annual sales topping $10 million. In this incarnation, Kresge had offered everything from candy and toys to housewares, notions, and even some apparel, all for a dime or less. Inflation soon put an end to that price ceiling (it was raised to a quarter before World War I and climbed higher over the years), but even into the 1960s, people still referred to such shops as dime stores. In that business, Kresge had thrived, for decades holding a secure second place behind Woolworth.

But after World War II, as the first chains of discount stores sprang up around the country, Kresge's leaders realized they faced danger. Many of the new discount stores were being built not in the traditional shopping districts but on the outskirts of cities, where land was cheaper—and where they were within easy reach of the suburbs that were now beginning their inexorable sprawl. There had been suburbs, in the modern sense, before World War II, of course; some, such as Chicago's Riverside, along the Des Plaines River, date from the 1870s. But the years after World War II saw an explosion of tract homes in vast new subdivisions, ever farther out.

It was this vast out-migration from the cities that Kmart would ride to greatness—and that changed the whole retailing landscape too, naturally. But to understand how this happened, it helps to go back to the first few years after the stock market crash of 1929, when home building fell by 95 percent, and bankruptcies and foreclosures multiplied exponentially. By 1933, half the home mortgages in the country were technically in default. At that bleak point, President Franklin Delano Roosevelt's New Dealers created the Federal Housing Administration, which they hoped would resuscitate the building trades by guaranteeing mortgages. FHA guarantees cut the risk to lenders, which meant lower interest rates for borrowers. The FHA also changed how the loans were structured. Instead of paying, say, half the cost of a home up front and signing a ten-year mortgage, as had been standard, home buyers now could put down as little as 10 percent and stretch out payments over thirty years. These changes would revolutionize home ownership, putting it within reach of millions of Americans for the first time and affecting where and how these millions would live—but not right away. The Depression's high unemployment and low wages still put homes out of reach for most workers, FHA or no FHA.

But then came the hyper-heated economy of World War II, when a flood of deficit spending created millions of new jobs. When the war ended, the country faced a postwar economic boom and a severe housing shortage. At that point, Congress created a program of easy mortgages under the Veterans Administration and boosted funding for FHA mortgages.* New federal income tax rules let home buyers deduct their interest payments, making mortgages even more affordable. Now millions of Americans could buy homes, in some cases without even having to make a down payment. But the rules didn't apply to all homes—or to all buyers.

During the Depression and the war, black migrant workers from the rural South, many of them put out of work by the mechanical cotton picker,

---

* From 1947 through 1957, homes sold with FHA or VA mortgages ranged between 40 percent and 50 percent of all homes sold.

had migrated in great numbers to northern cities in search of work. Along with other immigrants, they had wound up in the poorest, most neglected properties in the cities. Their old, run-down homes on small lots didn't meet FHA standards and didn't qualify for mortgages. In fact, FHA rules disqualified whole inner-city neighborhoods, in a policy known as redlining. The houses that did qualify were new, single-family homes being built by developers out on cheap, vacant land outside the cities. Whites who could afford to moved out of the cities to these new suburbs. In those days of legal segregation, most developers wouldn't sell to blacks, who were effectively ghettoized.

In effect, government mortgage policies helped turn cities into economic donuts; as the haves moved out, the inner cities—the donut holes where the have-nots lived—deteriorated.

Kresge, like many variety chains, still operated most of its stores in these downtown areas that were now starting to decay. By 1955, Kresge had 673 stores with sales of $354 million a year, but executives could see clearly what lay ahead. Neighborhoods were changing, middle-class customers were moving out, and in many places, Kresge was saddled with leases of up to ninety-nine years.[2] To compete with the new discount chains that, by the late '50s, were indisputably taking away business, Kresge began to experiment with building larger dime stores in the suburbs, and with offering self-service. But it was clear the company needed a whole new long-term strategy.

So, in 1957, company president Franklin Williams ordered one of his vice presidents, Harry Cunningham, to look into discounting and other ways of retailing. Just as Sam Walton would soon be doing, Cunningham spent much of 1957 and 1958 touring discount stores—flying more than 100,000 miles—visiting with any discounting executives who'd meet with him, and thinking.

Tall and stately, the baritone-voiced Cunningham looked like the Hollywood notion of an executive. At staid Kresge, he'd shown an unusual flair for innovation and a willingness to plunge forward with new ideas. Cunningham was born in 1907 on a farm near the town of Home Camp, in western Pennsylvania. In 1927, after his sophomore year at Miami University in Oxford, Ohio, he dropped out to become a newspaper reporter at the *Harrisburg Patriot*. He soon soured on the reporting life though; within a year, he met a Kresge executive who talked him into quitting the *Patriot* to join Kresge as a management trainee. All trainees there had to put in stints as stock boys; so Cunningham began his new career unpacking boxes at a Kresge in Lynchburg, Virginia. Given a moldering store in Grosse

Pointe, Michigan, to run, Cunningham asked sales clerks to note any customer requests on blue index cards. By carrying what they asked for, he doubled the store's sales in a year. From there, he had risen steadily through the ranks, moving to the company's headquarters in 1950 as an assistant sales manager. In 1951, despite being a relatively lowly figure in management, he had established himself as a maverick by pushing for Kresge to adopt the self-service style checkout system that supermarkets used (and which the Ben Franklin chain and Sam Walton would adopt the following year). Williams had made Cunningham manager of sales in 1953 and then appointed him to the company's board in 1956.

One of the favorite company anecdotes about him—another one of those stories meant to show how one should approach retailing—has Cunningham, while managing his first store, handling an irate customer who says he can't find eight items that bigger Kresge stores carry. As the story has it, Cunningham takes a list, drives to downtown Detroit, picks up the eight items, and delivers them to the man's house himself. This was a story told often in the late '70s, after Cunningham's retirement, when Kmart was starting to slip and there was a palpable feeling at the company that some of those up top didn't share Cunningham's devotion to doing whatever it takes to make a customer happy.

More than anything else, though, it was Cunningham's painstaking study of discounting, and the policies he carved in stone, that led Kresge to dominate the industry for three decades. Like Walton—only earlier—Cunningham quickly became convinced discounting was the way of the future. He also saw that many of the new chains were making mistakes that would soon leave them at risk. When Cunningham succeeded Williams as company president, in 1959, he had already decided to take Kresge into discounting. But this was an extremely conservative company. Better to get the board and upper management solidly with him, he thought. So he assigned a team to mount an elaborate study of discounting and how Kresge might get into the business. Meanwhile, he took hundreds of older, struggling Kresge stores, saddled with long leases, and remade them into a new chain of Jupiter stores. These were a hybrid of the variety and discount stores. They had fewer sales clerks than traditional Kresge stores and a much smaller selection of goods; but they sold those goods at deeply discounted prices.

In March 1961, Gene Sturges, the head of the team, brought his report to Cunningham. As he began to describe his conclusions, Cunningham interrupted him. This, he said, was something he wanted Kresge's entire executive and buying staff to hear. That afternoon, 45 top officers crowded into a conference room to hear Sturges.

Discounters were selling enormous quantities of merchandise, he told them, approaching $2 billion a year for the whole industry. In many ways, these companies—chains such as Korvette, Zayre, and J.M. Field—were outperforming variety stores, Kresge included. But they were vulnerable. Many were having trouble managing their operations as they tried to expand. They didn't have the experienced retailers, the sophisticated expense controls, and the deep pockets of a company like Kresge. The discount industry was fragmented. There weren't any dominant, well-entrenched players. And, he said, the opportunities were tremendous.

As soon as Sturges finished, Cunningham stood up and turned to his audience. "Gentlemen," he said, "the discount store is as much a part of Kresge's future as the variety store. And that is where we're going next."[3]

First, Cunningham quietly tested the Kmart idea at what had been slated to be a large Kresge store in San Fernando, California. The company would stick to the formula established there as long as Cunningham was in charge: Aim for volume by taking a lower margin and offering a lower price, of course—but sell nationally advertised, brand-name goods whenever possible, and sell in-house brands only when there was no name brand available. Guarantee satisfaction or your money back.

After several months of fine tuning in San Fernando, Kresge opened what it would officially call its first Kmart store on March 1, 1962, in the southwest Detroit suburb of Garden City, about a 30-minute drive from the company's downtown headquarters. It was huge, one-and-a-half times the size of even the largest Kresge store, 60,000 square feet, as long as a football field and two-thirds as wide. Cunningham felt so confident about the concept that he announced at the store opening that Kresge would open at least 37 more Kmarts over the next two years. And so many customers thronged that first store that he soon decided to make the next Kmarts even bigger, some up to twice as big.

Determined to snatch as much of the market as possible, Cunningham demanded that every available resource be devoted to the new operation. He convinced the board to cut shareholders' dividends in 1963 so the money could be used to open Kmart stores more quickly—infuriating many shareholders and sparking demands that he resign. By the end of that year, Kresge had built 53 Kmarts. They racked up $83 million in sales. At that point Walton, with his much more limited resources, was just thinking about opening his second Wal-Mart.

Like the Garden City store, most Kmarts would be planted in the sub-urbs of major cities. That would be the pattern: As Americans moved to the suburbs in growing numbers, they would find Kmarts awaiting them. The typical Kmart built in the early '60s would be a one-story building of 100,000 square feet (more than twice the size of a 1960s Wal-Mart), sur-rounded by a huge parking lot, and situated alongside a major road as the anchor tenant of a small shopping center. Often, the Kmart would be put next to a supermarket, to feed off the customer traffic. Kresge would sign twenty-year leases for the buildings rather than own them. In 1964, Kresge built 37 more Kmart stores, to become the largest discount chain in the country.

That Kresge should catch the wave of out-migration and ride it so success-fully shouldn't be surprising; for just as living in Newport and Bentonville alerted Sam Walton to the opportunities small towns offered, being based in Detroit gave the Kresge men an early insight into the new suburban markets. It was, after all, the Motor City's primary industry that, along with the FHA, helped create the modern suburbs that would suckle Kresge's Kmart stores.

Detroit had been an industrial center long before Henry Ford, perhaps inspired by Sears's warehouse automation, had invented the assembly line in 1909. But it was Ford who, by slashing the cost of production, and turn-ing the car from a luxury into something the working masses could afford, sparked the explosive growth of the automotive industry. That industry in turn propelled Detroit's hurtling growth. "Every time I reduce the price of the car by one dollar," Ford bragged of his Model T, "I get one thousand new buyers."[4] By the mid-1920s, Ford Motor Co. alone was building nearly 2 million cars a year. Even during the Depression, the number of cars in the country climbed, reaching 23 million by 1930. From 1900 to 1930, De-troit's population soared from 285,000 to more than 1.8 million.

As James Howard Kunstler described the era: "Worker housing was mass-produced on a scale almost as great as the production of cars. Vast, monotonous neighborhoods of one-story workingman's bungalows sprang up near the auto plants and on the fringes of towns. In fact, the fringe pushed out so rapidly that each successive boundary road was named to give people a proximate idea of their distance from downtown: Six Mile Road, Seven Mile Road, Eight Mile Road, and so on."[5]

In 1925, a commission appointed by Detroit's mayor—and, naturally, led by an automotive executive—called for tearing out the city's streetcar lines and building twenty superhighways radiating out into the surrounding counties. The onset of the Depression derailed this proposal to derail Detroit; but already, the steady march of single-family homes had created a city far too spread out for any form of mass public transit to be economical. During World War II, the federal government built highways to link these outer suburbs where many workers lived to its Willow Run bomber plant and to Chrysler Corp.'s tank factory in the suburb of Warren, out beyond 12 Mile Road. After the war, more highways followed. To speed cars along, highways were built below street grade, with limited access, and only a few overpasses, spread far apart. Like giant moats, these highways girdled the old neighborhoods, strangling them the same way stripping a ring of bark slowly kills a tree by cutting off the flow of sap. And even as homes and small businesses in the older parts of Detroit were demolished to make way for the expressways, or were cut off by them, the easy access these roads gave to once-remote rural areas spurred development farther out, creating a vast ring of still newer suburbs.

In Detroit, as elsewhere, the old, cheap inner-city housing was all that was affordable to the thousands of blacks who had streamed up from the South to work in arms factories during World War II. As the migration continued after the war, soon there were far more would-be workers than there were jobs for them. More and more blacks moved into the older, cheaper neighborhoods in the city, and white workers fled to the shiny new suburbs—a flight that would become a mass exodus after a savage race riot in 1967. It was a process being repeated, on various scales, in dozens of other cities across the country.

But for Kresge, these new suburbs and its new Kmart division were a perfect match. By 1966, with sales of $576 million, the new division accounted for more than half of Kresge's sales. Driven by Cunningham's sense of urgency, the company was opening Kmarts at the rate of one a week. At one point in 1967, it stunned rivals by opening 15 Kmarts in 15 days. By 1968, when Walton had 8 Wal-Marts among his 24 stores, and sales of $12.6 million, the Kmart division's sales hit $1.2 billion, from 273 stores. Even in 1970, as a recession rattled many of the smaller retailers, and sales slumped, Kresge opened 74 new Kmarts, and sales climbed 17 percent to $2.56 billion. That year, Kresge passed its perennial rival, Woolworth (with $2.5 billion in sales), to become the country's third largest general merchandise retailer, behind Sears and J.C. Penney.

Kmart's prowess was not lost on Walton. During those years he visited every Kmart store he could and copied anything and everything that looked good. "I was in their stores constantly because they were the laboratory, and they were better than we were. I spent a heck of a lot of time wandering through their stores talking to their people and trying to figure out how they did things," he said in his autobiography. "So much about their stores was superior to ours back then that sometimes I felt like we couldn't compete."[6]

It was Cunningham, Walton would later say, who "really designed and built the first discount store as we know it today . . . and should be remembered as one of the leading retailers of all time."[7] He wasn't just being polite; Walton had great respect for Cunningham's savvy and eagerly picked his brain whenever he had a chance. Initially, at least, Cunningham doesn't seem to have seen the folksy Walton and his tiny backwoods outfit as any kind of competition, and he was helpful and open with him. But you can learn much about people from the questions they ask, and Cunningham quickly recognized Walton as someone to take very seriously indeed.

He kept an eye on Wal-Mart's progress. And after he retired in 1972, and took a seat on Kresge's board of directors, Cunningham would warn his successors repeatedly that Walton and his small regional outfit posed a very real threat.

Cunningham's hand-picked successor at the helm was Robert Dewar, a genial, balding, professorial type given to bow ties, who had begun his career at Kresge twenty-three years earlier as a lawyer. During World War II the small, mild-looking Dewar had been a Navy bomber pilot in the South Pacific. At Kresge, he had worked his way up the financial side. He was not a merchant. But he had been Cunningham's right-hand man since before the first Kmart opened. Cunningham, brimming with confidence in his own abilities as a merchant, had plucked Dewar from among the bean counters to be his legal and financial expert. When he appointed Dewar as president in 1970, and then as chairman and chief executive in 1972, many of the store managers and merchandising men at Kresge were horrified. To put the company in the hands of someone who'd never run a store? Such a thing was unheard of at Kresge. But from Cunningham's point of view, what Dewar knew or didn't know about merchandising didn't much matter. Harry Cunningham was staying on the board, and he knew enough for both of them.

Many years later, when the '70s were seen as the time Kmart started to go wrong, Dewar's never having run a store would be wielded against him like a bludgeon. And it's fair enough, in a way, to lay the blame with him for misguided initiatives. But in another sense, it was Harry Cunningham who was to blame. He seems to have seen Dewar simply as a caretaker, a man whose job was to keep the ship at exactly the heading he was handed. Cunningham encouraged both Dewar and the company's top merchandising men to see things the same way.

Not that any clouds were visible on the horizon back in 1972, though. As Dewar took the helm that year, Kresge seemed unstoppable, a juggernaut far outpacing competing discounters. That year, as if signaling where its future lay, the company moved its headquarters from downtown Detroit to a sprawling new campus in the nearby suburb of Troy.

But seemingly minor changes now began to alter the long-term strategies Cunningham had laid out—a trimming of this sail, a slackening of that line—alterations that would eventually add up to run the company awry. Dewar himself, talking about the decisions made in those days, tends to adopt the passive voice: "There was a feeling we ought to consider" doing this, that, or the other, he'll say. In any event, Dewar, with Cunningham's evident acquiescence, now decided that to keep growing quickly, Kresge couldn't simply stick to Cunningham's formula of building big stores, stores of 80,000 square feet or more, in suburbs. There was a feeling that the suburban market would soon be saturated and that Kresge needed to change its approach.

Mindful of Wal-Mart's success in small towns, Dewar had Kresge design scaled-down stores, as small as 40,000 square feet—less than half the size of a standard Kmart—for smaller communities. But Kresge should have studied Wal-Mart more closely. Wal-Mart's equivalent-sized stores were only in its tiniest towns, towns less than half the size of those Dewar wanted to target. Even as Kresge began testing his new concept, Wal-Mart was doing so well in the sort of middle-sized towns Dewar was looking at that it was expanding the size of its stores, which were already bigger than the downsized Kmarts. The same was true of several other regional discounters. But Dewar and the other Kresge men either didn't notice or took no heed of what these companies were doing. When the first two mini-Kmart stores sold like gangbusters, a delighted Dewar ordered the program rolled out. Only later, when they went back to see where things had gone wrong, did Kresge executives realize why those first two stores had done so misleadingly well: "They were in test markets where they couldn't fail, because there was no competition," said Larry Parkin, later a director and executive vice president of the company.

Between 1972 and 1979, Kresge would open 1,100 of these smaller stores. Enough of them would do well at first, just like the two test stores, to keep the program going. But as it turned out, even in towns where the shrunken Kmarts arrived first, they couldn't hold their own against the larger rival discount stores that so often soon followed. In 1977, Kresge tried to deal with the problem by rolling out a new 55,000-square-foot mini-store. But even so, in the long run, most of the stores proved too small to be profitable as well as expensive either to abandon or expand.

Dewar became fascinated with the idea of invading Europe and Japan; encouraged by Cunningham, he devoted far too much time and effort to exploring possibilities in Germany, France, Italy, Great Britain, and Japan that never quite seemed to pan out. In 1973, at Kresge's annual meeting, Dewar eagerly promised shareholders that the company would open its first store in Europe by 1975. But red tape and a recession in Europe in 1974 forced him quietly to scuttle that plan. In the end, it would be another twenty years before Kmart actually crossed the Atlantic—and then its stay would be short and not particularly sweet.

As for merchandising—choosing and selling the goods in the existing Kmart stores—Dewar left much to Ervin Wardlow, the highly opinionated and fast-talking chief operating officer, and to his lieutenants. This was understandable; these men, after all, were *supposed* to handle the merchandising. But, too, because these men were merchants, they had the confidence of the buyers and the store managers in a way Dewar didn't. "We felt he got the title, but he wasn't really our boss; he wasn't the one in charge," recalls one store manager. Many managers from then still claim dismissively—and wrongly—that Dewar rarely visited stores; in fact, Dewar habitually devoted several days a week to store visits.

All the same, Dewar went along with the merchandising men's decision to drop Cunningham's policy of selling established name-brand apparel. Instead, they turned more and more to what are called "private-label" goods—items made for Kresge and sold as a Kresge house brand. The plan seemed sensible. Private-label goods can carry a fatter profit margin, because retailers typically pay the maker much less for them than for similar name brands. The problem, though, was that many of Kresge's private labels weren't very good. A lot of the clothing was shoddy, even ugly. By the mid-'70s, Kmart was being nicknamed the Polyester Palace, hardly the kind of image likely to help sales. Shoppers didn't entirely abandon Kmart; but they began turning as often to other discounters who still offered more attractive name brands.

Worse, under the caretaker mentality that now took hold, Kresge neglected spending to spruce up existing stores, many of which, as the years passed, looked increasingly shabby. The company relaxed into complacency about its assortment of merchandise, failing to devote as much energy as Wal-Mart or other rivals to stoking the fires of consumerism by constantly bringing in new products, whether the latest fashions in apparel or "improved" housewares and sundries.

And Dewar made another, still more fateful, decision. As early as the late '60s, Kresge had experimented in a small way with using computers to order goods and track inventory. But by 1973, when Walton had 22 of Wal-Mart's 64 stores on a computerized ordering system, and most major retailers from Sears on down were testing computers, Kresge still used its antiquated system of having managers at each of the company's 673 stores fill out order books by hand and mail in each day's invoices to headquarters—more than 40,000 invoices a day in all, which would be piled up, sorted by hand, and sent off to vendors. Orders could take weeks, even months. That year, seeing what was happening at rival retailers, several Kresge executives proposed replacing the order books with computers, which could send in orders over telephone lines. They argued that transmitting invoices electronically would speed up orders by days, keep more goods in stock, boost sales, and, in the long run, cut costs.

But Kresge had always had a decentralized structure that gave managers out in the field great authority. Anything that smacked of taking power out of the hands of store managers, as centralized ordering did, was bound to be seen as an attempt by headquarters to take power away from the field—so it provoked furious opposition. The merchandising men argued that it was the job of the store manager to know from experience what merchandise was available, what was going out of stock, and when to make an order. Go to some computer system to do that, and you'd lose all that expertise, they argued.

Dewar, for his part, wasn't about to ram this down the merchants' throats. He wasn't sure himself that computers were that necessary. So he vetoed the idea as too expensive, saying he didn't like the notion of spending millions on what he considered an experiment.

As a sop, he agreed to buy two mini-computers to test at two Kmart stores; but the test was practically meaningless, because while these stores would put their invoices on a computer tape, they couldn't transmit them. Instead, they mailed in the computer tapes each day, the same as paper invoices. By 1976, Kresge—now with 1,647 stores, including 1,206 Kmarts, and more invoices than ever flooding in—tried another small experiment, using computer technology to send orders for goods from its headquarters to a few of its biggest vendors. Again, a few executives recognized the huge potential to speed up and cut the cost of getting goods into stores, and they clamored to computerize the entire ordering system. And again, Dewar sided with the merchandising men, as he would throughout his tenure. If they insisted that filling out order books by hand and mailing the invoices worked just fine, it must be so. If they feared using a computer program to reorder goods automatically, if they argued that store managers and clerks were more capable than any computers could be at knowing what goods to order and when, why should he cavil? Computers cost too much anyway.

There were executives at Kresge who recognized various of Dewar's decisions as mistakes at the time, of course. But few spoke out. This company had a hidebound corporate culture utterly unlike that of Wal-Mart, where Walton encouraged those lower down to debate and challenge ideas, and where decisions, even by Walton, were rarely considered absolutely final. At Kresge, it was considered reckless to venture an opinion until you knew what the person above you thought. To second-guess a superior was foolhardy; and as most executives rose through the hierarchy, they expected their juniors to show the same deference they themselves had had to display. As had been the case with every man at the top since Sebastian S. Kresge himself, once Dewar made a decision, that was it; debate ended. (The sense that Wardlow and his lieutenants operated their own fiefdom was an exception, of course; but then, they were merchants and Dewar was not.)

Still, under the head of steam Cunningham had built up, Kresge coasted through much of the '70s. The company kept adding stores, and sales kept climbing, reaching $8.4 billion by 1976. That year, Kresge opened 271 Kmart stores, more than 10 times the number of new Wal-Marts, and accounting for nearly half of all discount stores opened by all retailers that year. The next year, the company officially changed its name to Kmart Corp.

But by 1978, even though Kmart's sales climbed by almost 18 percent to $11.7 billion, Dewar's mistakes were becoming clear. Raging inflation was squeezing retailers, and Kmart had left itself particularly vulnerable. The growth in sales was slowing—and in profits, too. Years of neglected upkeep had left many of the stores in embarrassing condition. Older Kmarts were often poorly lit, with cartons of merchandise piled on tables and shelves bare of hot-selling items. Increasingly, rival discounters were moving in and trouncing Dewar's mini–Kmarts—and full-sized Kmarts, too. Wal-Mart and other regional discounters, such as Caldor in the Northeast and Dayton-Hudson Corp.'s Target chain in the Midwest, had worked harder at keeping their stores attractive and at keeping goods in stock. Eventually, even the merchandising men had to concede that out-of-stocks were increasing dramatically, as Kmart's old paper-invoice ordering system became more and more unwieldy. Dewar finally agreed to begin gradually installing back-office computers in Kmart stores that could transmit orders and other data back to headquarters each night, when phone rates were lower.

But the system would take nearly four years to roll out, and it was too little, too late. By midway through 1979, it was clear that sales and profit for the year would show their smallest gains since the 1974 recession. Once price inflation was factored out, sales at existing stores were flat or even down slightly. All the trends pointed to a drop in profits in 1980.

From outside the company, it seems obvious that what happened next was that Cunningham and the board decided that Dewar had to go. By tradition, Dewar should have held the reins until 1986, when he would reach the usual retirement age of sixty-five. But it was not to be.

As Dewar remembers it, he decided on his own to "dramatize the merchandising operation at the stores" by stepping aside in favor of somebody with a stronger background as a merchant. In his version, he felt no pressure from anybody to retire. "I just sensed that having served for the number of years I had, that it made sense to step out," he says. But then, Dewar also denies that there were problems with merchandising, or with the condition of the stores.

However it happened, the jockeying to replace Dewar hit full swing by late '79. Wardlow campaigned for the job; but it soon came down to two other executives on the board who, for months, hotly debated their respective ideas of how to get the company back in gear. Walter Tenninga, the chief financial officer and vice chairman, said Kmart should focus on new ventures outside of discounting and should find promising businesses to acquire. Bernie Fauber, who'd climbed through the merchandise side to become the chief administrative officer, argued that Kmart should focus on its core business by building more Kmart stores and working on ways to improve existing stores.

In the end, Fauber had an unbeatable trump card—he was backed by Cunningham. In November, Dewar stepped or was pushed aside and Fauber became chief executive. The board announced that in May, at the next annual meeting, he would be made chairman as well. Within a few months, Tenninga, who had twenty-three years at the company, resigned. Wardlow retired within a year.

Fauber, a stern, intimidating man who was the same age as Dewar, might have been an unusual chairman at most companies: He'd never been to college, having joined Kresge straight out of high school in 1941. He'd started as a stock boy at the Kresge store in Lynchburg, Virginia, where Harry Cunningham had begun his career thirteen years earlier. But at Kmart, this was a standard-issue background. Of all the previous chairmen, only Dewar had graduated from college; and of the top seven officers now below Fauber, only two had college degrees. Even more than at Wal-Mart, Kmart liked to hire people directly out of high school as clerks and then move them on up. During Kmart's frantic expansion in the '60s, it had been forced to hire college recruits, because it needed more managers than could be promoted out of the hourly workers; but the company remained a place where an ambitious hourly worker had as good or better a crack at becoming a management trainee as did somebody with a college degree applying from outside. Compared to Wal-Mart or almost any other retailer, Kmart tended not to recruit managers from other companies, preferring to promote from within. This made for good opportunities—but it tended to reinforce the highly insular character of the corporate culture.

Fauber began his tour at the top all but donning a hair shirt for his predecessor's sins. At the 1980 annual meeting, he publicly apologized to shareholders for the fact that many stores seemed dirty and run-down, and that the layout and design of Kmart stores, unchanged in years, was obsolete. He promised to fix both problems and to improve the goods and bring in more shoppers.

Among the many changes he would make, perhaps the one that carried the most symbolic value was dropping all the private-label polyester apparel for cotton and poly-cotton blends. "Our customers won't have to suffer a polyester attack in our stores anymore," a spokesman told the *Wall Street Journal*.[8] Fauber ordered buyers to bring in more brand names for everything from clothing to house paints. New store layouts followed that tied a department's square footage to its sales per square foot, with new racks that put more goods at eye level.

Wall Street greeted these moves with bouquets. Gushing articles in *Forbes* and *Business Week* predicted that Kmart would soon overtake Sears as the world's greatest retailer.*

But Fauber knew he had to get under the hood to get the company's engine—its Kmart stores—running on all cylinders. He launched a two-year study of Kmart's weaknesses and what to do about them. In 1982, as the study was wrapping up, Fauber shocked the company by closing the 25

---

* However, *Business Week* did inject a note of skepticism by observing that "the snail's pace at which the chain has computerized its record-keeping until now astounds many observers."

weakest Kmart stores. He also cut back the pace of building stores, to free money to fix the ones already out there.

Fauber also decided—finally—to completely overhaul Kmart's system for tracking sales and orders. By the end of 1982, the technology that Dewar had approved so late in his reign was finally rolled out in full, giving all of Kmart's 2,370 stores computers and hand-held scanners that could read tags on shelves. (To give one example of the effect of the scanners, department managers could now inventory and reorder goods in an hour and a half, instead of a day and a half.) But Kmart still didn't have another key piece of technology: Electronic cash registers that could scan sales tags to collect information as each sale was made and feed the data electronically back to buyers at the company's headquarters. Dewar hadn't wanted to spend the money.

Wal-Mart had these registers. Walton's willingness (once convinced) to spring for such technology had helped Wal-Mart become far more efficient than Kmart at tracking goods, reordering them, and keeping them in stock. And Fauber knew all about it because, as it happened, in a casual meeting back in 1978, he had discovered that one of his neighbors was a consultant helping Wal-Mart install that system in its stores. Now, four years later, Fauber wanted Kmart to have that same technology to stay competitive.

But he, too, was intimidated by the enormous expense of the project, and he made the mistake of trying to do it by halves. To save money, Kmart's technicians tried to graft a scanning system onto their existing equipment and software; but it wasn't up to the job, and they couldn't get it to work. At first, the project's director kept the problems quiet; but in May 1984, a rival manager forced a confrontation, and a flabbergasted Fauber discovered that the project was already eighteen months behind schedule on what had seemed a generous seven-year timetable.

Exasperated, Fauber decided to bring in a new team and start from scratch. And he took a step that, in the insular world of Kmart's corporate hierarchy, was nothing short of extraordinary: He appointed an *outsider* as a vice president and handed the project to him. He hired the Wal-Mart consultant he'd met as a neighbor a few years earlier, David Carlson.

From outside of Kmart, it's hard to appreciate how radical a move this was. Kmart's policy of promoting from within was among the strictest in the industry. In his first days at headquarters, Carlson was told more than once that he was the first outsider to be made a vice president since the turn of the century.

Carlson faced a herculean task. When he arrived in July 1985, three years into the project to modernize Kmart's ordering system, only 23 Kmart stores had scanning registers in place. And, absurdly, because of infighting between rival managers, those stores were split between two incompatible scanning systems. Worse, the whole point of the system—getting goods ordered faster—was being undercut by Kmart's Byzantine bookkeeping methods. The company's own buyers avoided using Kmart's distribution system whenever they could, because under the bookkeeping rules, buyers got less credit (and fewer bonuses) for goods Kmart distributed itself, even if their cost was exactly the same.

Carlson's first move, with Fauber's backing, was to junk both of the existing scanning systems and start over. Kmart now shifted into overdrive to catch up. In 1987 the company would buy one-fourth of IBM's total production of scanning registers for the year; and it would commit to buy a huge supercomputer to crunch numbers in Troy. Nevertheless, it would take until 1990 to hook up the more than 2,400 Kmart stores around the country.

But even as an army of technicians hooked store after store into this fabulous, expensive new system, there was another, far more formidable obstacle: Kmart's managers. They had no interest in using the data these high-powered new computers could provide. By 1987, 200 stores were online, enough to provide a solid database. But many of the executives complained that crunching the numbers was too complicated. They didn't want computers in their offices. They echoed Dewar's old line that people made better merchants than machines did; they were unwilling to see that the computers and programs were just tools. One executive, chatting with Carlson one day in 1990, as the system was finally being completed, dismissed all the new technology as irrelevant, bragging that he'd never even used an automatic teller machine, let alone a computer.

It was the cult of the store manager asserting itself. Unlike at Wal-Mart, where Walton had scoured the country for techno-whizzes and experts in distribution, logistics, communication, and any other discipline he felt he knew nothing about, at Kmart almost everything was run by former store managers. It was ingrained in the company culture, part of the holy writ, that a good store manager could do anything. And so distribution, personnel, training, communications, and so on were all handled by former good store managers who inevitably had no training in distribution, personnel, training, communications, and so on. There was a common mindset, and it was dismissive of anyone who hadn't come up the merchandising side. That made Carlson suspect, of course. And when Tom Nigolian, a rare senior vice president who hadn't come up through the stores, argued for using all this new data more aggressively to figure out a better selection of merchandise, he was largely ignored. After all, what did he know? He'd never managed a store.

Some of the new computer men tried to convince the executives to let them do what they called trending—using the sales data to project ahead, and estimate demand and future orders. But that seemed too esoteric. This was something a store manager ought to be able to do intuitively. They weren't interested. They were like a man, thought a frustrated Carlson, who bought a new Porsche and then drove it looking only into the rearview mirror.

8

The Edge

It's too bad, really, that talk about the high-tech aspects of retailing made eyes glaze over in Kmart's executive suites, because what the predigital age executives were trying so hard to ignore would be one of the most vital developments of the '80s and '90s. Like harness makers shaking their heads at the first horseless carriage, dismissing it as newfangled nonsense, they didn't realize that their own way was already obsolescent. It wasn't just that a vast gulf had developed between how Wal-Mart and Kmart approached the business. Something more fundamental was happening: As surely as it was once transformed by the railroad and the telegraph, retailing was now being remade again by the use of computers to collect and sift through mountains of data and the use of telephone lines and then satellites to transmit that data and to link stores, buyers, warehouses, and manufacturers in one vast web.

It is an ongoing transformation. By the late '90s, retailers could track people's particular shopping patterns, building vast mosaics to tell them not only which brand and flavor of toothpaste young white housewives, middle-aged single black women, or elderly Chinese-American widowers prefer, but what those preferences implied about the deodorant they'd choose, too. Some retailers even tracked which parts of the stores shoppers visited *without* buying something. Using what they called "just-in-time" distribution, retailers were replacing traditional warehouses with laser-guided, automated systems in which goods arriving on a truck from a factory were split up and repacked on the fly to roll right into other trucks that zipped them off to stores, with (ideally) barely a pause in between.

Men such as Jack Shewmaker and David Glass, who were quick to grasp the implications of these technologies, put Wal-Mart at the forefront of this revolution; and it would be hard to overstate how crucial Wal-Mart's head start would be to its success. By 1982, when Kmart was still struggling with tracking when a tube of toothpaste was sold and for how much—when clerks in some Kmart stores were still writing orders by hand—Wal-Mart's in-store computers were doing things Kmart executives weren't even dreaming of.

In part, that was because Shewmaker set Wal-Mart down a digital path less traveled. Many retailers were starting to use scanning systems to track sales data in the early '80s, and the vast majority used a code that had been developed for the department store industry and that was backed by the Department of Commerce's Bureau of Standards. This system, known as OCR,° had the feel of something designed by committee: It wasn't that hard to install; but, early on, it forced clerks to type in a numbered code for each item. This led to longer checkout lines, grumpy customers, and, in-evitably, lots of mistakes by harried clerks.

Grocery stores, on the other hand, had begun using a different system that was more expensive, but also more sophisticated, known as the uni-form product code.† It's more familiarly known as the now-ubiquitous bar code. On this system, clerks simply swiped the label across a scanner, which automatically read a set of lines printed on the package or sales tag. Those lines, like the OCR code, told the computer what the product was and how much it cost.

UPC scanning was faster and much less prone to mistakes by clerks. It was also, though, considered impossible for department stores or general retailers to use. While a typical grocery store carried between 12,000 and 15,000 items (including different sizes and versions of products), a general retailer such as Wal-Mart, Kmart, or Sears typically carried 50,000 to 60,000 or more items. No UPC system back then had anywhere near the capacity to handle that variety.

But, unlike the fancier goods at department stores, nearly a third of the merchandise Wal-Mart and other discounters carried—toiletries, paper products, cleaners, etc.—also was carried by grocery stores, which meant manufacturers were going to slap on a bar code anyway. Shewmaker rightly

---

° *OCR* stood for "optical character recognition."
† UPC codes, now seen on almost all products, required higher-quality (and more expensive) printing, to work properly.

assumed that improvements would take care of the capacity problem. Then, too, 80 percent of Wal-Mart's goods went through its distribution centers (compared to less than 30 percent at Kmart). Because workers at the centers already were putting tickets on clothing, towels, sheets, and other soft goods, Shewmaker knew it would be simple to have them attach bar codes to those items, too.

By 1983, after testing the system for a couple of years to get the bugs out, Wal-Mart had UPC scanners in 25 stores and was adding stores as fast as possible. When, as we now know, UPC became the industry standard, retailers who'd invested in OCR had to play catch-up, and spend millions of dollars to switch over.

But bar codes were just one part of the picture. The scanners were tied into an ordering system linked to Bentonville and the distribution centers, and in turn to manufacturers. Wal-Mart had begun linking its computers directly to those of its biggest suppliers years earlier. It even shared with them its own sales projections, so the makers of the goods could better anticipate orders and time their deliveries. Wal-Mart used bar codes to route and track goods through its distribution centers. Another part of the system, also being rolled out then, let the centers transmit messages to the stores detailing what goods were arriving on what trucks and when.

Piece by piece, Wal-Mart was building a system that would give its executives a complete picture, at any point in time, of where goods were and how fast they were moving, all the way from the factory to the checkout counter. Instead of poring over last month's or last week's reports from each store or region, executives in Bentonville could call up the data on the computer from one day to the next; they could easily follow from day to day how quickly (or slowly) any item—a style of dress, say, or a fishing pole—was selling in one region compared with another. This made it easier to tailor the assortment of goods according to local tastes and to experiment. They could display an item several different ways in different stores, and then quickly order all the stores to adopt the way that worked best. All of this also meant Wal-Mart could keep less inventory on hand (tying up less cash), because it could reorder goods more quickly and be more certain of when they would arrive.

Having more—and more of the right stuff—in stock boosted sales and cut costs. By 1983, in no small part because of its computers and the way it was using them, Wal-Mart was opening a huge cost advantage. For every dollar of goods sold, that year, Kmart spent 5 cents on distribution (about average, in retailing); Wal-Mart spent less than 2 cents per dollar, the lowest figure in the industry. What this meant, of course, was that other costs aside, Wal-Mart could sell its goods for 3 percent less than Kmart and still enjoy the same profit margin.

Wal-Mart was also using its computers to track cash flow, bank transactions, work hours, and labor costs as a percentage of sales. Executives were analyzing how to schedule workers to avoid idle time—the beginnings of a move toward more temporary and part-time labor.

And then there was the satellite system.

Glenn Habern, a vice president in charge of the computers, had become increasingly frustrated as Walton's demands for more and faster data bumped up against the limitations of the phone lines over which ever more stores transmitted their data. If only they didn't have to use phone lines. Wouldn't it be wonderful to have their own satellite system, with dishes at every store? The possibilities would be almost endless: voice communications, just like with phones; but also huge amounts of data, going both ways—and even video broadcasts from headquarters. But maybe it was a pipe dream. The technology wasn't there yet, not really. The only retailers even *looking* into satellite communications were far larger and richer than Wal-Mart, big national powerhouses such as J.C. Penney. A million different things could go wrong with something so untested. And it would be so expensive one could almost picture Walton's hair standing on end at the notion.

So Habern did the only sensible thing. He floated the idea with the one man at Wal-Mart who might be even more rabid about technology than he was: Jack Shewmaker. Shewmaker, naturally, thought it was a great idea, and decided the two of them should look into it without saying anything to Walton or anybody else. Shewmaker was soon just as entranced as Habern, convinced it could be made to work. He knew it would be a tough sell with Walton. Such a system might cost more than $20 million. That was equal to roughly a fourth of Wal-Mart's whole 1982 capital budget (what it spent to build and expand stores and warehouses). Put another way, it was nearly three times what the company had just paid for the whole Kuhn acquisition.

But Shewmaker seized on one selling point he knew would hit home with Walton. Given nearly 600 stores to visit, and more opening every week, Walton couldn't get out to each store as often as he'd like. With a satellite system though, said Shewmaker, he could sit in front of a camera in headquarters, give one of his patented pep talks, and have it beamed live over television screens to workers in every Wal-Mart store and warehouse in the country.

Sure enough, Walton was highly intrigued by that prospect. Still, as one might expect, he was as cold-eyed as ever, questioning sharply whether the system would pay for itself. It was a hell of a lot of money. But Shewmaker's argument was convincing. The bigger and more spread out the company became, the slower, more complicated, and more expensive it would become to stick with what they already had.

In the long run, it would prove to be a fabulous investment—cheaper than a telephone network would have been to build and maintain; faster, too; and more useful in a thousand ways, big and small. By 1988, Wal-Mart would have the largest privately owned satellite communications network in the country, a system with six channels that not only let Walton give his pep talks, but on which a buyer could tell department heads in every store at once about new products and demonstrate how to display them. From Bentonville, they transmitted training videos on everything under the sun. By 1989, Wal-Mart was even putting transmitters on its trucks, so drivers could beam their exact location to headquarters every 15 minutes. That way, if a truck was running late, crews at the Wal-Mart store wouldn't waste time waiting around on the loading dock. Such efficiencies helped Wal-Mart average $103,000 in sales per employee by 1988, compared with $82,000 at Kmart.

One of the biggest boons, though, was what it did for credit card sales. Wal-Mart, like most discounters, had started out strictly as a cash-and-carry operation. Today, when one can use a credit card almost anywhere, even at the post office, it is easy to forget that the credit card industry only blossomed in the 1960s. By the '70s, credit cards were well on their way from being a novelty to becoming a national habit, and Wal-Mart, like most retailers, accepted them.

But it was a grudging acceptance. Early on, discounters had shied away from cards, and for several good reasons. One was that each time a customer used a card, the retailer had to pay a fee to the bank that issued it. Another had to do with calling the banks. Most cards had a "floor limit" of $25 to $100; on any sale above that, the store had to phone the bank to get approval. The problem was that, on the one hand, fraud was rampant on sales below the floor limit; on the other, before 1973 it took an average of five minutes to get authorization. Either way, it cut into profits; and for a discounter, with checkout stands at which customers might be stacked four or five deep, five minutes for one sale might as well have been an eternity.

In 1973, a national computer network for credit cards debuted and cut the average authorization time to 56 seconds. Credit card use exploded. Over the years, the authorization time steadily dropped. But now—fast forwarding again to 1988—Wal-Mart executives found that by using their satellite system for credit authorization, they could cut the then-current average time by more than half, to an astonishing seven seconds. This meant faster checkouts and so, happier customers, of course. But the time savings also let Wal-Mart start doing authorization for *all* charges, not just those above the floor limit. Credit card fraud plunged—saving enough to more than pay for the system.

By 1992, when Shewmaker's satellite system was even more sophisticated (and Wal-Mart controlled even store thermostats from headquarters), Walton would sing its praises in his autobiography, and dwell on its use in loving detail: "I can walk in the satellite room, where our technicians sit in front of their computer screens talking on the phone to any stores that might be having a problem with the system, and just looking over their shoulder for a minute or two will tell me a lot about how a particular day is going. Up on the screen I can see the total of the day's bank credit card sales adding up as they occur. I can see how many stolen bank cards we've retrieved that day. I can tell if our seven-second credit card approval system is working as it should be and monitor the number of transactions we've conducted that day. If we have something really important or urgent to communicate to the stores and distribution centers—something important enough to warrant a personal visit—I, or any other Wal-Mart executive, can walk back to our TV studio and get on that satellite transmission and get it right out there."[1]

But in 1983, when work began on the system, all of these benefits were far in the future. It seemed then as though the project might turn into a fiasco. The cost kept creeping higher, eventually reaching $24 million. When it did work—which wasn't often, at first—Walton hated the time lag that satellite transmission creates in phone conversations. "Sam liked to [have] killed me the first two years," Shewmaker later said.[2]

This was a bad time for Shewmaker shares to be dropping on the Sam Walton exchange. Only the previous fall, Walton had discovered he had leukemia and had spent months wrestling with the question of whether to gamble on the experimental interferon treatment being proposed by his doctor, Jorge Quesada. While Walton downplayed his illness, it's probably no coincidence that this was when he began thinking about whether to have Shewmaker or Glass succeed him.

Walton had thrown the men at each other, often sending both of them together to meet with analysts in New York or to speak at retailing functions. At the same time, mindful of the cliques that had developed under

Mayer and Arend, he watched their rivalry carefully—because while the divisions weren't quite as stark this time, each man had his camp within the company, and they clashed regularly as each made forays onto the other's turf.

In some ways—beyond the fact that as president he outranked Glass—Shewmaker seemed to have the edge. He often hunted and played tennis with Walton; Glass did neither. In fact, Glass barely socialized with Walton at all. His wife Ruth refused to play the usual role of the corporate wife. Back when they were living in Springfield, Ruth, lonely and miserable, had been watching the televangelists Jim and Tammy Faye Bakker on TV one day when she was suddenly overwhelmed by what she recognized as the call of the Lord. She had been saved. Encouraged by her Christian friends, she had begun speaking to Christian women's clubs, traveling to testify for the Lord, and eventually appearing on the Bakker's *PTL Club* (for "Praise The Lord") show, *The 700 Club*, and similar programs. She didn't have the time or inclination to entertain corporate guests or go to company events; and David Glass, on his own, seemed to become even more subdued in public.

While Glass was well respected, he was seen as a numbers or systems man; and his work focused on the less visible underpinnings of the company, such as improving distribution. Shewmaker, meanwhile, was widely regarded, by other retailers, Wall Street analysts, and many people at Wal-Mart, to be a brilliant merchant, the best the company had seen outside of Sam Walton himself.

Many credit Shewmaker, for example, with institutionalizing "everyday-low-pricing," Wal-Mart's strategy of avoiding sales promotions and constant markdowns by offering prices that were supposed to be the same (and, of course, low) all the time.* Avoiding promotions saved on advertising. It cut labor costs (since workers didn't have to change displays and prices back and forth all the time); and it prevented cherry-picking, as retailers call shoppers' scooping up of the specials on sale and then leaving without buying anything else. By holding constant sales and promotions, many stores in effect train shoppers to wait until there's a sale to buy anything. Everyday-low-pricing was supposed to do the opposite, and at Wal-Mart, it worked.

But if such innovations led many to consider Shewmaker a sort of retailing genius, Shewmaker thought so too; and while he didn't put on airs, he was so sure of himself, so supremely confident of his own abilities and in

* While the first Wal-Mart store had promised everyday-low-pricing back in 1962, Wal-Mart still had frequently resorted to promotions and markdowns over the years.

his decisions, that he was often aggressive and brusque with those under him. His outgoing manner and frequent store visits made him popular with store managers; but with his direct underlings he was impatient and hot-tempered. He had trouble delegating authority, seeming to doubt anyone else could do whatever the job might be as well as he could.

Glass, on the other hand, though he was stiff in public and generally more reserved, was very nearly as aggressive and adept at solving problems as his rival. He'd proven himself to Walton with his work in automating and expanding Wal-Mart's distribution system, for example. But Glass was far more diplomatic in his dealings, both with other executives and with those under him. And, like Walton, Glass was more willing to delegate jobs to others and to give them room to operate.

"Jack was a damn good man, and tough as hell; but with David, well, David isn't going to raise his voice and bloody you in front of your peers, and Jack had no compunction about doing that," remembers one confidante of both men. Another executive said, "We'd lost several good men over the years because of the way Jack treated them."

The cocksure Shewmaker didn't help himself by locking horns on a variety of issues with Rob Walton, who was Wal-Mart's general counsel and who, as future custodian of the Walton family's 39 percent stake in the company, would one day succeed Sam as chairman of the board. One of Shewmaker's great strengths—his willingness to push hard, to go nose-to-nose when he knew he was right, which was often—turned out also to be his great weakness: He didn't seem to know when to ease up—even, at times, with Sam Walton. "That was one place Jack went wrong," says James Jones, the banker and board member. "Glass knew when to give and when not to."

Take the flap over Charles Lazarus, the chairman and chief executive of Toys "R" Us. In early 1984, Walton decided to appoint Lazarus to Wal-Mart's board. Toys "R" Us was the prime example of the latest mutation to evolve in the retail jungle: "category killers," retailers who applied the discount-supermarket strategy to a single category of goods, in this case toys. Lazarus founded Toys "R" Us in 1957, sold it nine years later, and then took over again after it emerged from bankruptcy in 1978. In the six years since, by building huge airplane-hangar–sized stores filled with name-brand toys sold for the lowest prices around, Lazarus had turned the company into a powerhouse that was now growing even faster than Wal-Mart, and that had seized more than 10 percent of the U.S. toy market.

Walton was fascinated by Toys "R" Us and wanted the fifty-nine-year-old Lazarus on board so he could dissect him at leisure. Shewmaker, though, was horrified at the idea of opening Wal-Mart's innermost secrets and strategies to the head of what was, after all, a rival retailer. Lazarus would face a terrible conflict of interest. He was bound to be more loyal to his own company than to Wal-Mart, Shewmaker argued long and heatedly—maybe too heatedly, given that with the problems and the costs of his satellite system still soaring, he wasn't at a high point in Walton's regard.

One day that summer, not long after Walton had gone ahead and appointed Lazarus to the board, over Shewmaker's objections, the Wal-Mart founder called both Shewmaker and Glass into his office. He told the pair he'd like them to switch jobs. Glass would now be president, Walton said, and Shewmaker would be chief financial officer. To soften the blow a little, he told Shewmaker he would also appoint him vice chairman of the board.

"It was the biggest surprise Jack had in his life," recalls one executive who bumped into the stunned Shewmaker just after the meeting. Shewmaker hadn't gone down quietly—but Walton made it clear his mind was made up, and so, after some fervent discussion, Shewmaker had acquiesced. What else could he do? He was too loyal just to quit.

For official consumption, Walton claimed that he was making the switch as a training exercise, a form of "cross-pollination," just another example of his making his executives familiar with every part of the company. As a token of their equal status, the two men would receive the same salary.° Both Glass and Shewmaker knew better, of course. Walton might as well have tapped Glass on each shoulder with a sword.

In fact, Walton had been thinking about anointing Glass since late the previous year. He'd discussed it with Rob Walton, who was all for it; then the two of them polled a couple of other board members about the idea of making the switch. "It was the second time Sam had brought it up to me," said Jones, who considered Shewmaker nothing short of brilliant. "I said, 'What's your problem with him?' and he said, 'He's so abrasive . . . we can't control him.' He and Rob just couldn't put up with his strong personality.

"I said I'd fight them all the way and call every board member myself," remembers Jones, who didn't think much of Glass as a merchant. Walton had let the matter drop, for a time. But after a few more go-rounds, Walton called Jones again, saying he was going to go ahead and make the switch. Jones railed against the idea, and as soon as he got off the phone with Walton he called the other board members. Most of them said they liked Shewmaker better, too, but added that they would support the switch. How could they go against Sam?

° The year after the swap, each man was paid $465,000, plus stock options.

Shewmaker kept his crushing disappointment to himself, but at head-quarters, the sudden change of fortune created great tension between the two camps—especially as many Shewmaker men now had to report to Glass, and vice versa. As at any corporation, everyone in middle management felt the seismic shift, but no one knew what the aftershocks might bring. Would Shewmaker leave? Who would go with him? Did he still have a chance? What did this mean for his loyalists? Out in the stores, managers found the switch confusing, but many of them felt fonder of Shewmaker than of the more reticent Glass. Shortly after the change, both men spoke at a gathering of store managers held in Little Rock, to plan for the Christmas season. Glass received polite applause; Shewmaker, a thunderous standing ovation.*

As if to bolster Glass's image, the following year Walton launched a program that asked any employees who had gripes or suggestions to call or write directly to Glass. He got 18,000 letters, and "every single one is followed up," claimed Don Soderquist, to a financial writer.[3]

If Shewmaker himself thought he still had any chance at the crown—which seems unlikely—he must have felt it slip steadily away over the next few years. To outward appearances, he and Glass were absolute equals—given the same amount of time to speak at managers' gatherings and annual meetings, sent together to meet with Wall Street analysts, and so on. Shewmaker still hunted occasionally with Walton. And he worked as hard as ever. "Jack's motto is TGIM—Thank God It's Monday," cracked one employee at the time. "If Jack had his way, Friday would go into Monday and he would eliminate everything in between."[4]

Shewmaker also turned down every approach from rival retailers who tried to lure him away. When Jones asked him why he didn't take up one of these offers, Shewmaker said, "I may be crazy, but I just can't find it within me to go to another company and try to tear down and beat the company I spent my life trying to build."

But it became increasingly clear that Walton was not going to change his mind. Glass, too, seemed to be working harder than ever, putting in endless 16-hour days as if to make sure he was leaving Walton no chance for second thoughts.† And then, one evening in February of 1985, after a long day of meetings, Glass was at home helping his daughter Dayna with

---

* In a pointed message reflecting how many outside of the company saw the switch, *Mass Merchant Retailer,* an industry magazine, named Shewmaker retailer of the year the following year.

† The workload on executives was brutal. When Ron Loveless retired as a senior vice president in 1986, burned out by job stress at the age of forty-two, he told the *Arkansas Gazette,* "If you don't produce, you'll be gone."

her homework when he suddenly felt a squeezing pain in his chest. He could hardly breathe. He staggered back to his bed. Within minutes, Ruth Glass insisted on driving him to the hospital.

A good thing she did: He was having a heart attack. She phoned Walton, who rushed down. After talking with the doctors there, he offered to have Glass airlifted to a hospital in Tulsa that was better equipped to handle the situation.

The Tulsa doctors said Glass would have to have a multiple-bypass operation. But Glass absolutely refused. Walton, who'd come along with him, now began calling around to find the best heart specialists he could. As soon as Glass was stable enough, he had him flown down to Houston, to the same medical center where Walton had gone for his interferon treatment. The cardiologists there agreed with Glass. He didn't need surgery, they said, if he would agree to proper rest and medication, and then to improving his diet and getting regular exercise. Glass bought himself a treadmill (which he hated, but used religiously); within weeks, he was back at work, putting in as heavy a schedule as ever.

Finally, in February 1988, two months before his seventieth birthday, Walton announced that he was turning his post as chief executive officer over to Glass. That same day Wal-Mart blandly announced that Shewmaker would be retiring to pursue "personal business interests," such as breeding Angus and Hereford cattle on the ranch he'd bought near Bentonville in 1983.

Shewmaker had expected it, of course. But he still fell into a funk. His temper around the office grew blacker. When he suddenly backed out of a long-arranged speech he'd promised to deliver at a Procter & Gamble gathering in Cincinnati, a panicky P&G executive had to beg Walton to intercede. "Don't worry," Walton chuckled, "he'll be there."

For all that he was unwilling to hand Wal-Mart's helm over to Shewmaker, Walton wasn't blind to his talents. To Glass's chagrin, he asked Shewmaker to stay on the board and gave him a contract for $100,000 a year for five years to act as a consultant. And Walton took pains to give him a proper send-off, inviting more than two hundred guests to a farewell dinner for Shewmaker in Springfield, Missouri. Wall Street analysts and executives from Wal-Mart's biggest suppliers flocked in. At the dinner, joking about competing with Shewmaker at quail hunting, Walton presented him with a 20-gauge shotgun—with its barrel bent into an "L" shape. Shewmaker pretended to aim down the barrel. "Well, Sam," he said, only half in jest, "you're never going to let anybody get an edge on you in anything, are you?"

And so at forty-nine, after eighteen years, Shewmaker retired from day-to-day involvement with the company, taking with him more than $23 million in Wal-Mart stock.

As for Glass, he would find out all too soon just how great the difference is between being the heir apparent and assuming the throne.

9

Something Borrowed,
Something New

Sam Walton liked to think of himself as having his ear to the ground. And what with his endless visits to stores (both his own and his competitors'), his habit of scanning all the trade journals and financial papers, and the deceptively simple way he had of drawing rival retailers into overly revealing discussions, he had good reason to feel that way.

Even so, it was almost seven years before he caught on to the potential of a brand-new form of discounting that sprang up in San Diego in 1976. Of course, few others caught on any sooner—in large part because this new type of retailing was, well, so *new*. To many people it didn't seem like an obvious winner.

This radical new idea was the warehouse club: a giant boxlike store so stripped down it made a Wal-Mart look downright luxurious. The clubs looked like warehouses, with concrete floors and pallet-loads of goods stacked on steel shelves 18 feet high. There was mustard by the quart and beans by the gallon, other foods shrink-wrapped by the case, car tires, appliances, office supplies, stuffed animals—even knockoff Louis XIV dining-room chairs with needlepoint seats. Unlike discount stores, warehouse clubs carried some very upscale goods, too—as long as they sold quickly. The array of goods was broad but shallow: one or two models of toasters, say, instead of the eight or ten different models a discount store might offer. Where a typical discount store might offer a selection of 50,000 or 60,000 items, a warehouse club carried only between 2,500 and 3,000.

But the really odd part, the part that made other retailers rub their chins, was this: You had to pay to shop there—you had to buy a membership for $25 a year. This seemed incredible, at first glance. Why would anyone *pay* for the privilege of shopping?

The answer, of course, was that people paid to join because it paid off. The prices for the goods were miles below those of any other retailer—prices that were essentially wholesale prices. A big chunk of the clubs' customers consisted of people who owned small businesses and who could buy office supplies or goods to resell more easily and cheaply there than they could by going through traditional wholesalers.

Unlike true wholesalers, though, the clubs also did a booming business with ordinary shoppers, people anxious to snap up bargains for their own personal use. The whole idea of the clubs sprang from the same idea that had created mail-order businesses, chain stores, supermarkets, and discount stores: cut prices as low as you can and make your profit by going for high turnover. Remember how each of these previous retailing concepts eventually left room for an even lower-priced successor to crawl in at the bottom? Well, since the rock-bottom days of the '50s and '60s, discount stores—Wal-Mart included—gradually had let their costs, prices, and gross margins ratchet upward a few notches, as they put in nicer fixtures and furnishings and spent more on advertising. Through the crack that opened at the bottom came the warehouse clubs, which now took the low-price/high-volume concept even farther than discounters had. Wal-Mart and other discounters typically might sell a few popular items at their cost, as loss leaders to bring in shoppers; but then they would enjoy a gross margin of, say, 25 to 35 percent on most of the other goods. Warehouse clubs kept their margins on all goods to an incredibly low 8 to 10 percent.

The only ways to make such a razor-thin margin pay off were, first, to keep costs down remorselessly—absolutely no frills, no advertising, no fancy displays—and second, to generate a massive volume of sales. That was why the selection was so limited—if you ran a warehouse club, you couldn't afford space on your shelves for anything that didn't move fast.

And "fast" may not be strong enough a word. Once the man who invented the concept, Sol Price, got it working right, his warehouses sold goods at such breakneck speed that they completely turned over their inventory every two weeks, four times faster than that most efficient of discounters, Wal-Mart. All retailers had to keep a certain amount of cash tied up in inventory—the actual goods sitting on shelves or in warehouses. But Price moved stuff so quickly he had a *negative* inventory; that is, he sold most of the merchandise *before* he had to pay for it. This meant, in effect, that his suppliers were financing his inventory for him. By the early '80s, the average Price Club, as they were called, was blowing more than $2 million of merchandise out its doors each week.

As word began to filter out of California about the stupefying amount of business Price was doing, Walton recognized that this might pose not only a threat to discounting, but also a huge opportunity, and that it was an opportunity others would be bound to spot soon, too. He decided to check things out for himself.

He knew a lot about Sol Price. Price was another discounting pioneer; he'd founded the highly successful Fed-Mart discount chain back in 1954, in Southern California. Back then, the thirty-nine-year-old Price was a lawyer. Though his father had been a women's wear maker, Price himself had no real retailing experience. Still, like Walton, he'd spotted the opportunity in discounting; he'd raised $50,000, found a couple of partners, and opened a discount store.

Originally, Fed-Mart had sold only to government workers (hence the name); unlike other discounters, though, Price had charged a $2 membership fee, meant to offer a feeling of exclusivity. He also figured paying members would be less likely to shoplift or bounce checks. Aside from that twist, Price had chiseled at the same retailing walls as other early discounters: He'd fought with existing retailers who charged that he was ignoring the so-called fair trade laws, a tattered set of rules from Depression days that were supposed to protect competition by setting minimum prices for goods. Newspapers, afraid of losing other retailers' business, had refused to run Fed-Mart's ads. The Better Business Bureau had rejected his application for membership.

But, just as everywhere else in the country, those trying to block discounting might as well have been trying to stop the tide from rolling in. Fed-Mart did so well that Walton had studied it particularly closely in 1960 and 1961, when he was getting ready to launch Wal-Mart. Later, Walton would say, "I guess I've stolen—I actually prefer the word 'borrowed'—as many ideas from Sol Price as from anyone else in the business.

"For example, it's true that Bob Bogle came up with the name Wal-Mart in the airplane that day, but the reason I went for it right away wasn't that the sign was cheaper," he said. "I really liked Sol's Fed-Mart name so I latched right on to Wal-Mart."[1]

By 1975, Fed-Mart was a 45-store chain with $300 million a year in sales.* That year, Price sold control of the company to a German retailing mogul, Hugo Mann. Price—whom his own son Larry described as a control

---

* Wal-Mart, by comparison, had $236 million in sales that year from 104 stores.

freak—was supposed to stay on to run the chain, but he had a hard time not being the top man. At the first board meeting after the sale, he got into a huge row with Mann, over various changes the new owner wanted to make. So bitterly did they quarrel that at the next meeting, Mann fired him and locked Price out of his office. Price had to sue Mann in court to collect his salary and to get access to his own files. But Mann and his subsequent managers couldn't make Fed-Mart go. Over the next seven years, without Price and his two sons Larry and Robert (who quit as Fed-Mart officers as soon as their father was canned), the chain gradually slid into the red and finally was liquidated.

Sol Price, meanwhile, quickly came up with a new idea. Chatting with people around San Diego who owned restaurants, convenience stores, newsstands, and other small businesses, he realized that many of them had to turn to five or more different wholesalers to buy their supplies and merchandise, often on unfavorable terms. If he could offer them what they needed in one place, at a reasonable price, he could carve out a new business.

With $800,000 of his own money and funds from new investors and old Fed-Mart executives, Price opened his first Price Club in 1976, at the edge of town, where land was cheaper. To become a member, you not only had to pay a fee, but actually to prove that you had a business. You could be a one-person business or a professional—a doctor or lawyer buying office supplies—but you had to show some sort of permit or license.

The Price Club hit $16 million in sales its first year—and lost $750,000. At Price's skeletal margins, he needed even higher volume. "We couldn't figure out what had gone wrong," Price told a *New York Times* reporter. "Was it the membership fee? Did we have the wrong type of merchandise?"[2]

Price might have asked, too, whether enough small business owners understood what he was offering. He had to get more customers. Then one of Price's shoppers made a suggestion harking back to the early Fed-Mart days: Why not broaden the base a bit and let government workers join too? Why not, indeed? After mulling over the idea, Price decided to let a slew of groups join: federal employees, hospital and utility workers, members of certain unions, members of credit unions—in short, any group of people whom he had pegged as unlikely to bounce checks. Of course, they had to pay to join, too, making them still less likely to bounce checks or pull funny business.

Here was the extra lift the company had needed. The concept of a membership warehouse was still unfamiliar to practically everybody, so there was a lot of educating to do, but gradually, sales and profits started picking up and then soaring as people caught on to the idea of buying stuff at wholesale prices. So what if the only size of Peter Pan peanut butter was a 40-ounce jar? It cost less than half of what you'd pay for three 12-ounce jars in your local grocery store. People were so attuned to getting bargains that once they came into a club they just couldn't help but pick up all sorts of things.* "My father-in-law is dangerous in there," one member complained to a *New York Times* reporter. "He buys things he'll never use up, like 12 rolls of film, a case of motor oil, 10 rolls of masking tape. My mother-in-law tries to keep him out of Price Club, as a matter of policy."[3]

Soon, members were spending, on average, more than $100 a visit.

When Sam Walton flew out to San Diego to sniff around in late 1982, he took Rob Walton with him. Is it any surprise that Walton senior managed to wangle them both into a Price Club, despite their not being members? Surely not. After scoping out the operation from tip to floor, the deeply impressed Waltons called on Sol Price.

The two men had much in common, as discounting entrepreneurs of the same generation. Walton doubtless approved of Price's pinchpenny office in a modest one-story headquarters far from downtown San Diego. Just as at Wal-Mart, no executive had an assigned parking space. Inside, one could look in vain for Persian carpets, oak paneling, or fancy furnishings. Bookcases were made of concrete blocks and plain wood boards; and Price's box of an office, linoleum floored, was as small as Walton's, barely big enough for his desk, a few filing cabinets, and a chair for each of his two visitors.

Both Price, now sixty-five, and Walton, two years younger, were fighting their own physical decay: The previous year, Walton had been diagnosed with hairy cell leukemia, and Price with Bell's palsy, which had paralyzed the left side of his face.

But for all that, Sam Walton and Sol Price came from right angles to one another in their approaches to life and work. Price liked to claim he read the *Daily Worker* instead of the *Wall Street Journal*. Early on, when Price

---

* Joseph Ellis, an astute retail analyst at Goldman Sachs and among the earliest to cover warehouse clubs, noted some of the bargains he found on visits to various clubs, once Price had competition: Hartmann leather attaché cases at $230, versus $300 at most retailers; 200-square-foot boxes of aluminum foil at two for $5.79, versus $4.99 a box at a local discount store; a gold Rolex Oyster wristwatch at $1,699, versus $2,800 in jewelry stores.

Clubs didn't accept credit cards, he said ironically that the reason was that "it's against my religion for people to go into debt to shop."[4] He was considerably more generous with benefits and wages than other discounters, Walton included. And, unlike Walton in those days, Price gave money to charities generously and often, through a foundation he created and to which he handed $70 million.

At the same time, Price was renowned as autocratic and ruthless, even with his own family. He clashed with his son Larry, who leased space from the company to run tire-installation centers in Price Clubs. In 1985, after a spat between them over a family matter, Sol Price abruptly canceled his son's leases, cutting him out of the business. An arbitrator awarded Larry Price $3.7 million; and then the son hired a divorce lawyer to sue his father for more.

On first meeting Sam Walton, Price pegged him as a typical Southerner, gracious, full of compliments, and a little full of beans. He seemed, Price thought, to want to give the impression that everybody in the world was smarter than him.

He recalls Walton saying, with a humble expansiveness, "Twenty-five years ago I saw your Fed-Mart in Houston, and I knew it was a big thing, but I didn't have the money to begin in a big town, so I went back to my small town and started there. Now I have 350 stores, I'm worth $700 million, and I'm on the New York Stock Exchange—and it's all thanks to you."

"Well, then," answered Price, without missing a beat, "don't you think that I'm entitled to a finder's fee?" Walton seemed thrown for a moment, apparently not realizing that Price was kidding.

Over the years the two men would develop an odd relationship that might best be described as a commercial friendship. Each, understandably, professed great respect for the other's business prowess. When Walton visited Southern California, often with Helen in tow, the couple would meet Price and his wife for dinner. But Price, a man of far-ranging interests, always found the dinners one-dimensional. "We would talk about how to keep buyers from being corrupted, things like that," he remembers. Whatever topic Price might introduce, Walton would relentlessly steer the current of conversation back into the one channel he wanted to troll. "He was pretty much all business," Price said.

Price's business, to Walton, seemed like an idea well worth stealing. As soon as he got back to Bentonville, he began brainstorming with his executives about how to move Wal-Mart into warehouse clubs. He flew out to San Diego again for a retailing convention, and he and Helen Walton met

the Prices for dinner and another one-track conversation. When he got
back, Walton decided to open his first warehouse club in Oklahoma City, in
the 100,000-square-foot shell of a shuttered Woolco discount store.

Out of politeness, or perhaps pricked by his conscience, Walton phoned
Price shortly before he opened his first club, to tell him. Price, who'd seen
where things were headed even before their last dinner, told Walton he
wasn't at all surprised.

Walton called it Sam's Wholesale Club.° It opened in April 1983.

But Walton wasn't alone in horning in on Price's one-time monopoly.
Just as in 1962, when discounters seemed to pop up all over the country at
once, like mushrooms after a spring rain, 1983 yielded a bumper crop of
warehouse chains. In February, in Indianapolis, The Wholesale Club chain
opened its first store, guided by John Geisse, one of the founders of the
Target discount chain back in 1962. At nearly the same time, Walter Tenninga, who'd lost his bid to run Kmart, resurfaced in Chicago as the
founder of the new Warehouse Club chain. In July, the Pace Membership
Warehouse chain opened its doors in a Denver suburb; in September, a former Price Club executive and a partner launched the Costco chain in Seattle. More warehouse club chains followed in 1984, including Super Saver,
Price-Savers, and BJ's Wholesale Club.

Conspicuously absent from this list: Kmart. Bernie Fauber, its chairman, toyed with the idea of warehouse clubs, too, but only briefly; by 1984,
he opted instead to launch into a frenzy of acquisitions, adding home-
improvement, drugstore, and bookstore chains to the company fold.†
Fauber's decision left Walton in the same catbird seat Harry Cunningham
had enjoyed back in 1962 when he founded Kmart: In a brand-new industry, he had the deep pockets. All the new warehouse club chains aped
Price's formula to one degree or another; but none could afford to pour in
money the way Wal-Mart could.

By the end of the year, Wal-Mart had three Sam's Clubs in business.
Within three years, it would open 40 more warehouse clubs, whipping past
Price in store count. Sol Price seemed to be in no rush to stake out turf. He
seemed to be as interested in the real estate end as in the stores themselves, always buying the property and working to attract other big-box ten-
ants to create shopping centers. Walton leased the buildings for the Sam's

---

° In 1990, the word "wholesale" would be dropped from the name, because of a lawsuit filed in North
Carolina by the Better Business Bureau, which argued successfully that most of the goods weren't ac-
tually being sold for resale.
† These were, respectively, Home Centers of America, which Kmart redubbed Builders Square Inc.;
Pay Less Drugstores Northwest Inc.; and Walden Book Co.

Clubs, saving several million dollars per store in up-front costs and leaving more capital for expansion.

Walton took direct charge of the work of starting the new chain, which he seemed to enjoy inordinately. "It was almost what you'd call a second childhood for me," he'd say later.[5]

At first, Wal-Mart copied Price slavishly. Price, after all, obviously was doing it right, and to get the necessary volume, these clubs had to be located in bigger, more urban communities than Wal-Mart typically targeted. Then, too, the merchandise was so different, much of it more upscale than anything Wal-Mart's buyers were used to handling. So if Price Clubs stacked cases of fine wine by their entrances, then so would Sam's Clubs— at least, until the buyers learned the hard way that Oklahomans don't drink wine as eagerly as Californians do.

Early on, Walton returned time and again to scope out Price's stores, making notes to himself on a microcassette recorder about what Price sold and for how much. In one store, a manager caught Walton and forced him to hand over the cassette tape. Walton scribbled out a note with it to Robert Price, Sol's son, saying Price was certainly entitled to listen to it, but that he had other notes on there he'd sure like back after Price was through. Four days later, Price sent it back to him.

Sol Price says he never really worried about Wal-Mart. He figured Walton wouldn't get as aggressive as he could with Sam's Club, out of fear the chain might, as Price put it, kick the shit out of his own Wal-Mart stores. To his mind, Sam's Club was fighting with one hand tied behind its back. He was more worried about chains such as Costco, that were nearer his territory.

But, really, it wasn't long before everybody had to worry about everybody. There were only so many markets that could support the kind of massive turnover a warehouse club needed to be profitable. Warehouse chains raced like mad to be the first into new markets. After all, most all the chains offered pretty much the same goods—so why would anybody who'd laid out $25 for a membership in one club even consider becoming a member of another?

Back at the beginning of 1983, before the first mad rush, there had been only eight warehouse clubs in existence, all of them Price Clubs. Less than four years later, there were more than 200 clubs among the eight largest chains alone. It wasn't long before the chains began to bump elbows—leaving the smaller players battered and bruised—for example, the Super Saver chain, which was owned by Howard Brothers, a regional discount store outfit based in Monroe, Louisiana. Galloping to claim a territory, Super Saver opened 21 stores across the South by the end of 1986—but 10 of those stores were in the same cities as Sam's Clubs. After three years of fighting for customers and swallowing steady losses, the Howard Brothers sold the chain to Wal-Mart in 1987, for $36 million.

Walton veered sharply from Sol Price's strategy in one regard: Price, by expanding very deliberately and by focusing more than his rivals on the wholesale end of the business, got far higher sales out of each club—more than twice what Wal-Mart got out of each Sam's Club, for instance. Walton, meanwhile, raced to open stores as fast as possible and aimed to saturate markets to keep rivals out—even if that meant that, say, his six clubs in Houston or five clubs in Dallas wound up cannibalizing each other's sales. Better to lose sales to his own stores than to somebody else's, Walton figured.

By 1988, Price Club and Wal-Mart's Sam's Club dominated the industry. Walton had become confident enough to dive into an even more ambitious experiment, a titanic new type of store that made even the massive warehouse clubs look like dime stores: the hypermart. Where the average Wal-Mart took up about 62,000 square feet (about the size of one and a quarter football fields) and the average Sam's Club 100,000 square feet (or two football fields), Walton's first hypermart would be *220,000 square feet*, the size of nearly five football fields side by side.

The idea was that the hypermart would offer the extra-slim margins of the warehouse club in a store that combined the merchandise of a Wal-Mart with the food offerings of a giant supermarket—at heart, an updated and even bigger version of the Big Bear supermarket store of the 1930s.

Many on Wall Street, and many retailers, greeted the announcement of this Brobdingnagian monstrosity as logical, even inevitable—the apotheosis of a discount store, one commentator called it, as if to suggest that we were now arriving at the evolutionary culmination of all the trends that had dominated retailing in recent decades, that here, finally, was the ultimate big box on the edge of town.

And it was true—at least, in the same sense that the brontosaur represented the ultimate big dinosaur of the Jurassic. Like the brontosaur, the hypermart would turn out, in the end, to be too big for its own good.

Naturally, this would only seem obvious in retrospect. After all, Walton knew the idea could work. He'd seen it. Walton didn't get the idea for the hypermart from the long-ago Big Bear, but from a trip to Brazil he'd taken in the early '80s, where he'd been wowed by the crowds he'd seen at stores run by Carrefour, a French retail business. Carrefour had invented the *hypermarché* in (curiously enough) 1962. Over the years, it had expanded into Spain and then to South America. But Walton doesn't seem to have realized that the hypermart had flourished in Europe and South America mainly because U.S.-style supermarkets and discount stores had never developed in these countries, making the hypermarts the main alternative to tiny neighborhood food stores and sundries shops. Then, too, in France, arcane zoning laws had effectively protected the hypermarts from competition early on. That changed in 1973, when terrified small shopkeepers nationwide banded together and won a law requiring government approval for any new *hypermarchés*—pushing Carrefour and other French firms to look abroad for expansion. But by then, of course, they were so firmly rooted in France that they didn't need the protection they'd enjoyed for so long. In the wide-open free-for-all of American retailing, it would be a very different story.

In the United States various one-shot versions of the Big Bear store had appeared here and there over the decades. Then, in the 1960s, a Michigan businessman, Fred Meijer, began opening large discount stores (100,000 square feet) that also offered groceries and had a bakery and restaurant in each store. Another discounter, Fred Meyer, based in Portland, Oregon, took the same approach in the Northwest. By 1987, Meijer had nearly four dozen stores in the northern Midwest, and Meyer had double that number in his territory. But though they combined food and general merchandise, these stores operated more like typical discount stores than like hypermarts. The difference was that true hypermarts, because their enormous scale made them more expensive to build and operate, had to generate the same kinds of frenetic turnover that warehouse clubs relied on.

Several retailers—including Sol Price's Fed-Mart—had tried and failed with hypermart experiments back in the '70s. Then, in 1984, just as Walton, back from Brazil, began thinking about taking a crack at Carrefour's concept, another French retailer, Euromarché, slipped gingerly into the American market by teaming up with some American partners to open a hypermart in Cincinnati, a 200,000-square-foot store called Bigg's. The store had a perfect location, just off a freeway; within 10 miles were more than half a million households with an average income of $33,000. When the Bigg's struggled for its first few years, analysts said managers just needed to fine-tune the mix of products to suit middle-American tastes.

To Walton's thinking, the hypermart offered a way to crack the big urban markets that Wal-Mart had mostly skirted so far, with a store that could immediately dominate the competition. The one problem was that even with Sam's Club growing very rapidly, Wal-Mart didn't really have much experience with buying, distributing, and selling food (which, being perishable, was trickier to handle). As one might expect, Walton attacked this problem by going out, finding executives with the expertise he lacked, and spiriting them away. He swiped a top officer from Fred Meyer, another from Pace Membership Warehouse, and a whole slew from supermarket chains including Safeway, Cub Food, and HEB. At the same time, he teamed up in a joint venture with Cullum Companies, a big Dallas-based supermarket outfit, to have them supply the food for his first hypermart while a Wal-Mart food team got up and running.

Three days after Christmas in 1987, Wal-Mart and Cullum opened their first Hypermart USA in a Dallas suburb. Besides groceries and general merchandise, the store had a deli, bakery, seafood shop, and fast food section. Heavy advertising and lots of news coverage brought in a crush of people nearly too big to handle, more than 50,000 shoppers in the first week. A month later, Wal-Mart opened a second Hypermart in Topeka, Kansas—this time, opting to handle the food end without Cullum.

Maggie Gilliam, the First Boston analyst, cautioned that each huge hypermart would have to crack $85 million in sales a year *just to break even*. But Gilliam was sold on Walton and Wal-Mart's prowess. She suggested that the huge Dallas store was, if anything, too small. The great thing about this concept, she argued, was that the $50-million price tag to build a hypermart, the great expertise needed to get the right balance of food and other goods, and the huge turnover needed to succeed would keep the number of competitors to a handful and play to Wal-Mart's strengths. "We believe very strongly," she said regally, "that the hypermarket concept is going to be the next great trend in retailing."[6]

Ah, well. As is clear now, she couldn't have been more wrong. But Gilliam was far from alone in her belief. Most analysts, and many retailers, considered the march of hypermarts across the American landscape inevitable. That February, Carrefour, which had sent five scouts over to the United States a year earlier, thundered into Philadelphia with its first hypermart, a 330,000-square-foot behemoth in which clerks wore roller skates to get around.* Auchan, another French retailer, announced plans to open a hypermart in Chicago by 1989. Euromarché announced that it would open a second store soon.

And then Kmart—the only discounter still bigger than Wal-Mart—announced that it, too, would charge into the hypermart business.

---

* In an apt comparison, the *New York Times* writer Anthony Ramirez noted that "transplanted to Egypt, Carrefour and a bit of its parking lot would cover the same area as the Great Pyramid of Cheops."

10

Sometimes a Pretty Good Notion

What was going on at Kmart? For much of the '80s, under Fauber, snapping up bookstores, home-improvement chains, even cafeterias, the company had seemed interested in any form of retailing but discounting. And then, abruptly in 1988, as if throwing down the gauntlet to its upstart rival, Kmart not only said it planned several hypermarts, but that same spring, it abruptly bought a 51 percent stake in a six-store warehouse club chain on the East Coast, signaling a move into that business, too.

If there was a sense of jackets being removed and shirtsleeves being rolled up, it was for good reason. Kmart had a new chairman, president, and chief executive rolled into one feisty and forceful form, that of the forty-six-year-old Joe Antonini. He'd been tapped to take over when Fauber retired in the fall of 1987. And he was a man in a hurry.

Popular within Kmart, Antonini seemed to be a singularity at the company: someone who'd spent his entire career climbing up the Kresge/Kmart hierarchy without falling into the inflexible, ostrich-head-in-the-sand mindset that permeated Kmart's corporate culture. On the contrary, Antonini, cheerful, charming, and energetic, seemed anxious to look outside the company for help in waking Kmart up again and keeping it in front as the country's dominant discounter. He had studied Wal-Mart and Sam Walton avidly. And he was clearly determined to beat back their challenge—by sheer force of personality, if nothing else.

"He had such charisma," remembers Jeanne Golly, a former Kmart vice president Antonini lured away from a New York public relations firm. At their first meeting, Golly was amused and then beguiled by the infectious enthusiasm this dapper, round little man radiated. "I just felt like I'd be doing God's work by working alongside him, turning around this $25-billion company," she said.

Antonini's friendly ebullience provoked that kind of hyperbole. His verve seemed so refreshing at stodgy Kmart. Much of Wall Street and the business press treated his arrival as practically the second coming of Harry Cunningham. Here, they declared, was just the kind of inspiring dynamo who could rouse Kmart to its former glory. A *New York Times* reporter gushed that he "could have stepped out of one of those classic American rags-to-riches tales."[1]

"Rags" is a bit of poetic license, really. But Antonini was a perfect illustration of that generational upward mobility that lies at the heart of the American dream. His grandfather Antonio Antonini, a stonemason, had immigrated to West Virginia from Abruzzi, in central Italy, in the early 1920s, arriving, as the story has it, with little more than a strong pair of hands and a willingness to work. His skills, though, gave him an alternative to working in the virtual indentured-slavery of the local coal fields, where most immigrants wound up. He settled in Morgantown, and did well enough to send for his teenage son Theodore within a few years.

Theodore married another immigrant, from Naples, who became Catherine Antonini. Joe Antonini, born in 1941, was the first of their five children. He took strongly after his father, an outgoing, very social man who never seemed happier than when surrounded by people. For years, Theodore Antonini ran his own shoe repair shop in the basement of Morrison's Department Store, on High Street, Morgantown's main commercial artery. Eventually, he opened his own street-level storefront, also on High Street, called Morgan Shoe Repair.

As a boy, Joe Antonini worked in his father's shop and then as a clerk at Morrison's. He would claim, as Kmart chairman, that he had known from then, when he was fourteen, that his destiny lay in retailing.

Like all the Antoninis, he went to Morgantown High School. Short but athletic (he would be 5 feet 7 inches fully grown), he played basketball and baseball. And he was a dervish in school activities, playing saxophone in the school band, joining various clubs, and serving on the school council and all sorts of assemblies.

He worked his way through hometown West Virginia University by forming a rock 'n' roll dance band, The Bonnevilles. In 1964, straight out of college, the twenty-two-year-old interviewed with several retailers, including R.H. Macy & Co., in New York. But the owner of Morrison's and a family friend of the Antoninis, Max Maddox, talked Joe out of going to Macy's. That store's golden age was past, he said. The future, Maddox told him, lay with big discount stores like the Kmarts that Kresge was now opening all over the place.

But though Antonini heeded Maddox's advice, it would take him years to get to the Kmart division. The Kresge tradition called for management trainees to begin work as stock boys, and so it was with Antonini—in his case at an older Kresge store in Uniontown, Pennsylvania. In the usual way, the company moved him often early on; with one interruption for a seven-month stretch in the Army, he put in stints as an assistant manager at Kresge's stores in New York, Pennsylvania, and Connecticut.

After four years, he was promoted to the company's headquarters in downtown Detroit as an assistant sales manager. Two years later, in 1970, he got his first store to run, a Kresge in Buffalo, New York, that "was so old that it had no delivery chute, so we had to bring merchandise up in a basket and we had to sweep the floors with sawdust," Antonini said.[2]

Still, he handled it well enough that three years later, Kresge moved him to Baltimore and made him a district manager supervising 15 stores. Finally, in 1976—four years after Harry Cunningham, the father of Kmart, retired—Antonini finally was awarded his own brand-new Kmart store to run, in Maryland.

He was ready.

In those days, under Cunningham's technophobic protégé Robert Dewar, Kresge was just beginning its glacial conversion to computers from its antiquarian handwritten system for ordering goods. There wasn't anything Antonini could do to speed that up, but he figured out another shortcut, with spectacular results. Typically, a Kmart store manager would send off to headquarters one big order combining all the goods needed in all the departments—from bras to windshield wipers. And it was up to the manager to anticipate demand, using his instincts. In practice, when a manager guessed too low, shoppers hoping to snap up an advertised bargain might find empty shelves; and the shelves might stay empty for weeks, because the practice of combining orders could lead to long delays in restocking hot items.

Antonini, just by letting each department order its own goods directly, as needed, slashed in half the time needed to restock most items, to one week. On average, new Kmart stores took three years to turn a profit. But with more goods in stock, Antonini's new store turned a profit its first year. That grabbed the attention of executives in Detroit. Over the next seven years, Antonini was promoted four times, winding up as director of sales promotions in Kmart's eastern regional office, in East Brunswick, New Jersey.

There, under Fauber, he got his next big chance, again by applying common sense to handling merchandise. A little background here may be helpful: Back in 1962, when Kresge launched its Kmart division, it had followed the usual discounter's route of contracting with a slew of other companies to run various Kmart departments, including men's and women's apparel, jewelry, shoes, automotive parts, and sporting goods, among others. By leasing departments to other operators early on, Kresge cut both its financial risk and the amount of cash it had to pony up to open Kmart stores. Then, too, the shoe and jewelry and other outfits running these departments were presumed to have more expertise in selling their lines of goods.

Over the decades, Kresge/Kmart had bought many of the lessees. But instead of folding them into its Kmart division, Cunningham and then Dewar had turned them into wholly owned subsidiaries that operated side by side with Kmart as independent fiefdoms, with each doing its own buying and its own distribution. Eventually, Kmart executives figured out that all this duplication was absurdly wasteful and that they could save a bundle by consolidating these subsidiaries. But—as with everything the company did in the '70s and '80s—this move happened at practically a geologic pace.

And so it wasn't until 1983 that Kmart got around to consolidating the buying and distribution of its separate men's and women's apparel subsidiaries. Even then, Kmart Apparel would stay in its North Bergen, New Jersey, stronghold and operate independently from the Kmart stores division until 1991. As one result, when Kmart finally did computerize sales and ordering, the apparel division wound up using a different system to track goods than the rest of the company, with different scanning equipment, a different type of price tag, and different procedures that employees had to learn.

Each division was its own world. "We didn't have any crossover," recalls Larry Parkin, who was the head of Kmart's western region in 1983. "Very few people ever went from the parent company to apparel, and none from apparel to the parent company." So solid were the walls between divisions that Parkin was a bit dazed when Fauber shook up the corporate hierarchy that year by ordering him and Antonini to move to the apparel side. Even though they were being handed what was obviously a big assignment—they were to take charge of merging men's apparel, women's apparel, and fashion accessories into one unit—Parkin wasn't sure what to think. Was he being moved up, or out of the way?

"I asked, 'Where do I operate out of, North Bergen or Troy?' " Parkin said. "They said, 'Troy,' and I said, 'Fine.' "

But for Antonini, who was being catapulted a half-dozen rungs up the corporate ladder to become executive vice president of the apparel division, this was his chance to bat cleanup. Never mind that he would be in North Bergen, and reporting to Parkin, now vice chairman of the division: The opportunities were terrific.

Though Kmart had continued its fast expansion through the late '70s and early '80s, the cost of opening hundreds of stores and of cutting prices to battle for shoppers during the whipsaw inflation and recession of those years had chewed away at the company's net profit margin. Anyone who could batten that margin a bit would be a hero, and apparel offered many ways to do that. The markup—the difference between Kmart's cost on an item and the retail price it charged—was higher on apparel than on most other goods. All Antonini had to do was find a way to boost sales without slashing the markup. The key, he knew, would be to convince shoppers that clothing that didn't cost much didn't have to look cheap.

Fauber had already taken one big whack at Kmart's Polyester Palace image by junking the shoddy private-label polyester clothing and bringing in cottons, woolens, and cotton-poly blends. Now Antonini and Parkin moved to improve the quality of the Kmart clothing brands that were left and to bring in national name brands that shoppers loved. This would be an uphill struggle, since many apparel makers still refused to sell their most popular brands to discounters. Companies like Levi Strauss, the jeans maker, feared that selling through discounters would cheapen their image—and cost them department store accounts.

Antonini began advertising Kmart's clothing lines with slick spreads in *Cosmopolitan* and other women's fashion magazines. He ordered studies of regional differences in taste—discovering that in Florida, for example, spring fashions could be rolled out as early as October instead of in January, the usual time everywhere else. Another study showed apparel makers hadn't paid much attention to the fact that the average American was more overweight than ever; so Antonini added extra-large and double extra-large sizes for men and women, and they sold like crazy.

Other studies convinced him that instead of selling its own brands of apparel piecemeal, Kmart ought to design whole lines of coordinated fashions and then advertise and promote them as if they were national brands. That was the way to make a private label work, he thought: Create a brand identity—and to create one with instant name power, use a catchy celebrity as the brand's sponsor.

Using celebrities was nothing new, of course. In the 1940s, Montgomery Ward had featured such budding young stars as Susan Hayward, Lauren Bacall, and Gregory Peck in its catalogs. Kresge itself, back in 1968, had signed Olympic figure-skating champion Peggy Fleming as a Kmart spokeswoman. But Antonini took the idea a step further, swiping an idea from a more-upscale rival, Sears, that no other discounter had tried.

In late 1980, Sears launched an entire fashion line under the name of Cheryl Tiegs, a famous cover model who had proven wildly popular with women shoppers in studies Sears had conducted. The line, massively advertised inside Sears stores, with Tiegs's face plastered on posters, wall photos, floor displays, and price tags, had shocked the industry by selling $100 million in merchandise its first year.

Part of the reason this had been so shocking was that Sears, though it sold lots of clothes, hadn't been considered a fashion powerhouse. Kmart's reputation was worse; even the most avid women discount shoppers didn't think of it as a place to buy fashionable clothing, studies showed. But Antonini was convinced Kmart could work the same magic Sears had and rid itself of that Polyester Palace albatross once and for all.

When a fashion representative came to him with a proposal for a new celebrity fashion line, he jumped on it. He signed the popular, clean-cut television star Jaclyn Smith to act as a spokeswoman, and then created a full line of coordinated women's fashions under her name. It became an enormous hit. Crowds lined up in stores to see her. By 1986, the Jaclyn Smith line and other Kmart private-label lines that followed accounted for half the company's apparel sales—up from one-tenth of sales three years earlier. Apparel's share of total Kmart sales climbed to 24 percent, up from 20 percent. The gain in profits was even fatter. It was a tremendous coup, and one, Parkin readily said, "where Joe really took the ball and ran with it."

Antonini also convinced Fauber to invest in apparel factories in the Far East. To save costs, Kmart, like most other big retailers, increasingly was having its private-label goods made in the Far East, instead of in the United States. But because shipping took longer and because factories there weren't as nimble or technologically advanced as in the United States, orders had to be locked in place months in advance. By investing in its own factories, rather than buying from independent factories or middlemen, as most other retailers did, Kmart gained more control over production, letting it ship far faster.

Fauber rewarded Antonini by making him president of the apparel division in 1984, then a senior vice president of Kmart the next year, and then bumping him up to executive vice president in early 1986.

Later that year, as Fauber began contemplating his own retirement, he chatted with board members about who should succeed him. Antonini, though only forty-five, was one of the four candidates. Fauber asked each man to prepare a presentation for the board, outlining his vision of Kmart's future. Each candidate would meet privately with the board at a retreat to be held at a resort in Traverse City, in northern Michigan.

Nervous, not really daring to believe he had a good crack at the top job, Antonini called his trusted friend Marjorie Alfus and asked her to write a speech for him. He had met Alfus when he was in North Bergen, where she worked as an attorney, negotiating Kmart's contracts with manufacturers. Highly intelligent, well-read, tough, and imperious, Alfus hadn't been sucked into the Kmart corporate culture. Antonini found in her someone willing to give him brutally frank critiques of company policies and decisions—an anomaly at Kmart, which seemed to operate on the principle that the nail that sticks out gets hammered down. For her part, Alfus had taken a shine to the earnest younger man, who seemed to her to be on the fast track.

Now, when he called, she thought Antonini seemed surprised to have a shot at the presidency. He seemed sure that one of his more established rivals—such as Parkin, the man he'd reported to in North Bergen—was likelier to win the post. But they crafted a speech, and Antonini practiced it over and over, polishing his delivery, refining his presentation of Kmart as the retailer of the future.

As it happened, several board members already were leaning toward Antonini because of his stellar record at Kmart Apparel. Whatever doubts any of them held seem to have evaporated after his confident, polished presentation. "Can you *believe* it?" he asked Alfus gleefully, phoning her after Fauber had stunned him with the news that the job was his.

In August of 1986, Antonini was appointed president and chief operating officer. At the annual meeting, the following March, he was named chief executive; and when Fauber retired in September, Antonini became chairman, too. Fauber sponsored him for membership in the exclusive Bloomfield Hills Country Club, the gathering place for Detroit's business barons, including such automotive royalty as Chrysler's Lee Iacocca.

Antonini had arrived.

Now, he knew, his work would really begin. The boisterous new chairman was determined to do things right. Even before moving into his new office on the fourth floor, he decided to create something brand new at Kmart: an ad hoc committee, a "kitchen cabinet" operating outside the Kmart bureaucracy, that could give him unvarnished advice and feedback.

Alfus would be on it, of course, along with Mike Wellman, a bright marketing vice president; Patrick Kelly, a business professor at Wayne State University who had worked with Kmart before; and Barbara Loren, a
free-speaking advertising and marketing consultant who'd impressed Antonini with her savvy two years earlier, when, on Fauber's orders, she'd
made a presentation to Kmart Apparel.

Antonini told the group he wanted them to range far and wide, to dig
into and offer him advice on any and all aspects of Kmart's business and
how to improve it. Not that they had to look far for problems.

All they had to do was visit a store. Fauber had begun renovating some
of Kmart's oldest stores, but it hadn't been his top priority. Even as Antonini took the reins, the average Kmart store was fifteen years old—and
looked it. Many had water-warped floors, broken light fixtures, and cheap
displays awkwardly set in middle of the narrow aisles. While Wal-Mart
slapped up many of its buildings fast and cheap, too, it had a standing program of renovating stores every five years, keeping its older stores in far
better shape than Kmart's. Then, too, because Wal-Mart so often replaced
its oldest stores with bigger new models, more than a third of its stores
were less than three years old.

Then there were the goods on the shelves—that is, when they were on
the shelves. Antonini knew he had to ramp up the use of computers and
satellite communications to collect better sales data and reorder goods
more quickly. It was one more field where he would have to play catch-up
with Wal-Mart and other smaller rivals. One of his first announcements,
after being named chief executive, was that Kmart would spend $1 billion
over the next five years to roll out new technology faster, so it could track
sales and keep in stock better.

And, of course, Antonini also desperately wanted to correct what he
considered Fauber's blunder in ignoring the soaring warehouse-club business. Now that he was in charge, Antonini wanted in, and fast. It was obvious to him that Wal-Mart and Price Club were making mints with their
warehouse clubs. With Kmart's greater size and reach, surely it could
quickly carve out a healthy slice of the market. In March of 1988, Antonini
bulled the board into buying a 51 percent stake in Makro Inc., an upscale
warehouse-club chain owned by a Dutch concern, with six stores in the
eastern United States.

The Makro stores had been designed in the same style as the company's
stores in the Netherlands, and they offered the same sorts of *haute* goods
as had sold well there. But while most warehouse clubs offered a few fancy

items to pique members' interests, at Makro it was too, too much. Americans seemed confused by stores that offered so many gourmet foods in a loading-dock setting. A year after Antonini bought Makro, it was still deeply in the red.

But Makro was just an appetizer anyway. Antonini had ordered his subordinates to troll for other chains that Kmart might acquire—and they quickly got a nibble from Pace Membership Warehouse.

Pace had been founded in 1982 by Henry Mainsohn, who had been a vice president at a regional home-improvement chain, and Charlie Steinbrueck, who had come from Grand Central, a Salt Lake City–based regional discount chain. In seven years, the two men had created a chain with 47 stores and $1.5 billion a year in sales, putting it firmly in the industry's upper tier. But it was obvious to both men that a shakeout was coming. For Pace to stay a player, they agreed, either they would have to raise an awful lot more capital to pay for a fast expansion, or they would have to find a retailer with far deeper pockets who was hungry for an acquisition.

Sam Walton, who wanted to fold Pace into Sam's Club, had begun haggling with them in the fall of 1988. But when Mainsohn and Steinbrueck heard that Kmart was in the market for another warehouse-club chain, they immediately switched their sights. Kmart was hungrier—and so likely to pay more, they figured.

"Sam never paid a premium for anything," Steinbrueck said. "We knew Kmart had bought half of Makro, which was an absolute disaster. They'd really paid a high premium there, and that had never turned a profit . . . so we knew Kmart was likely to pay a premium for our company."

Steinbrueck claims that, without saying anything directly, he and Mainsohn made sure Antonini knew there was another suitor—and let him connect the dots drawing an arrow to Walton. As they intended, this was like waving a red cape before a snorting bull. To Steinbrueck—as to many Kmart managers—Antonini seemed obsessed with Wal-Mart and Walton and what they were doing. His whole manner seemed to signal a personal rivalry. Old hands still talk about the time, in early 1988, at a meeting with Kmart's district managers, that Antonini loudly dismissed Walton as a "snake-oil salesman." It was typical of the kinds of comments he would make about his adversary.

But his public contempt may have expressed fear more than anything else. Antonini knew better than to dismiss Wal-Mart's strengths. He'd been in too many Wal-Marts. That was why he made Kmart adopt so many of Wal-Mart's ways, from stationing a "people greeter" at the door of every store to eliminating most sales promotions in favor of "everyday low pricing." The $1 billion he committed to revamp Kmart's ordering and communications was meant to put it on a par with Wal-Mart's model.

His interest was anything but academic. Kmart was still far larger, with $27.3 billion in sales in 1988, compared with $20.6 billion at Wal-Mart, and with 2,200 stores compared with 1,325. But Wal-Mart was growing far faster, and it was more profitable. All of Antonini's spending to fix old stores and bring in new technology, at the same time that he was trying to cut prices, hammered Kmart's earnings. In 1988, for the first time, Wal-Mart posted higher net profits: $837.2 million compared with Kmart's $803 million.

Meanwhile, mighty Sears, the one retailer still running ahead of them both, was stumbling. Sears had been the world's biggest retailer since 1965. Back in 1972, in Chicago, when construction began on the new company headquarters, the Sears Tower, it seemed appropriate that this would be the tallest building on earth. More than half the households in the United States owned Sears credit cards. That year, Sears by itself accounted for 1 percent of America's entire gross national product. But as if to illustrate the old adage that whom the gods would humble they first raise up, at this apex of domination Sears's leaders were exhibiting a deadly hubris.

Since its beginnings as a mail-order concern in 1887, Sears had built its franchise by promising quality products at low prices. After World War II, as discounters multiplied, Sears had been protected for a time by its reputation, by the power that its size gave it to demand the best prices from its suppliers, and by its national presence: Everybody lived near a Sears, or near a Sears catalog store, or at the very least got the Sears catalog in the mail.

But as discounters—especially Kmart—had grown bigger and stronger, they began to steal Sears's customers. In the early '70s, leaving its own commitment to low prices behind it, Sears tried to counter this threat by moving upscale, stocking higher-priced, high-fashion merchandise the discounters didn't offer. But that move backfired: It pushed Sears's blue-collar customers deeper into the arms of Kmart and other discounters and didn't pull enough shoppers away from the tonier department stores Sears was now trying to horn in on.

So in 1977, Sears executives abruptly spun about-face. For that year's Christmas season, they slashed prices on three-quarters of the merchandise down to the bone, even selling some products below Sears's cost, on the theory that customers coming in for the bargains would take home higher-margin goods too. Customers mobbed the stores like locusts, cart-ing off enormous quantities of goods in the biggest shopping frenzy anyone at Sears had ever seen. But the hordes whipped right past all the full-price items that were supposed to bring in the profits, and the huge sale turned into a disaster. Sears had been cherry-picked to death. It racked up one of the biggest sales gains in its long history, but profits plunged by $130 million from the year before.

The debacle stunned senior executives. For the next few years, Sears seemed to drift like a rudderless scow. From 1973 through 1980—except for modest upticks in 1975 and 1976—Sears's earnings fell steadily.

Sears's stumbles in marketing itself were matched by its bumbles in handling its suppliers. After the 1977 Christmas fiasco, the company decided to trim many of its slower-moving lines and told suppliers it would stop carrying items that didn't sell quickly enough. It was a prudent move, in one sense, but Sears's executives really should have expected what happened next: Many of its manufacturers, such as Whirlpool Corp., the appliance maker, turned to discounters to make up their sales, offering them strong name brands they hadn't been able to carry before.

To cut costs, Sears trimmed its staff in stores, but it paid less attention to pruning the layer after layer of middle management it had larded on over the years. And the company fell victim to its own corporate culture. Managers in Sears's various divisions were deeply suspicious of their rivals in other divisions; the buying side and selling side operated as if the two halves of the retailer were separate companies. All the internal rivalries and divisions created massive drag as company chairman Edward Telling, in the early '80s, tried to turn Sears around. Telling, a lifelong Sears man who masked his literate and intellectual nature behind a country-boy facade, knew he had to take Sears in a new direction.

But that new direction seemed to be away from retailing. Besides its stores, Sears also owned Allstate Insurance Co. and a separate real estate and financial services arm. Now Telling restructured Sears as a holding company in which the insurance, real estate, and financial operations held equal status with its Merchandising Group—the side that included the Sears stores. Telling talked about all the big opportunities he saw in boosting financial services, in particular. Wall Street and rival merchants read this, not unreasonably, as a signal that at the world's biggest retailer, retailing was no longer the main focus.

Still, the head of the merchandising group, Edward Brennan, wasn't about to cede the high ground to Kmart or any other rival, if he could help it. Brennan, a third-generation Sears man with a seemingly encyclopedic knowledge of retailing, led a flashy remodeling of the Sears stores' layout—

designing what he called the Store of the Future. He launched a new national advertising campaign, promising shoppers that "there's more for your life at Sears." The stores picked up new lines, such as Levi's jeans (making Sears, overnight, Levi Strauss's largest customer). The company upgraded its registers and scanners to adopt the latest technology. Brennan, who disdained what he called off-price retailers, was determined not to be beaten by them. "If you truly fail at something," he said, "then you ought to be thrown out."[3] He ordered his staffers to shop the competition—Kmarts and other discounters included—and steal any techniques better than those at Sears.

All this helped—but not quite enough. So in late 1988, Brennan decided to test his own advice. At a single store in Wichita, Sears stopped holding sales, marked down the prices on all its goods, and adopted Wal-Mart's policy of everyday-low-pricing. The standard practice at a typical Sears store, in those days, was to put some 9,000 items on sale each week. That meant changing the displays, remarking prices, and moving around merchandise. Not having to do all that would save a lot of money—if customers would still come in.

The test scared Wal-Mart enough that it ran strident newspaper ads warning shoppers not to be fooled by people imitating Wal-Mart's everyday prices. But Brennan was impressed. Sales at the Wichita store gained a few percentage points compared to similar Sears stores elsewhere, but profits leaped by 40 percent. He decided Sears should adopt everyday-low-pricing across the country, cutting some of its prices by as much as 50 percent.

In late February of 1989 the company took the astonishing step of closing all of its stores for a day and a half while thousands of employees, working until 3 A.M., plastered new price tags on 30,000 different products in every store. Meanwhile, a huge advertising campaign on television and radio and in the newspapers blared about Sears's "Sale that Never Ends." When the stores reopened on March 1, customers jammed the stores as if it were Christmas Eve.

But even though many of the new prices were competitive with those at Kmart and Wal-Mart, Sears still faced a big problem: It couldn't operate as cheaply as the discounters, at least, not while making anywhere near the kinds of profit margin it needed. On those products where Sears was cheaper, Kmart and Wal-Mart soon cut their prices to match. They could afford the fight; their overhead—especially at Wal-Mart—was far lower. Sears spent three times as much per item as Wal-Mart (and about 30 percent more than Kmart) on distribution, on getting goods from the factories to the stores.

And, too, Sears still clung to outdated policies—misguidedly trying to protect its Sears cards, now redubbed Discover cards, by refusing to accept Visa, Mastercard, or American Express.

The fact was, Sears was changing too little, too late. It would remain a big and powerful retailer, but its glory days of the late '60s and early '70s were fading. While no one at Sears had noticed, discounters such as Kmart and Wal-Mart and Target had slipped into Sears's former role as the place most people went first to pick up everyday buys: socks, underwear, towels, motor oil, dishes, videotapes.

By the mid '80s, analysts were predicting that Sears's days as the world's biggest retailer were numbered. The only question was whether the crown would be snatched by Kmart or Wal-Mart.

Antonini seemed to want to answer that question by taking Kmart in half a dozen directions at once, even as he tried to fix up the Kmart stores and the distribution system. He branched the company into the "category killer" arena, opening huge office-supply stores under the name Office Square, and sporting goods stores on steroids called Sports Giant. And, zealously watching Wal-Mart, Antonini decided to follow Walton's lead by tackling hypermarts. He had Kmart team up with Bruno's Inc., a 150-store Birmingham, Alabama, supermarket chain that would handle the food side.

In January 1989, Kmart opened its first hypermart in Atlanta's eastern suburbs, a 225,000-square-foot store with 600 employees, that Antonini cockily predicted would crack $100 million a year in sales. Called American Fare, the hypermart had the usual concrete floor, but tried to disguise its warehouselike appearance by draping colorful signs and banners everywhere; green trellis work and glass on the building gave it a bright, airy effect. It offered more brand-name clothing and fancier goods than the usual Kmart store. The fixtures were fancier too, more like what one might expect in a department store. On the food side, meanwhile, Bruno's had added a solid array of gourmet items to the usual selection of groceries, all at discount prices.

Antonini was confident enough to fly down dozens of retail analysts from New York and elsewhere, and his aplomb seemed justified. "I think this time dowdy old Kmart may have got it right," said William Smith, an analyst at Smith Barney, after his tour.[4] Walter Loeb, an analyst at Morgan Stanley, said he expected the giant store easily to meet Antonini's predicted sales.

There were skeptics. Kmart said it expected to pull shoppers from a 30-mile radius; but a market research firm from Chicago, Leo Shapiro & Associates, said American shoppers weren't likely to change their food buying from supermarkets to hypermarts unless they happened to live closer to the hypermart.

As it turned out, Shapiro's researchers were right. But the numbers needed to succeed were so huge that both Walton and Antonini seem to have felt some doubts themselves. Even as workers scrambled to prepare for the American Fare's grand opening, both Wal-Mart and Kmart already were experimenting with scaled down versions of the hypermarts that they would call supercenters. Wal-Mart had opened its first supercenter nearly a year earlier, in Washington, Missouri, a 126,000-square-foot store that gave about a fourth of its space to food and offered roughly half the food selection of a typical supermarket. Kmart, meanwhile, had opened two Super Kmarts in November 1988, taking a slightly different approach. For years, Kmart had plunked many stores down in strip malls next to grocery stores to draw off the traffic the grocery stores generated. Now, instead of putting up new buildings, it experimented with having two existing Kmarts simply take over those spaces next door.

But that project wasn't on the front burner yet. Antonini was in a bigger rush to get in on the warehouse-club business, and with something better than the Makro stores. At first, Antonini had sent one of his lieutenants, Joe Newsome, to dicker with Steinbrueck and Mainsohn over buying Pace. But when they "let slip" that Walton was wooing them, Antonini took over.

He knew that the Pace stores and Sam's Clubs didn't overlap in many markets. If Wal-Mart added the 47 Pace warehouses to its 105 Sam's Clubs, it would take a nearly insurmountable lead in the industry and lock up a lot of markets that Kmart would then either have to skip, or spend an awful lot to muscle into. Snatching Pace away, on the other hand, would give Kmart a solid base from which to take on Wal-Mart's warehouse club division.

Neither Mainsohn nor Steinbrueck had any interest in staying on after they closed the deal; but Antonini knew he needed their expertise. The terms weren't a problem; Antonini was hungry enough to agree to pay a generous $326 million, and he easily convinced Kmart's board to go along. But for that price, Antonini insisted, Steinbrueck had to agree to stay on and run the operation for three years. As Steinbrueck recalls, Antonini promised a hands-off relationship. Steinbrueck could run things his own way, he said, but he had to be part of the deal.

Steinbrueck agreed. They closed the sale in November.

It was a coup for Antonini, who seemed to be doing everything right— and who was lionized by Wall Street analysts and the press alike. He was delighted, even thrilled by all the attention. In 1987, Detroit's Columbus Day celebration committee had named him its man of the year. An industry magazine, *Discount Store News,* declared him 1988's "Discounter of the Year," one of a half-dozen awards that were showered on him that year.

All the attention seemed to stoke rather than sate his ambition. He appointed himself the face of Kmart, appearing on television commercials the same way his new country-club buddy Lee Iacocca had done at Chrysler. "I promise you," he said, beaming at the camera, "you're going to love shopping at your new Kmart."[5] He explained that he was doing this as a way of proving to people that he was committed to getting Kmart on the move. And, no doubt, he meant it—but, in truth, he loved being recognized and famous too.

And he had his eyes on what he considered the biggest prize of all: sweeping past Sears and holding off Wal-Mart to make Kmart the biggest retailer in the world—making Joe Antonini, by extension, the greatest merchant in the world.

11

Darkness on the Edge of Town

Back in 1945, when Sam Walton opened his first variety store in Newport, and then again in 1950, when he came to Bentonville, he and his store had been welcomed by each town with open arms. This was true in 1962, too, when he opened his first Wal-Mart Discount City in Rogers, Arkansas.

Through the '60s and early '70s, as Wal-Mart stores grew bigger and better, most folks in the small Southern towns Walton was targeting were only too happy to see one of his discount stores come to town. It was a sign of progress, a symbol that this was a place where things were happening. It wasn't at all unusual for small towns to write or even send delegations to Bentonville begging for the signal honor of being home to a Wal-Mart.

Walton cagily played on that desire. Even when he had his heart set on going into a particular site in a particular town, he would act utterly nonchalant, as if any of half a dozen other sites would do as well. Whenever he thought he could get away with it—which was often—he would politely but firmly demand concessions: a break on property taxes, use of tax-exempt bonds to finance construction, infrastructure subsidies, a rezoning, even a change of town boundaries so he could get city services at his site out on the edge of town. This approach, set in the days when Sam and Bud Walton, and then, briefly, Jim Walton, had taken charge of real estate, became even more pronounced under Tom Seay, who was put in charge in the mid-'70s of finding places to put stores.

Seay, whose erect bearing betrayed the several years he'd spent in the Army's quartermaster corps before winding up in Bentonville, was another of Walton's chance hires; the two men met after services one Sunday at the First Presbyterian Church, in town. Seay had just quit his job with a local developer to go back to school for an MBA, in search of a better opportunity. He found it with Walton, who could always use another real estate man. While studying for his degree, Seay worked at the Wal-Mart store in Rogers; after a year of familiarizing himself with Wal-Mart's operations, he was put briefly under Jim Walton's aegis; he then took over the real estate operation when Sam's youngest son left.

Now, as Wal-Mart evolved—as the stores got bigger, the prices lower, the selection better—Seay began refining Walton's strategy, analyzing all the existing stores to figure out from just how many miles away each store could draw customers, and just how densely the company should saturate an area with stores. Through the '70s, at Walton's orders, Seay mostly avoided competing with Kmarts, or even with TG&Y, a large variety store chain. Following Walton's model—and working closely with a real estate committee consisting of Walton and his top executives—Seay targeted small towns where Wal-Mart could immediately dominate the market.

And in those small towns, where the mayors and city councils and chambers of commerce were almost comically anxious to please, Seay worked every cost-cutting angle he could think of, playing neighboring towns off against one another, just as Sam had, to wangle whatever breaks or subsidies local leaders were willing to hand him. It was pretty easy, really. But gradually, toward the end of the decade, as Wal-Mart stores grew ever more dominant, attitudes began to shift. He began running into resistance.

It was the small business owners on town squares and main streets—like pitchers in a sandlot baseball game suddenly facing Ty Cobb—who were the first to quail at the menace from the big box full of bargains.

One such place was Donaldsonville, Louisiana, a somnolent small town and parish seat° on the west bank of the Mississippi River, between Baton Rouge and New Orleans. The arguments each side raised there perfectly encapsulate the nature of what eventually would become a national debate. When Wal-Mart decided in 1980 to open a store in Donaldsonville, Seay had a local attorney, Hugh Martin, ask the city council to appoint a board that could declare Wal-Mart's planned site an "industrial expansion" area. That would let the company issue tax-free industrial revenue bonds to

---

° Louisiana is divided into parishes, rather than counties.

build its store. It was the same sort of routine break the company always asked for—and got. There seemed little reason to expect any different outcome here. Hadn't the local paper just rhapsodized about the feeling of new growth, the new jobs and greater variety the Wal-Mart store would bring?

But this time, at that council meeting on a steamy night in June, one local business owner after another stood up and demanded that the council say no. Wal-Mart didn't need this kind of unfair advantage when it was going to hurt all their businesses anyway, they argued.

Wal-Mart's man from Bentonville, Bob Martin, hotly retorted that "weak businesses will still go out of business, whether we come into town or not."[1] But all the clamor led a majority of the council, led by Mayor Lala Regira, to vote no.

Meanwhile, business owners and a group of would-be neighbors loudly opposed Wal-Mart's request to rezone the site it wanted from residential to commercial. After a yearlong debate, Wal-Mart gave up and picked a second site, also on the edge of town.

The fight polarized the community. Opponents—including most of the local merchants—maintained that Wal-Mart would pull shoppers away from downtown, hurting or maybe even killing Donaldsonville mainstays such as the Lemann's Department Store. An opulent three-story landmark of stuccoed brick, Lemann's had operated continuously in town since 1836, making it the oldest department store in Louisiana. But neither Lemann's nor smaller businesses could hope to compete with Wal-Mart on price, the merchants said dourly, warning that money spent at Wal-Mart would be shipped in bags to Bentonville, instead of being spent again in town.

On the other side were those—including many of the poorer black residents—who felt the new store represented progress and who derided its opponents as being afraid of honest competition. Look around you, argued the company supporters: Folks living in Donaldsonville already were heading out of town to malls down by Baton Rouge to shop. A Wal-Mart might keep more of those shoppers in town. Anyway, they said, Wal-Mart's low prices and great variety of goods not only would save locals money, but probably would draw shoppers into town from outlying communities.

Wal-Mart itself—after Bob Martin's little salvo—regrouped, working on council members behind the scenes. There was no rush. Louisiana offered plenty of other sites to build in; Wal-Mart only had seven stores in the state. By the end of 1981, Wal-Mart came back to the council, now headed by a pugnacious new mayor, Ralph Falsetta, who keenly favored the company. He gladly agreed to appoint a bond board and to extend the city limits out to the new proposed store site. But local merchants, led by a department store owner and, curiously enough, a politically well-connected mortician, fought a rearguard action, trying to foil the state approval needed for the bonds. By early 1983, Wal-Mart opted to begin construction without the bonds—though it kept wangling for them.

Now both sides took their fight to the state bond commission. At the hearing that February in Baton Rouge, tempers boiled over. Funeral-home owner E. J. Ourso argued—quite rightly, as it turned out—that turning down the bonds wouldn't slow construction one bit. "I have $10 million in assets in one of my companies, and I didn't borrow a dime that I didn't have to pay prime interest for," he thundered, adding, "I'll stand up and fight for this principle." Mayor Falsetta, sitting behind Ourso, promptly jumped up and offered to fight Ourso right then and there. "Wait till you get back to Donaldsonville," drawled commission chairman B. B. Rayburn. "The folks down there might enjoy it."[2]

The commission voted down the bonds and then voted them down again at a rehearing in April. In August, Wal-Mart opened a 45,000-square-foot store—smaller than average, but mighty big for Donaldsonville. Shoppers thronged the grand opening. And that, it seemed, was that.

Except for one thing. Or more properly, one person: Glenn Falgoust, who would become Donaldsonville's last angry man. Falgoust, thirty-three years old, had grown up on a sugar-cane farm about 20 miles out of town; after college and a few years of working in New Orleans, he'd moved back to Donaldsonville in 1971. He had run his own auto-parts store downtown for ten years. He'd worried a bit about Wal-Mart, but not enough to get very involved in trying to keep it out.

Once it was clear the store couldn't be stopped, Falgoust had resigned himself to competing as best he could. So he was shocked to see other business owners, people he'd known for years, giving up even before the Wal-Mart store opened. When his main rival, who ran a Western Auto store directly across the street from him, announced he was closing the store, Falgoust asked him why. "My bills are paid," said his friend, Joe Acosta, "so I'm going to get out while the getting's good." (Falgoust took this to mean that Acosta didn't want to compete with Wal-Mart; but Acosta, reached years later, said he was just tired of the business and hated it. "They would have driven me out of business if I'd stayed, I'm sure," he said, "but I wanted out anyway.")

The owner of a variety store down the street decided to shut down. "My lease is up," he told Falgoust. "Why should I go into debt to get my teeth kicked in?" In the months after the Wal-Mart opened, several other small shops—a shoe store, a clothing store—also closed.

As it happened, Louisiana then was well into what would later be known as the "oil-patch crisis," a severe recession that hammered all of the country's oil-producing states through the mid-'80s. The same soaring oil prices that had primed the economic woes and severe inflation of the late '70s across the country had created a boom in the economies of oil states such as Texas, Alaska, and Louisiana. Now the worm turned. In March 1983, oil prices peaked at $37.50 a barrel; and Saudi Arabia, fearful of sparking a global depression, jawboned its fellow OPEC members into bringing the price down to $30 a barrel. That move seemed to break the psychological state of panic that had gripped the oil-importing countries. As David Halberstam observed, "It was not a shortage of oil so much as fear of a shortage that caused the crazy escalation of prices."[3] Now, as that fear subsided, prices eased to $29 a barrel, then $28, and soon fell to $22 a barrel. By late 1986, they would sink as low as $10 a barrel.

The plunging price of oil led to vast cutbacks in the oil industry; the loss of 148,000 jobs over six years and plummeting state revenues from the drop in taxes on gas and oil rippled through the Louisiana economy. Other parts of the state—the Gulf Coast, for one—were hit harder than Donald-sonville; but it, too, slipped into recession.* Still, to Falgoust's mind, the real culprit squatted out at the edge of town. He could see for himself how much business he was losing. He had been selling 1,000 bicycles a year; but Wal-Mart could sell them at retail for less than what he paid his wholesaler. Same with lawn mowers. How could he make it without such high-margin items?

As he would struggle over the next few years to change his merchandise, to offer better service, and to find other ways to compete, Falgoust also would begin keeping track each time another business in town closed its doors. Eventually, too, he would begin researching Wal-Mart—compiling evidence, in effect. He, for one, would not let his business go gently into that good night.

•   •   •

---

* The Baton Rouge area, including Donaldsonville, was more reliant on the state's huge chemical industry than on oil; but an exceptionally strong dollar from 1980 through 1985 crippled exports and led to the loss of thousands of jobs in that industry, too. The area recovered quite quickly after 1988—and far faster than the rest of Louisiana, according to studies by Loren C. Scott, an economics professor at Louisiana State University who has written annual economic studies of Louisiana for two decades.

Most places, what resistance Tom Seay and his team ran into in the early '80s was minor and not very well organized. None of the fights—such as they were—drew more than local attention. A few business owners here or there might doomsay a bit, especially if they had friends in towns where Wal-Mart already operated. But in the end, it made little difference. At least, until Steamboat Springs.

Seay had gone to Steamboat several times on ski vacations. He'd been enchanted—and had quickly sized up the place as an ideal market to tap as soon as Wal-Mart expanded into Colorado.

Founded in 1875 as a trading post for French fur trappers in the Yampa River Valley, in the middle of the Rocky Mountains, Steamboat took its name from the chugging sound made by a local natural hot spring. Trappers had eventually given way to ranchers and coal miners; and the arrival of the railroad in the early 1900s made the town one of the largest cattle-shipment points in the West.

As the seat of sprawling Routt County, even by the late 1970s the town didn't depend solely on the skiing and tourism for which it was becoming famous. Ranchers and miners still mixed comfortably with ski bums and wealthy visitors. Compared with the glitter and ostentation of Aspen or Vail, Steamboat seemed more down-home; its old clapboard buildings and simple frame houses gave the town a feeling of rootedness missing from many other Colorado resort towns. The small shops that lined Lincoln Avenue, the main street through downtown—a hardware store, a Ben Franklin, a Gamble general store, a drugstore—catered to locals, not tourists. Denver, the nearest big city, was more than 160 miles away.

In 1985, Wal-Mart reached Colorado, and Seay quietly came to town again to look at potential sites. In town, rumors that Wal-Mart was coming began to spread in the spring of 1986. A few people knew the town planner had already discouraged Wal-Mart from applying for the first site Seay had spotted, a vacant plot near the Holiday Inn at one edge of town. That fall, Wal-Mart resurfaced as the prime tenant for a proposed mini-mall, also, of course, on the edge of town.

In the buffet line at the Cove, a modest Mexican restaurant downtown, merchants gathering for their monthly meeting in October talked about little else but whether the city would okay the permit that the huge store would need. At 41,304 square feet, this would be only two-thirds the size of the average new Wal-Mart. But that would still make it 11 times the size of Roy Struble's Gamble store. Many locals, tired of driving 42 miles to the Kmart in Craig to find bargains, were thrilled. But Struble and other shopkeepers, both on Lincoln Avenue and at the base of the ski slopes, were terrified.

Struble warned that friends of his in other towns with Wal-Marts said they couldn't meet the chain's prices even selling at their own cost. Tom and Nancy Clapsaddle wondered how their 2,000-square-foot Lyon Drug store could ever hope to match Wal-Mart's variety, let alone its prices. Within days of the meeting at the Cove, they and 42 other business owners petitioned the city council to turn down Wal-Mart's permit. They also asked the council to require an economic impact study for any store of more than 10,000 square feet.

The Clapsaddles, worried about losing the business they'd run for fourteen years, joined an uneasy alliance of shopkeepers and others with their own reasons for opposing Wal-Mart. These ranged from owners of luxury condominiums on the slopes who disdained the idea of a downscale behemoth hunkered at the base of what they considered their mountain, to locals who worried that Wal-Mart would be followed by a slew of other national chains, turning Steamboat into the kind of Anytown, USA, they'd moved there to escape from.

There was already one big fight going on in town over development: Steamboat Ski Corp., which ran the local ski resort, wanted to build a new resort at nearby Lake Catamount. This idea was furiously opposed by local conservationists, who feared the resort would draw tens of thousands more visitors to the valley and lead to even more development. For them to fight Wal-Mart, too, seemed only natural.

The first skirmish came at the planning commission. Commissioners said Wal-Mart's standard design, essentially a big, windowless, concrete-block box, didn't meet town planning guidelines. Wal-Mart would have to include a covered walkway connecting the store to the rest of the mall and pour less asphalt out front, to start with. But Seay's real estate men weren't accustomed to taking orders from local yokels. Carl Ownbey, Wal-Mart's point man for this store, flatly refused the commission's demands. They weren't reasonable. Most of what Wal-Mart planned was just like what the commission had already approved for an earlier proposal a supermarket had made for that site, he pointed out. Ownbey's logic was faultless, but the commissioners were no more inclined to be flexible than he was. After a rancorous public hearing in December, the city council rejected Wal-Mart's permit application—for aesthetic reasons.

The one person unhappiest at this point was Patricia Sandefur, who owned the property. She thought she'd washed her hands of things when she sold the land to the developer who'd lined Wal-Mart up for the project; but when the developer ran short of cash and couldn't make his payments, she got the land back. Now she was suddenly being harangued by people she'd always considered her friends, who complained endlessly to her about what she was about to do to the town and to their businesses.

The project had to have a big tenant, an anchor. Already, she'd been hit once: The past spring, the City Market grocery had been poised to move to her site from downtown, but suddenly, the Steamboat Ski Corp. had enticed the grocery to switch to a rival mall it was building right across the highway. What Sandefur didn't know was that the ski corporation's attorney, Bob Weiss, was now helpfully feeding the Clapsaddles and other Wal-Mart opponents tidbits of advice on how to scuttle the proposed store.* What she *did* know was that everybody was ganging up on her, and it was horrible. For the first time in the thirty-one years she'd lived in Steamboat, she felt uncomfortable going downtown to shop.

Ownbey couldn't have been any happier about the delay. Wal-Mart was building stores across the rest of Colorado without these kinds of problems. This situation had to be handled decisively.

He and the developer, with Sandefur along for the ride, decided to play hardball. They hired a top-dollar land-use attorney from Aspen, Nick Mc-Grath. In January 1987, they sued the city, individual city council members, and ten John Does—local business owners to be named later. The suit demanded $2 million in damages and $1 million more each year until the project was approved. It claimed that the local merchants and council members had conspired to keep Wal-Mart out for anticompetitive reasons.

As one might expect, council members were livid. They immediately had the city attorney cannonade back with a countersuit charging that Wal-Mart, Sandefur, and the developer were abusing the court system and trying to harass, humiliate, and intimidate the council members. When a reporter for the local weekly, the *Steamboat Pilot,* asked McGrath to comment, he icily sneered, "It'll be a cold day in hell before they win any of those counterclaims.

"All I'll do is fight harder," he promised.[4]

But at the same time, Ownbey and Sandefur tried another tactic. Figuring that, merchants and greenies aside, more townsfolk would say yes than no to a Wal-Mart, Sandefur hired several locals to gather signatures, for $5 an hour, on petitions asking for a referendum on the issue. Paying for signature-gathering was illegal under Colorado law, but McGrath blithely assured her and Ownbey that the law was unconstitutional and would never

---

* Nancy Clapsaddle confirmed this in an interview. Weiss, for his part, said, "I may have said something to them [Clapsaddle and other opponents], but I don't think it was with any conscious intention . . . to get Wal-Mart over to our site."

hold up in court. When the city clerk rejected the petitions and the council backed her up, McGrath went straight back to court.

Inevitably, newspapers in Denver got wind of the fight, and wrote a few stories. Then, in May, *USA Today* described the melee: "The USA's richest man is getting a cold shoulder from this Rocky Mountain ski town." Not a fan of the press in any event, Walton had declined to be interviewed. But he was not happy about the story, which, though giving both sides their due, had a David-and-Goliath tone.

"Wal-Mart will be poison to this town," it quoted opposition leader Mark St. Pierre, an art gallery owner, as saying. "I'd much rather pay more for my hardware and kids' clothing than see neighbors and friends forced out of business by a guy who's already got more money than he could spend in a hundred lifetimes."[5]

Here were Walton and Wal-Mart, being described to more than a million readers coast to coast as greedy enemies of small-town America. And more national press and television coverage followed the *USA Today* article, echoing these themes. The company's image seemed to have mutated almost overnight. After decades of quietly gobbling up the business of one small town after another, Wal-Mart was suddenly blinking uncertainly in the dock while a prosecutor cried with a flourish, "Guilty!"

It seemed to come out of nowhere. Even a month before the *USA Today* piece, the *Wall Street Journal* had published a front-page article entitled "Arrival of Discounter Tears the Civic Fabric of Small-Town Life," dissecting the impact of a Wal-Mart store on daily life and small businesses in Pawhuska, Oklahoma.

The impetus for the story had come from a lawsuit filed by five Oklahoma druggists. They accused Wal-Mart of breaking an old 1941 state law that required retailers to sell their goods above cost—one of the flurry of fair-trade and chain tax laws passed by many states in the '20s, '30s, and early '40s to attack chains such as A&P and Sears. The suit claimed Wal-Mart's practice of using loss leaders—scores of items, from toothpaste to disposable diapers, sold below cost to pull in customers—was illegal in Oklahoma.

But the nub of the story wasn't whether Wal-Mart was breaking the law: It was that Wal-Mart was sapping the lifeblood of small towns by killing local businesses. "Last year, a whole block of downtown stores here closed," reporter Karen Blumenthal wrote. "The five-and-dime is gone, and so is the J.C. Penney. The population, already down to about 4,200, is still slipping. 'Wal-Mart didn't cause the trouble,' says Bonnie Peters of Peters Hardware, 'but they haven't helped any.' "[6]

The story went on to detail how the Western Auto store was being converted into an antique outlet and how Peters Hardware dropped Corning dishes and Oneida silverware because it couldn't come close to Wal-Mart's prices. And it quoted the owner of a TV and record store, now closed, as saying "Wal-Mart really craters a little town's downtown."

On the Oklahoma lawsuit, Walton pulled no punches fighting back. He had the company hire four of the state's top lobbyists and spent about $80,000 trying to get the fair-trade law repealed. Through a retail trade group, Wal-Mart ran newspaper ads around the state calling on readers to "stop higher consumer prices" by writing their representatives. Wal-Mart greeters at the stores gathered 200,000 names on petitions calling for lower prices.

In the end, though, a state house committee tossed out Wal-Mart's repeal bill. Toward the close of 1987, Wal-Mart also lost the lawsuit. It settled out of court during its appeal and agreed to raise prices at all of its stores in the state.

And now Walton also retrenched in Steamboat. Word filtered back to Bentonville that the American Civil Liberties Union, concerned that the suit was meant to silence opponents, would step in as soon as McGrath, Wal-Mart's attorney, named any of the John Does in the alleged conspiracy. That was all Wal-Mart needed now: a fresh round of stories painting it as a bully.

In two years in Colorado, Wal-Mart had opened 17 stores without anything remotely resembling the headaches Steamboat Springs was causing. After reviewing the mounting legal bills and everything else with Seay and the other executives on the real estate committee, Walton finally ordered the plug pulled.* In November, Wal-Mart and the city council agreed to drop their lawsuits.

At that point, Weiss, the Steamboat Ski Corp. attorney, called Ownbey and asked if Wal-Mart would like to build on its land across the highway. Ownbey said sure, but added that the ski corporation would have to carry the water on this one. Then Ownbey called Sandefur and regretfully told her about the new plan. She thanked him for his politeness and wished them luck.

---

* Accounts vary as to how worried Sam Walton was about the company's image. But a person close to the decision making in this case confirmed accounts given by several people in Steamboat Springs, including Steamboat Ski Corp. attorney Bob Weiss, as to one other big consideration. "They're incredibly cheap," he said. "They don't like paying for litigation anyway, and McGrath is incredibly expensive." McGrath declined to comment.

The new plans were ready by April 1988. The store would be bigger, 55,000 square feet; but Wal-Mart would give an inch or two to the planning commission. The site would be landscaped, the walkways covered, and Wal-Mart would forgo the slogans—such as "We Sell for Less"—that it usually splashed across the outside of its stores.

People who've lived in a small town know how quickly disagreements can become very personal. Over the next six months, as Weiss and the ski corporation shepherded the plans along, hundreds of scathing letters pro and con swelled the editorial pages of the local papers. Bowing to a city council demand, the ski corporation paid for a $26,000 study of Wal-Mart's likely effect on local business. To no one's surprise, the study concluded that some would fail, but that the town would benefit.

Wal-Mart opponents shellacked the study, which adopted wholesale parts of an earlier study the ski corporation had commissioned touting the benefits of its Lake Catamount proposal. For months, St. Pierre, the Clap-saddles, and other allies searched for any item they could find on the effects of Wal-Mart stores elsewhere. At every possible public meeting, they attacked the ski corporation study as worthless and presented anything new and negative they'd gleaned.

Finally, on two nights in October, more than 450 people crammed into the town's community center for city council hearings on whether to approve the Wal-Mart store. Those who couldn't fit inside crowded around the windows to listen in.

Wal-Mart flew in Don Shinkle, the head of its tiny public relations division. Just before the hearings, he and Ownbey met with Weiss, who fretfully proposed that Wal-Mart and the ski corporation sweeten the pot by offering $100,000 to the merchants association for downtown improvements. He wanted Wal-Mart to put up half the money. Neither one of them could approve it, so under his prodding, they called Seay in Bentonville, who said okay.

At the meeting, Shinkle, a pudgy former television newsman who'd joined the retailer three years earlier, promised the crowd that Steamboat would get "the Taj Mahal of Wal-Marts" and that the store and its workers would be active in the community. Shinkle told the crowd about the $100,000. They were underwhelmed. He answered a great many hostile questions and listened stoically to the hooting laughter as one of many opponents, taking the microphone, dismissed Shinkle's promise of trees and flowers to dress up the Wal-Mart site by saying "it's like putting panties on a pig."[7]

Out of the seemingly endless parade of people filing up to testify, Wal-

Mart opponents ran a two-to-one lead. The vote promised to be close. One council member who worked for the ski corporation would have to abstain. Three of the other six clearly leaned toward Wal-Mart; two others just as clearly leaned against. That left councilwoman Julie Schwall as the swing vote.

In the first go around, two years earlier, she'd testified forcefully against Wal-Mart, vividly describing her anguish at how a similar discounter had wiped out the downtown of the small town where she grew up in North Carolina. That speech had helped get her elected to the council a few months later, and many of those who had voted for her expected her to help keep the giant retailer out.

But this time around, Schwall hadn't committed herself. Now that she was on the council, she wasn't sure her personal feelings were a good enough reason to vote no. For the past week before this hearing she had agonized over which way to go. Dozens of people had stopped by her art store or had phoned to sound her out. Several promised to mount a recall campaign against her or boycott her store if she voted to let Wal-Mart in. She was drowning under pressure.

All night, as people testified, many in the crowd watched her, too. When the time finally came to vote, she sided with Wal-Mart, which won 4-to-2. The packed room suddenly deflated. And how did the Wal-Mart contingent react? They didn't. Shinkle, anxious to avoid any appearance of gloating, had warned his people beforehand to keep cool if they won the vote. Afterwards, an emotionally wrung-out Schwall said that, convinced the development met city regulations, she had decided to put her personal feelings aside.

Disheartened opponents gathered a few days later at the city library. If anything, the hearings showed most people didn't want a Wal-Mart—so why not get a citywide referendum and vote 'em out?

Members fanned out across town with petitions. Violin teacher Charla Palmer, who'd rattled into town eight years earlier in a beat-up, overloaded old Volkswagen van, planted herself in front of the downtown post office. She toted along a 6-foot inflatable dinosaur meant to represent Wal-Mart, and a sign reading WHERE THE PEOPLE LEAD, THE LEADERS WILL FOLLOW.

In nine days, they gathered 927 signatures. The city attorney refused to accept the petitions, saying building permits weren't subject to referenda. They appealed to the city council—which agreed to vote on it. Again, the lines seemed drawn—but this time Schwall, only too happy to let the whole town settle this issue, said she would switch sides. That would mean a 3–3 tie, which, under council rules, would send the matter to the voters.

But a few days before the vote, Schwall tore up her knee in a skiing accident that put her in the hospital. She wrote to the council saying she would support a referendum; but without being there in person, she couldn't vote. By identical 3-to-2 margins, the council voted not to wait for her and to reject the petitions.

Sitting in the crowd at that council meeting was Richard Tremaine, a land-use attorney who had just moved to Steamboat from a suburb of Washington, D.C. Tremaine had known all about the Wal-Mart fight, and he'd heaved a hearty sigh of relief when he'd heard that the council had approved the store. One less dogfight to get dragged into, he figured.

Even as he had been packing for the move, though, a Wal-Mart foe had phoned him, saying she got his name from a local attorney Tremaine knew slightly. He had agreed, reluctantly, to come to the council meeting; but after watching its performance, he quickly agreed to take the referendum issue on.

Less than a month later, on a nippy day in January 1989, he filed a suit to toss out the council's decision. On April 13, a district court judge sided with Tremaine and ordered the city to hold a referendum on Wal-Mart's permit.

The city attorney immediately said he'd appeal. But back in Bentonville, Sam Walton, Seay, and other Wal-Mart executives weren't so eager, as they discussed what to do. What if they let the referendum go forward and Wal-Mart lost? How would that play anywhere else? What if they appealed and lost? Would it set a precedent? Seay wanted to battle on. But Walton said maybe it would be better to back off and let it go, for now. Unsurprisingly, his view carried. A few days later, Shinkle announced that Wal-Mart would drop its plans in Steamboat rather than force a vote.

"I truly believe Wal-Mart is a kinder, gentler company," Shinkle told reporters. "And while we have the votes to win, an election would only split the town more."[8]

Opponents took this as so much hot air. Wal-Mart was just scared it would lose, Palmer thought; it would rather take a hike than risk being publicly humiliated. But who cared? They'd won. They had beaten Wal-Mart. The story got national play: A Little Town Says No. The day after the announcement, a bemused Tremaine fielded a call from a man with a strong Southern twang, who identified himself as a bank president in Arkansas. "I just wanted to call and say 'Congratulations!' to the man who kicked Sam Walton's butt," the caller said warmly.

Not everyone was so sanguine. Nancy Clapsaddle, for one, had a feeling this would not be the end. And, of course, she was right.

And yet, this single, static image of Wal-Mart kicking the dust from its shoes and walking away from a small town would take on a greater significance than anyone then suspected. Here, for the first time, Wal-Mart articulated a stance that later would come back to haunt it. Sam Walton would express it in its ultimate form in his autobiography by saying: "We have almost adopted the position that if some community, for whatever reason, doesn't want us in there, we aren't interested in going in and creating a fuss. I encourage us to walk away from this kind of trouble because there are just too many other good towns out there who do want us."[9]

By the early 1990s, when it was clear that Donaldsonville and Steamboat had been the first few droplets presaging a torrent of opposition to come, groups battling Wal-Mart would wield Walton's own words against his company. Dropping the first part of his quote, they would flourish the rest of it—"if some community, for whatever reason, doesn't want us in there, we aren't interested in going in"—as a promise not to go where it wasn't wanted. If they couldn't stop Wal-Mart, at least they could make it look hypocritical.

And, really, all the talk of not going where it wasn't wanted was just that—talk. Wal-Mart wasn't used to being rejected. The company was more used to receptions like the one it got in Loveland, Colorado, which had just offered to provide $2 million in road, power, and water improvements, along with $300,000 in state funds to train workers, if Wal-Mart would deign to go there to build a massive distribution center for all its new Colorado stores. Even while Walton, Seay, and the others had brooded over what to do in Steamboat, businessmen in Craig, Colorado, less than an hour's drive down Highway 40 from Steamboat, had come to the retailer hats in hand, humbly but eagerly offering their town as an alternative. But Steamboat had been too obviously the best choice; this time, Wal-Mart hadn't bothered to try to play one town off against the other, as it had so many other places.

There had been opposition before—in Donaldsonville, in some small towns in Iowa, in a few other places—but not like what was happening now. One week after Shinkle's announcement in Steamboat, the city council in Lincoln, Nebraska, rejected a proposal to build a Wal-Mart and a Sam's Club there, saying the stores would hurt existing businesses. In Saline, Kansas, where Wal-Mart wanted to abandon its existing building to build a larger store, local businesses managed one delay after another for the re-zoning the project needed. Opposition was building in Jackson Hole,

Wyoming, where the local paper had devoted considerable ink to the Steamboat contretemps. Shortly, the company would face another referendum in Iowa City.

But in Steamboat itself, even as Shinkle announced that Wal-Mart was striding away, the struggle would continue out of public view. Sam Walton had agreed that while Wal-Mart would hang fire, the ski corporation should carry on the fight. If things turned around, Wal-Mart would come back.

Bob Weiss, the ski corporation attorney, never had the slightest doubt that Shinkle's announcement was just public posturing. Wal-Mart worried too much about adverse publicity, he thought. This gave them an out. But they wanted Steamboat just as much as ever—and they'd be back, he figured.* He began helping the city attorney with his appeal.

The court fight would drag on for two more years. But other changes were underway—changes Seay and Walton had anticipated and that had led them to target Steamboat. And those changes would guarantee Wal-Mart its day.

The first was that the town lost its remoteness. Back in 1986, the Yampa Valley airport, 25 miles away, had been expanded to handle full-sized jets. New nonstop flights from Los Angeles, Chicago, Dallas, and Houston made it easy for rich urbanites to zip in and out, boosting not just tourism, but the appeal of buying property. This was especially true for Californians, thousands of whom were searching for real estate outside their own overheated market. By 1989, when Shinkle made his announcement, the Yampa Valley land rush had begun. Steamboat had never seen such a frenzy. One house in town, offered at $125,000, was snapped up sight unseen by a Californian for $160,000.

That fall, an aggressive Japanese resort development company bought the Steamboat Ski Corp. and immediately began designing new golf courses and housing developments. Over the next year, 350 rural properties around Steamboat were rezoned from agricultural to residential, many of them becoming second or third homes for out-of-state snowbirds.

The second change came in the resolve of many of the business owners: It eroded. The city hired a small-business consultant to hold a state-funded workshop on how local businesses could compete better. The consultant— who just happened to be a big commercial developer—hammered at the gathered shopkeepers with the idea that it was inevitable that Wal-Mart or some other giant discounter would roll into Steamboat. They simply had to

---

* Shinkle, asked in 1997 about the announcement, said, "It wasn't a ploy in any way, shape, or form— we'd just had enough."

accept that as fact. Businesses hoping to survive would have to change their ways: Find niches the discounters didn't fill, sell kitsch to tourists, and so on.

As this notion reverberated through their ranks, the Lincoln Avenue shopkeepers were further shocked by the findings of a new study that hit town. Published in late 1988 by an economist from Iowa State University, Kenneth Stone, it was the first formal study to look at what happened to the economies of small towns after a Wal-Mart store opened. The figures, to a small-town merchant, were terrifying.

Wal-Mart had invaded Iowa in 1982; and, as in Donaldsonville, worried local merchants in many of the towns had tried to block permits or zoning changes or had looked for other ways to stall or stop the big retailer. At the time, Stone, forty-six years old, was working for Iowa State's extension service, analyzing rural retail trade and helping small businesses figure out their strengths and weaknesses. Hearing of some of the local battles, he decided to look into the matter. He figured some of the Iowa shopkeepers might be interested in his findings; maybe some economic journal would be, too. Stone didn't give much thought to the fact he was creating a bombshell.

He picked 10 small-to-medium-sized towns in Iowa and pored over years of state retail-tax records to see what happened to sales after a Wal-Mart opened. He also looked at 45 nearby towns without Wal-Marts. He found that Wal-Mart—just as its boosters had argued in Donaldsonville and elsewhere—did act as a magnet, drawing in customers from outlying towns, draining business from them, and boosting the total sales of the town it was in. Tax figures showed that the spillover of new shoppers often helped local restaurants, bars, and those businesses that didn't compete directly with Wal-Mart, such as furniture stores.

But he also found that a typical Wal-Mart would take more than three-fourths of its sales from existing stores in town. A 50,000-square-foot Wal-Mart, with sales conservatively estimated at $130 a square foot, could be expected to grab more than $5 million a year in sales from existing local businesses, especially groceries, hardware stores, drugstores, bookstores, hobby and toy stores, and apparel shops.

Imagine how those figures sounded to small-town Iowa shopkeepers. Word spread far and wide, as fast as phones could be dialed. Stone soon found himself sending copies of his study to hundreds of towns around the country. But while reams of local merchants found the report chilling, Sam Walton and his executives were equally aghast. It had been bad enough to have merchants in town after town put up roadblocks because they suspected a Wal-Mart would hurt them. Now it was all down in black and white. This was bound to spark angrier and more widespread oppostion.

Stone fielded one angry phone call after another from Bentonville: from attorneys working for Rob Walton, from Shinkle—even from Shinkle's secretary. They rumbled about legal action, though it turned out to be nothing more than rumbling. But reporters, town planners, and business groups also flooded him with calls, asking for copies of the report, asking him to come and speak to them, begging for advice about what to do if Wal-Mart came to their town. Stone, a tall, thin, bifocal-wearing man who considered himself a bit of a bore as a speaker, might not get a ticker-tape parade in Bentonville—but he was about to become a small-town consulting star, courtesy of Wal-Mart.

One of his first appearances was at the chamber of commerce in Ottumwa, Iowa, where a Wal-Mart store was about to open. Midway into his speech, Stone was interrupted by the angry local Wal-Mart store manager, who stood up and accused him of lying and of making up his numbers. A few weeks later, back in the area, Stone tried to sneak into the Wal-Mart to check it out, but the manager spotted him and said, "Say, I talked to Mr. Walton about you."

And so he had. But Walton knew he couldn't sue Stone. There was only one thing to do: fund his own study right away, this time by academics closer to home who could find nicer things to say. After soliciting proposals from several schools, Walton had the company pay the University of Missouri $10,000 for a study that looked at 14 Missouri counties hand-picked by Wal-Mart. Predictably, the study gave a beamish view, saying that far from being hurt by the giant stores, the counties "almost all showed growth or revitalization after the opening of Wal-Mart."[10]

It seemed a surprisingly naive ploy, in one way. As soon as the study came out in late 1989, it was savaged, both by other academics and by the national press.* But that mattered less than what happened at the same time: It was uncritically picked up by dozens of smaller newspapers that served just the audience Wal-Mart wanted to reach with its soothing message. For years afterward, Don Shinkle gamely flogged the study to reporters as proof that Wal-Mart wasn't hurting anybody.

---

* The Missouri study did admit that the number of businesses in the 14 counties had dropped, but countered that the remaining businesses were bigger, with more employees. It also described two towns, Butler and Maryville, where economic conditions improved after Wal-Mart arrived, at least as measured by sales taxes. Unlike Stone, though, who took into account other changes in the general economic condition in Iowa, this study ignored the effect of an overall improvement in Missouri farm economies in the mid-'80s.

The derision stung its authors, though. Dr. Edward Robb, one of the Missouri academics, groused a few months later to a *Chicago Tribune* reporter that "we got lots of stories that suggested the university sold its soul to Wal-Mart for $10,000. If we were going to sell out, we'd be sure to get a lot more money."[11] He seems to have gotten his wish. In 1992, Walton gave a $3-million donation to the university's business school, for an endowed professorship and student scholarships.

Ironically, for all that Walton considered Stone a troublemaker, the Iowa economist had no personal bias against Wal-Mart and often shopped there himself. As part of his careful study, Stone had made a point of suggesting strategies small businesses could adopt to compete: Offer merchandise Wal-Mart doesn't carry; offer better service and longer hours; cut prices; aim for more upscale shoppers.

In Steamboat Springs, though, as was likely true in many other towns, such nostrums didn't ease the sting of the smack in the face that his findings represented. Nancy Clapsaddle, the drugstore owner, had hoped that Stone's study would stiffen shopkeepers' resolve against Wal-Mart. But it had the opposite effect.

Ken Stratton, who owned the Ben Franklin store, said it made him feel he was seeing the writing on the wall. Maybe, he thought, he could survive by aiming at rich tourists. He decided to close the Ben Franklin and turn his building into a little mall of tourist-trap gift shops.

Roy Struble, who owned the Gamble store, decided to hang it up too. He'd been considering retiring in the next few years anyway. He loved the hardware business—had ever since he was a kid in Galesburg, Illinois, when his father had roamed through the region as a sales rep for Shapleigh Hardware, a St. Louis firm. But after forty years of running his own shop, Struble didn't feel like gearing up for a new fight.

First, he tried to sell his business; but he couldn't find a buyer on decent terms. The whole Gamble chain, based in Minneapolis, was ailing financially; and ever since the company had shuttered its Denver warehouse a few years earlier, Struble's goods had been shipped all the way from Minneapolis, making it tough to stay in stock. No one was interested. He decided just to close his doors and sell the building.

As for the court fight over the referendum, it finally ended in March 1991, when, after defeats at every level for the city, the Colorado Supreme Court refused to hear one last city appeal. The council set a town vote for June 11. By then, all four of the general stores in town had either closed or announced their plans to do so. Many of the other downtown shopkeepers had capitulated to what they now saw as the inevitable by dropping most of their sundries to stock souvenirs they hoped to foist on tourists.

Joan Hoffman, a local artist who'd worked against the Wal-Mart, had watched the shift with mounting unease. "Before the bulldozers ever hit the ground for Wal-Mart," she said later, "there really was no place left in town to buy cheap socks or clothing."

In the weeks leading up to the vote, Wal-Mart opponents seemed muted. Weiss, the ski corporation attorney, couldn't believe how quiet it was. But over the preceding two years, with Wal-Mart officially out of the picture and the court fight limping interminably along, the opposition had gradually, almost invisibly, deliquesced. Nancy Clapsaddle, for one, became exhausted with running a small business and trying to carry on a seemingly never-ending campaign at the same time. She couldn't keep the energy level up. Other leaders—St. Pierre, for example—moved on. Others, like Hoffman, had turned their attention to fighting off the ski corporation's Lake Catamount project.

"It just seemed to slip away," Clapsaddle would later say, sighing. "And it was such a relief just to let it slip."

Even so, Weiss couldn't let himself feel optimistic about the vote. The turnout for special elections was always pitiful; and surely opponents would be more motivated to make the effort to get to the polls. And then, just weeks before the vote, a rival developer suddenly began calling for building the Wal-Mart on the west side of town, saying it was more appropriate than at the base of the ski slope. The city council washed its hands of the matter by adding a second referendum question, asking voters whether, if they voted down the permit on the first referendum, they'd approve a Wal-Mart anywhere else in town.

The competing developer peppered the local papers with ads, and the ski corporation shelled out for counter-ads. But Wal-Mart stayed out of it. Weiss pleaded with Ownbey for Wal-Mart to run an ad asking people to vote for them, but Walton and the real estate committee in Bentonville wouldn't go for it. What if they ran such ads and then lost? They were just as nervous about the national implications as they had been back in 1989. Weiss kept pounding at them, but to get Bentonville's okay, the proposed ad had to be watered down and then watered down again. Finally, a week before the vote, Wal-Mart ran one full-page ad simply promising to start construction that summer if voters approved the store.

By mid-morning on June 11, at the high school (one of three polling places) it was clear that the turnout would be the highest of any special election in memory. The final tally was announced that night: 1,020 for Wal-Mart, 787 against. The city attorney, Ron Stock, jubilantly phoned Weiss with the results and offered to buy him a drink to celebrate.

Nancy Clapsaddle didn't feel the least bit surprised. "At least we kept them out for five years," she thought to herself. Almost immediately, she and her husband began planning how to change their business. They put in a soda fountain and a jukebox, and went from focusing on being a drugstore to offering greeting cards and party goods.

Julie Schwall—whose single vote might have changed the course of everything that happened—would say in later years that she wished she'd voted against Wal-Mart to begin with. Oh, they'd addressed her aesthetic concerns, and she still felt the company was entitled to its property rights. And yes, overall sales tax revenues to the city increased by hundreds of thousands of dollars. But over the coming years, she came to feel more and more strongly that her vote had opened the floodgates for the homogenizing tide of other corporate chains that soon washed over Steamboat, making it that much more like anywhere else, eroding its uniqueness. Later, she would try to persuade the council to ban permits for freestanding fast-food restaurants—such as McDonald's and Pizza Hut—but without success.

Years later, Nancy Clapsaddle, too, would look with regret at the ways Steamboat changed in the ensuing years. But she wouldn't fix the blame on Wal-Mart. The tourist boom, fanned ecstatically by city officials, had attracted the horde of chain restaurants and stores that corporatized the town; and that would have happened with or without Wal-Mart, she figured.

The most common reaction may have been that of Charla Palmer, the violin teacher who'd collected anti–Wal-Mart signatures with the inflatable dinosaur. Just after the vote, she'd thought ruefully that if only there hadn't been all the delays, they could have stopped Wal-Mart dead. But years later, when she shopped at Wal-Mart twice a week, Palmer would say that if she had it to do over, she wouldn't protest at all.

"I don't see any negative effects," she said. "Downtown is full and bustling—and in retrospect, this community needed a place to buy basic things like material to sew with." She would feel occasional pangs of guilt at spurning the few downtown shops that still carried sundries "because I know my money isn't going to a family I know." But, she would add, "I have to decide: Do I want to spend $3 more for something, or get it at Wal-Mart?"

Sometimes, she felt sorry for the Wal-Mart workers, all of whom were nice and friendly, but nearly none of whom seemed to live in town. Like the near-minimum-wage workers at the ski area and at the fast-food chains, many of the Wal-Mart workers couldn't afford to live in Steamboat, and drove in or rode the bus 42 miles every day from Craig, the nearest place with cheap housing. But such passing thoughts didn't keep Palmer from shopping at the place that offered the best prices in town. Like most people, she'd been well trained in the paramount importance of getting a bargain.

For Wal-Mart, the Steamboat store, which finally opened in late September 1992, would be one more smoothly spinning cog, growing consistently more profitable each passing year. More importantly, though, the Steamboat fight was one more episode that helped cement, by the late '80s, Walton and Seay's strategy of being as secretive as possible when trying to build a new store. Keeping negotiations quiet when buying land or leasing a site makes sense for any company, of course. It helps keep prices from getting inflated. But more and more, Wal-Mart was finding that as soon as word leaked out, it could expect troublemakers to spring up, stalling or blocking the permits, zoning changes, bonding approvals, and other concessions that it relied on to keep its costs down and its growth up.

In the long run, Wal-Mart's eventual victory in Steamboat would mean less to the company than would the reverberations from the battle—and especially from that moment in 1989 when Wal-Mart seemingly gave up. That year, a steady stream of articles in the national press echoed one theme, the flavor of which may be gleaned from this sampling of headlines: The *New York Times*—"When Wal-Mart Comes to Town: For Main Street Merchants, the Arrival of the Giant Discounter in Independence, Iowa, Was the Final Blow." *Newsweek*—"Just Saying No to Wal-Mart: Iowa City Fears for the Loss of Its Downtown." *U.S. News & World Report*—"How Wal-Mart Hits Main St.: Shopkeepers Find the Nation's No. 3 Retailer Tough to Beat." *St. Louis Post-Dispatch*—"Retail Wars: Wal-Mart Leaves Mark on Rural Merchants."

The *New York Times* article, by writer Jon Bowermaster, was typical, quoting the disheartened mayor of Independence, Iowa, over coffee at a diner on Main Street. "Wal-Mart threatened us," says Frank R. Brimmer. "They told us if they didn't build here, they'd build in a nearby town, and that would have been equally hard on Main Street. Our people were going to shop there whether it was in Independence or 25 miles away. You simply cannot beat Wal-Mart, so we joined them."

Later in the story, Bowermaster tells of speaking with Robert TeKippe, the owner of a Coast to Coast Total Hardware store who was doing everything he was supposed to—offering extra services, longer hours, goods Wal-Mart didn't carry—only to see his business fall off anyway. "The biggest difference now," a tired TeKippe told Bowermaster, "is that you've got to work so hard, so many hours, just to break even, to say nothing of making a buck."

Story by story, a new public image was being forged for Wal-Mart, despite the company's efforts to counter it through such gestures as having every store offer a $1,000 scholarship each year to a local college-bound high school student. The real knock-down-drag-outs over new stores were still few, compared with how many stores Wal-Mart was opening; but there was the slightest whiff on the breeze, like the faint suggestion of smoke that signals a distant forest fire.

The troubles were just beginning.

12

So Help Me Sam

On a breezy, cool March morning in 1984, Sam Walton, wearing a blue pin-striped suit, stood uncertainly in front of the offices of Merrill Lynch on Wall Street. David Glass, looking entirely too pleased with himself, helped Walton step into a grass skirt and fasten it around his waist. He handed his boss a sky-blue Hawaiian shirt splotched with purple flowers, which Walton, looking increasingly self-conscious, put on, followed by a couple of leis, and then a wreath of flowers, which perched like a crown on his balding pate.

Knots of curious bystanders stopped and stared. Three waiting hula dancers slipped off their coats and shoes and donned their flowered headdresses. Two ukulele players began strumming away.

Smiling weakly for the gathered television cameras and press photographers, the dancers swiveling away behind him, Walton awkwardly stuck his arms out and haltingly danced the hula down the street.

He had, after all, promised. Half a year earlier, he'd sworn to the workers that if Wal-Mart's pre-tax profits for the year reached 8 percent of sales (one percentage point higher than the company's record), he'd hula down Wall Street to celebrate.

This goofy image—one of America's richest men, arms akimbo, dancing about as gracelessly as any sixty-five-year-old corporate chairman might do—would become one of the defining images of the Sam Walton mythology. It would be replayed on videotape for all the workers in every Wal-Mart store. It would make the papers and the evening newscasts, of course; Walton himself would include a photo of his hula in his autobiography.

While it does seem to have been one of the rare occasions on which Walton actually was embarrassed by one of his own stunts (New York's financial district doubtless offering a less supportive environment for such a stunt than a Wal-Mart store thronged with company employees), he succeeded brilliantly at what he wanted to do: to "make our people feel part of a family in which no one is too important or too puffed up to lead a cheer or be the butt of a joke."[1]

Store openings, Saturday morning meetings, and other activities always included silly stunts by senior managers. Jack Shewmaker earlier had danced the hula at a Wal-Mart store; when the stock hit a new high in 1983, Glass too did the dance for employees at the company headquarters. One manager in Texas wrestled a bear; another, wearing pink tights and a blond wig, rode a white horse around the Bentonville town square. Groups of employees—truck drivers, accountants, store clerks—were encouraged to perform, at meetings, Wal-Mart songs and cheers they'd written. Store managers were exhorted to hold contests and silly events that got customers involved and that made being there fun for workers. One of Walton's favorite examples: a Moon Pie eating contest at an Alabama store that—at least in company lore—was concocted out of desperation as a way to unload thousands of extra snack-food items a manager had ordered by accident.

Jana Jae, a country fiddler from Tulsa, remembers her first gig, entertaining at a manager's meeting at a lodge in Lake Fort Gibson, Oklahoma, in the late '70s. Walton had brought his favorite hound dog with him. "When I started playing, Ol' Roy, who was laying at Sam's feet, woke up and started walking to the front of the stage. Now I didn't know this, but he had a reputation for decorating the hallways, so all the managers watched to see what he'd do. He got right up to the mike, turned up his head, and started howling." As the managers roared, Jae bent to the microphone and said, "I don't know who owns this dog, but if he likes our music well enough to sing with us then his owner ought to come up and sing too."

Walton demurred at that offer, but Jae wound up performing at hundreds of Wal-Mart events and got to watch him in action time and again. "He would do whatever it took to get people's attention," she remembers. "He'd interrupt people constantly." If a manager's report started to get eye-glazing, Walton would break in to make sure people heard the important points. "He'd say, 'What do you mean $500 million? Can we do better than that? You think we could double that figure?' " Jae said.

To Walton, all this was a way of keeping workers in the increasingly far-flung empire interested and involved. As he said in his autobiography, discussing the Saturday morning meetings, "Without a little entertainment and a sense of the unpredictable, how in the world could we ever have gotten those hundreds of people—most of our managers and some associates from the general offices here in Bentonville—to get up every Saturday morning and actually come in here with smiles on their faces? If they knew all they could expect in that meeting was somebody droning on about comparative numbers, followed by a serious lecture on the problems of our business, could we have kept the meeting alive? No way. No matter how strongly I felt about the necessity of that meeting, the folks would have revolted, and even if we still held it, it wouldn't be any good at all."[2]

Wal-Mart's biggest and most spectacular event every year, and the foremost celebration of its corporate culture, was the annual meeting. The actual business of the meeting—votes on new directors or proxy matters, the financial review—seemed all but incidental to the giant pep rally for the troops that was the real focus of the day. Wal-Mart still flew in the analysts and held a weekend full of events for them, such as a picnic lunch at the Walton's home* and a canoe float down the Sugar River (a flier for which promises a taste of Alice Walton's "Ozark-Cajun 'Bone-Mending' River Stew" and is illustrated with a drawing of a woman, presumably Alice, clad in overalls and a tattered straw hat, smoking a corncob pipe, and stirring a giant pot full of dead snakes and chickens).

But the company not only invited employees to come to the annual meetings, it began hauling them in by bus for the event. By 1984, the only place in town big enough to accommodate the 1,800 people who showed up was the Bentonville High gym. Before a stage buffed out with enough red-white-and-blue bunting for a political convention, Walton joined the crowd in kicking things off by singing "The Star-Spangled Banner." He spent much of the morning giving awards to various stores, managers, and employees; and urged everyone to buy more Wal-Mart stock. At the Saturday manager's meeting the next day, guests included Govenor Bill Clinton of Arkansas, and four members of Congress, including Representative Jack Kemp of New York.

"It's not really a corporate stockholders' meeting, is it?" Walton asked

---

*To which many employees were invited, too.

the crowd at the 1985 meeting. "It's a happening—it's a revival." Wearing a blue T-shirt emblazoned with a giant numeral "1" and the words GO FOR IT! over his white dress shirt and tie, Walton worked the crowd for more than an hour before the meeting formally started. As always, he had other executives get up to talk, especially Jack Shewmaker, David Glass, and Rob Walton, for whom this seemed to be a form of training; but it was indisputably Sam Walton's show. And it was a show. Every year the company seemed to bring in more celebrities to enthrall the multitudes. That year, country music singer Chet Atkins and NBA and former Arkansas Razorbacks stars Sidney Moncrief and Darrel Walker were among the guests, the latter pair bemusedly playing along with Walton's suggestion they face off in a pickup basketball game against Glass and Shewmaker. Other years would bring a succession of Miss U.S.A.s and scores of stars and performers from Joe DiMaggio to Reba McEntire, with the bill for each celebrity usually footed by Wal-Mart's suppliers. Employees, too, would compete in talent contests in the months beforehand for a chance to perform at the meeting—inevitably singing popular songs rewritten to be about Wal-Mart.

By 1987, to find enough room for the 6,000 shareholders who came that year, Wal-Mart had to move the meeting out of Bentonville to the University of Arkansas's Barnhill Arena in Fayetteville. Announcing a stock split at the meeting, Jack Shewmaker told the story of the widow of a Vietnam vet who that year had been cleaning out her closet when she found 200 shares of Wal-Mart stock her husband had bought in 1970. With stock splits, Shewmaker told the crowd, including the one just announced, the woman now would have 40,000 shares worth more than $1 million.* That kind of stock performance, of course, helped explain the enthusiasm of the crowds at these meetings, but only in part. The vital spark came from the energetic Walton, greeted that year as usual with a standing ovation. The workers brought into Barnhill for the meeting—even those who hadn't met him in person before—*knew* Mr. Sam. When he asked them to cheer, to stand up and sing, to help the company pass Kmart to become the biggest discount chain, they cheered and stamped and hollered with an enthusiasm stunning to analysts or institutional shareholders who hadn't been to a Wal-Mart meeting before. "Sam Walton may have a million dollars, but he has a million volts of electricity too," declared one young worker brought in from

---

* Actually, Shewmaker understated the stock performance. Someone holding 200 shares from the time the company went public in 1970 would have had, by June 1987, a total of 51,200 shares worth $1.7 million.

an Orlando, Florida, Wal-Mart store for the 1987 meeting."[3] Like hundreds
of others, he was elected by the workers at his store to represent them. *

Walton was confident enough to do something increasingly rare at other
corporate meetings: take unscripted, unscreened questions from the
crowd. When a woman shareholder that year stood up and said Wal-Mart
should "quit tearing down the trees" to build its stores and parking lots and
added, to cheers from the crowd, that the company should "beautify our
parking areas," Walton apologized and said, "We have been careless about
that," and promised to improve the particular store the woman complained
about. Such promises didn't always result in action (as shareholders who
asked the company to appoint more women officers could attest), but Walton rarely if ever left a questioner unmollified.

Once the satellite system was up and running, the annual meetings
were broadcast to all the stores, too. Every year, the production got more
involved, the meeting longer, the flag-waving more intense. In 1989, the
meeting began with videos of patriotic scenes played on three giant screens
as 7,000 people recited the pledge of allegiance; then, as the lights came
up, a prayer followed, led by Walton at the edge of the stage, down on one
knee, head bowed, and Wal-Mart baseball cap in hand. By Walton's last annual meeting in 1991, people were arriving before 7 A.M. for a meeting that
would last until noon.

All the motivating was critical, because if you wanted to succeed at Wal-
Mart, it swallowed your life. A typical assistant store manager in Oklahoma,
who felt his 52-hour workweek was modest for the company, said, "We
have to work long hours if we want to move up to manager. When you're
salaried, you have to pay the toll." Other assistant managers said they
worked 60 and 70 hours a week. "You could count on working a seven-day
week at least once a month, and of course that could go right into the next
week's work," said one man who found the pace too stiff and quit.[4]

Even ordinary hourly workers—officially exhorted never to put in time
off the clock—had myriad obligations and Wal-Mart activities they were
forcefully "encouraged" to volunteer for. And, of course, the pay was still
measly—enough so that, in 1988, Arkansas state senator Jay Bradford attacked Wal-Mart for "dumping their overhead" on state taxpayers, saying

---

* Most workers were brought in by bus or, in the case of more distant stores, by plane. Other workers
were told to carpool, driving their own cars. Wal-Mart paid them for gas, but gave no mileage al-
lowance.

many of the retailer's part-time, near-minimum-wage workers made so little money, they had to get by on public assistance. His effort to open company payroll records to inspection to prove his argument fizzled, though.

Regardless, Wal-Mart's paterfamilias knew that for workers to keep putting in long hours at modest pay, they had to feel they had a stake, that they were valued. He knew how important it was to workers to feel a personal connection to him; so he always wore the same plastic name tag as all the store clerks, with *SAM* spelled out in capital letters. In headquarters, with his executives, Walton could be—and was—tough, blunt, and demanding. But on store visits, he was attentive and avuncular, getting hourly workers away from their managers to get their feedback.

"He was a master at getting people to talk," said Jae. "He'd gather everybody together, grab a bag of peanuts, and go into the back of the store. Or at Sam's Clubs, he'd go in front, have everybody sit on the floor, and get down on one knee to talk to them. He'd get down on your level. He'd make them talk about *their* ideas. He'd look at a person and talk to that person, and the rest of the world would disappear. He'd do whatever it took to draw you out."

And so, he continued visiting stores, shaking hands and looking people in the eye, trying to memorize people's names—even when there were far too many stores for him to get to all of them. And he wrote folksy and personal letters in the company newsletter, *Wal-Mart World;* just as, once he started appearing on the satellite system, he talked to workers as if he was sitting with them chatting in their living rooms.

He had to work harder at it as the number of employees swelled ever higher. And, of course, it became that much tougher to seem like old ordinary Sam when it became obvious to everyone, courtesy of *Forbes* magazine, that he was rich as a Rockefeller. Richer, actually.

When *Forbes* published its first list of the 400 richest Americans in 1982, it estimated Walton's fortune at $690 million, placing him seventeenth on its list. Though *Forbes* had erred considerably on the low side, Walton was sore as a gumboil at being named at all—complaining, like many others on the list, that it would bring unwanted attention. Not that his ire made any difference. The next year—reflecting both better research by *Forbes* and the high-flying price of Wal-Mart stock in a raging bull market*—he'd vaulted to second place, his estimated $2.15 billion placing him just behind Gordon Peter Getty, an amateur composer and the son and sole

---

* Between the start of a bull market in August 1982 and early October 1983, when Forbes published its second list, Wal-Mart stock rose 212 percent.

heir of oilman Jean Paul Getty. In 1984, Walton ranked second to Getty again, this time with $2.3 billion.

But then the Gettys sold their oil company, and the great fortune was broken up to settle legal claims by other Getty family members—and so in 1985, with an estimated $2.8 billion, Sam Walton was officially crowned, by *Forbes*, the richest man in the country.

The announcement abruptly focused frenzied and at times bizarre attention on him. Scores of reporters, photographers, and television crews clamored for interviews. Walton refused to give any, which, of course, only added to his allure. *People* magazine featured him as a sort of magnate of the week. The *New York Post* ran a huge photograph of him getting his usual $5 haircut at John Mayhall's barbershop in downtown Bentonville, eagerly noting in an accompanying story that Walton never left a tip. "America's Richest Nobody," the *San Francisco Chronicle* called him, in a typical take on the subject.

He wasn't at all comfortable acknowledging his wealth. He only very reluctantly agreed to increasingly pointed suggestions from other executives and Wal-Mart's security staff that he have an alarm system installed in his house. Same with putting a telephone in his truck, for security reasons—though he then always left it turned off. If anything, though, his great wealth only seemed to add to his luster in the eyes of Wal-Mart workers. Many took to asking him to autograph dollar bills on his store visits; and, though it bothered him, he smiled and signed them anyway.

It may have been just as well for Walton's aw-shucks image that he didn't give interviews then; discussing this period in his later autobiography, he lashes out at the media "scavengers" and moans bathetically about all the people who called and wrote asking for money—a complaint that might draw empathy from an H. Ross Perot or Bill Gates, but probably not from most other folks. *Forbes* answered beefing by the billionaires it listed, Walton included, by suggesting an easy way off the list: Give your money away. It described tycoons who'd done just that—including chain-store heir Stanley S. Kresge, who as early as 1924 had poured tens of millions into his Kresge Foundation and who, when he died in 1966, left nearly 20 times as much to charity as to his heirs. His son Stanley Kresge, a trustee of the foundation, told the magazine: "There's no adverse feeling. He did what he wanted to do, and we were provided for fairly reasonably."[5]

Given how Sam Walton had structured his family's holdings, there was no risk of his children settling for a mere few million bucks apiece. Not that, in any event, he was keen on giving money away, his own or the company's. He would later say, "Wal-Mart really is not, and should not be, in the charity business."[6] Still, pressed by Helen Walton, in 1981 he established the Wal-Mart Foundation to manage the company's donations; that year, it gave out a whopping $64,700 to charities, or about .1 percent of the company's 1981 net income. By 1987, he boosted the foundation's giving to $4.3 million for the year. This still left Wal-Mart dead last among major retailers, by the usual measure of generosity: the percentage of its earnings a company donates to charity. The company's stinginess was remarkable. That year Wal-Mart gave away .4 percent of its earnings. The average for all U.S. corporations was two and a half times higher, at just over 1 percent. Kmart gave 1.5 percent; Sears, 2.4 percent; and Dayton-Hudson, which ran the Target discount chain, 3.8 percent of its earnings—better than nine times as much as Wal-Mart.

But, in his usual way, Sam Walton got a lot of bang for his nickel. He got tremendous publicity out of having each store give away a $1,000 scholarship to a local high school senior each year. That was the advantage of being in all those small towns: Wal-Mart's donations were compared not with those of other giant corporations, but with those of mom-and-pop local businesses. Walton encouraged workers to raise money through bake sales, car washes, pancake breakfasts, and other drives in the stores, for which the company foundation would put up matching grants, to a limit. This got workers involved, made the drives highly visible to customers, helped counter criticism that the company's giant stores were hurting small towns, and cost Wal-Mart far less than if it just made corporate donations on its own.

By any standards—except, perhaps, those of economist Milton Friedman—getting workers involved in charitable activities is a wonderful idea; and had the company backed up its exhortations with as muscular a program of corporate giving as, say, Dayton-Hudson, the impact could have been powerful. But at Wal-Mart, relying on the philanthropy of workers and customers was just another way to keep costs down without looking miserly.

Walton never hesitated to have Wal-Mart grab credit for its purported generosity—even if that meant shamelessly taking kudos for the donations of others. The classic example of this came in the aftermath of Hurricane Hugo, which devastated the Carolinas in 1989. Wal-Mart trumpeted itself as giving $1.1 million worth of goods to the victims of the disaster and won national acclaim on TV newscasts and in newspapers for its generosity. In fact, that $1.1-million figure reflected the retail price of the goods, not the considerably lower cost Wal-Mart would have paid. But in any event, many of the goods, perhaps even most, were donated not by the company, but by

various manufacturers. Wal-Mart simply used its trucks to ship the donations and then took credit for them. Many of the vendors were understandably irked—but who wanted to risk losing their biggest account by
saying anything to reporters? Even years later, Wal-Mart executives refused
to say what percentage of the donations came from vendors. But Wal-
Mart—and Sam Walton—got terrific press out of the ploy, which seems to
have been the point.

To be sure, many truck drivers and other volunteers from Wal-Mart
worked as tirelessly as mules during the relief effort—people such as Martin Novak, the head of the company's Douglas, Georgia, distribution center,
who took charge of coordinating the flow of relief supplies into Charleston,
South Carolina. Workers in hundreds of stores helped raise money for relief. But, then, there were plenty of other volunteers in the Carolinas from
Target, Kmart, Homelite, and Brendle's (two local outfits), and many other
companies, too.

Wal-Mart executives did hear the rumblings of resentment from their
vendors. When the company helped provide relief after Hurricane Andrew
hit Florida in 1992, it publicly credited its vendors with being involved in
the effort though, again, Wal-Mart wouldn't say how much it actually contributed.

As for Sam Walton himself, what moved his spirit of charity was his wife's
sharp elbow. In 1985, Helen persuaded him to donate $3.6 million for
scholarships to three small Arkansas colleges for students from Central
America. She was behind donations that helped build a fine arts center and
a gym at two of those same colleges. And, again under Helen's relentless
prodding, Sam Walton established the Walton Foundation and two other
foundations, to make other charitable contributions, such as tennis courts
for Bentonville High School and funds for the local offices of Planned Par-
enthood. Helen Walton's charitable inclinations also led her, in 1989, to be
elected to the board of trustees for the Presbyterian Church (USA) Foundation; she later gave that foundation $6 million.

But Sam Walton's own Depression-era frugality didn't change. When
he did allow himself splurges—holding a family meeting at some fancy resort hotel, for example—it was out of sight of people from Bentonville or
Wal-Mart. And he always wanted to go someplace he could visit stores. In
1985, after agreeing to go with Helen and the grandchildren on a cruise to
Alaska, Sam Walton drove them all crazy with his frustrated prowling because he couldn't get off the ship.

In town, the Waltons preferred to keep a low profile. Take their home: Walton certainly could have afforded something as grand as William Randolph Hearst's San Simeon, but that wasn't his style.

Back in 1958, mostly at Helen's instigation, Sam had agreed to hire an architect to build the family a nice home. They bought a 20-acre lot in a wooded area on the east end of town and hired a young architecture professor from the University of Arkansas, E. Fay Jones, who had been a student of Frank Lloyd Wright's.

Jones dammed a small stream that burbled through the property to create a reflecting pond and a 14-foot waterfall and then designed a 5,800-square-foot house, made of Arkansas fieldstone, glass, and cedar beams, that bordered the pond and waterfall, with a wing bridging the stream. The design, long and low, was elegant but unobtrusive. Jones remembers worrying that what he'd designed might be out of the couple's reach; but Helen's money paid for most of the $100,000 cost.*

That house burned down one night in April 1972, struck by a bolt of lightning during a spring storm. The Waltons, blasted out of bed by the boom, escaped unscathed, but most of the house was consumed before firemen could put out the blaze. Helen Walton called on Jones again. This time, with all the children grown and living away from home (Alice was in her senior year of college), she had him redesign and enlarge the house for entertaining. "It had the same basic outlines," Jones said, "but they could afford nicer materials" not to mention central air-conditioning, an extravagance Sam Walton hadn't seen the need to spring for, the first time.†

As she had with the original house, Helen Walton took charge of working with Jones on the redesign. Sam Walton sat in occasionally. Mostly, as Jones recalls, "Sam would say, 'Now Helen, do we really have to do this?' and she'd say, 'Yes, Sam, we do.'"

While the home was being built, the Waltons lived in a double-wide mobile home on the property. Later, their son Rob built a house about 100 yards away, a bit uphill of his parent's homestead. Rob also bought a $1.5-million home in Aspen, Colorado.

Of all the Walton children, only John, the second-oldest and most independent, seemed to have left Bentonville for good. He had turned his crop-dusting into a substantial business, funded and owned by Walton

---

* The equivalent of about $556,000 in 1998 dollars.

† One person mightily impressed by the house was David Glass, who in 1996 hired Jones to design a nearly 9,000-square-foot stone and stucco home in Bentonville. Less low-key than the Walton home, Glass's palace included a fountain, pool, and extensive outdoor terraces on the property. Jones also designed a home in Fayetteville for Alice Walton.

Enterprises, the family holding company. After briefly moving to Casa Grande, Arizona, where his crop-dusting business was headquartered, he remarried. In 1984, he put the business in the hands of a manager and moved with his new wife to San Diego. She soon gave birth to a boy, whom they named Luke. John Walton teamed up with an Australian boatwright to found another company, Corsair Marine, that built trimarans, sailboats with two additional hulls on outriggers. Corsair Marine's trimarans featured retractable outer hulls, letting the boats dock in a standard berth and even be hauled on trailers.

Back in Bentonville, Jim Walton, still running Walton Enterprises, also took charge of the family's Walton Foundation, Sam Walton's vehicle for giving tax-deductible donations. Jim had married too, in the fall of 1978. His wife, Lynne McNabb, who'd spent several years working in New York as an editor at a publishing house, opened a bookstore in Bentonville. By 1987, they'd settled down to as peaceful an existence as a couple could have with four children. Jim Walton had a house built on the same creek that meandered through his parents' property, just a few blocks away.

Alice Walton, too, got married, in 1974, two months before her twenty-fifth birthday, to Laurance Eustis III, a handsome young investment banker from New Orleans. She opted to hold a small wedding ceremony and reception in Sam and Helen's rebuilt home. The Eustises settled down in New Orleans, and not long after, Alice left Jim Jones's bank to become an account executive at E.F. Hutton, one of few female brokers in a testosterone-driven business.

And here she entered a series of tribulations. By early 1977, she and Eustis formally separated; within a year, they were granted a no-fault divorce. Though both kept mum about why they split up, friends of Alice Walton point to a basic incompatibility. Alice, maybe more than any of the other children, took after her father, Sam: She was smart, tough, hard-headed, incredibly ambitious, and often cold—and she hadn't yet developed her father's folksy patina. "Eustis was a nice guy," said one close friend of Alice's, "but he just couldn't cope with her."

Alice Walton remarried almost immediately, this time to Hall Moorehead, a contractor she met while he was building a swimming pool at her home. This pairing turned out even less suitably, and friends say her new marriage was in trouble before the end of the year. At the same time, she was heading toward a rocky headland at E.F. Hutton.

The late '70s were lean years for most brokerage houses—part of a sixteen-year trough between the great bull market of the '60s and the even greater bull market that would begin in 1982. Investors were looking elsewhere. Stock equity funds were shrinking, and so were brokers' commissions. It was in this climate that Alice developed an aggressive trading program in stock options* with another E.F. Hutton account executive, Donald LoCoco. It was a high-risk strategy that produced fat commissions for her, LoCoco, and E.F. Hutton; and it was a strategy many other commission-starved brokerage houses were diving into, too. But when turns in the market led to heavy losses, and complaints from clients began to mount, the Securities and Exchange Commission decided to investigate the brokers pushing these trading programs.

E.F. Hutton was the third brokerage house the SEC trained its sights on for making what it called "unsuitable" trades. In early 1979, the commission accused Alice, LoCoco, and ten other E.F. Hutton employees in eight cities of violating antifraud provisions of securities laws in connection with their options trades. According to the charges, trades that she and Lo-Coco made had netted the pair about $129,000 in commissions, while costing customers $197,000 in losses. The SEC staff said the two, along with others at the brokerage, made false and misleading statements, didn't fully disclose how risky the strategies were, and illegally used trading strategies unsuited to the "financial situations, investment sophistication and investment objectives" of some of their clients.

The firm and most of those accused—Alice Walton included—agreed to settle the charges without admitting or denying them. She would later deny the charges and say she settled only to avoid a drawn-out legal fight. Ten years later, when she applied to register an investment firm of her own with the SEC, she claimed on the form that all the investors who complained had been solicited by LoCoco and that "if these persons were misinformed as to the guidelines and objectives of the program it was the fault of Mr. LoCoco," not Alice Walton. The SEC staff, though, seem to have felt that she was no innocent bystander. As part of the settlement, she was suspended for six months from holding any job with a broker, dealer, investment company, investment advisor, or affiliate; LoCoco was suspended for two months. No other E.F. Hutton employee in the settlement drew a suspension longer than three months.

Walton left the firm. She got divorced again, and moved back to Arkansas. Then came her accident in Acapulco.

Alice, like both of her parents and her brother Rob, had a reputation as a fast driver. The Walton's leaden feet had long been a popular topic of banter in Bentonville. Helen's pastor, the Reverend Gordon Garlington, joked

---

\u option is the right to buy or sell a security at a certain price by a certain date.

that Helen's silver Lincoln Continental should be nicknamed the Silver Bullet. One year, Sam and Helen gave each other police radar detectors for Christmas. Sam Walton himself constantly speeded, relying on his sharp eyesight and quick reflexes to stay out of trouble—not always successfully. He once rear-ended one of his own company trucks while driving to Springdale, an incident his executives ribbed him about more than once. In 1983, when Bentonville city leaders decided to throw an "appreciation day" for Sam and Helen Walton—what with Wal-Mart being the town's biggest employer and all—some of the Wal-Mart managers stuck a float in the parade that consisted of a Wal-Mart semi with a wrecked junker attached to its rear end and a policeman sauntering along behind it. Helen, in particular, seemed greatly amused.

That same year, the Waltons decided to hold their regular family meeting—to discuss Walton Enterprises investments and so on—at a beach resort near Acapulco, over the Thanksgiving holiday. One day, while the rest of the family relaxed, Alice rented a Jeep and roared up a narrow, winding road through the mountains above the town. Somehow, she lost control on a curve and plunged into a ravine, shattering one leg. After emergency treatment at a hospital in Acapulco, she was flown back to the United States. Unfortunately, she picked up a virulent infection in the bone—and underwent more than two dozen operations as doctors tried to control it. She spent more than a year convalescing, and the injury would leave her with apparently permanent recurring pain.

During the mid-'80s, Alice Walton managed the investments of the family's six Arkansas banks. She opened discount brokerage operations at three of the banks and took charge of investing $180 million in trust money.

Then in 1988, with $19.5 million from Walton Enterprises and $5 million out of her own pocket, she opened her own investment firm in Fayetteville, Arkansas, about 20 miles from the 900-acre horse farm she'd settled in near the small town of Lowell. She named her firm Llama Company, after a pet llama she'd bought. "He cost more than I wanted—now he's on our letterhead, I can write him off," she joked.[7] She said the firm would underwrite bonds, mostly for small to mid-sized Arkansas businesses, and would manage investments for pension funds and banks.

The company would do well. But early one beautiful misty morning in April of 1989, speeding down the highway in her 1987 Porsche on her way from the farm to work, Alice Walton slammed into a woman trying to cross the road, killing her instantly. Fifty-year-old Oleta Hardin, mother of two fully grown sons, had been waiting for a ride to her job at a nearby canning factory when she decided to step down off her porch out onto the edge of the road to watch for her friend, who was running late.

Neither she nor Alice Walton saw each other until too late. Hardin was carried up onto the hood of the car, her head smashing through the windshield before her body was thrown off as the Porsche skidded to a stop.

Hysterical, spattered with blood and shards of glass, Alice Walton ran back to the body, but there was nothing to be done. Walton was treated for shock and very minor injuries. Oleta Hardin's husband, Harold, who worked the night shift at a nearby tool plant, arrived home from work barely an hour later to find a policeman waiting on his front porch with the terrible news. He was still in shock when Alice showed up a little later that day and tried as best she could, stumblingly, to apologize to him.

Though Alice Walton had been speeding—and had been ticketed twice for speeding in the previous year—the police decided not to file any charges. Witnesses said she couldn't have avoided hitting the woman, as police explained to Harold Hardin. He accepted their explanation. "It wasn't her [Alice's] fault," Hardin said later. "Oleta stepped on the road in front of her too close for her to stop."

Other than a payment from Alice Walton's auto insurer, Hardin said he was offered no compensation by the Waltons and didn't ask for any.°

As part of that same appreciation day at which Sam Walton had been teased about his driving, the town renamed one of its main thoroughfares Walton Boulevard, named a junior high school for Sam, and dubbed a day care center for Helen. It was a sign of Sam Walton's growing importance that, even though he was far from being a major campaign contributor to any party,† the dignitaries who showed up to honor him at a banquet that night included Governor Clinton, Senator Dale Bumpers, and, on videotape, Vice President George Bush. President Reagan telephoned his congratulations, which were broadcast on huge loudspeakers.

To mark the occasion, the local newspaper, the *Benton County Democrat*, issued a special edition lionizing Walton—who happened to be its

---

° Writer Vance Trimble, in his 1991 biography of Sam Walton, quotes Hardin as blaming Alice for the accident, saying that if she had been watching, she could have stopped. Trimble also quotes Hardin as saying Walton's lawyers offered him $2,500 for funeral expenses and that he hired a lawyer to get an undisclosed, presumably larger amount in an out-of-court settlement. Interviewed in 1997, though, Hardin said he never blamed Alice Walton, wasn't offered money, and never demanded any.

† Sen. Dale Bumpers of Arkansas once said that waiting for political contributions from the Waltons was like leaving the landing lights on for Amelia Earhart.

owner. He'd bought the paper in 1972, later turning it over to his son Jim to manage as another asset of the family holding company.

But Walton was lionized in plenty of other places. Mind you, a lot of the coverage was hampered by the fact that almost nobody could get an interview with him. But the articles continued, all the same, focusing on those tidbits of his public persona—how he drove an old truck and so on—that reinforced Walton's down-home image. The fascinating thing about the coverage was that—just as with Walton's hula on Wall Street—it showed how Walton had developed a genius for making even the seemingly hokey and ordinary work to his ends in ways that weren't always obvious.

Take the company's greeters, those aggressively friendly and often superannuated workers who stand at the entrance to every Wal-Mart store, saying hello to customers as they come in and asking if they need help finding something. By company lore, a store manager in Crowley, Louisiana, first came up with the idea. When Sam Walton visited the store in 1980, he was so enchanted with the notion that he decreed that all the stores should have greeters, because it sent such a warm, friendly message to shoppers. All this was essentially true. But—as shouldn't be surprising—there was a more bottom-line reason Walton loved the idea: The Crowley store had a major shoplifting problem; and the greeter kept an eye on people leaving to make sure they weren't walking out with anything they hadn't paid for. Dan McAllister, the manager, had figured it would be less jarring to customers to be greeted by an old codger than by, say, a uniformed guard.

That was what Walton loved about the idea: It cut down shoplifting. The warm-and-fuzzy image boost was just gravy. Not everyone grasped the beauty of the idea as quickly as Walton had. Many of his executives, and many store managers, considered using greeters stupid and wasteful, and resisted using them. By the end of the '80s, though, half a dozen other chains would adopt them too—including, at Joe Antonini's insistence, Kmart.

One of Walton's greatest public relations triumphs was his "Buy American" program. Accounts vary on where this idea sprang from. In his autobiography, Walton simply says he came up with it out of concern with the soaring trade deficit. But several board members remember him coming back in an uncharacteristically somber mood from a vacation he'd taken to Central America in 1984, with Helen. As usual, while she'd gone sightseeing, he had decided to visit factories that made goods for various U.S. retailers. He found the working conditions appalling—especially by contrast with the U.S. factories he'd visited. What specific factories Walton visited isn't clear; but it isn't hard to guess what he probably saw: sweatshops straight out of the nineteenth century. Other accounts[8] of working conditions in the Central American garment industry at the time describe typical factories as crowded, hot and dusty, poorly lit and poorly ventilated, often full of child workers putting in 12- and 14-hour days, paid so little many couldn't afford shoes.

When he came back to Bentonville, Walton started asking his executives whether there wasn't some way to have more of the company's goods made at home, in the United States. Not long afterward, Walton got a phone call from Governor Clinton. The two men knew each other fairly well. Though Walton was a Republican and not much of a political donor, he was also the state's richest man and largest employer; and Clinton had courted his support on various economic development schemes. Clinton also had been a guest speaker and glad-hander at several of Wal-Mart's annual meetings; and his wife, Hillary Rodham Clinton, had become friendly with both Helen and Alice Walton.

On this occasion, Clinton asked Walton if he could do anything to help rescue Farris Fashions Inc., an Arkansas clothing company. It teetered on the verge of closing, after losing contracts to make flannel shirts for Phillips–Van Heusen, which had opted to switch to a cheaper factory in China. Walton agreed to give it a shot. In several talks, he and the company's president, Farris Burroughs, knocked out a deal: Walton guaranteed to place a big order for flannel shirts and to pay Farris faster than usual; Farris, after failing to find a domestic supplier, agreed to cut costs by importing the flannel (a detail that would be left unmentioned in later press reports). To great local acclaim, Wal-Mart signed the first of several contracts with the company that not only kept its doors from closing, but eventually let it add enough capacity to grow from 90 employees to 350.

Clinton effusively praised Walton and Wal-Mart as patriots. Farris's managers, too, sang paeans with gusto. According to company lore, Walton, still talking about the growing U.S. trade deficit and how more and more goods once made by Americans were being imported, charged several executives with developing a Buy American program. In March of 1985, Walton announced his plan in a letter to 3,000 U.S. companies that sold goods to Wal-Mart.

In his letter—excerpted in press releases with which the company blanketed the media—Walton noted that between 1981 and 1984 more than 1.6 million American jobs were lost to imports, and that in 1983, imports (not including oil) had grown by a third to $70 billion, accounting for much of a record trade deficit of $123.3 billion. "Something can and must be done to reverse this very serious threat to our free enterprise system and our great country," Walton wrote. "Our Wal-Mart Company is firmly committed to the philosophy of buying everything possible from suppliers who manufacture their products in the United States."

Walton offered to give suppliers and manufacturers "the same advantages we are providing overseas vendors," such as longer lead time on orders; and he invited any interested companies to get in touch. As one might expect, the announcement that Wal-Mart would "Buy American" whenever possible drew avid praise from politicians, the press, and plenty of ordinary folks. Soon Walton called on other retailers to join in, too. His timing was impeccable. As so often with Walton, he seemed intuitively to have sensed, ahead of his competitors, a shift in the wind.

First, the background: Studies estimated that, in 1985, 43 percent of all apparel sold was imported. Hundreds of U.S. manufacturers had been moving production overseas, especially to Asia, the Caribbean, and Central America. In the case of the latter two regions, U.S. companies were getting active encouragement and financial help to go abroad from the U.S. State Department's Agency for International Development. Back in 1961, President John F. Kennedy had launched a massive economic development program for Latin America, called the Alliance for Progress. The idea had been to encourage democracy and fight Communism by raising the standards of living; but as it worked out, most of the effort, channeled through AID, focused on developing export industries and encouraging U.S. businesses to invest in Latin America. Several countries created free-trade zones where factories could locate. Then, in 1983, at the behest of President Reagan, Congress adopted the Caribbean Basin Initiative, a law that let the president exempt from tariffs many goods—including apparel—imported from Caribbean and Central American countries. The result had been a boomlet in U.S. manufacturers' moving production into these countries.

By 1985, a backlash was building. Unions were agitating in Washington, demanding something be done to stem the flow of jobs overseas. Polls showed many Americans were worried about foreign competition—and about their jobs. Congress was debating restricting imports. And meanwhile, most retailers and retail-trade groups were publicly trying to protect cheap imports and fighting on Capitol Hill to block any restrictions.

So, after Walton's Buy American announcement, when reporters approached Kmart and Target, executives at both companies said, in effect, that the lowest cost was their only consideration. A few other retailers, because of the debate on the Hill, were even silly enough to attack Walton by claiming that buying American would drive up costs for consumers. Predictably—and deservedly—they looked greedy, while Walton might as well have been wrapped in the Stars and Stripes. The *Washington Post* illustrated its story on the Buy American program with a drawing of Sam Walton as a bald eagle, wings spread to protect his nest. The *New York Times* lauded him as a man swimming against the tide.

Walton made the Buy American theme a centerpiece of the company's raucous annual meetings, featuring examples of products brought back from overseas and testimonials from factory workers and politicians. By early 1986, Wal-Mart was running national television commercials on the Buy American theme; and all of its stores had red-white-and-blue "Made in the USA" banners that read KEEP AMERICA WORKING AND STRONG. People loved it; polls showed Wal-Mart to be one of the most respected companies in the country.

But if one looked more closely, a far more complicated picture emerged. From the beginning, like other discounters, Walton had bought goods wherever he could get them cheapest, with any other considerations secondary. Following the usual pattern, he'd added name brands when he could and eventually had looked for higher-quality goods, too. Where they were made was irrelevant; and so, along with other discounters, Walton had increasingly looked to imports, which were usually cheaper because factory workers were paid so much less in China and the other Asian countries that were the biggest sources of imports. In fact, because getting the lowest price was so important to Walton, he'd been particularly aggressive about looking overseas. By 1981, Wal-Mart opened an office in Hong Kong to buy and order goods, and then quickly added a second office in Taipei, Taiwan.

Of course, *direct* imports by Wal-Mart and other discounters only made up a small share of all the goods sold; Walton, for instance, estimated that Wal-Mart's direct imports accounted for 5.8 percent of its total sales at the time he launched the Buy American program. The bulk of the importing was done by the manufacturers that sold goods to Wal-Mart and other retailers. That was the other part of the picture: As the discount industry grew bigger and bigger, and the price competition grew fiercer, makers of clothing, toys, shoes, and other goods came under increasing pressure to cut costs. Even the middle tier of retailers—companies such as Penney and Sears—pushed for lower costs, so they could compete more effectively with the discounters.

It was to meet those demands that many suppliers opted to shift production from the United States to wherever labor costs were cheaper. That was what had happened to Farris: Phillips–Van Heusen moved production overseas to meet demands from Sears and Penney for lower prices. It happened in dozens of industries. In the textile industry alone, more than 250 domestic factories closed between 1980 and 1985.

China became a favorite import source after 1981, when the Chinese government began subsidizing exports to help its textile and apparel industries grow. In 1983, when U.S. textile and apparel factories were demanding that the Commerce Department slap higher duties on those subsidized goods, executives from Wal-Mart flew to Washington to testify in China's favor.

The irony was that contracting with factories scattered around the Third World created all sorts of new problems. Because of the shipping distances involved and other complications, retailers had to place their orders much sooner, often as much as year in advance. Retailers had to pay sooner, too. Typically, retailers wouldn't pay U.S. manufacturers until 30 days after an order was shipped; but they had to pay overseas producers immediately on shipment, and sometimes before shipment. Because of the time and distances, retailers tended not to demand refunds as aggressively from overseas suppliers for returns, rejects, and defective items. And there was the cost and time involved in sending buyers overseas to inspect the factories, to make sure they were making the goods properly and meeting deadlines.

Walton's brainstorm, after his conversation with Clinton, was to wonder whether he couldn't get U.S. suppliers to cut their prices to Wal-Mart if he offered them the same kinds of terms he and everybody else were offering the overseas producers. He ordered his executives to weigh the hidden costs of doing business overseas. "We tried," said Al Johnson, an executive vice president at Wal-Mart, to "focus on what actual costs were associated with manufacturing off-shore."[9] These included, besides those just mentioned, the cost of storing goods in Wal-Mart warehouses after they arrived in the United States and the risks involved in buying great quantities of goods—especially clothes—long before the selling season. "We finally developed a formula that said you need to go through all of these steps to make a comparison between an import item and one that's produced domestically. Once we got that figured out, it was a little easier to make those comparisons," Johnson said.[10]

Price aside, it was easier, safer, faster and more convenient to have goods made domestically, and there weren't the cultural and linguistic barriers. Giving U.S. suppliers big orders well ahead of time would give them a chance to cut costs by ordering their materials, scheduling workers, and controlling inventories more efficiently. Walton knew that if he could push some U.S. suppliers to cut their costs in exchange for a few billing and ordering concessions, it would give Wal-Mart one more edge.

"One of our big objectives" in the Buy American program, says a Wal-Mart board member involved in the effort, "was to put the heat on American manufacturers to lower their prices."

This was the nub: Walton may well have felt sorry for those factory workers he saw slaving away in Central America; but the bottom line was the bottom line.

Walton was very direct with his suppliers that their bids had to meet or come within spitting distance of the prices foreign factories charged. "We're not interested in charity here," he said. "We don't believe in subsidizing substandard work or inefficiency."[11] But Walton also knew that even if he agreed to pay a few pennies more for a domestically made item, he'd make those pennies back from lower warehousing, ordering, and other costs.

And touting Buy American had another benefit, too: It put more pressure on overseas suppliers.

Speaking at a retailing convention in Dallas in mid-1986, Walton gave the example of Frazier Engineering, a Morristown, Indiana, factory that bid on a patio chair Wal-Mart was then having made in China for $4.98 apiece. "This Indiana factory called Al Johnson and said 'We think we can make this chair for you and we think we can beat your offshore price.' So Al and his merchandisers sat down with them and they talked about quantity, quality; we gave them lead time and offered to pay them on delivery [with a] letter of credit," Walton said, clutching a sample of the white wire chair in his hand.

"Well, this Indiana factory came through for us and made them for $3.50. The folks in the Orient heard about it this year and you know what happened?" he asked the audience. "They lowered their price. So it works both ways," he said triumphantly—quickly adding that Wal-Mart stuck with the domestic chair maker all the same.

For all the banners and commercials and other efforts to tout the program, Walton and his executives declined to estimate the overall percentage of imported goods Wal-Mart was selling—and for good reason. By 1988, Walton was saying that Wal-Mart had brought back to U.S. manufacture $1.2 billion in retail goods (or, at Wal-Mart's cost, between $400 million and $500 million), creating or saving some 17,000 jobs. But Wal-Mart's direct imports, as a percentage of sales, hadn't shrunk at all, because the company was buying more goods directly than before—including more imported goods. Wal-Mart's buying staff in Hong Kong and Taipei alone had grown to 90 people.

And not all the domestic deals worked out well. That Indiana factory, for instance, in trying so hard to cut its costs, went bankrupt after one year, and Wal-Mart went back overseas for the chairs.

Some rival retailers groused, usually privately, that Wal-Mart still imported more goods than ever. Kmart economist Robert E. Hayes claimed that Kmart bought more of its goods domestically than Wal-Mart. "The truth of the matter is that we have done a better job," he said, adding that Walton had really only done better from a public relations standpoint, as if that were a negligible concern.[12] But nobody really knew how much Wal-Mart was importing. Wal-Mart wasn't saying—and anyway, a lot depended on how one defined American-made. Was Farris's flannel shirt, stitched in Arkansas from imported fabric, American-made? Walton though so—and no doubt the workers at Farris agreed.

But from a public relations standpoint, it hardly mattered what percentage of goods Wal-Mart was importing. There were good examples of genuine "conversions" to U.S. factories, and Wal-Mart's stores were spangled with signs that read THIS ITEM, FORMERLY IMPORTED, IS NOW BEING PURCHASED BY WAL-MART IN THE U.S.A. AND IS CREATING OR RETAINING— JOBS FOR AMERICANS!

13

They Call Me
Mr. Sam

After Sam Walton turned the job of chief executive officer over to David Glass in 1988, one area that he turned his attention to more than ever was reaching and keeping alive a connection to the ever-growing army of employees, who numbered more than 223,000 by 1989. One tool he used was the company's *Wal-Mart World* newsletter, which, naturally, told workers all about Wal-Mart's efforts—on Buying American and everything else—in particularly glowing terms. Besides Walton's own artfully ingenuous letters to his employees, issues of *Wal-Mart World* often featured articles such as one in which an awestruck worker described a trip in Mr. Sam's plane. "I took the copilot's seat to enjoy the vista," wrote Tim Crane. "I should have known better. If you're around Mr. Sam, you are gonna work. I found myself taking notes and sorting papers as Mr. Sam took advantage of the autopilot to review district manager reports."[1]

Walton tried to rouse by example, singling out for praise workers such as the Florida clerk who drove 20 miles to another store to pick up parts for a customer whose picnic table was missing hardware and then went to the customer's house and helped her put the table together. "We have a customer there for life!" Walton exulted.[2]

The company incessantly reminded workers how they could benefit from profit-sharing. "Recently, one associate announced that her stock purchase plan investment of $1,200 in Wal-Mart stock rose to $138,000 in value in 17 years," said an introduction from Walton in one handbook given to new employees.[3] And, in fact, the '80s were extraordinary times for Wal-

Mart's stock. Later, the company would calculate that $3,000 invested in Wal-Mart stock at the start of 1981 would have been worth $105,600 ten years later.

But even so, it was getting tougher for the company to find and keep the happy, cheerful workers Walton wanted. As at most places where workers are paid at or near minimum wage, turnover was high. One answer was to seek out and hire older workers, seniors who presumably shared the work ethic of that older generation. And, as Wal-Mart moved into more suburban areas, it started giving job applicants drug tests. It made them take personality tests, too, to see if they'd fit into the culture and be productive, honest employees. If you wanted a job at Wal-Mart, you could expect to have to answer such questions as these:

A description of my childhood might be: A. Happy   B. Average C. Unhappy

I have felt like breaking something in the past.   A. Agree   B. Undecided   C. Disagree

Which one of the statements is true of you: A. I like a neat and tidy home. B. I don't mind a messy house as long as it's clean. C. I'm indifferent regarding neatness.

My friends see me as: A. tough   B. average   C. a pushover.

I sometimes have pretty wild daydreams.   A. Agree   B. Undecided   C. Disagree

Assuming you passed that test and were hired, you'd be given an employee manual featuring a curious combination of rigid rules and paternalistic advice, all meant to "Wal-Martize" you. "Look for the good in others. Avoid idle gossip" instructed the 1988 handbook. It also told you to be sure to live within your means. "There is no need for a union at Wal-Mart!" it declared. Along with very specific rules about such issues as how to dress and when to take breaks, the handbook also noted that if, as an hourly worker, you wanted to date another hourly worker, both of you had to get permission from your district manager.

When the company recruited for management trainees, it did so mostly at smaller colleges in the South and Midwest. "They're really cost-conscious. They want somebody that they feel would be a hard worker and can see the opportunity ahead; and that would be willing to come in at a little less salary and go to a location that's not metropolitan," said Sharon Lutz, assistant director of placement at the University of Texas in Austin. "They want somebody able to sacrifice, perhaps, during the first couple of years, but a person who can see that—based on merit and accomplishment—there is a definite opportunity with this young and growing company. Kind of a good-ol'-boy approach," she said.[4]

In 1989, on one of his satellite catechisms to the stores, Walton introduced a new pledge that perfectly expressed his place in the Wal-Mart firmament. Entreating workers to promise to stay attentive to customers—to greet any that came within 10 feet of them, among other things—he asked them to swear to do so, "so help me Sam."

One regard in which Walton hadn't changed was in his attitude toward women. Like many retailers and many businessmen of his generation, he was perfectly happy to have women working as store clerks and assistant managers; but he didn't think they were cut out for more demanding managerial positions. In 1985, for instance, there was not a single woman among the company's top 42 officers (vice presidents or above) listed in Wal-Mart's annual report, and there were no women on the board of directors. The feminism of the '60s and '70s, the notion of equal opportunity for women, had scarcely touched the company.

Some board members—Jim Jones, the banker, for one—had been trying for years to get Walton to appoint a woman to the board, without making much headway. Jones also wanted Walton to appoint a black board member. "Sam was really resistant to the idea," Jones said. Not so much because of prejudice, Jones believes, but because "he was afraid to bring on anybody from the outside."

Actually, there were several outsiders on the 15-member board, such as Charles Lazarus, from Toys "R" Us, and Sidney McKnight, the retired president of Montgomery Ward & Co., and Robert Kahn, a retail consultant from the San Francisco Bay Area with decades in the department store business. But—like most corporate boards—it was full of middle-aged, successful white businessmen, most of whom shared a pretty similar world view. To Walton and to most of the directors, this makeup made sense. The board included seven Wal-Mart executives, Sam, Bud, and Rob Walton among them; and all of the other eight directors had particular areas of expertise Walton figured would be useful to his business. Many, too, had long been associated with the company, such as Jones, or Jackson Stephens, the Little Rock financier.

But things were beginning to change. Kahn, who'd joined the board in 1980, also argued for appointing a woman director and even came up with the ideal candidate: Betsy Sanders, a vice president and general manager at

Nordstrom Inc. The plush and highly regarded Seattle-based department store chain was perhaps the one major retailer with an even better reputation for customer service than Wal-Mart. But though Sam Walton was impressed enough to offer Sanders a seat, Nordstrom didn't want one of their executives on another retailer's board, and she was forced to decline.*

Meanwhile, Helen and Alice began lobbying Sam on behalf of their own candidate: Hillary Rodham Clinton. She was a rarity in Arkansas: a powerful, articulate woman who resisted conforming to the Southern belle stereotype expected of prominent women there.† That may have been one reason the two Walton women felt a kinship with her. Sam Walton knew her too, of course, and not just because she was Bill Clinton's wife and a shareholder. The Rose Law Firm in Little Rock, where she was a partner, had represented Wal-Mart many times. And she had personally enlisted Sam Walton's help back in 1983, when she took charge of getting an ambitious education-reform plan through the Arkansas legislature—a plan that later would be called Bill Clinton's biggest achievement as governor.

At the time, Walton had been the chairman of "The Good Suits Club," a group of the state's deepest pockets and political movers and shakers. Officially called the Arkansas Business Council, the club was supposed to be devoted to bettering Arkansas. Hillary Clinton convinced them to back education reform, and got Walton and other moguls, such as chicken-processing king Don Tyson, to contribute to a political fund to pay for ads to push the initiative.

Arkansas's schools ranked among the worst in the country. They fell dead last among the 50 states in the percentage of high-school graduates going on to college. Half the school districts had no foreign language instruction; nearly a third offered no mathematics. Clinton's plan called for mandatory kindergarten, smaller classes, competency tests that students had to pass to get out of third, sixth, and eighth grade, testing of teachers, consolidating school districts, and higher sales taxes to pay for it all.

In addition to lobbying the "Good Suits," Hillary Clinton had held hearings around the state and waylaid recalcitrant legislators one-on-one. In the end, most of the reforms passed by a narrow margin. And Hillary Clinton's profile grew immensely.

---

* Sanders eventually did join the board, in 1993. By then, she had left Nordstrom to become a management consultant.

† For the sake of her husband's political career, she had made some concessions to Arkansas's Babbittry, most notably by agreeing to use Clinton as her last name, rather than her own surname, Rodham, which she'd kept after marriage. She also put aside her lifelong indifference to her appearance to adopt a more "ladylike" look, lightening her hair, wearing contact lenses, and dressing in softer, more fashionable clothing.

Still, when Helen and Alice pushed to put her on Wal-Mart's board, Sam Walton remained reluctant. It's hard to say whether her liberalism put him off. It's unlikely Walton knew about some of her most famous past episodes—such as the time in 1970 when, working as a staff attorney for Senator Walter Mondale's Subcommittee on Migratory Labor, she had confronted Coca-Cola president J. Paul Austin in the hallway outside a Senate hearing room. She had visited the squalid labor camps run in Florida by Coca-Cola's Minute Maid unit; and as Austin arrived to testify at a sub-committee hearing, she snarled at him "We're going to nail your ass—nail your ass."[5] No, that story probably hadn't made it back to Bentonville. But Walton most likely was aware of her work with, for example, the Arkansas Adolescent Pregnancy Child Watch Project, which was trying to lower the state's teen pregnancy rate (second-highest in the country) by having school health clinics distribute condoms and other contraceptives—a highly controversial tactic in such a socially conservative state.

But though he was quite conservative himself, Walton seems to have liked or at least tolerated Hillary Clinton personally; and it may be that he simply felt unsure what this tough, smart thirty-eight-year-old Wellesley and Yale Law School graduate would bring to his boardroom table. Nevertheless, in November of 1986, he diffidently agreed to appoint her as Wal-Mart's first female board member.

Hillary Clinton took her new $15,000-a-year directorship as a chance to push Wal-Mart along in several areas. Even before she joined the board, Walton had agreed to have an outside consultant study Wal-Mart's track record at providing equal opportunities for women and minorities. The record, to no one's great surprise, was abysmal.

The situation was abysmal in most of the retail industry, of course, and had remained so even after the Equal Employment Opportunity Act became law in 1972. The Equal Employment Opportunity Commission had only made one great sally into discrimination in retailing. It had tilted its lance at Sears, then the country's largest retailer and biggest employer of women. At Sears, as at most retailers, men held commissioned sales positions hawking big-ticket items, such as electronics and appliances, and women held near-minimum-wage hourly positions as sales clerks in lower-commission or noncommission departments. Among its findings, the EEOC said that the average commissioned salesman at Sears, after his first year, made twice what the averge noncommissioned female clerk was paid, no matter how long she'd been there.

The EEOC filed charges against Sears in 1979; and the company promptly doubled the number of commissioned sales women. But though there was a pretty persuasive case against it, Sears also decided to fight the charges at trial; and its move paid off. Sears was able to delay the trial until the Reagan administration took power in early 1981. Under new leadership far more sympathetic to big business, the EEOC rapidly backpedaled. Even as the case was being argued in court, the commission's new chairman, Clarence Thomas Jr., told the *Washington Post* "I've been trying to get out of this since I've been here."[6] In the end, the commission's lukewarm handling of the case before a skeptical Reagan-appointed judge led to a win for Sears.

But even though this seemed to take the pressure off retailers, by then a decade of EEOC enforcement in other areas had made the idea, if not the practice of equal opportunity for women and minorities, a part of the social fabric. Companies increasingly felt obligated at least to make a token effort in that direction.

On Wal-Mart's board, Hillary Clinton was interested in something more than a token effort, and she was not at all shy about making that clear. In league with a few sympathetic board members and executives, she made gradual headway.* By 1989, though there were still no women in the 22 highest positions, at senior vice president or higher, there were two women vice presidents among the company's top 88 officers—including one heading the "people division," in charge of hiring. That summer, in one of his monthly *Wal-Mart World* letters, Walton wrote: "I'm so pleased to see us beginning to recognize and promote women to responsible positions of management throughout Wal-Mart. For years, retailing management was considered the exclusive province of men. That's not so today. Wal-Mart's Executive Committee† realizes that we have a tremendous pool of future management talent in the ranks of our women associates and has made the commitment to train and develop them in the fullest."[7]

Sam Walton had learned to talk the equal-opportunity talk. But, in the end, that talk didn't lead to very visible progress. Wal-Mart steadily declined to make public any figures showing how many women it had running stores or in mid-level management. In 1992, after Hillary Clinton resigned from the board during her husband's presidential campaign, the issue came up again. At the 1992 annual meeting, when Bud Walton asked sharehold-

---

* In response to a shareholder's question at the 1987 annual meeting about why Wal-Mart had so few women managers, Walton said, "We haven't gotten as far as we would like . . . [but we have] a strong-willed young lady on the board now who has already told the board it should do more to ensure advancement for women." In a rare disclosure, he said 33 of Wal-Mart's store managers were women. Wal-Mart then had more than 1,100 stores—meaning 97 percent of its store managers were men.

† Namely, Sam, Bud, and Rob Walton, David Glass, Don Soderquist, John Tate (the union-busting attorney, now an executive vice president), and Paul Carter, the company's chief financial officer.

ers how to improve the meeting, someone shouted "Put some women on the board," and a huge cheer went up from the crowd, visibly embarrassing all the men on stage. By 1998, Wal-Mart had two women among its 14 directors, but had no women above the corporate vice president level, and only one woman among its top 38 executives. (There were two women senior vice presidents within the company's Sam's Club and Wal-Mart stores divisions.)

Not that, while on the board, Hillary Clinton didn't try. But changing a corporate culture isn't easy, especially when the man at the top is lukewarm at best about the idea. And at Wal-Mart, sexism was ingrained in myriad ways. At the big managers' meetings, for example, Walton tried to be solicitous of the managers' spouses by scheduling special wives' gripe sessions for them to vent their frustrations and concerns—but, of course, this assumed that the managers were male. And while other board members attest that Hillary Clinton was genuinely interested and pushed the issue, she was, of course, consumed by her own pressing concerns—such as getting her husband reelected as governor and then getting him elected president.

During the time she was on the Wal-Mart board, Clinton did take on another issue: getting the company involved in environmental activities. She talked Sam Walton into appointing an environmental advisory board, which she chaired, that would report to him. It included several outside members, an executive from Wal-Mart's biggest vendor, Procter & Gamble, and some Wal-Mart executives, including Bill Fields, a young senior vice president who initally would be the company's point man on this issue.

Fields, who was two years younger than Clinton, was a particular protégé of Walton's. He'd gone to Bentonville High School with Alice Walton and then had paid his way through the University of Arkansas by working at a Sears store. Fields had been planning to go into Sears's management-training program; but he graduated just as Sam Walton had decided to start recruiting college men, and Walton had talked him into starting out as an assistant manager at a Wal-Mart store.

Fields was notable for another reason: He had been a Ron Mayer man in the '70s and had left in Mayer's Ayr-Way exodus. But after that didn't work out, Walton had gladly welcomed Fields back to Wal-Mart, not holding anything against him.

Under Clinton, the board looked at dozens of ideas: encouraging recycling at the stores, using recycled paper for ads and signs, promoting "green" products, and even such pie-in-the-sky proposals as ecologically designed Wal-Mart stores. The general dictum, of course, was that whatever they came up with had to be bottom-line oriented, too. Other retailers—Sears, for example—were trying to reduce packaging, both to trim waste and save money. But when Wal-Mart officially launched its green effort in 1989, with full-page newspaper ads that said, "We're looking for quality products guaranteed not to last," it wasn't long before Kmart, Target, and other discounters followed suit.

Questions about the program sprang up almost from day one, especially about the "green" tags Wal-Mart would put on products that were supposed somehow to be environmentally "improved."

"The Wal-Mart program signaled the advent of the green consumer movement into mainstream America," Joel Makower, editor of *The Green Consumer Letter*, told *Audubon* in 1990. "But in fact, it could be a major contribution to killing the green consumer movement."

Why? "You walk down the aisle of a Wal-Mart store and you will see, for example, a roll of Bounty paper towels, 67 square feet of chlorine-bleached, unrecycled paper packaged in plastic. Why did it get a Wal-Mart environmental recommendation? The core tubes are made of 100 percent recycled paper. I have a fantasy that a bunch of marketing guys were sitting around after too many drinks, saying, 'How are we going to get Bounty into this Wal-Mart thing? Wait a minute, isn't the tube made out of recycled material? Let's push that, maybe they'll fall for it.' "[8]

Wal-Mart did rely on its vendors, and some of the green tags were mighty dubious. But the company did launch a serious recycling effort at its headquarters, claiming to reduce its trash by 80 percent. It bought recycling bins for many of its stores, offering to donate profits to United Way. It used recycled paper for ad circulars, signs, and stationery, and began an oil-recycling program at stores that had auto centers. And, in one more public relations success, it developed an "eco-store" prototype that opened with great fanfare in Lawrence, Kansas, in 1993.

Three years of planning produced a 112,264-square-foot store that cost about $500,000 more than the typical $2.4-million price tag for a Wal-Mart store that size. That extra cost more than paid for itself in the advertising mileage that Wal-Mart got out of the store. Some of its eco-claims approached the absurd. Wal-Mart explained that the building had an unusually high ceiling and cement-block sides laid out in such a way that, should Wal-Mart ever vacate, windows could be popped in, a second floor added, and the entire building could be turned into apartments. Apartments handily surrounded by 40 acres of parking, presumably.

But the store had many genuinely green features. Wal-Mart pointed out that the store's roof was supported by arching wooden beams made from second-growth timber, selectively harvested rather than clear-cut. The store had skylights to save on electricity, with electronic daylight sensors on the roof to dim or brighten fluorescent lights depending on how bright it was outside. There was recycled asphalt in the parking lot; a solar-powered sign out front; a holding pond to collect waste water and run-off from the parking lot to be used to irrigate the shrubbery.

At the store's opening, David Glass declared that "this is the beginning of a great new era," with the implication that in years to come, more and more Wal-Mart stores would be green. In fact, the company would open one or so green store a year, out of the hundreds of new stores—enough to let Wal-Mart keep touting its eco-sensitivity in its millions of (recyclable) advertising circulars.

At least once, Wal-Mart offered an eco-store as bait, in a quixotic effort to open a store in Boulder, Colorado, a university town and rich liberal enclave with hippie roots. Wal-Mart real estate manager Steven P. Lane made what he thought was a pretty good pitch to city council members, harping on how the store would be environmentally sensitive right up to its solar-powered sign. But when council member Spencer Havlick—who had been one of the organizers of the first Earth Day back in 1970—suggested that the whole *store* be solar-powered and that Wal-Mart should build affordable housing for its workers, since there was no way anyone on near-minimum-wage could afford Boulder rents, Lane fell silent. Havlick, a professor of environmental design at the University of Colorado, said, "Their proposal wasn't as green as they thought it was."

In the end, the effort to make Wal-Mart a model of environmental sensitivity had a few modest successes, when cost savings could be found. Many new stores used recycled asphalt for the parking lots, for example. But intentions and hype outstripped real progress. An environmentalist might be forgiven for asking how any company that builds thousands of stores surrounded by acres of asphalt, selling goods shipped thousands of miles to customers who inevitably drive emission-spewing cars to get there, could conceivably serve as a model for ecologically sensitive retailing, if there is any such thing.

Hillary Clinton, though she served as a catalyst of sorts at Wal-Mart, didn't wind up having as significant an impact as, perhaps, her supporters might have hoped. But then, consider her distractions. Intriguingly, it was two of her fellow Wal-Mart advisory board members, after one meeting in Bentonville, who helped her come to the decision that would lead Bill Clinton to run for president in 1992. The Clintons had been discussing his po-

tential candidacy and the problem posed by the fact that he had promised
Arkansas voters, when he was reelected as governor in 1990, that he would
serve out his term.

On August 14, 1991, after a meeting of the environmental advisory
board, Hillary Clinton asked two of the other members to go for a drive
with her. They were Garry Mauro, land commissioner for the state of Texas,
and Roy Spence, the head of an Austin, Texas, advertising firm that worked
for Wal-Mart. She'd known both men for nearly twenty years, since working with them in Texas on George McGovern's 1972 presidential campaign.
With Spence at the wheel, driving no place in particular, Hillary Clinton
said, "We're thinking of doing it. We're thinking about going forward with
this great adventure. What do you all think?"9 The two men encouraged
her, but she raised the promise her husband had made, so they hashed out
that problem. Out of that conversation, wrapped up sitting back at the
parking lot in front of Wal-Mart's brick headquarters, came what was later
called the Secret Tour, in which Bill Clinton quietly visited his supporters
in towns all around Arkansas and got their blessing to break his earlier
promise.

Meanwhile, Sam Walton had his own pressing concerns. It was in late 1989,
of course, that Walton found out he had myeloma. And just as when he'd
been diagnosed with hairy cell leukemia seven years earlier, he wrote a
memo about it, in as offhand a manner as he could, to be read by the manager of each store to all the associates. Typically, the first three-fourths of
his memo effusively thanked and congratulated everyone for Wal-Mart's
being selected as retailer of the 1980s by an industry magazine and for Wal-
Mart associates being honored collectively as the year's "outstanding retail
leader" by another retailing publication.

Only then did the seventy-one-year-old Walton ease into the subject of
his illness:

> The personal matter I spoke of earlier is really no big deal, but I'd
> rather level with you and share the facts concerning my current health
> than to have you hear a lot of rumors, many that likely will be exagger-
> ated or untrue.
>
> As most of you know, since 1982, or about 7½ years ago, I've been
> contending with a form of Cancer called Hairy Cell Leukemia. My
> treatment generally has been very successful here at M.D. Anderson in
> Houston, along with the excellent doctors I've been using both in Ben-

tonville and elswhere. Currently, though, I'm continuing to take a drug called interferon and my Leukemia seems to be in remission at this time.

Last week, I was informed that I have contracted another form of Cancer called Multiple Myeloma, a bone disease; and that has apparently accounted for my many aches and pains these past 60 to 90 days. And even so, I've been bird hunting, which has probably accelerated this condition.

So, bottom line, this type of Cancer as with my Leukemia is a disorder of the cells of the bone marrow. They may be connected, but my doctors feel at this time there is no connection. They have also advised me that they have good success treating this type of cancer if it is detected in time. Over the past few days, I have undergone two chemotherapy treatments and some radiation, and I feel so much better already. I'll probably be here in the Houston area receiving treatments for two or three weeks, then hopefully within a month or two I'll begin my visitations over our Wal-Mart country.

Again, my friends, we all believe we have, as I've said often of you and Wal-Mart, continuously through the years "swam upstream" utilizing opposite strategies and working principles different from our competition—and it's worked. We can continue to excel in the 1990s. With your dedication, prayers and concerns, your Chairman will be back soon helping as I can in the years ahead as a most interested spectator and stockholder.

You are great and are certainly our real front-line Wal-Mart leaders! We have great servant leaders in our management ranks and I know we will have a great decade in the 1990s.

Bless you and all thanks again. Your friend, Sam.

Walton opted not to disclose what he already knew: that the disease was almost certainly incurable. Even as he was being treated, Walton arranged to visit a Sam's Club and a couple of Wal-Mart stores in Houston—though, instead of walking through the store and doing his usual glad-handing, he agreed, on doctor's orders, to sit in a back room and let the workers come to him. That year, at the annual meeting, he seemed his old self, bounding around the stage, leading cheers, and predicting that by the year 2000 Wal-Mart could reach $130 billion in sales. "Can we do it?" he shouted out to the crowd of 9,000, cocking his head. "*Yes we can!*" they roared back.[10]

For much of the following two years, Walton tried to continue his old routines as much as possible. He'd work more from home, because he needed to lie down and rest more often. He would even, as time went on, miss more and more of the Saturday morning meetings, and other management sessions.

With Walton's health declining, his family and Wal-Mart executives pressed him again to write the memoirs he'd scrapped right after the myeloma diagnosis. There was another writer, Vance Trimble, writing an unauthorized biography. Trimble wrote Walton a steady stream of letters pleading for an interview; those letters may also have encouraged Walton to reconsider putting out his own version of his story. When Walton had canceled his earlier book, he'd bought out the contract of the writer, Eric Morgenthaler, the *Wall Street Journal* reporter, and Morgenthaler had turned over all his notes and transcripts of his interviews with Walton, the family, and Wal-Mart executives. Now, having all that material on hand made it easier for Walton to agree to do an autobiography after all. It also helped that the writer John Huey, of *Fortune* magazine, was now available. Walton had wanted Huey, who could hunt quail and talk that good ol' boy talk with the best of them, to write the book the first time; but tied up with other commitments, Huey had steered Walton to Morgenthaler.

Now Huey was free, and eager to do the book. Walton agreed to the project—getting a reported $4-million advance from Doubleday, which he said he would donate to charity.

By the end of '91, he was too weak to continue his store visits. On one of his last visits, "I remember him struggling hard to put his coat on, and he didn't want anyone to help him, and he just couldn't get it on," said Jana Jae, the singer. "You could tell he hurt when he walked, and he was just working through the pain."

It was obvious that he was sinking steadily. He tired more and more easily. When his efficiently motherly young secretary, Becky Elliott, noticed that he was having a hard time staying warm in his office, she told him she was going to buy a space heater—only to have him insist, "No, no, I'm fine." While he was out, she had installed at the top of one wall across the office heating strips that would come on automatically, with a very slight popping sound, whenever anyone entered the room. "A week went by, and he didn't say a word, but he didn't complain about being cold," Elliott said. "One day he said, 'Becky, what is that popping sound I keep hearing?' " When she told him what she'd done, he smiled indulgently—until she confessed they'd cost $500. "He didn't like that," she remembered. "It was more than he would have okay'd if I'd taken it to him first."

In March of 1992, when President Bush, accompanied by the First Lady, presented Walton, at the auditorium in Wal-Mart's headquarters, with the Presidential Medal of Freedom, one of the country's highest civilian honors, Walton had to be rolled out in a wheelchair for the ceremony. His skin was sallow and puffy, but his gaze was still piercing. Walton insisted on standing, at obviously great effort, when Bush placed the medal around his frail neck. The citation with the medal began: "An American original, Sam Walton embodies the entrepreneurial spirit and epitomizes the American dream." As Bush gave him the medal, the throng of Wal-Mart workers who'd crushed into the room erupted into a roaring, standing ovation that went on for minutes. Walton stood the whole time, waving feebly, clearly proud and touched, as he steadied himself with one hand on the wheelchair behind him.

Within days of the ceremony—which Walton told workers was "the highlight of our career"—the company founder had to be taken to the University of Arkansas Medical Sciences Hospital in Little Rock. Friends and family streamed by to see him. One of his last visits—and the one that seemed to perk him up the most—was from the manager of a Little Rock Wal-Mart store, whom Walton grilled, one last time, about his store's sales figures for the week.

On April 6, 1992, he died.

He was lauded as the most influential retailer of the century, and with good reason, for nearly every great retailer of the coming years would follow his business examples. But, in the way he'd remade himself relentlessly into a merchant, Walton also had taken his place in the line of obsessive empire builders who have defined successive American ages, a line stretching from such figures as Thomas Alva Edison, Henry Ford, J. P. Morgan, and Andrew Carnegie to Bill Gates and beyond.

More than any of his predecessors, though, Walton not only created a business empire and amassed a vast personal fortune, but also had focused his energies on making his business into an ever-expanding, self-pepetuating, self-correcting machine that he intended to reflect his values and goals long after his death. A few observers compared the culture and the corporate mores he'd tried to institutionalize to a sort of retailing church or cult; and it was in many ways an apt comparison.

The day after he passed away, the Walton family held a small, private funeral, their seclusion protected by as heavy police security as the town could muster. David Glass led a public memorial service that evening at the Bentonville High stadium. A separate memorial service at the company headquarters was broadcast to all the stores over the satellite network. Don Soderquist, the chief operating officer, led that service, which included speeches by radio commentator Paul Harvey and by Govenor Clinton, who skipped the New York primary election day to attend.

Mr. Sam was gone. What would become of Wal-Mart now?

14

Little Hands, Big Money

In the television studio at Wal-Mart headquarters from which Sam Walton so often had delivered his homespun soliloquies over the satellite system, David Glass now sat down for an unprecedented interview with an NBC television correspondent. It was early December 1992.

Walton generally had avoided reporters. In fact, not long before his death he'd turned down an interview request from the same news show—*Dateline NBC*—that Glass had now agreed to talk to. But in the eight months since Walton's death, many things had begun to change.

Cool and composed, his left leg casually crossed over his right, Glass fielded a few softball questions from correspondent Brian Ross about Sam Walton and Wal-Mart's Buy American program. Behind him, watching intently, Don Shinkle hovered off-camera as both NBC's and Wal-Mart's cameras rolled.* But then the questions turned much, much tougher. Ross told Glass he'd visited 11 Wal-Mart stores and found, in one department after another, goods made in Bangladesh, Korea, and China under signs saying MADE IN THE USA.

Glass sat still. "It shouldn't have been signed that way on the rack," he said. "That's—that would be a mistake at the store level."

Ross looked at him quizzically. "But rack after rack, in a number of stores in Florida and Georgia, we found that," he said.

"On apparel racks?"

---

* Wal-Mart videotaped the interview (as it would a second one), apparently as a way of protecting itself.

"Yes," Ross said, showing him a children's parka made in Bangladesh that he'd bought at a store in Georgia.

"You know," said Glass slowly, "you'd be foolish to put a—a garment that said 'Made in Bangladesh' on a rack that was signed 'Made in America' and expect to fool people."

Ross asked a series of hard questions, suggesting he had evidence that one of Wal-Mart's big suppliers in Hong Kong was involved in a quota-busting scheme. Citing evidence from U.S. Customs officials, Ross said the company, Sino Overseas, was putting fake tags on hundreds of thousands of pieces of clothing made in China, to make it look as though they came from other countries.* Glass didn't have a good answer.

Ross asked whether Wal-Mart did much business in Bangladesh. Not a lot, Glass said.

"We were told that in Bangladesh, on a regular basis, children, young children, are employed to make clothes for you, for others," Ross said. Glass stared at him for a moment and then said that to his knowledge Wal-Mart didn't buy from any vendors that used child labor. Ross asked if he could show him something.

"Sure," said Glass with a shrug.

On a small television monitor, Ross rolled a videotape. He had been to Bangladesh—and visited, with a cameraman, a factory making Wal-Mart clothing. The workers looked to be boys and girls, some as young as nine years old. Glass craned forward to see. "This is a factory full of children, and they're making shirts for Wal-Mart—your private-label shirts," Ross told him. When Glass said he didn't recognize the shirts, Ross pulled one out of a bag.

"This is the shirt I brought back," he said, handing it to Glass. The normally taciturn Glass, looking increasingly somber, said carefully, "We make a concentrated effort not to buy merchandise from manufacturers where it is made with child labor." Behind him, Shinkle dithered. He knew the interview was turning into a disaster—but wouldn't it look even worse if he barged in and stopped it with the cameras rolling?

Ross now told Glass that the factory he'd visited, the Saraka factory, was one of the country's most notorious. He gave Glass a handful of black-and-white photographs of the bodies of 25 children who'd died, locked in during a fire at the factory two years earlier, less than a year before Wal-Mart moved production there. As Glass, poker-faced, thumbed through the photos, Ross said, "The children who—who work in this plant are locked in

---

* Sino Overseas denied any involvement in illegal smuggling.

until all hours of the night, until they finish that day's production." His cameraman zoomed in tight on Wal-Mart's chief executive.

"Yeah," said Glass, sitting back and making a tent with his crossed fingers under his chin, "there are tragic things that happen all over the world."

Ross looked at him incredulously. "That's all you want to say about it?"

Shinkle couldn't wait any longer. "Excuse me, let's—" he started to say, as Glass, staring at Ross, said "I—I don't know what else I would say about it."

At that, Shinkle ordered a halt to the interview, and Wal-Mart's crew cut the lights and cranked up music to prevent NBC from doing any further taping. Glass walked off and took Shinkle and some other Wal-Mart people back into the studio's control room. An angry voice—whose it wasn't clear—floated back out to the studio. "Are you happy now?" it demanded. Ross was very happy. Astonished at his luck, he packed up his crew and left.

This was going to be very, very bad, the Wal-Mart men knew. Charges of child labor, smuggled Chinese goods, misleading MADE IN THE USA signs. And that interview! They had to do something. Glass said he wanted someone sent to check out that Saraka factory immediately. And, after some tense debate, Glass decided he would try to recoup by doing a second taped interview with Ross. Rather than phone Ross directly, though, he called and complained about being ambushed to Jack Welch, the chairman of General Electric Co., which owned NBC. Welch called NBC president Robert Wright. Wright talked to Ross, who readily agreed to go back and interview Glass again.

Two weeks after the first interview, Ross and his crew flew back to Bentonville. Ross's producer, Rhonda Schwartz, had phoned Bangladesh, and they knew a Wal-Mart man had visited the Saraka factory. By now, Ross expected, Wal-Mart would certainly have cleaned up the problem. Probably they would say that it was just a local mistake, that they'd been appalled to find children there, but that they'd corrected it as quickly as they could. No doubt they would say it wouldn't happen again. It would make Ross's story a bit less dramatic, but that was fair enough, he supposed.

This time, Glass would be prepared to handle him. At least, that was the theory. What actually happened was that Ross polished him off like a piece of buttered toast.

Before the interview, Glass took Ross and Schwartz off to his modest office for a tête-à-tête. He told them offhandedly about his call to Welch; but Glass tried to be friendly, seemingly anxious to get this interview off to a better start. Once they set up in the studio, Glass began by telling Ross that

Wal-Mart had inspected the Saraka factory and others Ross had cited—but, he added firmly, they hadn't found any evidence of children working there.

What Glass didn't tell Ross—but later described in a letter to several members of Congress—was that the "inspection" had consisted of having a merchandising vice president from Wal-Mart ask various Saraka workers how old they were. Glass's letter said the workers all assured the Wal-Mart man that they were over fourteen, Bangladesh's minimum working age.[*] Saraka's manager, too, promised that all the workers were of legal age, Glass wrote.

What actually had happened in that factory? According to an executive for an investment firm that was a big Wal-Mart shareholder, shortly after the *Dateline NBC* story aired, two Wal-Mart officials, Randy Laney and Rhonda Parish, conceded privately that Wal-Mart had found children working in its Bangladeshi factories.[†] This wasn't for public consumption, of course; Laney and Parish made the admission in a conference call with two executives for the investment firm.

Back in Wal-Mart's studio, though, with both sides rolling cameras, Glass laid out his denial.

"Well," he began, "I think the stories of children being locked in and exploited are certainly something that we've not been able to verify, and—"

Ross interrupted: "You—you—your man was there and he saw no children working in that factory?"

"No."

"Or any of the other factories?" Ross asked.

"Children," Glass said, pausing, "you and I might, perhaps, define children differently. In Bangladesh—"

Again, Ross broke in. "Should a twelve-year-old girl be in school or making clothes for Wal-Mart? Anywhere in the world?"

What else could Glass say? "No, we—a twelve-year-old girl should not."

---

[*] Glass's letter didn't say whether it was the manager or someone else who translated their envoy's questions to the workers, and their answers. Of course, the workers doubtless knew that anyone admitting to being under fourteen would be fired. Glass's letter also didn't address another problem: Bangladeshi law at the time mandated a maximum 5-hour workday for workers under eighteen years old. Neither it nor the minimum-age law were enforced by the government to any meaningful degree. Workers in the Saraka factory reported working from 14 to 18 hours a day, and sometimes sleeping on the factory floor between shifts.
[†] Laney, interviewed in 1998, said he remembered taking part in the conference call, but said he didn't recall what he said. "I can't recall whether we found kids in the factory or not," he said, adding, "I remember we made every effort to certify they [the workers] were of the right age."

"But they are," Ross insisted. "We saw them."

Still doggedly trying to put his denial across, Glass said, "Well, we have not been able to substantiate that."

But Ross kept pushing. "How can you believe that, given what we showed you?"

"Why should I not believe that?" Glass retorted.

"The pictures of those young children don't contradict the assurances you received from an employer or a boss in Bangladesh?" Ross asked.

Glass, looking as though the interview wasn't going quite as he'd expected, stammered, "The—the picture—the—the—the pictures you showed me mean nothing to me. I'm—I'm not sure where they were or who they were, you know. Could have been of anything, I'm not sure."

"I'm telling you," Ross said directly, "they're not 'of anything'; they're of the Saraka factory, of children making Wal-Mart clothing."

"Well," said Glass, "I'm—I'm comfortable with what we've done."

And that, more or less, was that. The interview rambled on a bit longer. Among other observations, Glass said Asian workers just looked young because they were so small. Afterward, Glass seemed satisfied that he'd acquitted himself well. As he and Ross walked back to Glass's office, the chief executive confided in the reporter that his people had let him down a bit the first time, that he hadn't been prepared.

But it wasn't long before Glass began to realize that perhaps neither he nor Wal-Mart was going to come off quite so well as he initially believed. When Ross got back to NBC, Wright sat down with him to watch the tape. Wright was stunned at how poorly Glass had handled the interview. He asked Ross why Glass seemed so unprepared. Ross shrugged.

At Wal-Mart, as the advance preparations for damage control began, executives muttered about the unions being behind this—which, as it happened, was at least partly true. But then, that was something that Glass, Shinkle, and the rest really should have anticipated. After all, these questions that Ross raised had come up before.

Nearly a year before Sam Walton's death, in May of 1991, on Mother's Day, the United Food and Commercial Workers International Union had held a press conference and handed out leaflets in front of Wal-Mart stores in ten cities, calling on Walton to have Wal-Mart stop buying goods in Bangladesh because of the use of child labor there. Pat Scarcelli, a union vice president, had specifically fingered two shirt brands sold at Wal-Mart as being made by children at a factory in the capital city, Dacca. The media had almost entirely ignored the event; but the Wal-Mart men should have known that the UFCW wouldn't let the matter drop and that Wal-Mart ran the risk, sooner or later, of being called to account for how its goods were made.

Had Wal-Mart investigated the earlier allegations and taken swift action in Bangladesh, the most dramatic part of the *Dateline NBC* exposé might never have existed. But that doesn't seem to have been seriously considered. As a practical matter, Wal-Mart's approach to overseas child labor—like that of just about every other major retailer—amounted to don't ask, don't tell.

Of course, nearly every retailer's goods were made in similar overseas factories—a point Scarcelli had acknowledged in promising that the UFCW would look at Bangladeshi suppliers for Kmart, Sears, J.C. Penney, and Target, too.

And, in truth, the entire apparel industry was one continuing and underreported scandal. Even as the UFCW was pointing to child workers in Dacca, one could find sweatshops quite nearly as appalling in the United States. In September of 1991, New York labor inspectors found labels for Wal-Mart brands being made in illegal sweatshops in Manhattan's Chinatown district. In one of these crowded, dingy shops, sixteen and seventeen-year-old Chinese immigrants without work permits had put in a month of sewing without being paid. "Training," the factory's owner called it. In that case, also largely ignored by the press,* Shinkle had promised to cut off the suppliers if Wal-Mart could confirm any laws were broken.

A year before that, federal labor inspectors in Los Angeles had found a seven-year-old boy and two other children making clothing for a supplier to Wal-Mart, Penney, and Sears; raids had found more than a dozen more children working in other sweatshops. The raids got almost no attention outside of Los Angeles. Perhaps it was too complicated a story—too many layers between seven-year-old David Valladares, working in a tiny apartment in a Santa Ana barrio at one end of the supply chain, and the giant retailers at the other end. Here's how that chain of supply worked, in this instance: Wal-Mart and other big retailers ordered clothing from En Chante Inc., an L.A.-based dress and sportswear maker; En Chante contracted with a sewing shop, Su Enterprises Corp., to make some of the garments; and Su Enterprises farmed out some of its work to a score of smaller contractors, including the one for which the children were working in an illegal home-sewing arrangement.

To be sure, the hundreds of U.S. sweatshops, largely clustered in New York, Southern California, and Texas, tended to be small and fugitive in na-

---

* The sweatshop raids were covered by a *Minneapolis Star-Tribune* reporter, Mike Meyers.

ture, in comparison with huge overseas factories such as Saraka, which had some 500 workers. But they shared one thing in common with their bigger overseas counterparts: deniability. Retailers denied knowing about sweatshop conditions; after all, they bought from vendors who were supposed to watch out for that sort of thing. The vendors argued that they had to deal with tremendous pressure to provide the lowest possible price, which meant subcontracting to the lowest bidders. The subcontractors inevitably argued that they were providing jobs and that they were under so much price pressure that there was no way to pay as much as minimum wage, meet all the regulations, and still survive. And the workers rarely complained, those in the United States because they were usually illegal immigrants afraid of being deported, and those in countries such as Bangladesh because that was the way things were done.

Meanwhile, enforcement of minimum age and wage laws was next to nonexistent in many countries—as every retailer knew. Even in the United States, regulators couldn't keep up. Hugh McDaid, an investigator for the New York State Labor Department's apparel industry task force, estimated in 1991 that New York alone had 4,000 sweatshops, with a total of 12 state inspectors trying to keep an eye on them. When sweatshops were raided, everyone involved claimed to be shocked—shocked—and piously promised not to let it happen again. Within a few weeks or months, the sweatshop owners often reopened somewhere nearby—readily finding workers desperate for jobs and contractors willing not to ask any hard questions. As for the overseas factories, the only Americans who ever saw their insides were the ones buying the goods. Until now, that is.

Wal-Mart's trouble this time around was that the Bangladeshi children had been caught on videotape, live and in color.

As for the union connection, one might wonder why the UFCW—with so much of its membership in grocery stores or food factories—had involved itself in policing apparel-industry sweatshops, rather than leaving that fight to some textile or apparel union. The answer—along with the reason that the UFCW had targeted Wal-Mart—lies in the union's history.

The UFCW came into being in 1979 out of a merger between a meat packers' and a retail clerks' unions. Other unions had joined in following years. The UFCW included grocery store and retail clerks, shoemakers, barbers, beauticians, and members of several other trades. Eventually, it became the largest union in the AFL-CIO; and it was unusually militant.

Overall, the strength of organized labor in the United States had steadily declined since World War II. Back in the mid-1950s, 35 percent of American workers were unionized. By 1990, just 16 percent were. Union elections had shriveled—especially during the Reagan and Bush years, when enforcement of labor laws and protections of workers' rights had eroded steadily. It was tough to organize workers: Would-be organizers faced losing their jobs, while the company that fired them faced, at worst, an order to make up back pay or post a notice on a back wall somewhere admitting the violations. There were no additional fines for companies, no punitive provisions in the law.

Even so, the UFCW had been one of the few large unions that actually gained membership through the '80s and early '90s. It did this mostly by organizing in tough, low-wage, high-turnover industries that other unions avoided, such as food processing. And instead of relying on the nearly toothless National Labor Relations Board, UFCW leaders figured out other ways—other laws they could use—to pressure companies to recognize the union and to come to the bargaining table voluntarily.

It's worth looking at how the UFCW approached these struggles to see the mindset the union would bring to targeting Wal-Mart. In 1987, for instance, a UFCW organizer discovered that for years, a staunchly anti-union Mississippi catfish farm had forced workers to show up at a certain time every morning, but then made them stand by—without pay—for anywhere from one to three hours until the fish were delivered for processing. So the union filed a lawsuit on behalf of the 1,800 workers to collect millions of dollars in lost pay—including pay for workers who might want nothing to do with the union, but who, of course, wanted the money. Suddenly, to the catfish plant's owners, the cost of signing a contract seemed cheaper than fighting a lawsuit with a potentially crippling liability. The company capitulated and let the workers organize.

In another case, IBP Inc., an enormous, fiercely anti-union meat-packing company based in Nebraska, locked out the union at one of its plants. The UFCW spent four months investigating the company's accident and injury reports; then it filed a complaint with the federal Occupational Health and Safety Administration charging that IBP hadn't reported hundreds of injuries. That sparked a federal investigation, congressional hearings, and a $9.7-million fine—which was cut by 90 percent when IBP agreed to redesign the jobs to make them less dangerous. IBP also agreed to settle the strike and to let the UFCW organize another plant.

There was no question, to the UFCW, that Wal-Mart, the largest nonunion company in the country, posed a threat. Two-thirds of the union's members worked in grocery and retail stores that competed with Wal-Mart.

These stores paid anywhere from $1 to $5 more per hour than Wal-Mart paid its workers, and they spent more on benefits, too. If those stores lost customers to Wal-Mart's lower prices, the owners and managers would be sure to demand lower wages and cost-cutting measures so they could compete.

Until the late '80s, there hadn't been many clashes, because the bulk of Wal-Mart's stores had been built in small towns in the South and lower Midwest, in "right-to-work" states where labor laws and unions were weakest. But then the company's phenomenal growth began taking it into union territory—including such UFCW strongholds as California and the Northeast. And it wasn't just that Wal-Mart took away a bit of business every time a shopper bought soap or toiletries there instead of in a unionized supermarket. Now, with hypermarts, supercenters, and Sam's Clubs, Wal-Mart was offering food, too.

In 1988, when Wal-Mart announced plans to build a hypermart—with its usual huge grocery section—in St. Louis, the UFCW local there immediately announced a campaign to organize the workers, launched an anti–Wal-Mart leafleting campaign, and began working behind the scenes to stop the store by blocking the permits it would need.

Within two months, Wal-Mart canceled its plans. Instead, Tom Seay announced, Wal-Mart would open a much smaller, standard Wal-Mart store (without groceries), along with a Sam's Club, which would sell a small selection of foods in bulk. Seay, blaming parking problems and other difficulties, denied that union pressure had anything to do with the decision (and it was certainly true that, by this point, Walton was having doubts about the hypermart concept); but local newspapers and the union itself both declared a UFCW victory.

Meanwhile, UFCW strategists, helped by organizers at the AFL-CIO's Food and Allied Service Trades department, began gathering information about Wal-Mart. In early 1989, union leaders gathered at AFL-CIO headquarters in Washington, D.C., to plan their Wal-Mart campaign. One organizer told the gathering that Wal-Mart had become a trendsetter for the retailing industry and was sure to be the dominant retailer of the 1990s. "This company," he said, "is coming head on at the heart of this union. . . . They are going to determine the future of the retail and food industries into the next century, unless we can stop or organize them."

As they all knew, trying to organize one store at a time, or getting the company to sign a contract with workers at a single store, would be nearly hopeless. In the past, Wal-Mart had hit back hard at such efforts, firing would-be unionizers and, according to some workers, threatening to shutter any store that organized. No, to unionize Wal-Mart, they would have to think on a much bigger scale. They would have to wage a years-long battle involving locals across the entire country. "The question is not whether you want to take this company on," the organizer said. Rather, it was "Do you want to wait until it is too late, or impossible?"

The company's corporate culture, too, would be a problem, one organizer who'd approached Wal-Mart workers noted. "Even when they're shit on by local management," he said, "they feel Sam wouldn't want it that way and that if Sam only knew what was going on, then things would get better."

Strategists reviewed the profit-sharing, the stunning performance of Wal-Mart's stock, the company's incomparable efficiency in distribution and information technology. They analyzed the Kenneth Stone study, with its chilling implications for their union grocery stores. They talked about the Buy American program and Wal-Mart's sterling public image.

This would be the toughest foe they'd ever faced. To get this company to the table, they would have to level the playing field. The strategy to do that grew straight out of the UFCW's efforts against other tough anti-union outfits. They would investigate Wal-Mart's operations with a magnifying glass: Gather any information that might dent Wal-Mart's image with the public and its own employees. Look into the Buy American program, and where and how Wal-Mart goods from overseas were made.

Research would be the key. "We'll follow the money," one organizer said. They would peer into how the company financed stores; investigate how well Wal-Mart complied with laws on equal opportunity and work safety; look for insider loans or sweetheart deals between the company and the Walton family; and comb through court cases for anything else that might be useful.

Meanwhile, they could encourage opposition anywhere Wal-Mart tried to build a store. The Stone study might help—they could use it to point out the danger to small merchants. They could gather data and information about strategies that stopped or slowed the company in one location and pass those along to other groups.*

After a brief debate, the union leaders agreed to begin what they would code-name the "Whale" project.

Wal-Mart wouldn't expect these kinds of attacks, the organizer said. They would have to run a tight operation—avoid anything that might tip off the company too soon.

---

* At the meeting, the union leaders agreed to target other nonunion big-box retailers too, but their primary focus was on Wal-Mart.

As it happened, though, Wal-Mart caught on to the campaign quite quickly.° By the fall of 1989, Walton, David Glass, and Don Soderquist devoted a satellite broadcast to warning all the stores to watch out for union activity. In October, Walton wrote in his monthly message to the associates that he didn't think an organizing campaign was imminent, but warned:

> At this time, we believe they will be more interested in an all out effort to discredit our Company and blemish us in any way possible, personally and corporately, such as, making statements that our "Buy American" program is a hoax and advertising gimmick. You and I and our vendors and our customers know this is not so. The union may try to create trouble for us with zoning boards and commissions all over this country to stop or slow our expansion and growth, and will make statements that Wal-Mart is not good for the communities we serve—that we only take and not give. . . . If the union should choose to try to stop us on a national basis with tactics such as these, they could spend millions of dollars and wage a long, tough and nasty fight. It is hard to know what strategies the union will try, but let's be prepared for anything.[1]

Walton then asked all employees to watch out for "any strange or unusual happenings in your individual units, especially when strangers ask too many questions" and to call John Tate—the company's chief unionbuster—if they noticed anything that smacked of union activity.

One of the earliest forms that this "union activity" took was helping to organize opposition, particularly as Wal-Mart invaded California beginning in 1990. As usual, Seay's real estate men and the developers the company worked with played towns off against one another and demanded—and got—sales-tax rebates, write-downs on real estate, and cash from town redevelopment funds. Take Cathedral City: Just before Wal-Mart arrived, it charged residents a $98-per-household fee for police services because the town coffers were so deeply in the red. Despite the deficit, town officials agreed to give Wal-Mart's developer a sales-tax rebate for up to 90 percent of the $1-million cost of buying the store's site, and they waived building permit fees of several hundred thousand dollars. This time, though, UFCW

° Tate claimed in an interview for this book in 1997 that he had an informant at AFL-CIO headquarters. Union leaders, too, claimed they had a mole in Bentonville. There's no obvious evidence to support either claim. Neither Wal-Mart nor the UFCW seems to have discovered much about the other that couldn't have been gleaned from thorough outside research.

and AFL-CIO agents helped local business owners and community activists organize a group to try to scuttle the deal.

Sparking resistance was easy. Some towns—such as Fontana, Rialto, and Rancho Cucamonga—had agreed to give millions in incentives to keep Wal-Mart from going to a neighboring community. When they discovered that Wal-Mart was taking their money and at the same time quietly signing deals to build other stores as near as 7 miles away, many town leaders felt betrayed. Spotlighting such deals, the union helped organize and fund grassroots anti-Wal-Mart groups all over the state. Only rarely did they stop a proposed store cold, but they slowed Wal-Mart down and often drove up the company's costs of building the stores.

In Lompoc, though Wal-Mart eventually prevailed, a union-backed group challenged traffic studies, the environmental-impact statement, and sales-revenue estimates. It organized a boycott of the *Lompoc Record,* a pro-Wal-Mart local paper, until the paper agreed to print opposing viewpoints. The group got the store proposal to be put to a town referendum and then organized a voter-registration drive to make sure union sympathizers would vote.

The UFCW also backed fights against Wal-Mart in Illinois, Maryland, Michigan, and Missouri. The union was largely up-front about its role in these fights; often, local union officials testified at public hearings. So Wal-Mart executives can't have had any doubt about what was going on.

In early 1991, the UFCW kicked off a campaign targeting Wal-Mart's shoe imports, calling on the company to sell more U.S.-made shoes. The union focused on Missouri, which had lost 5,000 shoe-factory jobs over the previous decade—including a factory that had closed in David Glass's hometown of Mountain View.

At the same time, the union came up with another tactic. Researchers discovered that Sam Walton had allowed various of his in-laws to engage in a whole slew of inside business deals with Wal-Mart—deals that the company either hadn't disclosed to its shareholders or had mentioned only in obscure SEC filings most shareholders never saw. Here was Sam Walton—who insisted his company's buyers not accept so much as a cup of coffee from a vendor, who often said that every dollar spent foolishly came out of their customers' pockets—cutting in his in-laws on the gravy train. It seemed a superb opportunity to embarrass everyone involved.

Earlier, the AFL-CIO's Food and Allied Service Trades department had bought 20 Wal-Mart shares, giving it all the usual shareholder's rights. So, on May 16, less than a month before Wal-Mart's annual meeting, FAST sued in federal court to make the company disclose all the deals in a new proxy statement. Sam and Bud and Rob Walton were, by all accounts, livid. But they were caught dead to rights.

Five days later, Wal-Mart spent more than $280,000 to send all of its shareholders a "supplementary proxy" telling them about the suit, and about some of the deals; then company attorneys asked a federal judge to dismiss the suit as moot. But FAST demanded more disclosures and, after several days of furious negotiations, got its way. FAST's suit had called on Wal-Mart to divulge that the company leased eight stores from Helen Walton's brother Frank Robson, seven stores from Bud Walton's son-in-law E. Stanley Kroenke, a developer, and another store from Bud's two daughters, Ann and Nancy, and their husbands, Kroenke and William Laurie. FAST had also wanted Wal-Mart to reveal its dealings with two businesses owned by the Walton family's Walton Enterprises: Essick Air Products, which was selling air coolers to Wal-Mart,° and the Bank of Bentonville, which was serving as the trustee for various Wal-Mart benefit plans with enormous financial holdings. All these dealings, Wal-Mart now acknowledged.

As it happened, the union researchers had missed a few deals. Wal-Mart also disclosed that Stan Kroenke had stakes in 27 stores leased to Wal-Mart, for total rents of more than $6.3 million a year; and that Frank Robson had stakes in 10 stores, leased to Wal-Mart for $2.8 million a year.† Wal-Mart also disclosed that the company had loaned Helen Walton's brother $2.4 million to expand the stores he was leasing back to the company.

Seay and others at Wal-Mart staunchly maintained that none of these leases were sweetheart deals and that every one of them had been reviewed by Wal-Mart's real estate committee (which, of course, included Sam and Bud Walton). But Curtis Barlow, a Wal-Mart vice president in the real estate section with fourteen years at the company, had a different view. In 1991, he was assigned to look over a proposed Sam's Club site in Dallas that Stan Kroenke wanted to lease to Wal-Mart. Kroenke wanted $10 a square foot, or about $1.3 million a year, for a 130,000-square-foot building. Barlow told the real estate committee that, given Dallas rents, Wal-Mart shouldn't pay any more than $6 a square foot.

"We can do better," Barlow said. "We should push for our numbers instead of his numbers." But the committee quickly agreed to Kroenke's price; and after the meeting, Barlow said Seay pulled him aside and scolded him, saying, "You're not being a team player." Then, Barlow said, Seay

---

° Wal-Mart paid $1.5 million for the coolers.

† Kroenke's share of the rents amounted to $3.8 million a year, Robson's to $2.5 million. The company had disclosed the leases in an SEC filing.

warned him that "if I ever got into a position where it was me against the family, that I would be the loser . . . [and] that I could either accept it and go on and do the things the way they wanted things done, or I should look at going someplace else."[2]

Seay denied making those comments and said that paying a higher rent was reasonable because Wal-Mart needed to move fast to lock up the site ahead of any competitors. In any event, a few months after the meeting, Barlow was told that his job was being eliminated, and he was offered a demotion. Instead, he quit.

It was in 1991 that the UFCW and FAST really began pushing on child labor. Earlier, the unions had sent investigators to Bangladesh, posing as businessmen, to visit the apparel factories. Besides the Mother's Day press conferences, the unions also sent members to the annual shareholders' meeting of Gitano Group Inc., a Wal-Mart supplier the unions accused of using child labor. But even though the unions had photos of children on the assembly lines at factories that supplied Gitano, among others, the accusations didn't get much play, in print or on television. They shopped their evidence to the television news program *60 Minutes,* and a producer there agreed to look over what they'd found. But, ultimately, *60 Minutes* didn't chase the story.

Meanwhile, FAST's secretary, Jeffrey Fiedler, made the first of several trips to Hong Kong and China to look into whether Wal-Mart and other retailers were selling goods made by forced prison labor. Fiedler teamed up with a former political prisoner who knew about China's prison-labor system from the inside: Harry Wu.

Born in Shanghai in 1937, Wu Hongda, as he was then known, grew up in a wealthy family, the third of eight children. He went to a private British school and then to college in Beijing. For the first few years after the Communists took power in 1949, the Wu family faced little trouble. But then Wu's father, a banker, lost his job because of his bourgeois background, eventually becoming a school teacher.

In 1957, in an apparent opening to dissent, Mao launched the Hundred Flowers campaign, in which the Chinese were invited to criticize the Communist regime, with the idea that criticism would improve the party. Wu, then a college student, said he thought the party had treated former members of the upper classes too harshly and that China shouldn't have supported the Soviet invasion of Hungary. But after just a few weeks, Mao abruptly stopped the Hundred Flowers campaign. Wu and thousands of others who had voiced criticisms were branded counterrevolutionaries and sent to the countryside to live with peasant families. After three years, Wu was allowed to come back to Beijing. But even though he apologized to the party for his earlier comments, in 1960 he was sentenced to "reeducation through labor" in a prison camp, or *laogai*.

Wu spent the next nineteen years in prison camps. During a famine in the early '60s, he had scraped food out of rats' nests and trapped insects and frogs to eat—even stealing food from other prisoners to survive, he said. In following years he worked in a coal mine and on farms run by the prison system. Finally, in 1979, three years after Mao's death, Wu was released. It took him six more years to get a passport and permission to go the United States. Wu became an American citizen, taking the first name Harry.

But though he'd escaped, Wu couldn't forget all the prisoners he'd seen die and those he knew were still slaving in the prison system. In 1988, as an associate at Stanford University's Hoover Institute, he began researching China's prison system and founded the Laogai Foundation to publish information about the more than 1,000 prison-labor camps, which include mining, agriculture, textile, chemical, and tool-making operations, among other industries. Posing as a businessman or tourist, he traveled back to China in 1991 and surreptitiously visited 20 *laogai* camps, shooting footage with a hidden video recorder. He presented evidence to a U.S. Senate committee that prison-labor goods were being illegally exported to the United States and that as much as 40 percent of the goods made by China's *laogai* system were produced for export.

None of Wu's evidence directly proved that Chinese prison goods were being sold by Wal-Mart; but some of it was pretty suggestive. That Christmas, FAST helped organize a leafleting campaign against Wal-Mart and Toys "R" Us, calling for a boycott of toys made in China. In 1992, Fiedler decided to put a resolution before Wal-Mart's shareholders, asking to have Wal-Mart's board appoint a committee to investigate whether any products imported from China were being made by forced prison labor. But Fiedler and the union's strategists didn't ask Wal-Mart to put the resolution on its proxy statement; instead, they got permission from the SEC to print and send out their own proxies.*

That let FAST demand Wal-Mart's shareholder list—which, of course, included the names and addresses of some 171,000 Wal-Mart employees who owned stock on their own or through a company plan. Glass and the

---

* Another shareholder group that year had proposed a proxy resolution to have Wal-Mart reveal how many women and minority workers it employed. Wal-Mart refused to put the resolution on the proxy, leading to a lawsuit that the shareholders won in April of 1993.

Wal-Mart executives agreed among themselves that the union obviously would use the list to try some sort of organizing—so they refused to turn it over. FAST sued. In court, company lawyers tried to argue that the resolution was just a ploy to get workers' names. It was a pretty good argument. But as it happened, FAST's long-term plan didn't call for any organizing for years to come—so the union said it would be happy to let Wal-Mart delete all the employee shareholders before it turned over the list. The judge, finding this quite reasonable, ordered Wal-Mart to turn over an edited list, and FAST sent out its proxies.

Of course, the resolution didn't stand a ghost's chance of passing without the support of the company and the Walton family, which between them controlled 44 percent of the shares. But then, that wasn't the only point of this exercise. Earlier, the Amalgamated Clothing and Textile Workers Union had dropped a similar shareholders' resolution it had proposed to Sears, after both sides agreed to a deal: Sears said it would make its suppliers sign contracts saying no goods would be made in prisons; and the company also agreed to keep a list of all its suppliers' factories, to cross-check them against a list of Chinese prison sites, and to conduct its own surprise inspections.

Wal-Mart executives maintained that there was no problem. In a letter to FAST, company attorney Robert Rhoads said that Wal-Mart already had a policy against buying goods made by forced Chinese labor. He said Wal-Mart's contracts required vendors to guarantee their goods weren't produced with forced labor and that Wal-Mart inspectors visited factories to see if they were following these policies.

But FAST argued, with good reason, that these guarantees were suspect. In China, the Communist Party controlled the *laogai* prison system and state-run manufacturing enterprises—which were often one and the same. Not all factories used prison labor, but United States companies buying goods in China often couldn't even find out what subcontractors a manufacturer might be using. As an example, FAST quoted from an SEC filing made by a Wal-Mart shoe supplier, Millfeld Trading Co.: "In China, manufacture of [Millfeld's] products is arranged through government agencies, which are responsible for selecting the particular manufacturing facility. [Millfeld] had limited input in selecting the facility. . . ."[3] Millfeld noted that it didn't have any contracts with the various suppliers that made the materials for its shoes. This meant, FAST said, that to promise Wal-Mart that its goods weren't made with forced labor, Millfeld had to rely on what it was told by the Chinese government. Meanwhile, solid evidence showed that the Chinese government had set up an elaborate system of double names for its *laogai* factories to disguise the fact that goods were being made with forced labor.

If Millfeld couldn't guarantee where its goods were coming from, FAST asked, how could Wal-Mart? Union researchers had dug up at least 314 products Wal-Mart itself imported directly from China. The imports included more than 150 tons a month of denim clothing under Wal-Mart's "New Order" private label. These jeans came from a factory in Shanghai not far from a prison textile factory that was one of China's largest producers of denim cloth.

FAST's proxy quoted an executive at Elan-Polo, another Wal-Mart supplier, as saying that one of its Chinese subcontractors operated a prison factory and a factory "next door" to the prison. Citing evidence that people released from Chinese prisons often are forced to live nearby and continue working at the prison, FAST said Elan-Polo's dealings needed to be investigated.

To top off everything, during the legal fight over the shareholder list, FAST had wangled an internal Wal-Mart memo written by a company buyer in Hong Kong addressing the question of prison labor. "Where we are most at risk," the memo said, "is with Direct Vendors or Importers who are using State-Owned factories for production, or with any who are using subcontractors [which was nearly all of them]. . . . This is not always easy to detect, and since it is a known fact that it is a violation of U.S. law, it is often covertly done."

One day before the Wal-Mart annual meeting, FAST president Bob Harbrant called Rob Walton to ask him to support the resolution. Their conversation only highlighted the vast gulf between their viewpoints. Harbrant insisted that the resolution wasn't just a union ploy; Walton insisted the company had a solid policy in place; and neither man seems to have believed the other for an instant. Rob conceded that Wal-Mart couldn't guarantee that none of its goods were made with prison labor; but said the company did what it could to make sure forced labor wasn't used and acted instantly if it ever found anything amiss. Harbrant tried to convince him that there were too many unknowns for Wal-Mart to be able to know; but he didn't persuade Rob Walton at all.

The next day, going into the meeting at the University of Arkansas's cavernous Barnhill Arena, Harbrant, Fiedler, and Wu were stopped by a Wal-Mart security guard, who made Wu turn over a camera he'd brought with him. But Harbrant and Fiedler had assigned other union members, wearing Wal-Mart T-shirts and caps, to come in separately—and, streaming in with 15,000 other shareholders, they were able to tote in video cameras and shoot film undisturbed.

Wal-Mart served the shareholders free soda, pretzels, and cookies, all made in America, as red-white-and-blue signs proudly announced. The usual parade of celebrities—singer Conway Twitty, the latest Miss U.S.A., and perky gymnast and tout Mary Lou Retton, among others—were on hand to liven up the proceedings. There were the usual company cheers, flag-waving, and songs. Much of the meeting was a memorial for Sam Walton, who'd died two months earlier. It began with a video tribute to him on three huge screens; at another point, a Wal-Mart employee even pretended to talk with Walton in heaven, declaring that Mr. Sam wanted everybody to sing "God Bless America." They did.

When the time came, Harbrant read his resolution aloud and then turned the microphone over to Wu, who was given three minutes to make his case. In his halting, accented but impassioned voice, Wu told the shareholders briefly about his nineteen years as a political prisoner working in forced-labor camps and stressed that he was asking Wal-Mart to make every attempt to ensure it wasn't importing products made with slave labor. He specifically asked the board to investigate whether the company's New Order jeans used prison-made denim.

"The need for an investigation is not an admission of wrongdoing," he said. "It is a recognition of the reality of the pervasiveness of the gulag. It would show a willingness and determination not to be used by the Communists. It would tell the world Wal-Mart is a responsible corporation."[4]

Rob Walton cut Wu off, telling him his three minutes were up and to close his comments. Then David Glass gave a three-minute rebuttal, saying Wal-Mart already had strong policies in place. "I view this as nothing more than a disruption of our meeting, and I recommend that you simply mark your ballot against it," he said. Later, announcing that 94 percent of the shares had voted against the resolution, Rob Walton told the cheering crowd with satisfaction they could "pitch it" away.[5]

Leaving the meeting, a somber Wu told Harbrant and Fiedler that he hadn't seen a meeting like that since the last Communist rally he'd been forced to attend in China.

Fiedler, meanwhile, had been digging up whatever he could on child labor, especially in Bangladesh. Earlier, he had run across a news photo showing the 1990 fire in the Saraka factory. On a hunch, he'd called the AFL-CIO's office in Dacca and had had them buy photos of the fire and morgue shots from a Bangladeshi newspaper. Now, not long after the Wal-Mart annual meeting, he ran the Saraka factory name through a Department of Commerce database showing import shipments. Bingo. Not only was the factory open again; it was making clothes for Wal-Mart.

Late that summer, Fiedler chatted about his findings with Rhonda Schwartz, a *Dateline NBC* producer who had been to Bangladesh. Schwartz and Brian Ross decided to do their own investigation. When Schwartz called Don Shinkle in early fall, she told him, in vague terms, that they were interested in doing a story about Wal-Mart, including its overseas operations. She was surprised at how eager he seemed to let NBC do a story. But that came from the top: Glass was less reticent about the press than Walton had been. Already, he'd granted interviews to several national business magazines and had been rewarded with flattering profiles. When Schwartz went to Bentonville for her initial research, Shinkle casually foisted her onto his younger and less experienced assistant, Jane Arend. She handled Schwartz's calls and requests. Everyone at Wal-Mart seemed casual about it. And that was how, a few months later, Glass came to be sandbagged on camera.

Shortly after the second interview, Ross heard from others in the news department that Glass had threatened to pull $175 million of GE products off Wal-Mart's shelves if the *Dateline* piece aired.[*] Other Wal-Mart executives called Michael Gartner, president of NBC News. "They bitched, and made it clear that they were a big buyer of GE products," Gartner said. But Gartner said he never felt pressured to kill the story. NBC president Robert Wright's only comment to him, he said, was "just make sure it's there." The day of *Dateline*'s office Christmas party, Ross and Schwartz went over the script word by word with NBC's attorneys, hauling out the fat files of documentation they'd mustered for each and every charge.

Meanwhile, in Bentonville, Glass and other Wal-Mart executives brainstormed on how to avert the fiasco that loomed ahead. Of course, the company would deny whatever charges the program made—and they knew from the interviews what those would be. But the executives came up with other strategies.

They put together a 45-minute in-house video that was made mandatory viewing for all Wal-Mart employees the morning before the broadcast. On the video, Glass said he expected that parts of a long interview he'd

---

[*] Glass denies making any such call. General Electric, through a spokesman, declined to comment. No GE products were pulled after the story aired.

given NBC would be taken out of context to make Wal-Mart look bad. He said Wal-Mart had investigated all of NBC's allegations and found no evidence to substantiate them. At the same time, he said that even before the NBC interview, Wal-Mart had canceled contracts with distributors who'd engaged in questionable practices. Glass said that some Wal-Mart stores had made the mistake of leaving MADE IN THE USA signs on racks that held imported clothing, but that obviously there wasn't any intentional deception involved.°

To fight back in public, executives decided to draft others to defend Wal-Mart, in what would be made to look like a spontaneous outburst of support. Wal-Mart's public relations people designed newspaper ads for the company's vendors to sponsor, defending the Buy American program. Suppliers were given sample ads with phrases such as "Thanks, Wal-Mart" and "We Support Wal-Mart's BUY AMERICA Program" in huge print. Wal-Mart buyers were to ask vendors to use their own words, to make the ads seem their own. Wal-Mart "recommended" that vendors, depending on their size, either buy full-page ads in national newspapers such as *USA Today* (for $65,810) and the *Wall Street Journal* (for $110,629) or buy ads in local newspapers. Wal-Mart helpfully included a list of newspapers, phone numbers, and names of whom to contact, and what the rates for a full-page ad would be ($2,790 at the *Biloxi Sun-Herald,* for example). Vendors were supposed to say the ads were their idea and were warned not to run them before Wednesday morning, the day after the broadcast.

Hours before the December 22 broadcast, Glass issued a press release apologizing for the misleading "Made in the USA" signs "in some of our stores" and said that Wal-Mart was pulling a jacket made in Bangladesh that had a label with a U.S. flag on it in red, white, and blue. Otherwise, the carefully worded release denied everything.

The actual broadcast, seen by 14 million households, was one of *Dateline NBC*'s most-watched programs—in part because the heavily promoted show also included an interview with teen love-triangle gunwoman Amy Fisher. But the Wal-Mart story was every bit as tough as the company had feared. There were the shots of the children in the Saraka factory; the interviews with Glass; hidden-camera footage of Ross rummaging through the racks at Wal-Mart stores, pulling foreign-made goods from under MADE IN THE USA signs. There was Jeff Fiedler on camera, walking down a Hong Kong street with Ross, and talking about the 288 million pounds of goods Wal-Mart had imported from China and Hong Kong in the past year.

° The day after the broadcast, newspaper reporters following up would find imported merchandise under MADE IN THE USA signs in stores from South Carolina to Ohio.

Worse, Ross had found a North Carolina sweater factory that Wal-Mart had featured in one of its Buy American television ads. It had closed—400 jobs lost when Wal-Mart shifted to cheaper factories overseas, an investor said. Finally, there was the alleged quota-busting, again with hidden-camera footage. Ross said that Wal-Mart had ignored repeated warnings from U.S. Customs officials about smuggled goods; Glass insisted on camera that the warnings were just "casual lunch conversation" and that Wal-Mart had canceled its contracts with Sino Overseas, the suspect company. Glass said the cancellation had nothing to do with NBC's story, adding that Wal-Mart acted because of "growing concern over the last few months."*

"You didn't take any action until we asked you about it some two weeks ago," Ross said.

"Well, that's incorrect. We were—" Glass began, when Ross interrupted, asking, "When did you cancel the contracts?"

"Within the last week," Glass said—still insisting that it "had nothing to do with this interview." Glass, on camera, neither admitted nor apologized for anything.

The next day, Wal-Mart's counterattack began with a barrage of ads—including a full-page ad in *USA Today* paid for by General Electric's lighting division. Some reporters noticed that they all looked suspiciously similar, but Shinkle insisted that vendors were defending Wal-Mart completely on their own. Early on, an advertising executive at one supplier—Ben Stark, at Faultless Starch/Bon Ami Co.—admitted the obvious, that Wal-Mart was behind the ads. No sooner had his admission been picked up by the news wires and made its way to Bentonville than Stark rushed to make a retraction.† Even years later, other vendors would only admit the ad campaign was Wal-Mart's idea as long as they weren't identified.

All this was coordinated with a phone-in and letter campaign, in which Wal-Mart employees and suppliers were encouraged to call and write GE and NBC with complaints about the story. The flood of calls, many of them abusive, paralyzed NBC's switchboard. "At one point," Ross said, "I was

---

* U.S. Customs officials in Hong Kong confirmed in interviews for this book that, for more than two years, they repeatedly warned Wal-Mart buyers and visiting company executives about the quota-busting problems—even giving them documentary evidence—and were ignored. One customs inspector said that the third time he personally told Wal-Mart's head buyer in Hong Kong about the problem, "he said to me, 'I've told the people in Bentonville about this, and told them I share your concern. All they told me was not to worry about it, that we're not the importer of record.' "

† Reached in late 1997 at Faultless Starch/Bon Ami, Stark first said he had no recollection of the incident, and then called it "ancient history" and declined to discuss it.

told, 'You caused this—you get down there and help answer phones.' "°
Glass also attacked Ross and NBC as having lied about their intentions.
Shinkle publicized a saccharine letter that NBC News's Jane Pauley had
written to Shinkle back in March, before Walton died, saying, "The Wal-
Mart story I would like to tell is part a 'gee-whiz' success story and part
'how to' for recovering America's competitive edge. I specifically can rule
out the 'scourge of small town America' angle. . . . I want to tell a positive
business story. . . ."

Shinkle didn't mention that *Dateline NBC* producer Rhonda Schwartz
had contacted him separately that fall, for what was clearly to be a different
story. As Ross recalls, he and Schwartz made it clear from the start they
would talk about the Buy American program, about imports and how they
were made, and similar topics. Ross and Schwartz said they weren't aware
of Pauley's letter until just before their story aired.

In its stores, Wal-Mart skipped the Christmas music to replay over
and over a bizarre commentary by radio personality Paul Harvey, in which
he quoted from Pauley's letter, accused NBC of being deceitful and unfair in attacking Wal-Mart, and complained that "since the news-media
watch dogs tasted the blood of Richard Nixon, their appetite has been insatiable."

Wal-Mart's ad campaign through its vendors continued for weeks. So did its
other efforts to defend itself, such as a commentary by David Glass that ran
in various newspapers. Most of the *Dateline* allegations could be countered
or dealt with: Fixing signs in the stores was easy; plenty of vendors were
willing to say Wal-Mart had given them jobs in the United States; canceling
the contract with Sino Overseas had closed the door on the smuggling
problem. As for those youthful-looking Bangladeshis, hadn't they all said
they were old enough to work?

But that last issue was one that wasn't going to go away. NBC wasn't
keen to rush into battle again; Ross's proposals for follow-up stories were
left hanging fire, but less than a week after the broadcast, Wal-Mart got a
proposed shareholder's resolution from Franklin Research & Development
Corp., a Boston-based investment firm that held lots of Wal-Mart stock.
Franklin specialized in "socially responsible" investing; and executives

---

° NBC logged more than 7,000 calls and letters about the story, the biggest reaction to any *Dateline*
show to that point. They were, spokeswoman Tory Beilinson told *Fortune* magazine, "mostly from Wal-
Mart employees, from sales clerks on up, yelling at us for slinging mud at the company."

there were worried about the child-labor charges. So they drafted a resolution calling for Wal-Mart to adopt a tough code of standards to make sure its vendors weren't using prison or child labor.

Few U.S. companies had formal standards. Back in 1991, Levi Strauss & Co. was accused of using a contractor on the island of Saipan that was keeping Chinese women workers in conditions of virtual slavery. Levi Strauss had fired the contractor. But then managers looked at how to keep this from happening again. So, in early 1992, Levi Strauss became the first major company to adopt a broad code of conduct for its suppliers, covering everything from how workers were treated and paid to the environmental impact of production. The jeans maker also promised to inspect its factories regularly and cancel contracts with any that broke its rules.

Robert Dunn, one of the executives who helped design the code, made no bones about the fact that the company saw its image at stake—that this was a way to protect the brand and the company reputation. And the standards paid off. After *Dateline*'s exposé on Wal-Mart, many retailers moved to drop any clothes made in Bangladesh. But Levi Strauss, pointing to its standards, was able to keep its Bangladesh-made clothing on store shelves.

Franklin analysts Stephanie Leighton and Simon Billenness cited Levi Strauss's standards in their first of a score of conference calls with Wal-Mart's treasurer, Randy Laney, and company attorney Rhonda Parish. "That first call, they were still doing damage control," Billenness recalled. Laney and Parish spent much of the call disputing the various charges, he said; and though they said that yes, Wal-Mart had found children making its clothes in Bangladesh, they added that this was against company policy and that Wal-Mart hadn't known about the situation.°

"We said, 'If you write *formal* policies and make them public, *then* it's real,' " Leighton said.

Over the course of several months, Wal-Mart drafted a code of conduct with Franklin's help. During one conference call, Billenness insisted that to be meaningful, the code had to apply to subcontractors, too. "They were uneasy about that—not sure it could work," he said. "Then suddenly a voice piped up. 'Hi, this is Rob Walton, I just came in.' So I explained about the subcontractors, and he said, 'Yup, that makes sense, we'll do that.' "

"That was the one decision they made on the spot," Billenness said.

The final standards represented a complex series of compromises, with

---

°As noted, Laney said when interviewed in 1998 that he doesn't recall whether children were found in the factory.

a mix of the quite specific and the vaporously vague. Forced or prison labor was forbidden. Workers had to be at least fifteen years old. Vendors had to comply with local laws and "fairly compensate their employees by providing wages and benefits . . . consistent with prevailing local standards." Work hours had to be "reasonable"; Wal-Mart said it would "favor" vendors who kept workweeks under 60 hours, and that workers "should" get at least one day off a week. It would also favor vendors that didn't discriminate in hiring by race, sex, color, gender, disability, sexual orientation, religion, or political opinion.

As for enforcing the rules, Wal-Mart suppliers were to police their own facilities and subcontractors and certify the results to Wal-Mart. Wal-Mart said it would have the right to do its own inspections, too.

Franklin hailed the standards as state of the art and proof that Wal-Mart was willing to take responsibility for how its goods were made. Fiedler, at FAST, derided them as naive, and questioned how seriously they'd be enforced. As he saw it, without an outside monitor keeping an eye on the company, the code would be little more than a public relations exercise. Billenness didn't agree, though he conceded that "setting standards is 5 percent of the work; ensuring compliance is 95 percent." Wal-Mart's Bill Fields, who was now president of its Wal-Mart Stores division, very quietly announced the standards at the bottom of a Mother's Day press release devoted to charity fund-raisers for children's and mothers' groups.

Fields called the code precedent-setting; and he was right. Other companies, too, had begun looking at adopting codes after the *Dateline* show, but Wal-Mart's announcement spurred a stampede by retailers and apparel makers. Sears, following up its deal with the textile union, announced its own code. So did Dayton-Hudson, Kmart, J.C. Penney, Nordstrom, Liz Claiborne, Nike,* Reebok, Woolworth, Phillips–Van Heusen, and scores of others. Within two years, rare indeed was the retailer or manufacturer that didn't have a code of conduct. Now, it seemed, American shoppers could buy with a clear conscience.

There was just that one nagging little question: Just how well were these codes really being enforced?

---

* Nike, too, promised to improve its guidelines after a CBS story in July 1993 detailed how a Nike contractor in Indonesia was paying workers $1.30 a day for 12-hour workdays, while exposing them to glue and paint fumes.

15

Breaking the Code

When it came to the question of how well workers overseas making U.S.-bound goods were treated, there was one group of Americans particularly keen to find the answer: Unions—if for no other reason than the threat that overseas factories posed to their members. For example, during the 1980s, more than 65,000 footwear workers in the United States lost jobs, as shoemakers shifted production overseas. Nike Inc., based in Oregon, was one of those companies—which made it a particular target of the AFL-CIO. And though Nike made its contractors sign a code promising to abide by local labor laws, a trickle of stories out of Indonesia (on CBS, in the *Los Angeles Times, Harper's Magazine,* and the *Portland Oregonian*) reported that Indonesian workers making Nike shoes often were forced illegally to put in unpaid overtime and took home less than Indonesia's minimum wage of $1 a day.

Phil Knight, Nike's founder and chief executive, dismissed the notion that his company was exploiting workers—though he'd never visited any of his contract factories there, he told the *Oregonian*. Nike's manager in Indonesia, John R. Woodman, was even more curt. The factories were supposed to follow local law, he said. As for the workers, "they're better off than they would be without that job," he told the *Los Angeles Times*. "That's difficult for people who don't understand Third World economics to understand."[1] Nike didn't seem to worry much about a few news stories that fretted over its treatment of nameless overseas workers. But then again, it didn't have to: To put out its own image message—"Just Do It"—Nike spent $180 million on advertising in 1992, including $20 million for an endorsement contract with Chicago Bulls basketball star Michael Jordan.

The argument that Phil Knight and a few others raised in defense of sweatshops claimed that such factories were an essential step on the way to turning Third World countries into industrialized nations. "People argued that we were taking advantage of the poor Japanese workers 20 years ago," Knight argued. "Now Japan makes no Nikes and imports $100 million of them."[2] By such logic, far from exploiting workers, the Nikes of the world were providing opportunities—a foot up, as it were.

Knight, though, was an exception—facing criticism head on by saying, in effect, that sweatshops were better than no shops. Executives at other companies may have agreed with his logic, but most weren't about to debate such a point in public. But then, most didn't have to—because the likelihood of getting caught in flagrante delicto was extremely low.

To get an idea of just how the codes worked in practice—and of the complexity of the issues involved—it may help to take a brief jaunt to Guatemala, circa early 1995, and to some of the more than 400 apparel factories that exported some $680 million worth of clothes a year to the United States. The work was simple; cloth manufactured, designed, and cut in the United States or elsewhere was shipped to Guatemalan factories, where the pieces were sewn together, wrapped, and then sent to the United States. Guatemala's only real selling point in this process was some of the cheapest labor in Latin America.

Begin in Chimaltenango, a dusty town clinging to the rugged Sierra Madre, an hour's ride via smoke-belching bus from Guatemala City. Behind a cinder-block wall, well off the highway, squatted a warren of tin-roof shacks facing narrow, dirt-packed alleys. This is where thirteen-year-old Ana Manuela Par lived. Sitting on one of four beds crammed into the single-room home she shared with 11 other family members, the tiny pig-tailed Mayan girl shyly talked about her life.

Her great ambition was to learn to read. She dropped out of school in third grade to help support the family. Her father, Pedro Par Etec, who worked at whatever manual labor he could find, considered school a luxury the family couldn't afford. Despite four full-time workers, the Par family—like 70 percent of Guatemalans—fell far below the country's poverty line.[*] They had no electricity, no plumbing. On Sundays, Ana Par would spend all

---

[*] In 1995, $3,100 for a family of four, according to Guatemala's Labor Ministry.

day at the bustling local market, making and selling corn tortillas with her mother. The rest of the week—and many nights—she spent standing on a production line at a massive apparel factory, furiously folding and sewing women's wear. Typically, she worked 54 hours a week—except during rush jobs. Then, she said, "We work six days a week from 7:30 in the morning until 10:30 at night," or 90 hours. She made clothes for Wal-Mart and Penney.

So did many of her twelve- and thirteen-year-old friends. Guatemala's minimum legal working age was fourteen. Asked how they got hired, Ana and her friend Ana Carolina Par volunteered that they just lied about their ages. No one checks or asks for proof, they said, giggling. Neither girl knew anything about any codes of conduct. Because neither could read, they didn't even know for what retailers they were making apparel.

Finding workers like the Par girls was easy. All one had to do was wait outside an apparel factory at the end of a shift and ask around. Visits to 14 apparel factories here readily turned up dozens of child workers, along with workers paid less than the country's minimum wage of $2.80 a day, workers forced to put in unpaid overtime or locked into factories until they met their production quotas, workers who described being beaten when they worked too slowly, women who were fired for getting pregnant. Then there were the workers fired or subjected to death threats for trying to organize; and cases in which whole factories were shut down and moved after workers formed a union.

Not that Guatemala was unique. Studies by United Nations and U.S. government agencies described similar conditions in other Central American, Caribbean, and Asian countries. Such conditions, on their face, would seem to violate U.S. retailers' codes of conduct. Which brings one back to that nagging little question of enforcement.

At this point, two years after most retailers had adopted the codes, companies such as Wal-Mart, Penney, and Dayton-Hudson were happy to talk about them. Shinkle described Wal-Mart's code as having sharp teeth, because suppliers knew they could lose their contracts for violations. Penney's director of buying in Guatemala City, José Asencio, said similarly, "Our suppliers know how strict we are regarding these conditions."

But when confronted with specific examples of problems, retailers retreated—because, in fact, few went any farther than simply making contractors sign a piece of paper.

"We don't have a fleet of people to inspect plants—we have to rely on our contractors to police themselves," said James Davine, director of imports for Dayton-Hudson's Target discount chain. "I don't want to sound callous, but we probably have 150 major contractors, and sometimes we don't know which factory something is coming from."

At Penney, Kenneth Russo, vice president for sourcing, echoed such thoughts. "When you go into a factory, it's very difficult to make a judgment whether someone is twelve or fourteen," he said. Penney's inspectors, he said, are trained to check on the quality of the garments, not on how old workers are or how they're treated, so they "don't ask unless it's a blatant issue."

"We do business in over 50 countries, with literally thousands of individual factories," Russo said. "To be alert and aware of all the issues we're faced with around the world, well, it's just very difficult."

Wal-Mart, too, said it had inspectors visit factories, but assumed its vendors were doing the right thing. "Obviously, you can't be in every place at all times," said Don Shinkle. "We have to rely on our vendors to make sure our standards are met fully."

Factory owners in Guatemala were far more cynical about the codes. Young Il Kim (nicknamed Fernando), manager of the Sam Lucas factory where the Par girls worked, could readily explain why. Neither Penney, Wal-Mart, nor any other retailer ever asked him about the workers, he said. Retailers sent inspectors all the time, but only to make sure the finished product was up to snuff.

"They're interested in a high-quality garment, fast delivery, and cheap sewing charges—and that's all," Kim said.

"Penney's? They don't really check" on workers' ages or how they are treated, agreed Michael Patillo, whose Fabrica del Prado plant in Guatemala City made skirts for that retailer. In fact, Penney's Asencio conceded that his office's inspectors, who monitored plants in five Central American and Caribbean countries, had never reported an apparent violation of Penney's code.

One could argue that even unenforced, the codes seemed to make some difference. In the factories in and around Guatemala City, there seemed to be none of the seven- and eight-year-old workers common in some other industries in Guatemala. In a country with a long history of child labor, this suggested that perhaps factories at least limited themselves to child workers of ten or eleven who might arguably pass for fourteen. Still, in more remote rural areas, garment factories hired workers as young as six—and overall, children accounted for as many as one in four of Guatemala's garment workers.*

---

* According to a survey by the U.S. National Institute for Statistics.

Workers couldn't count on being protected by Guatemala's labor laws, which, thanks to corruption and indifference, were practically meaningless. Government labor officials estimated that half of the 80,000 workers in the apparel industry were paid less than minimum wage. Factory owners, workers, and government officials agreed that the commonest way to settle a complaint was by bribing the inspector. "There is a lot of trafficking of influence," said labor inspector Juan Castillo Rodriguez matter-of-factly, sitting at his battered desk in a grimy office in Guatemala City. At factories exporting to the United States, "workers often aren't paid for overtime," he said.

"It's common for these companies to close the doors and force workers to stay all night working," he said, shrugging. "There are many minors working."

Legally, factories weren't allowed to make youths between fourteen and seventeen work more than seven hours a day. But that law was ignored as faithfully as all the others. Ana Mendoza de Rivera, chief of the Labor Ministry's child-worker protection office, said, "We don't have the people to investigate" what she estimated to be 300,000 child workers under fourteen across all industries. Her office, with a staff of five, had no telephone.

"Many children want to work" because their parents' wages are too low to support the family, Mendoza said.

Child or adult workers were free to file complaints, but a visit to the nearby federal labor court illustrated the futility of such an act. In the clerk's office, hundreds of pending cases, unfiled, spilled off tables and gathered in drifts along the floor. Neither of the country's two labor courts, established in 1992, had managed to resolve a single case in their first three years.

In these kinds of circumstances, genuine pressure from retailers to improve conditions could, in theory, make a huge difference in workers' lives. But factory owners uniformly said the only pressure they felt was to do whatever it took to pare costs to the bone—so that paying overtime or the full minimum wage, for instance, put one at a competitive disadvantage.

"The ethics of the world market are very clear," said Carlos Arias Macelli, one factory owner. Retailers and manufacturers, he said, "will move wherever it's cheapest or most convenient to their interests."

The other potential worker protection—unions—were a scary proposition in Guatemala. During the country's decades-long civil war, trade unions were targeted by the military-dominated, conservative government. In the first half of the 1990s, more than 40 unionists were murdered or "disappeared," including several working for makers of United States–

bound apparel, according to human rights organizations.[3] Kidnappings, death threats, rapes, and beatings were also common. Human rights observers generally blamed right-wing death squads, allied to business and military interests, for most the violence. In any event, by 1997, Guatemala's national police hadn't charged anyone in connection with the murder of a single trade unionist in the previous ten years.*

Understandably, would-be organizers or union members found these tactics pretty intimidating. That people kept trying is an indication of how appalling work conditions were. It's worth looking at a few examples to see just how things typically worked.

Blanca Álvarez was sixteen years old when she tried to organize a union at the Industrias RCA factory in 1994. She explained why. "Many Fridays we'd have to work until midnight. They would lock us in, and we would have to sleep on the floor of the factory; then we'd start work again at seven in the morning," she said. "And they made us work the extra hours without pay." Workers weren't told in advance if they'd have to stay the night. But the last straw was that the factory was crawling with rats—which scurried over and sometimes bit the women while they tried to sleep. When the workers organized, the factory owners fired them all and moved the sewing machines to another building.† The owners also circulated a blacklist to other apparel factories.

When workers began organizing in the fall of 1994 at Disenos y Maquilas S.A., an apparel factory making clothes for Kmart and Penney, an assistant plant manager and a gun-toting guard drove seven union leaders into the countryside, according to the workers, and ordered them to sign resignation papers on the spot. "They said we would disappear or be killed if we didn't sign," said José Amilcar del Cid Arias, one of the seven. They signed.

How did retailers respond when told of the incident by a human rights group? They asked their supplier, GHR Industries of New York, to look into it. Both Penney and Kmart declared themselves satisfied after GHR's vice president, Robert Rahn, told the retailers he'd gotten assurances from the factory that there was nothing to the claims and that no one had filed

---

* Such human rights abuses led the U.S. Trade Representative's office to announce a review of Guatemala's trade benefits in August 1992. The threat of ending the benefits was supposed to help stop the abuses; and the review did lead Guatemala to establish the labor courts. But little more happened, because State Department officials leaked word to government and business leaders that benefits would not be suspended, to avoid hurting the country's weak, nominally civilian government.
† Though the firings were illegal under Guatemalan law, Álvarez and the few workers who sued didn't expect to win. Their case still hadn't reached the courts several years later. Moreover, in Guatemala, a company that is sued by workers is allowed to pick the judge who will hear the case.

any complaints with the police or the attorney general's office. As it happened, that simply wasn't true: Detailed complaints had been filed. Rahn also neglected to mention one other little fact: GHR owned the factory, and he was the factory's president.*

For a retailer to let a contractor investigate itself might seem problematic, to say the least. But even after GHR's ownership of the factory was brought to their attention, both Penney and Kmart continued having clothes made there.

While it would be hard to spend much time in Guatemala, or visit many factories there, without becoming aware of how workers were treated, Wal-Mart and most United States retailers usually took action only when they were forced to—say, by a group such as the U.S./Guatemala Labor Education Project. This Chicago-based, union-funded group tried to encourage organizing and improve work conditions in Guatemala. It operated on a shoestring, keeping a one-man office in Guatemala City. The project tried to pressure factory owners there by taking abuses to United States retailers, using the threat of public exposure to get the retailers to push their contractors to clean the factories up.

But the project had to walk a delicate line. In December of 1992, for example, more than 500 workers occupied a Korean-owned apparel factory. East-West,† to protest the illegal firings of 30 workers who'd tried to form a union. Their complaints had been the common ones: forced and unpaid overtime, beatings, sexual abuse of women workers by managers, low wages, and filthy conditions. After trying unsuccessfully to broker a settlement between the workers and the factory owner, the project's local agent, Rhett Doumitt, discovered that East-West was making clothes for Wal-Mart, the Gap, and Phillips–Van Heusen. So the project's director in Chicago, Stephen Coats, warned all three companies that the project was about to launch a public campaign calling attention to the problems. In his letter to Wal-Mart, Coats wrote: "Our request of you is simply that you contact the company [East-West] directly or through your contractors, and tell it that failure to respect the basic rights of its workers . . . to provide back pay, to end physical and sexual abuse, and to end its reprisals could jeopardize Wal-Mart's contract.

"Let me be clear," Coats wrote. "We are not seeking the termination of

---

* Confronted with these facts in 1994, Rahn fell back on other evasions, claiming that only two workers alleged being kidnapped and that neither actually worked for the factory at the time. Documents filed with the attorney general showed both claims were false. Rahn also claimed the workers were laid off for financial reasons—even though the factory advertised immediately for replacement workers.
† Translated from the Spanish name, Este-Oeste.

your contract . . . but the assurance that U.S. companies will hold their contractors responsible for respecting Guatemalan labor law and for respecting the basic rights of their workers."

But rather than deal with the issue, Phillips–Van Heusen's licensee yanked its contract from the factory. Worried the workers would lose their jobs, Coats canceled the public campaign. Meanwhile, Wal-Mart asked its contractor, Hampton Industries, about the abuses and was told everything had been taken care of. But when Coats checked, workers were still complaining about being beaten by supervisors and other problems. So Coats talked to Wal-Mart again and told Hampton he was doing so. Now two things happened: Under pressure from Hampton, East-West rehired the fired workers with back pay, and cleaned up and ended the other abuses, workers said. But at the same time, Wal-Mart ordered Hampton to cancel its contract. "For the record, Wal-Mart cannot be involved with any factory where human rights violations are a problem. Please source our merchandise elsewhere," wrote John Lupo, a divisional senior vice president and Wal-Mart's general merchandise manager, to Hampton. Two months later, the factory closed, throwing hundreds of people out of work.

And here was the catch: By pulling out and closing down a factory, Phillips–Van Heusen and Wal-Mart effectively punished the workers and Coats's project for trying to improve their situation—which, intentionally or not, made workers even more hesitant to make a fuss the next time.

This could happen anytime publicity threatened. Take Sam Lucas, the South Korean–owned factory in which the Par girls worked and which Labor Ministry officials cited as law-abiding and modern. In contrast with other factories, Sam Lucas was clean and well ventilated, with good lighting and a separate area off the work floor where workers could eat. But workers there echoed the complaints of the Par girls about overtime, beatings, and other problems. At the factory, manager Fernando Kim had his own complaints.*

"Our company invested here because of the low wages and a good quota" for export to the United States he said. Grumbling about a hike in the minimum daily wage to $2.80 (U.S.) the previous year, he said, "Now it's difficult for us to make a profit." As for the obligatory overtime, he grimaced. "We don't like to stay up all night any more than the Guatemalans do, but if you have to, you do."

Initially, during an interview for a story to appear in the *Wall Street*

---

* Of 14 factories visited in 1995, only four agreed to visits or interviews. Sam Lucas's Kim agreed to an interview at the request of Guatemala's apparel-export association, which offered the factory as an example of one of the best operations in the country.

Journal, Kim flatly denied that there was any child labor; then, pressed, he said that few Guatemalans could document their age. "We always ask, and they always say they're 16 or 17 years old," he said.

Kathryn Connors, a senior vice president for Leslie Fay Inc., Wal-Mart's contractor at the factory, said that while Leslie Fay inspectors visited Sam Lucas frequently, they didn't check on workers; Leslie Fay relied on the factory's payroll records, which, of course, showed that all the workers were legal.

Asked about Wal-Mart's policy on violations, Don Shinkle talked tough about the obligations of vendors such as Leslie Fay. "Our policies are written in terms anyone can understand, and these people have agreed to comply," he said. "If a problem comes up, they don't just lose the contract, they lose the entire business relationship."

Asked specifically about the underage workers and other problems at Sam Lucas, Shinkle said Wal-Mart would investigate. Meanwhile, in a desperate effort to avert the loss, which he said would close down five of the factory's 12 lines and force him to fire 300 people, Kim ordered all 1,200 workers at the factory to produce proof of age. He began firing anyone without documents, declaring that this would be the factory's new policy. Among those to go: the Par girls. Kim spent the entire night at the factory, going over the personnel records worker by worker.

The next morning, Wal-Mart conducted a surprise inspection. The factory passed, Shinkle said. But, he said, since the *Wall Street Journal* planned a story about child labor, the contract would be terminated anyway. Asked whether Wal-Mart would consider continuing to work with the factory and perhaps find a way to help the children go to school, as Levi Strauss had done when one of its contractors in Bangladesh was caught using child workers, Shinkle said no. When a reporter or anyone else pointed out a problem, he said, the penalty had to be severe.

Wal-Mart's code—as Shinkle had earlier said—called for punishing the contractor, Leslie Fay, which was supposed to be obligated to enforce the code. Instead, Wal-Mart ordered the factory terminated, and Leslie Fay shifted production to the Dominican Republic—where labor conditions and the use of child labor in apparel factories were about the same as in Guatemala, according to studies by the UN and various human rights groups.

What happened at Sam Lucas showed how far the promise of the codes—that Americans could shop with a clear conscience—remained from the reality. Wal-Mart and other companies that had adopted codes generally didn't search out violations—and could expect only rarely to be called to account. It was difficult, time-consuming, and expensive for reporters or labor agents or anyone else to trace the links connecting children or mistreated workers in a specific factory to the retailer selling the clothes they made. In Guatemala, as in many other Third World countries where apparel factories flourished, the factories themselves were walled and guarded to keep strangers out. Most workers couldn't read and often didn't know what labels or companies they made clothes for; at most factories, only the workers at the very end of each assembly line even saw the labels; and they could be fired for stealing if they took labels away. There were layers and layers of deniability between the factory at one end and the retailer at the other. And when someone managed to get into a factory, to get the labels, to trace the shipments, and to show that these garments made by these eleven- and twelve-year-olds were winding up on the shelves at Wal-Mart or Penney or Kmart or Sears, then the retailer could simply pull its contract from that particular factory and move to another where conditions were often no better— at the same time showing workers at the abandoned factory just what would happen if they demanded better conditions. The few organizations devoted to plugging away at the issue—groups such as Coats's project in Guatemala—faced the risk of costing workers jobs if they pushed too hard.

And, in reality, while workers wanted better treatment, and while children such as Ana Manuela Par would have liked to be in school instead of on an assembly line, the workers made it clear that they wanted these jobs—that, as Nike's Phil Knight argued, bad jobs were better than no jobs at all. Jouncing along in the back of a sardine-tin public bus, on her way home from working an 11-hour shift, thirteen-year-old Leti Iscajoc said that if she were ever caught and fired as underage, she wouldn't go back to school; she'd find another job.

"When we opened this factory," Sam Lucas's Kim said, "a lot of workers didn't even own shoes, and came in to work barefoot. Now they all have shoes." This defense of child labor and harsh, poorly paid conditions would be offered time and again. In 1996, for example, defending Honduran sweatshops, *New York Times* writer Larry Rohter noted that apparel factories there had absorbed so many jobs that wages were being pushed up in even more exploitative industries, such as agriculture, mining, and domestic work.° Rohter also said that if child workers were pushed out of apparel jobs, they might wind up in even lower-paying, harder jobs in another industry.

° Rohter failed to note that wage increases weren't keeping pace with inflation, so that workers' real buying power was eroding in Honduras through the mid-1990s.

While economically true, this relativistic argument boils down to saying that as long as there are even worse and more exploitative jobs out there, making children work 12- and 14-hour days at barrel-scraping wages is morally and ethically defensible.° Business men and women making this argument often follow it by saying that to stay competitive, their company *has* to go wherever it can get goods made for the lowest cost. The flip side of this was to claim that anyone pushing for higher wages or better conditions was hurting the workers by pushing their jobs to a country with still lower standards.

But this argument isn't just morally repugnant. It's a lie. Companies— even discount retailers that compete primarily on offering the lowest price—recognize that other values can be more important than getting absolutely the lowest cost. That recognition lay at the heart (at least in theory) of Wal-Mart's Buy American program, for one.

There were alternatives. In the case of overseas sweatshops, take Levi Strauss's handling of the problem: It was a pioneer in adopting a code of conduct for its vendors; and unlike other companies, it assigned inspectors expressly to police working conditions in its overseas factories (though the company conceded that its inspectors missed much because, to avoid offending factory owners, they didn't delve too deeply). And consider what it did in 1994, when the jeans maker discovered that a Bangladeshi contractor was using child workers under fourteen. Levi Strauss could have simply canceled the contract and said it was shocked, surprised, and appalled. But company officials knew that the children would probably wind up working either at another factory or at some even harsher job. So Levi Strauss executives agreed to open a school for the children at that factory, to pay them what they would have earned if working, and then to offer them jobs at the factory when they turned fourteen.†

° There's a macro-economic corollary to this argument, captured nicely by essayist Ted Fishman: "Invest in developing countries . . . and the tide of money wrought by cheap, brutalized labor eventually would lift all boats and bring democracy." This development theory argues that open capital markets eventually make repressive regimes more open because investors demand reliable information and a legal system that can resolve business disputes fairly. In practice, though, as Fishman pointed out, many "emerging-market" countries in Asia and Latin America set up special economic zones for foreign investors and factories, with separate courts for business complaints, so that higher profits aren't accompanied by any reform of government bureaucracies, the political system, or the broader legal system. Fishman's quote comes from his article "The Joys of Global Investment: Shipping Home the Fruits of Misery," (*Harper's Magazine*, February 1997), p. 35.
† This wasn't simple compassion, of course. Pete Jacobi, Levi Strauss's president of global sourcing, said that protecting Levi's brand name was crucial. "If that means we have to pay a little more to be sure that our company's reputation and brand image aren't sullied, then so be it," he told *Global Production,* an industry magazine.

At the time, some critics called it a public relations move and said such a gesture would hardly make any difference for the thousands of other child workers in Bangladesh. But it certainly made a difference for the children in that factory. And, in fact, under continuing public pressure from various groups in the United States, the Bangladesh Garment Manufacturers and Exporters Association agreed just a year later to work with UNICEF* to develop an industry-wide schooling program based on Levi Strauss's model.

Wal-Mart never seems to have considered taking Levi Strauss's approach to its problem in Guatemala, perhaps because that would have meant admitting that there were child workers making the company's clothes—and perhaps because that might have opened the door to similar demands elsewhere.

Intriguingly, back in late 1992 David Glass had make several substantive promises about how Wal-Mart would, as he put it, "eradicate any and all illegal child labor in factories which work on Wal-Mart goods." A few days before the *Dateline NBC* exposé aired, Glass was contacted by an international labor rights group, asking about problems at the Saraka factory that had been mentioned in a Bangladeshi publication. The group sent copies of its letter to several members of Congress, the Children's Defense Fund, and the National Consumers League. On Christmas Eve, two days after the broadcast, Glass wrote back to the group's director, Pharis Harvey, with copies to everyone who'd received the original letter. Glass disputed the child-labor allegations—but then promised to end this nonexistent problem. He wrote that all factories making goods for Wal-Mart "will be inspected and certified by independent examiners . . . at least annually." Next, he promised, "Wal-Mart is establishing a fund for factories and/or garment associations in order to help educate the children of Bangladesh."

Five years later, the company could offer no evidence that Glass or anyone else at Wal-Mart ever followed through on either promise.

There's a weird disconnect here. David Glass was considered by his friends and family to be a fine, upstanding, morally correct, and honest man. Don Soderquist was a devout Christian once named lay churchman of the year by a national Baptist organization. And yet these two men ran a company that profited from the exploitation of children—and, in all likelihood, from the exploitation of Chinese prisoners, too. Time and again it was put before them, by *Dateline*, by Harry Wu, by the *Wall Street Journal*, by others. And yet their response was to do the very least they could, to

_____
* United Nations Children's Fund.

hold up, time and again their feeble code, as if its mere existence—forget monitoring, forget enforcement—was enough; as if by uttering once more that "our suppliers know we have strict codes" would solve any problem. And nothing would change.

Maybe they just didn't give a damn. Maybe they simply couldn't, or wouldn't, believe the evidence before them. Maybe they convinced themselves that all that mattered was getting the lowest price they could, that getting cheaper goods for their customers and protecting Wal-Mart's profit margins had to be more important than anything else—that when they walked into Wal-Mart headquarters, their job required them to set to one side their own sense of morals and ethics.

But Wal-Mart's reluctance to make its code meaningful would not go away, as Glass would soon discover yet again. In early 1995, Wal-Mart announced that it was launching a new line of women's apparel. Like Kmart with its Jaclyn Smith line, Wal-Mart was moving into private-label celebrity-name brands. The star on whom this particular line would hang seemed perfect: a wildly popular, wholesome, perky Christian television performer and singer, Kathie Lee Gifford.

No one outside of Wal-Mart—not even Gifford—thought to ask, at the time the line was announced, where or how the new Kathie Lee line would be made.

But soon, one person would ask. And Gifford and Wal-Mart would have some explaining to do.

16

Say It Ain't So, Joe

Toward the end, it was as though a curse had descended on Kmart's sprawling, sterile headquarters. It resembled nothing so much as a fortress of gloom, from which a bleak miasma seemed to emanate that reached to every corner of the Kmart empire. From the boardroom, where talk turned to filing for bankruptcy, to the cubicles and hallways and distant store aisles, where workers waited with dread for yet another round of massive layoffs, wondering if this time, their number would come up, if their store would be among the hundreds more to close, there was a sense of inevitable collapse, as of a once-majestic tree, its trunk hollowed by rot, slowly toppling to the ground. It was a sense that continued even after Joe Antonini had been ignominiously driven out and was presumed to be off in the wilds somewhere, licking his wounds. In those days, it was hard to remember how sunny the prospects had seemed both for Antonini and for his company, just seven years earlier. It seemed so very long ago.

In his first days as Kmart's chairman, president, and chief executive, Joe Antonini spun changes at the company in every direction, like a Catherine wheel spitting off sparks. He ordered departments reorganized, computers rolled out faster, prices cut by the thousands, and a new layout to be designed for Kmart's discount stores.

He even became the first senior executive at Kmart to put a computer in his office, so he could keep track of sales and other data. "Oddly enough," said Jay Scussel, a vice president under computer maven David Carlson, "after his was installed, there was a sudden wave of demand from all the other senior executives."[1]

In 1989, as Kmart was on its way to $29.5 billion in sales for the year, he announced a plan to reach $50 billion a year in sales by 1995. He'd promised lower everyday prices, better customer service, new and refurbished stores, better merchandise, and, well, just about anything else that would make Kmart better.

Even as he tried to improve the Kmart discount stores, Antonini tried to make the company rely on them less by expanding into other kinds of retailing. His ultimate vision—the way of the future, he called it—was of huge "power centers," malls anchored by Kmart stores and packed with warehouse clubs and a slew of big specialty "superstores"—office supplies, sporting goods, books, etc.—also all owned by Kmart. And so Antonini snapped up one specialty chain after another.

Building power centers wasn't a bad idea. Arguably, it was even visionary—and Antonini was big on vision. But the simple fact was that chasing this new vision, for Antonini, was more fun than the more mundane but essential job of cleaning up the mess his predecessors had left. At some level, Antonini knew what he really needed to do. Just after becoming chairman, in one of his first interviews, he'd said "The most successful retailers in the United States tomorrow will be the ones with the most effective, low-cost base of operations."[2]

But instead of doing everything in his power to make sure Kmart had the lowest-cost base of operations, that it streamlined and fixed its distribution and communication and computer systems, Antonini wanted Kmart in on every big retailing idea around. He didn't ignore distribution and fixing the discount stores—in 1989, Antonini announced a $1.3-billion program to modernize and expand the discount stores over the following few years; then in early 1990, he upped that to $2.3 billion over five years, and eventually he bumped it again to $3.5 billion. But consider: At the time he announced the program, only 10 percent of Kmart stores were less than three years old, compared with 40 percent of Wal-Mart and Target stores. Over the course of Kmart's $3.5-billion store modernization and expansion program, Wal-Mart, without any special fanfare, would spend three times that much on its stores. And Wal-Mart's stores were newer and in better shape to begin with because, though it had fewer stores than Kmart when Antonini came to power, it routinely spent more on sprucing them up.

But the extra time, effort, and money Antonini might have spent on fixing his discount stores went instead to a series of other expensive distractions. In 1988, it was opening the Office Square office-supply stores; in 1989, the Sports Giant stores; in 1990, acquiring the Sports Authority chain and folding in the Sports Giant stores; in 1991, buying control of the OfficeMax chain; in 1992, buying the Borders Inc. bookstore chain and launching Kmart stores in the Czech Republic and Slovakia; in 1994, going into Mexico and Singapore. And, of course, there were the hypermarts, supercenters, and warehouse clubs. Antonini was determined to delve into anything that could give him the sales volume to make Kmart the world's biggest retailer.

One of Antonini's pet projects was taking over Pace Membership Warehouses and tilting at Wal-Mart's Sam's Club. Antonini had very definite ideas about that—as Pace co-founder Charlie Steinbrueck was shocked to find at one of his first meetings with Antonini and Larry Parkin in late 1989. During the negotiations earlier that year, Antonini had promised a hands-off relationship; Steinbrueck took this to mean that under Kmart, he would still run his own show. But what Antonini meant and what Steinbrueck heard turned out to be two very different things.

"The first thing they did was step in and take over all our real estate," the process of picking out and buying sites for stores, Steinbrueck said. Antonini, anxious to make up for lost time, wanted to expand Pace as quickly as possible. All that planning now would happen out of Troy.*

What difference did that make? Plenty. Pace had generally avoided taking on Sam's Club, Price Club, and other rivals head on. Of course, by 1989, avoiding competition was becoming a lot tougher. Most of the smaller chains had been knocked out of the market or gobbled up, and those that were left—Sam's, Price Club, Costco, and Pace—were all racing to stake out turf and build new stores as fast as possible. But to Steinbrueck, Antonini seemed to go out of his way to make Pace knock heads with Wal-Mart.

"He had such a passion," said Steinbrueck. "It was always 'What's Wal-Mart doing? What's Sam's doing?'—not 'What should *we* be doing?' "

It was a question of tactics. Steinbrueck wanted to build more warehouses in cities where Pace already had clubs, such as Atlanta, to lock up those markets before any Sam's Clubs arrived; but Antonini wanted instead to charge into Sam's Club strongholds. Early on, he sent Parkin, his erstwhile rival and now the man in charge of the hypermarts, supercenters, and warehouse clubs, on a trip with Steinbrueck to a score of cities with Sam's

* "The planning was handled out of Troy, but Charlie was still totally involved," remembers Parkin.

Clubs. They were to scout for sites where Pace could go in behind enemy lines, in New Orleans, Birmingham, Nashville—even Little Rock.

Steinbrueck felt that he could make some headway with Parkin on where and how to build stores. But then, at the beginning of 1991, Parkin retired. Steinbrueck began to argue with Antonini more directly, to push harder and harder. He hadn't come up in the Kmart system and wasn't used to showing the kind of deference with which everyone else treated Antonini. He hated going to Troy, anyway. Kmart's headquarters seemed so stiff, cold, and formal—aside from Antonini himself, everybody was "Mr." this or that; no first names. And the building was a maze of cubicles in which it was all too easy to get lost.

In that sense, the headquarters reflected the corporate culture. Pace's executives tried early on to figure out ways to save money by cooperating with Kmart's specialty stores division on things like buying goods; but they soon gave up. There were so many levels of management to push things through, such complicated chains of command. And the executives at Kmart's various divisions looked on each other more as rivals than allies. At one point, a couple of Pace executives realized that some of Kmart's suppliers were charging Kmart far more for certain goods than Pace Club was paying its suppliers for the same items. They came up with a plan to supply Kmart stores with the goods out of the Pace warehouses, cutting Kmart's cost and boosting Pace's sales—only to be told that Kmart didn't want to jeopardize its supplier relationships.

In the fall of '91, Steinbrueck flew to Detroit again for one of Kmart's regular real estate reviews, in a conference room on the fourth floor, the executive level. As Steinbrueck recalls the conversation, he and Antonini got into their usual debate about strategy—Steinbrueck wanting to avoid Sam's Club—and then they got more and more heated, shouting at each other across the table as a half-dozen other executives looked on, hardly breathing.

"You're a chicken-shit," Steinbrueck recalls Antonini yelling. "You're just afraid of Sam Walton."

"No," Steinbrueck shouted back. "No—it's just good business." Angry, his voice still raised, he went over what everyone there knew: This wasn't like discounting; the longer a club was established somewhere, the tougher it was to take away its customers. Why take on markets that Sam's Club had held for four and five years? People already paying a membership fee at one club weren't likely to switch.

Antonini didn't see it that way. "You obviously don't think your people are as good as Sam's people," he sneered. It was just a question of merchandising, of outselling them, he insisted, according to Steinbrueck. (Antonini denied that this conversation took place.)

No one else in the room said a word. After a few minutes of glaring at each other, both men calmed down a bit. Antonini said he'd come out to Denver to see why they had such a fear of Sam. They could discuss this further then.

After the meeting, as everyone was leaving, two Kmart executives stopped Steinbrueck briefly in the hallway. "You were right, Charlie," one of them said, the other nodding agreement.

"If you really meant it," Steinbrueck thought to himself, "you could have chimed in."

Antonini's strategy amounted to playing a billion-dollar game of chicken—and it was a game that Sam Walton, David Glass, and their executives were perfectly happy to play, too. Like Pace, Sam's Club adopted an in-your-face strategy: attacking rivals on their own turf.

But there were big differences. Pace and the other two big chains, Price Club and the Seattle-based Costco Wholesale Corp., plopped warehouses all over the country. Wal-Mart, meanwhile, used the same approach to expanding Sam's Club's turf as it had with its discount stores, almost always building out from territory it already occupied, to keep the supply lines simple and efficient and to keep its costs down.

In 1991, Antonini had Pace invade Dallas and Houston, both Sam's Club territories, as a sort of tit for tat for Sam's Club's moves into Pace markets such as Atlanta. As soon as Sam's had arrived in Atlanta, it had started slashing prices to bring in customers. Dan Doerflein, Pace's voluble senior vice president of merchandising, was convinced that the Atlanta Sam's Clubs, at the prices they were charging, had to be taking half the usual gross profit margin. Sam's could afford it, because it was pulling huge amounts of money out of cities such as Houston and Dallas, where its hold on the market was uncontested. The Sam's Clubs in Texas charged higher prices than in Atlanta and were pulling in sales of more than $100 million a year per store, more than double that of the average Sam's Club.

So Antonini figured that by invading Texas, he could make a profit and force Wal-Mart to slash its margins there. At the time, a dubious Steinbrueck, forced to publicly defend a strategy he disagreed with, called it "a defensive move for us."

It turned out to be a huge mistake.

Steinbrueck tried to find voids in the market, areas where at least there was some space between them and the nearest Sam's Club. But Wal-Mart, which already had eight Sam's Clubs in Dallas, promptly added several more. The new stores might take sales from the existing Sam's Clubs, but Walton and Glass figured they were better off cannibalizing themselves than letting rivals get established. As they found out where Pace was building stores, Wal-Mart even relocated Sam's Clubs to go toe-to-toe with the invader.

When Price Club, too, invaded Dallas in 1992, its president, Mitchell Lynn, cockily dismissed Wal-Mart's plans to build more stores. "Isn't that a coincidence? Do you think they might be trying to scare us away?" he asked, adding, "it's going to be great fun."[3] And so it was, though not, as it turned out, for Price. Its first store in north Dallas, opened that summer, was tough to spot from the nearby expressway, because drivers' views were blocked by a huge billboard directing them to the nearby—and brand-new—Sam's Club. In a pointed appeal to Texan chauvinism, the billboard touted Sam's as "the original Texas club." The Price Club outlet struggled mightily for customers, finally closing after just fifteen months.

Pace's stores, too, struggled to carve out a profit in Texas. Meanwhile, the battle expanded across the country, sometimes to the point of absurdity. After Pace opened Puerto Rico's first warehouse club in the town of Baya-mon, Wal-Mart opened the second warehouse club on the island—also in Bayamon.

In tiny El Centro, California, near the Mexico border, Sam's Club, Pace, and Costco all opened stores within a few months of each other in 1992. "In an area with a population of 75,000, nobody flinched," marveled Thomas Vander Ark, Pace's vice president for strategic planning. Likewise, after Pace staked out Anchorage, Alaska, Costco invaded by building not one, but two, stores; and Pace retaliated with a second store of its own, giving the city of 250,000 as many warehouse clubs as other cities six times its size.

And it wasn't just a matter of building stores. When a new Sam's Club opened in Colorado Springs, for example, it promptly hired away the assistant manager of a nearby Pace Club to be its manager. The man, of course, knew all of Pace's membership, its pricing, costs, strategies, policies—everything that could help Sam's in its fight to seize that market. Vander Ark said the Sam's quickly made inroads on Pace's business and lured away some of its biggest-spending customers.

In public, all the chains accused the others of using underhanded tactics while professing their own innocence. "The to-die-for information was a competitor's membership list," said Vander Ark. That was understood—

though none of the chains, Sam's Club included, would admit to fishing for the lists. Herb Zarkin, president of Waban Inc., which owned BJ's Whole-sale Club, a regional New England chain, came the closest, admitting that managers hired away from rivals by BJ's often offered to bring the lists with them; but Zarkin said he always turned the lists down.

Then there was pricing. When Sam's Club moved into BJ's turf in Del-rand, New Jersey, Zarkin went for a look—and immediately was convinced that Sam's was selling M&Ms, Mars bars, and other bulk packages of candy at a loss. "We went into the Sam's and bought thousands of dollars of candy and sold them ourselves at the price we paid until they got the message," he said later. Zarkin made that the policy: Whenever a Sam's sold at what looked like below cost near a BJ's, he'd send over people to buy out all the merchandise, and then he'd sell it at BJ's at the same price.

In charging that Wal-Mart was selling below cost to knock off BJ's, Zarkin joined a long line of accusers. Over the years, hundreds of small-town mer-chants had accused Wal-Mart of using the same tactic against them. Back in 1987, of course, Wal-Mart had agreed to raise its prices in Oklahoma after a state court ruled that it broke that state's fair-pricing law.* And then in 1991, three pharmacies in the small town of Conway, Arkansas, sued Wal-Mart in state court, accusing it of trying to drive them out of business by selling hundreds of items, from Crest toothpaste to over-the-counter drugs, under its cost—Arkansas being one of 23 states that still had the old anti-chain pricing laws of the '30s and '40s on its books. With typical ag-gressiveness, the Conway Wal-Mart store's manager had set up store dis-plays directly comparing its price to each pharmacy's price on various items.

Pharmacies around the country helped fund the Conway suit (as they had the earlier Oklahoma suit), hoping that a win there might trim the company's sails elsewhere by making Wal-Mart worry about copycat suits. After a years-long battle and several appeals, Wal-Mart eventually won, when Arkansas's Supreme Court ruled that the pharmacies hadn't proven, as the law required, that Wal-Mart not only sold below cost, but had specif-ically *intended* to injure competitors and destroy competition.

Still, the case had its embarrassing moments for Wal-Mart. In Okla-homa, and in a later predatory-pricing suit in Colorado, the company had

---

* Wal-Mart lost despite the backing of the Reagan administration, which had the Federal Trade Com-mission intervene in the suit on Wal-Mart's behalf.

settled out of court under seal; but this time its pricing practices were dissected in public. After first denying that Wal-Mart sold under cost, the company's lawyers then claimed that if it did, it didn't intend to be predatory. When the pharmacies' attorney demanded pricing records, Wal-Mart attorneys claimed the company didn't have records of how much its goods cost; of course, it turned out Wal-Mart did keep such records, and eventually the company turned them over. When the case went to trial in the fall of 1993, David Glass tried to have a subpoena quashed before agreeing to testify; then, under oath, he first conceded that Wal-Mart did sell under cost and then claimed he'd had no idea that company attorneys ever had denied that.

Even before the Conway trial, Wal-Mart was embroiled in another pricing brouhaha that began with an attack by the Target discount chain. That spring, Target complained to the Council of Better Business Bureaus' national advertising division and ran full-page newspaper ads in six states accusing Wal-Mart of cheating on price comparisons that it posted in its stores. Target charged that Wal-Mart routinely inflated Target's supposed prices, compared different sizes without saying so, and left the comparisons posted for weeks after Target had changed prices.

Target's ads ran under headlines that read THIS NEVER WOULD HAVE HAPPENED IF SAM WALTON WAS ALIVE, adding that "he knew the difference between an honest fight and a dirty one." By using Wal-Mart's own icon against it, Target struck a nerve. Wal-Mart naturally denied everything— but it also launched a furious public counterattack.

Glass blasted back at what he called a smear campaign exploiting the memory of Sam Walton, saying that Target's unfounded, strident ads were "well beyond the boundaries of fairness and decency."

"We just need [Wal-Mart] to stop lying," retorted a Target spokeswoman.[4]

Wal-Mart then ran its own full-page ads, calling Target's volley an affront "to every value Sam Walton ever stood for."

While these sorts of hissy fits between retailers go on all the time (if not usually quite so publicly), Target's ads raised an interesting point—not in claiming that Wal-Mart cheated, for that clearly was true,* but rather in saying this never would have happened if Walton were alive. In a perverse way, the ads showed how effectively Sam Walton's sterling image had been set in the popular imagination. In reality, similar charges had been raised by

---

* Independent surveys by several news organizations after Target's initial ads appeared confirmed that, in fact, Wal-Mart did inflate Target's prices, did compare different sizes without saying so, and kept price-comparison signs posted long after prices had changed.

others often enough when Walton was still alive. But that wasn't what people remembered.

Following Target's lead, Kmart and Meijer, a Michigan-based regional discounter, jumped on board with their own complaints to the Council of Better Business Bureaus; Meijer also complained to Michigan's Consumer Protection Division. After a six-month state investigation, in March of 1994—without admitting any wrongdoing—Wal-Mart signed an agreement in Michigan state court saying it wouldn't mislead customers with inaccurate price comparisons and that it would update any comparisons at least weekly. Shortly afterward, the Better Business Bureaus' national advertising review panel also ruled against Wal-Mart. The company agreed to stop running price-comparison ads in its stores and to change its slogan, "Always the low price. Always," which the panel said wrongly implied that Wal-Mart always had the lowest available price on all items. The new slogan was the more general "Always low prices. Always."*

Neither of the two agreements, nor the news stories that followed, detailed some of the ways Wal-Mart fudged on prices. But letters and memos written by Michigan assistant attorney general Fred Hoffecker, including letters to Wal-Mart's attorneys, are pretty illuminating. Wal-Mart would use its buying clout to make suppliers give it special packaging that let it seem to be selling for less when it wasn't. For example, Hills Brothers made special coffee cans for Wal-Mart that looked like the cans Hills sold elsewhere, but that held 5 ounces less coffee—letting Wal-Mart advertise a lower price for what looked like the same product but wasn't.

Another favorite trick was to have two shopping baskets at the front of the store, one filled with goods from Wal-Mart, the other ostensibly filled with the same items bought at, say, Meijer. In one case, for example, Wal-Mart had two baskets showing the same goods being sold at Meijer for $172.33 and at Wal-Mart for $125.34. Both baskets were wrapped in heavy cellophane so shoppers couldn't pick up or even make out what all the items were. The wrapping hid the fact that the items weren't actually the same—comparing, for instance, a $20 watch with automatic quartz movement from Meijer to a $13 Wal-Mart watch that had to be wound by hand, without mentioning the difference.

---

* Sam Walton originally wanted to make the slogan even more aggressive: "Always the lowest price. Always." But he let himself be talked out of the "-est" after several executives argued that it would be seen as a promise—and one the company couldn't hope to keep on every item at every store all the time. Even the compromise slogan had left opponents unhappy for the same reason. Ironically, Target's attack helped persuade Glass to phase out the slogan in favor of the "Always low prices" version even before the advertising panel's decision. While the panel's decisions weren't legally binding, retailers generally agreed to follow the panel's recommendations as a form of self-regulation.

Wal-Mart also would have price tags on the shelves that were lower than what the price would scan for at the checkout stand, Hoffecker said. Wal-Mart maintained any problems were just mistakes at one particular store; but the same problem turned up in stores in Michigan and Florida.

Meanwhile, the competition for warehouse-club real estate had turned into a feeding frenzy, as everyone rushed to build first and lock up memberships in whatever markets were left. "It wasn't uncommon for several of us to helicopter into the same intersection on the same day, and all be competing with the landowner for the same piece of dirt," Pace's Vander Ark said.

In Paramus, New Jersey, BJ's Zarkin offered what he considered a more than fair bid for a site that had some traffic problems—no left turn out of the parking lot—only to be outbid mightily by Pace. Pace often bid aggressively—far more aggressively than Wal-Mart.

"Wal-Mart just grinds you down and grinds you down, until I was surprised I was still more than three feet tall," said William Buettner, a vice president at a Denver-based developer, Antonoff Miller Properties. "They don't know they've got the best deal they can get until they're tap dancing on your tombstone."

After haggling with Wal-Mart for five months over a piece of land in Billings, Montana, Buettner, in frustration, cajoled a bid on the site out of Costco. Then, at a charity event in Denver, one of Antonoff Miller's owners mentioned the Wal-Mart talks to a Pace executive. Pace immediately rushed in with a better offer for the development rights, which Antonoff Miller happily accepted. Buettner wouldn't reveal the price, but said it was more than one and a half times what the site otherwise would have leased for.

Wal-Mart's real estate men were livid. "I'd have the life expectancy of a second lieutenant in combat if I went into Bentonville, today," Buettner drawled at the time. As it happened, though, Costco had stolen a march on both rivals by buying a lot across the street on which it could build sooner, because the lot needed less work. Pace backed out of the deal.

Wal-Mart soon exacted revenge. After a business fronting for Costco signed an agreement to buy a lot in Great Falls, Montana, Wal-Mart's local real estate man stepped in with a better offer. The owner repudiated her deal with Costco and conveyed the lot to Wal-Mart. The next morning dawned at eight degrees—but that didn't stop Wal-Mart from breaking ground on its Sam's Club.°

° Costco filed suit in state court accusing Wal-Mart of unlawful interference with its contract.

The fight turned into a war of attrition. Smaller warehouse chains were gradually forced out of business or swallowed whole by the bigger fish. But even the winners were bleeding to death. As the economy slipped into a recession in the early '90s, sales sagged even as competition got fiercer. By 1993, sales, even in long-established clubs, were dropping lower and lower at all the surviving chains.

And Pace faltered, too. This sort of battle called for subsidizing low prices in new cities with profits from markets where Pace dominated—but Pace didn't have many places like that. And, like Kmart's discount store division, Pace couldn't match Sam's Club's distribution system, either for speed or efficiency.

Steinbrueck had decided early on to leave as soon as his three-year management contract ended in January 1993. By late 1992, as planning began for the following year, Steinbrueck proposed to Antonini and to George Mrkonic, Parkin's successor as head of the specialty stores, that Pace cut its losses in two of the toughest markets, Chicago and Dallas. As Mrkonic looked at it, he decided there were other markets, too, where the losses were too big to sustain. With the shakeout in the industry, there weren't many buyers. As much as it galled Antonini, he had little choice but to order negotiations to sell 14 Pace warehouses to Wal-Mart. The deal closed in May of 1993. Pace shut down three other clubs Wal-Mart wouldn't buy.

After the sale, Sam's Club marketers in many cities targeted businesses that belonged to the remaining 113 Pace warehouses, "telling them they ought to sign up with them because we'd soon be going out of business," groused Bruce Quinnell, Pace's chief financial officer. In June, the Price and Costco chains announced their merger, leaving Pace a distant third among the surviving national warehouse club chains.

One day that summer Mrkonic phoned Steinbrueck in Denver. For the first half of the year, he said gloomily, the Pace clubs had racked up an operating loss of $63 million. "We're really getting our lunch handed to us," he told Steinbrueck, saying he was at a loss as to what to do. Steinbrueck jokingly suggested they talk to Wal-Mart again. Mrkonic didn't laugh.

Antonini, by this point, was under heavy pressure from major shareholders to sell off Kmart's specialty chains, most of which were playing second fiddle to stronger rivals, as Pace was, and draining money and attention from the core discount stores. And the discount stores themselves were in serious trouble, too. Kmart needed cash. Maybe selling off Pace wouldn't be such a bad idea, at that.

•   •   •

Meanwhile, Kmart's supercenter program had gone askew, too. Antonini had been particularly keen on the idea of supercenters, discount stores with grocery operations. Hundreds of older, struggling Kmart stores in strip malls had groceries or vacant spaces next door—and the new head man had hoped to energize those stores by taking over those neighboring spaces and adding food to the Kmart stores' offerings.

By November 1988, Kmart had opened its first two experimental supercenters, with bare-bones, warehouse-style food operations. Shortly afterwards, Antonini excitedly laid out his strategy to a consultant he'd just hired, Gene Hoffman. A thirty-year supermarket-industry veteran, Hoffman thought the idea stank—but he was loath to say so, right off the bat.

Antonini hooked Hoffman up with Parkin. The two men inspected the test supercenters and toured Kmart's Atlanta hypermart—which, despite its early rave reviews, quickly headed overbudget and under its sales goals. And time and again they scoured every foot and feature of Wal-Mart's first supercenters and hypermarts, too.

Hoffman's initial reluctance to seem too critical quickly evaporated. Shoehorning groceries into tired old stores would never work, he thought; Kmart should find good locations and build new supercenters from scratch. Parkin agreed. The two men drew up a plan that would have sounded very familiar to Sam Walton, if he'd been on hand: Build the stores radiating out from a single center; saturate a region, and then grow out from there. Building that way, they agreed, would make it easier to stay in stock and get goods to the stores faster and more often.

Hoffman said bluntly that one of Kmart's biggest problems was its stodgy and lackadaisical corporate culture. "We've got to divorce this from Kmart's culture," Hoffman said of the supercenter project. "Let's create something that can come back and enrich the existing Kmart culture." Parkin was dubious. He'd been at Kmart thirty-four years and figured this would be a lot tougher than Hoffman seemed to appreciate. Only if the supercenters were a roaring success could they hope to have any impact, he thought; but he agreed it was worth a shot. Again, they decided to copy what worked. Kmart's supercenter employees would wear red vests so customers could spot them immediately. They'd encourage workers to make suggestions and to get involved in the store and in the community. "We modeled it in terms of how Sam Walton would have done it, in terms of the employees," Hoffman later said.

Antonini took some convincing, but he agreed, too. Perhaps because Parkin had once been his boss, back when the two men had worked together at Kmart apparel, Antonini let him and Hoffman run with their ideas on this one.

Otherwise, though, Antonini and Parkin seemed less and less often to see eye to eye. Parkin was too much the good soldier for their disagreements ever to blow up; but he felt he couldn't get Antonini to listen to bad news. Parkin, for example, decided very early that the American Fare concept wasn't working. The foods were too expensive, he kept telling Bruno's, the grocery operation that, as their joint-venture partner, was handling that side of the business. But Antonini didn't back him. It got to a point at which Antonini asked Parkin to stay out of meetings with Bruno's executives. Antonini, too, of course, eventually decided that the hypermarts were too big. Like Walton, he would abandon them in favor of smaller supercenters. But not as quickly.

Parkin just didn't like the way Antonini ran things. He seemed to listen more to all the new consultants and "experts" than to his own executives. Maybe it was a bit personal; Antonini had, after all, beaten him out of the top job. Maybe it was just time to go, the fifty-six-year-old Parkin thought.

Late in 1989, he flew out to Denver with Antonini on the newest corporate jet, to meet with the heads of the recently acquired Pace warehouse club chain. While flying over Nebraska, Parkin told Antonini he'd decided to retire at the end of the next year. He was going to move to Kansas and raise ponies. The timing meant he'd leave just before the first of the new-model supercenters opened. Someone else would have to take over rolling out that concept. Someone else could tilt at the windmill of changing Kmart's corporate culture.

Even without Parkin, the first of the new-model supercenter stores— the Super Kmart, they called it—was a tremendous success, with sales far beyond those at any regular Kmarts. The second store was a smash too. But then Antonini, eyeing the results, decided that this would be a great way to strengthen struggling existing stores, or to replace newer Kmarts that weren't proving as competitive as expected.

The idea of building supercenters gradually outward from one point got tossed out the window. As with the Pace clubs, Antonini ordered new Super K's to go in all over the country, which wiped out the distribution efficiencies Hoffman and Parkin had hoped to establish. Hoffman complained about the Super K's having the same problem keeping in stock as the Kmarts. He tried to convince Antonini that to firmly establish the Super

K stores, they should do whatever it took to stay in stock, even if that meant going to another Kmart for the goods. But Antonini didn't buy that idea.

"I kept saying this was the wrong way to do it, and eventually, I wore out my welcome," said Hoffman, who quit in 1993. With him went his great hope of creating the germ of a new corporate culture that could reinvigorate Kmart.

And it would be Kmart's corporate culture, as much as anything Antonini did or didn't do, that would doom the company to near-bankruptcy by the mid-1990s. It's important to remember that Antonini himself had been steeped in Kmart's way of thinking and doing things for three decades—as had nearly all of the senior executives working for him. They were all part of Kmart's cult of the store manager, the idea that someone who'd run a store could do any other job, regardless of whether they'd been trained for it. It was not a culture open to innovation and sweeping change—which is what Kmart desperately needed.

There were signs, early on, that Antonini was blind to the nature of this flaw in the company, and in himself. When Bernie Fauber, the previous chairman, had left, he'd advised Antonini not to wear all three hats—chairman, chief executive, and president—but to appoint somebody smart and independent as president. Antonini's ad hoc advisors pushed the same idea. A strong president could help shoulder the load of turning the discount stores around, they argued. But after his long climb to the top, Antonini wasn't about to give up any of his power. He kept the title himself, just as previous chairmen had.

Even for outsiders who could pinpoint Kmart's ailments, changing anything was like pushing against a giant jelly-blob: As soon as the pressure let up, everything sagged back to where it had been.

Early on, Antonini hired a retail consultant, Carol Farmer, to work with his kitchen cabinet. Farmer had worked with Target, Wal-Mart, and J.C. Penney; and she'd been involved in developing a new store layout that had swept the discount industry in the '70s.* In November of 1988, Antonini agreed to a proposal by his advisors to hold a three-day-long strategic planning retreat with all his senior executives, away from the Troy headquarters. Farmer was to run the session.

Since joining the Bloomfield Hills Country Club, Antonini had taken up

---

* This design was called the "racetrack" layout, because of an aisle that ringed the store.

golf with a passion. He ordered Farmer to hold the retreat someplace with a good golf school and to schedule each day's work so that he could knock off at 1 P.M. for a golf lesson and 18 holes. She found a resort in Orlando, Florida.

Farmer, seeing it as her job, raised problem after problem at the first session, critiquing Kmart's layout, its use of fluorescent strip lighting, its inability to stay in stock, and so on. When she made comparisons to Wal-Mart, Antonini grew irate. "Why is everybody so high on Wal-Mart?" he growled. "What are they doing that we aren't doing?"

Farmer stared at him. "Are you crazy?" she said. "They have an incredibly efficient distribution system, for one thing . . ." At another point, she had all the executives write a "mission statement," their idea of what Kmart should be about, what direction it should go.

"They were totally hopeless," she remembered. She was unstinting in her critiques, too. The meeting got so rancorous that, on the golf course that afternoon, Antonini told Mike Wellman, a marketing vice president and member of the kitchen cabinet, that if Farmer kept this up, he should find someone else to run the retreat. Wellman located Farmer and warned her to ease up.

To her, the attitudes of the Kmart executives couldn't have stood in sharper contrast to those of their counterparts at Wal-Mart. "The Wal-Mart people were so curious, so hungry to learn," she said. "Kmart was totally the opposite." The executives there seemed utterly averse to any risk-taking; they were bureaucratic turtles, keeping their heads low and staying in their shells. Sitting in the room with them, she said, she could feel her energy draining away. (Farmer never changed her impression of Kmart's managers; two years later, Antonini would fire her—according to her, because she wrote him a letter telling him that turning around the company would be impossible with the management team he had in place. Antonini denied that the letter led to her firing.)

Still, out of Orlando came some key decisions: Among other steps, they agreed to redesign the stores and launch an aggressive remodeling program. And to speed up distribution, Kmart would cut back its assortment of hard goods by nearly 25 percent.*

But back in Troy, the idea of carrying fewer goods to keep in stock better never got off the ground. Bill Underwood, the senior vice president of merchandising, hated the idea—and so he simply didn't carry it out. "Three months after Orlando, the assortment wasn't down, it was up; six months

---

* "Hard goods" includes essentially everything except apparel and linens, which are "soft goods."

later, up; a year later, still up," remembers Dave Carlson. Carlson showed the figures to Antonini. Nothing happened. Antonini didn't force Underwood to make it happen.

This was where Kmart's problems were: in execution. Antonini's advisors and consultants developed strategies; but many of them stayed on paper. Once the satellite and computer systems were rolled out, Kmart erased much of Wal-Mart's technological edge; but Kmart didn't use the data it gathered as quickly or efficiently. Even in November of 1993, an internal company report found that Kmart employees woefully lacked the training and skill to control inventory. The report said that, among other things, most of Kmart's buyers didn't know how to use their computers effectively to track sales and orders; some of Kmart's buyers didn't use their computers at all; and Kmart's cash registers often had out-of-date information and rang up wrong prices.* Then, too, there were still arcane bookkeeping conventions in place that unintentionally rewarded buyers for having vendors ship directly instead of using Kmart's distribution system. Such problems mostly were talked about only when Antonini commissioned studies or brought in outside consultants; but even then they never seemed to get solved.

Like their Wal-Mart counterparts, Antonini and the Kmart executives visited their stores; but nowhere near as often. And when they did—particularly in Antonini's case—they preferred visiting shiny new stores to troubled old ones. "It's depressing to visit an old store, even if I must say so," Antonini told a writer for *Forbes*.[5] Farmer suspected this was one reason the executives didn't seem to appreciate the urgency of getting goods back on store shelves; the newly opened stores they visited hadn't run out of popular goods yet. Farmer, who regularly sat in on the kitchen cabinet meetings, kept pushing for a focus on better distribution. "It was a constant battle," she said. "I'd take snapshots to Joe and show him" pictures of bare shelves in stores. It didn't seem to make any difference. Carlson's data showed that Kmart's inventory turns kept sinking, falling to below three turns a year by 1992, compared to Wal-Mart's four and a half turns a year. Some of Antonini's kitchen-cabinet advisors began to call him, among themselves, "Teflon Joe," because bad news just never seemed to stick.

But the bad news didn't bubble up from below anyhow; Kmart man-

---

* In May 1994, the Riverside County, California, district attorney filed suit claiming 72 Kmarts in that state overcharged customers. Kmart settled the suit for $985,000.

agers avoided raising problems or sticking their necks out in any way. Michael McClary, a corporate communications assistant, was assigned to do comparison shopping at Kmart, Wal-Mart, and Target stores in various areas, and then to write reports to go to Antonini. His reports inevitably would be rewritten and softened by his boss; and then again by his boss's supervisor. "Antonini's getting them a month and a half later, and they're completely changed," he said. Once, he sent a report directly to Antonini's office without clearing it—and was immediately hauled before a regional vice president. "I want to talk about your report; there's a lot of things in here that aren't true," the man told him. McClary insisted his comparisons were accurate. "We went round and round in his office. . . . I'm saying, 'Look, I'm sorry we're $1.80 higher on this, but that's the way it was.' He said, 'Well, Mr. Antonini wants me to explain why your report is so screwed up,' and I said, 'I'll be glad to explain it to him myself.' He said, 'No—you can't do that.' "

One consultant remembered a 1990 meeting he had with a group of executives where he made the mistake of asking the junior man, seated next to him, what he thought of a proposal. "I don't know. What do you think?" the man asked his senior, who turned to the man next to him, and on around to Parkin, the senior man present. "It was absurd—no one was going to say anything until the top guy said whether he liked it or not," the consultant said.

"Nobody had the guts to say anything bad," said Jeanne Golly, one vice president. "They'd all been there thirty-five years and were terrified of losing their retirement."

During lunch one day his first week, one new assistant in human resources was walking around a one-mile sidewalk that looped around the headquarters, when he saw two executives he'd been introduced to earlier. He waved and said, "Hi." They glanced at him and walked past without acknowledging him. "What was that about?" he asked Cheryl Hagel, another assistant he was walking with. "That's just the way it is here," she told him.

Antonini, early on, sent a memo around telling everyone to call him Joe rather than Mr. Antonini; but no one below him adopted that practice. Antonini remained personally popular with people lower down at the company until the end, but his enthusiasm and friendliness didn't change the way the company culture operated.

At headquarters, for many workers, putting in "face time" was more important than what work got accomplished. "We'd be hassled if we didn't come in Saturdays from eight until noon," remembers Hagel. "So we'd show up, and spend hours playing solitaire on our computers."

• • •

And what about Antonini's advisors—the kitchen cabinet he'd specifically appointed to give him blunt and unsparing advice? For their effectiveness, they might as well have been a coven of Cassandras.

Antonini had assigned one of his cabinet members, Barbara Loren, the former advertising executive, an office next door to his. From there, she'd worked on projects such as signing a deal with homemaker queen Martha Stewart and putting together Kmart-sponsored Christmas television specials.

At first, Loren was excited by the prospect of working with the ebullient Antonini, of getting the once-mighty retail engine back on track. And Antonini met often with his ad hoc advisors, especially in his first two years, when he seemed to be on a roll. But the slew of awards he won early on from industry magazines and groups, and the glowing press coverage, seemed to go to his head. He tore down the wall between his office and an adjoining space and put in trophy cases to display his awards and honors. He still worked with tremendous energy, often coming back to the office in the evening after going home for supper with his wife Kathleen and their two children. But he also seemed always to be jetting off to present grants or accept awards in person from some group or another, having Kmart sponsor events such as golf tournaments where he could schmooze with sports stars. More and more, he became, Loren thought, enamored of the celebrity of his position—and less and less willing to listen to criticism.

Unlike Walton, Antonini wouldn't have been caught dead wearing anything that could have been bought at Kmart; Italian silk ties, top designer suits, crisply starched designer shirts—this was his style, the style befitting a man running a huge corporate empire. At a store opening one day, Golly bragged to him that she'd dressed her entire staff on hand in Kmart apparel, as she always did for store openings; to her surprise, he frowned disapprovingly at the news. "For some reason, he didn't like that idea at all," she said. (Antonini denied that he disliked having staff wear Kmart apparel.)

As time passed and Kmart didn't turn around, and Antonini began to feel pressure, other flaws came to the fore, flaws that hadn't been apparent before Antonini's coronation: He began displaying a harsh temper, dressing down executives he was unhappy with, often quite brutally, in public—even at times over Kmart's satellite system in broadcasts to the stores. He regularly savaged Richard Miller, the executive vice president in charge of the Kmart stores, calling him stupid and inept on the broadcasts. "Joe ate him alive, just beat the shit out of him," said Parkin. Antonini would call people jerks, say that they disgusted him, that they weren't worth their salary; he'd berate them for failing to follow his instructions. "In front of 500 people, at huge meetings, he'd single out high-level people and just ridicule them," said Wellman. (In a written response to questions about his behavior, Antonini denied ever harshly criticizing executives in public.)

But, paradoxically, Antonini couldn't seem to bring himself to fire or demote executives he'd appointed, even when they clearly weren't doing a good enough job. Golly came to think of the executives as abused spouses.

The toughest of the cabinet members, the regal but hard-nosed attorney Marge Alfus, would get so angry in some of their meetings she'd stomp out of the room to collect herself. She thought Antonini was in over his head and kept pushing him to get himself a president. She and Wellman discussed approaching Jack Shewmaker and floated the idea with Antonini. But Antonini wouldn't hear of it.

All of Kmart's shortcomings were only highlighted by the recession of the early '90s. Sales growth at Kmart's discount stores, especially in apparel, slowed, and sales at older stores shrank. By the end of Antonini's first four years as chairman, sales at Kmart stores open a year or more had only risen an average of 3 percent a year, compared to an average gain of 20 percent at Wal-Mart. And a visit to almost any Kmart store showed why. At one in Warren, Michigan, checkout clerk Wanda Mazur groused that she often came up with a blank as she scanned items, because someone would forget to program in the price. Then when she'd call for a price check, the customer would wait and wait, and, after a few minutes, usually storm off. Customers would come in looking for specials on sale to find they were sold out before the sale even began. And it was the same all over. When Farmer visited stores, time and again she'd see managers sitting on old merchandise that should have been promptly marked down and cleared out to make space for newer goods that might sell at full price.

At an executive meeting in April 1992, when company inventory was $500 million over plan, Glenn Smith, the executive vice president for merchandising, said his people would have the number back on target by the next board meeting in May, three weeks away.* "But by that meeting, we

---

* What's the big deal with too much inventory? Simple. Normally, retailers don't pay manufacturers for the goods immediately. A 30-day delay gives them the chance to sell the goods and get cash from their customers that they can use to pay the merchants. When inventory sits around too long, it creates a cash-flow problem and, of course, cuts profits.

were $700 million over plan," said Carlson. "Glenn, saying that, should have been fired on the spot."

The cumulative effect of Kmart's failings became increasingly visible during 1993 and was reflected in the company's floundering stock. Each quarter, earnings fell below the previous year. Big institutional shareholders began to pressure Antonini and his somnolent board of directors to focus on the discount stores and getting them fixed. But there wasn't enough money. Neither the discount stores nor the specialty stores were generating enough cash. Pace was gushing red ink. And then there was the quarterly dividend, the payout per share of stock. Since 1964, Kmart had traditionally increased its quarterly dividend every year, sunny or grey. Antonini had continued that tradition—so the dividend, now 96 cents a share, was sucking hundreds of millions of dollars of cash that would have been better devoted to fixing Kmart's problems. Kmart's payout, compared to the price of its shares, was more than double that of the average stock and more than eight times as much as the ratio of Wal-Mart's dividend to its share price.

It's easy to say, with the benefit of hindsight, that the only way to raise the needed cash would have been to sell off almost everything but the core Kmart stores and to slash the dividend. But neither Antonini nor his board were about to risk infuriating shareholders by taking such a bold move as lopping at the sacred dividend; and Antonini was still far too enamored of his power-center idea to let go of his chains if he could possibly avoid it.

But as the losses mounted, he knew he had to do something. He made the cosmetic change of moving Richard Miller over to the small Super Kmart division, handing the main discount-store division to Joe Thomas, another dedicated long-time Kmart executive who would follow Antonini's orders without question. In October of 1993, Antonini said Kmart would consider selling small stakes in its Sports Authority, Borders, OfficeMax, and Builders Square chains. At the end of the month, Antonini agreed to sell Kmart's Pay Less drugstore chain to a California investment firm for more than $1 billion.

And then in early November, he agreed to cut his losses on the warehouse club business, selling 91 Pace stores to Wal-Mart for $774 million and closing the rest.

It was a stunning deal for Wal-Mart, cementing Sam's Club as the dominant warehouse club chain—albeit one that was still seeing slumping sales and a skeletal profit margin. For Kmart, about the best one could say was that it was better than nothing. Kmart netted about $300 million in cash on the sale, but then had to take a $450-million charge against its earnings for different various costs and losses, including shutting down 22 stores Wal-Mart didn't want. "We were excited," Carlson remembers. "Kmart would have given Pace away and written off the inventory, if we had to."

By the beginning of 1994, fewer than half of Kmart's 2,435 discount stores had been modernized, with better lighting and displays, and wider aisles. In general, prices compared with Wal-Mart's on many goods—on some price surveys, Kmart even came out ahead. Profits were another matter. And Kmart still couldn't keep in stock; it never had enough of the bestselling items and repeatedly had to take huge markdowns on clothing and other goods it had too much of. In the understaffed stores, service was often terrible, if shoppers could get anyone to help them at all. While Antonini boasted that sales in expanded, modernized stores were up 14 percent, the stores were on average 14 percent larger than they'd been—meaning the sales per square foot weren't going up at all.[6] "It wasn't the stores; it was the merchandise," said Carlson. "If you're not getting the turns, you don't need bigger stores; you need a better assortment of merchandise." For example, Kmart carried 13 different toasters, when the top two toasters accounted for 80 percent of the sales. "You don't need a bigger store to add a fourteenth and fifteenth toaster—you need to get rid of the bottom six toasters so you can stay in stock on the more popular models," Carlson said.

In early 1994, Kmart announced a loss of $974 million for the previous year—largely from taking a charge of $1.35 billion against earnings to fix up and replace older discount stores. Antonini announced that Kmart would close as many as 800 stores over the next few years—including nearly all the small stores he'd inherited from Dewar's ill-advised foray into mini-Kmarts, stores that were now being crushed by newer, bigger Wal-Mart or Target stores nearby. To raise money, Antonini announced a plan to create separate classes of stock for each of Kmart's four specialty store chains—Sports Authority, Builders Square, OfficeMax, and Borders—with the idea of selling 25 percent stakes in each to the public, to raise $600 million.

But $600 million wasn't going to begin to touch Kmart's needs. By this point, one big pension fund with a hefty investment in Kmart stock, the State of Wisconsin Investment Board, had had enough. Its investment director, James Severance, publicly demanded that Antonini sell off the specialty chains entirely and concentrate on fixing the discount stores, which, as everyone knew, were getting thrashed by Wal-Mart. He ran full-page newspaper ads comparing Kmart's stock performance in the Antonini years (up 3 percent a year) to Wal-Mart's (up 27 percent a year). And he called on other shareholders to vote down Antonini's proposal. The Wisconsin board owned less than one percent of Kmart's stock; but Severance had pushed successfully for change at other companies the board held stock in, and other big pension funds in New York and California quickly joined the chorus.

The ruckus was such that Kmart, in May, formally denied rumors that Antonini would resign as chairman. Antonini and the board members seem to have been surprised at the opposition—as if they hadn't expected anyone else to notice that the ship was sinking. They had a bigger surprise in store.

The day before Kmart's annual meeting in June, the country's biggest pension fund, the California Public Employees Retirement System, joined the revolt. "We have serious questions about who's minding the store at Kmart," said James Burton, a Calpers officer, announcing how he'd vote the fund's 2 million shares. At the meeting, Antonini himself poured on the charm and personally lobbied shareholders for votes. He had Kmart extend balloting for eight hours as he scoured for every vote he could get. He promised things would be turned around soon. He promised to cut up to $800 million a year in costs.

But the hostility was inescapable. "You can't be a master of everything, a jack-of-all-trades," yelled one shareholder, Chester Bogan, calling for dumping the specialty stores. "How can we have confidence in your leadership?" he demanded loudly, to vigorous applause.[7]

When the vote totals came in, the shareholders had rejected Antonini's proposal. "This is an extraordinary slap to the face of Kmart's management," retail economist Kurt Barnard told the *Los Angeles Times*, in a tone of genuine astonishment. Such a revolt was almost unheard of—and showed just how desperate Antonini's situation was becoming.

But even now, far from chastened, Antonini tried to avoid the obvious marching order. For weeks, he tried to work out another way of selling just a minority stake in the specialty chains. In August, after repeatedly denying they were considering doing so, Kmart's board sold the company's part-interest in a big Australian retailer, Coles Myer Ltd., for $924 million. In August, Antonini bowed to the inevitable and agreed to sell the specialty chains off entirely.

But the pressure from the shareholders didn't ease. By September, Antonini was forced to agree to appoint a president and chief operating officer to work with him. He also announced that the company would cut its management ranks by 10 percent, close 100 stores, and lay off 7,650 hourly workers and managers. Richard Miller, one of Antonini's favorite targets for abuse, retired and was replaced by one of the growing number of outsiders Antonini had begun to hire.

A month later, Kmart announced its seventh straight quarter of declining profits. In November, Kmart sold its OfficeMax and Sports Authority chains, and Antonini formed a task force to find his promised $800 million in cuts, even on top of the earlier closings and layoffs. But it was too little, too late. In January 1995, as the company announced yet another quarter of slipping earnings, the board and Antonini still refused to cut the dividend—even though, in 1994, the company hadn't made enough profit to cover the $440-million cost of the dividend and had had to sell assets to make up the shortfall.

For months, at Kmart's headquarters, gossip had centered on how soon the board would axe Antonini. It was a distraction from the bigger fear— that even more people were about to lose their own jobs. Now the board reluctantly agreed to force Antonini to hand his chairmanship to an outside director, Donald Perkins, the former chairman of the Jewel Cos. supermarket chain. At a half-hour news conference at Kmart's headquarters, directors insisted they still had confidence in Antonini's ability, as chief executive, to solve the company's woes.

After several months of looking for a president to serve with Antonini, the board had hit a wall. None of the good candidates—including one Wal-Mart executive—would agree to work under the autocratic Antonini unless the board would promise to specify just when they could take over the top spot. But the board had been reluctant to oust Antonini outright, as big shareholders kept demanding they do.

The 13-member board, just as under all the previous chairmen, had been a rubber-stamp outfit, not very involved in plotting corporate strategy or in keeping a close eye on Antonini; and to the extent they had, they'd supported Antonini's plans right down the line. Of the 10 outside members, all had pretty nominal holdings in Kmart stock, and only Perkins had any retail experience. Later, Perkins said he agreed to become chairman in the hope that by doing so he could give Antonini more time to turn things around. Kmart brought in four more outsiders as executive vice presidents to help in the turnaround under Antonini.

That same month, Mike Wellman flew with Antonini on a business trip. The beleaguered chief was still bubbling with plans to turn Kmart around. "I had to pinch myself," said Wellman. "I was almost back in 1988, getting enthused about his enthusiasm—until I was off the plane. Then I thought, Wait—this is horseshit. He's going to be out on his ear and so am I."

If the plan was to buy Antonini more time, it didn't work. How could it? Kmart was slipping into a black hole. The cash situation was so poor that Kmart could budget only $750 million that year to build, fix up, and expand stores—one-sixth of what Wal-Mart would spend. Inventory was still hopelessly out of whack, and as for profit margins, well, profit wasn't really the right word anymore.

On March 21, 1995, under mounting pressure from the company's biggest shareholders, the board forced Antonini to resign his posts as president and chief executive, and his seat on the board. Sitting in a chair in an otherwise empty room, he made the announcement on a videotape broadcast to all employees over Kmart's satellite system. "External factors," he said, were forcing him to leave. It was an indication of how low his stock had fallen that Kmart shares jumped a dollar a share to $13 as soon as the company announced he'd stepped down.

Two days later, on a television interview with a local Detroit station, Antonini seemed clueless as to why he'd been ousted. He blamed pressure from the media and shareholders, saying they didn't let him do his job. "Where I might have gone wrong during the past two years . . . was not keeping a real good close communications program with the investors," he said. "Kmart is fine," he repeated, time and again, adding that Kmart's only problem was that its base of stores was older than Target's or Wal-Mart's, and that he'd addressed that problem. "If we hadn't done what we did, Bill," he told the interviewer, "we would have been out of business."[8]

Years later, Kmart refugees—and there were a great many of them—remained bitter about the Antonini years. Parkin, watching from his horse farm in Kansas, said, "Joe screwed up a good company; I wouldn't mind saying that to his face."

When Antonini had taken command of the bridge at Kmart, it held 35 percent of the discount retail market; Wal-Mart held 20 percent. Seven years later, when he left, Kmart held 23 percent; Wal-Mart, 42 percent.

A month after Antonini's ouster, Kmart's board finally cut the dividend in half; by the end of the year, it would eliminate it entirely, to stave off bankruptcy. In June, the company named Floyd Hall, a fifty-six-year-old retailer who'd once headed Target, as its new chairman, chief executive, and president. Hall immediately closed 72 stores and axed 5,800 jobs.

Antonini might be out of work. But he wasn't alone.

———————17———————

Bambi Beats Godzilla

No, he thought. Not this time. As he cradled the phone in his left hand, listening, Al Norman all but shook his head. Normally, he was happy to help out Wendy Sibbison. After all, they'd known each other since their senior year in college, in 1968, at the University of Wisconsin. Their slight acquaintance there had grown into a friendship years later, when Wendy, after law school, had wound up in the same small town he lived in, Greenfield, Massachusetts.

Norman worked as the executive director of a nonprofit elder-care group; but he also moonlighted as a freelance political consultant. He had planned Sibbison's successful campaign for a seat on the town council in 1988. Now, on this warm afternoon in August 1993, she was asking him to help reorganize a struggling local group trying to stop a Wal-Mart store from being built at the edge of town.

Wal-Mart. The name didn't mean very much to him. Norman, forty-seven years old, had never seen a Wal-Mart store. He'd heard about the local fight. A few months ago Wal-Mart had won a referendum, by a 2-to-1 margin, on rezoning an industrial area so it could build a store there. The town council had approved the change in late July. Sibbison had voted no.

But that referendum had been just advisory. Now, Sibbison explained, the anti-Wal-Mart group, which called itself the Greenfield Community Preservation Coalition, had gathered enough signatures to force a binding referendum on the rezoning. But the group was woefully disorganized, she said, and the vote was set for October 19—less than ten weeks away. Wal-

Mart was backed by the council president, a lot of other local officials, and the local paper. Stopping this juggernaut would take a pro, she said.

As Sibbison explained the situation, she could sense that Norman felt lukewarm at best about the issue. The coalition leaders planned to meet in a few days, she told him. Would he come and propose a campaign?

"I don't know," he said. "It sounds like a lot of work, and I don't know if I have the time."

"How about at least coming to the meeting?" she asked. "We could really use your advice. Maybe you could make a few suggestions or suggest somebody else to hire." When he didn't answer immediately, she asked, "Will you think about it?"

Sure, he said.

After he hung up, Norman mulled his friend's request. Over the years, he'd dived into and won fights to block construction of a proposed nuclear reactor and, later, of a gas pipeline. But this was just a big store. How bad could Wal-Mart be?

On the other hand, the town of Greenfield had been the target of a lot of bad ideas over the years. Maybe this was another one. Wendy had talked about the threat to downtown. If Wal-Mart pulled enough customers away, how many of the already-struggling merchants would go under? As his ruminations continued, Norman's bone-deep distrust of large corporations began to stir.

It was a distrust that dated from his college days, if not earlier. In the spring of 1968, when he was a senior at the University of Wisconsin, protests against the Vietnam War dominated the campus. Norman had eagerly joined demonstrations against recruiting on campus by Dow Chemical and the military.

From there, he had gone to Columbia University to study literature. He wanted to be a poet. After getting his master's degree the following year, he dropped out of the program, seeing no point in getting a Ph.D. It was hard to live on verse. His father Lloyd had suggested journalism. At the time, Lloyd Norman covered the Pentagon for *Newsweek* as a Washington correspondent; he arranged a job for his son in the magazine's New York City office, writing book reviews and a "Where are they now?" column.

In his lunch hours, Al Norman had organized protests on Madison Avenue at which he and others read aloud the names of the latest casualties in Vietnam. Journalism, he soon decided, wasn't his calling. After barely a year, he quit and moved to Boston, and then to Amherst, where he earned a master's degree in education. Then he joined an anti-poverty program, working with children. That led to a job with a state legislator on related issues, then eventually to his current work as an administrator and lobbyist for a network of 30 nonprofit elder-rights groups.

It was that job that had brought him to Greenfield, an old colonial town of nearly 19,000 in western Massachusetts, about an hour's drive north of Hartford, Connecticut. Greenfield was an old tool-and-die-making center; and though in recent decades most of the tool factories had moved away, Greenfield remained largely blue-collar. It was a very pretty little town, if one ignored the strip malls out by the highway. Norman lived with his wife and three daughters in a shady old grey two-story house a few blocks from downtown. He had stayed active politically; Sibbison's town council campaign was only one of many state and local campaigns he'd conducted.

Now, the more he considered the idea of a Wal-Mart store, and the questions Sibbison had raised about how it might affect the town, the more he began to rethink his demurral. Wal-Mart, Kmart, any mart the size of what Sibbison said they were proposing—a 116,000-square-foot store on a 62-acre lot—just seemed too big for Greenfield.

He phoned her back. "Okay," he said, "I'll come to the meeting."

The coalition leaders met at the office of David L. Bete, Sr., the president of Bete Fog Nozzle, a maker of industrial spray nozzles with 140 employees. Bete's plant was near the site of the proposed Wal-Mart; and back in April, Bete had voted for the rezoning. After all, the store would bring jobs, and Wal-Mart had promised to spend $50,000 over five years to promote the downtown area. Then, too, to stave off criticism about reducing the available land for industry, Wal-Mart had offered to pay to clear, grade, and fill 68 acres of currently unusable land in a nearby existing industrial park.

But after the referendum, Bete had read a $36,900 economic-impact study that Greenfield's council had made Wal-Mart pay for. The study, written in a dense, technical style, had been released four days before the April vote, and hardly anybody had plowed through it. Even the local paper, *The Recorder*, had ignored it in the eight-page supplement on Wal-Mart and the rezoning that it published just before the vote.

But one man did make the effort—and savaged the study in a public hearing just before the referendum. Kevin O'Neil, the president of Wilson's Department Store, downtown, had decided the study didn't jibe with what he'd heard at a seminar that Ken Stone, the Iowa economist, had conducted in Brattleboro, Vermont. O'Neil had gone so far as to have the study analyzed by an independent economist and a land-use attorney, and then had brought the two men to the hearing to argue that the study's seemingly rosy conclusions were misleading.

O'Neil's comments convinced Bete to review the study himself. What he found troubled him. It concluded that Wal-Mart would bring 177 new jobs to Greenfield over the next decade and add $6.9 million a year to the town's commercial tax base, which was all well and good. But even under what it called a low-impact scenario, the study also projected that many existing retailers would close. Bete checked with other local business owners and with several economists. They agreed: Since Wal-Mart planned to build several other stores within 20 miles of Greenfield, the town couldn't count on its store to act as a magnet for shoppers from surrounding Franklin County. That meant Wal-Mart was likely to take two-thirds of its sales—between $10 million and $16 million a year—from the other Greenfield retailers.

Downtown already was struggling with competition from a strip mall off the highway on the west end of town and a half-empty mall on the north end of town. A fourth retail hub would only make matters worse. The likely store vacancies, particularly downtown, would drive down commercial property values, which in turn could hurt residential property values. Factoring in the lost jobs and lost tax revenue from shuttered businesses, the Wal-Mart would add, net, only eight jobs and as little as $33,800 a year in tax revenue. And that was under the most optimistic scenario.

Bete was equally worried that Greenfield had very little land zoned for industry, even with the acreage Wal-Mart had offered to clear. Bete didn't need land to expand his business; but without enough industrial land, how could Greenfield hang on to the growing industries it had, let alone attract new ones? To give up the prospect of $16- and $20-an-hour manufacturing jobs for $6- and $7-an-hour sales-clerk jobs just didn't make sense, he felt.

And so Bete and a few other business owners had joined the anti-Wal-Mart coalition shortly after the April vote. Bete had become the leader, mainly because the small-business owners were terrified of angering customers if they took a stand against the store. As the April vote showed, a lot of townspeople liked the idea of a Wal-Mart, with its low prices and wide selection.

O'Neil, the first businessman in town to critique Wal-Mart's plans, had received cut-up Wilson's charge cards and threats of a boycott from Wal-Mart supporters after speaking out—and he had merely called, at first, for making Wal-Mart locate someplace already zoned for commercial use.

O'Neil and other members of the group had testified at public hearings and had run a few ads in the *Recorder.* But Wal-Mart, too, had run ads and sent out mailings. Wal-Mart's local real estate manager, Sandra Watson, had worked hard to boost the company in a series of meetings with council members, town selectmen, and other movers and shakers, at the office of a local attorney. Days before the July 21 council vote on the rezoning, Wal-Mart had put on a reception and free feed at Brickers Restaurant, a popular local gathering spot. Don Shinkle had flown in from Bentonville. Wendy Sibbison had gone—scouting out the enemy, more or less—and had been dismayed to see what seemed like 200 people, including many of the council members, noshing and rubbing elbows with the Wal-Mart visitors.

The Wal-Mart opponents knew they'd lost even before the council's 19-to-7 July vote approving the rezoning. But one coalition member, attorney Cynthia Heslen, had reread the town charter beforehand, and found that citizens could take any council decision to a town referendum, if they could gather enough signatures in seven days. So she'd drafted a referendum petition in advance. She brought 70 copies to the council meeting and passed them out as soon as the vote was tallied.

At first, though, the other coalition members were so disheartened at their overwhelming defeat, after more than a year of work, that most of the petitions sat idle for several days. Then Bud Havens, the president of the town council and a strong Wal-Mart supporter, blasted Heslen in comments to local reporters, saying those sponsoring the petitions ought to be held accountable for the cost of an election.

Havens's barbs prodded opponents back into action. Ted Wirth, whose home abutted the proposed site, phoned Bete, who'd been away to Cape Cod on vacation. The two men and a few other coalition members set to work gathering signatures. On the sixth day after the vote, they stood on the town common in pouring rain, under a leaky tarp, asking people who signed to call their neighbors and get them to come down. A local-access cable-television channel invited Bete and the others to appear on a call-in show, *Guerrilla Television.* They splashed over on the spot, marching into the studio with water streaming from their clothes. Local newscasts covered the effort, attracting more townspeople.

By the next day, they had collected 600 signatures, easily meeting the requirement for a referendum. The council set the vote for October 19. It was at that point that Sibbison decided to bring in a pro.

"We have to raise money," she had said to Bete, "and we have to hire somebody." He agreed.

Her first call had been to Al Giordano, a newspaper reporter in nearby

Springfield who had organized a successful campaign to block a proposed nuclear reactor in Maine. Giordano turned her down flat.

"You know who's the best for this kind of thing?" he'd said, "Al Norman—why don't you call him?"

Of course, she'd thought. He'd be perfect.

But given Norman's tepid reaction when she'd called, Sibbison kept her expectations in check for the meeting at Bete's office. Then too, Bete, a staunch conservative, had made it clear he was apprehensive about Norman, whom he considered a wild-eyed liberal.

At first, Norman sat and listened as Bete, O'Neil, and the other coalition organizers concocted financial arguments against the store, describing how it would hurt incremental tax rates and so on. Suddenly he interrupted.

"This battle can't be won by quibbling over tax rates," Norman said, gruffly. "This has to be about our town, our community. You're trying to appeal to people's brains. We want to appeal to their hearts.

"This is a political campaign," he continued. "We want to make it clear Wal-Mart is the enemy here, and we don't want to appeal to the intellect to do that." He pulled out a sheaf of papers he'd brought with him. It was, Sibbison saw with delight, a game plan—a whole campaign already laid out for the next eight weeks.

The first thing they needed, he told them, was a snappier name. Greenfield Community Preservation Coalition? Please. This should be the "We're Against the Wal Committee."

Something had happened, Sibbison thought, watching Norman take over the meeting. Something had captured his imagination. He was "on." As Norman spoke, it was as though everyone in the room was being pumped full of energy. Norman showed them ads he'd designed. One showed a Wal-Mart store as a Pandora's box, the roof lifted, with snakes and rats, slugs and bugs slithering out. "We're not gaining a store," the ad copy read. "We're losing a community." The reticent Yankee merchants gathered in the room blanched at the brutal directness of Norman's approach. They would never have dreamed, on their own, of taking the Mr. Buy-American, mom-and-apple-pie, small-town image of Sam Walton's company and transmogrifying it into a nest of snakes and monsters.

But in their glances to each other, Sibbison could see that they were as fascinated as they were appalled—that the ads appealed to some deeply buried rebellious spark in them.

This would have to be run like any other political campaign, Norman said: grassroots organizing; intensive advertising; polling to figure out which voters were for or against the measure; and an organized get-out-the-vote effort on election day. They would need to raise at least $15,000, including his fee of $4,000, he told them. If they could raise the money, he'd do the job.

Only in retrospect would their decision seem obvious. Most of the business owners had stayed on the sidelines during the earlier debate, afraid to offend customers. Norman wanted them visibly involved: Their names would be on advertisements; in some cases, their faces, too. But as they discussed his proposed campaign, they quickly decided it was time to put up or shut up. They agreed to hire him.

Work got under way quickly. Norman had them print up hundreds of bumper stickers that read STOP THE WAL, to be plastered on as many cars as possible before the end of August. He had the group hold a press conference at which they unveiled a four-foot-by-six-foot bulletin board, dubbed "the Wal" by Norman, on which they tacked letters from locals and from Wal-Mart opponents in other towns. They invited interested people to record their views and said they'd have the board on the town common every weekend, and various other places around town. Norman wanted it to be a visual symbol of community opposition. As the comments piled up, a second and then a third "Wal" would be added.

At the press conference, the balding Bete, brandishing a wooden slingshot, his glasses pushed professorially down on his nose, told reporters he was "one David willing to fight the Wal-Mart Goliath."[1]

The group barraged the town with ominous radio and newspaper ads. "You can't buy small-town life at a Wal-Mart. You can only lose it there," warned one ad. Another ad, titled "Wal-Mart's Land Grab," superimposed a rendering of the proposed Wal-Mart development over a map of downtown Greenfield, to show that it would be bigger than the entire downtown commercial district.

Norman had immediately plunged into opposition research—and poured whatever he found into more ads. When he discovered that the campaign finance reports of a pro-Wal-Mart group, Citizens for Economic Growth, showed that every penny of its funding came from Wal-Mart, rather than from Greenfield residents, he prodded the local newspaper to run a story about that fact. When it wouldn't, he published an ad cackling, "Look Who's Contributing to Wal-Mart!"

The committee whipped up a four-page tabloid advertising insert that went to 6,000 local newspaper subscribers. Among other broadsides, the insert included warning letters from other towns; excerpted an *Arkansas Times* story saying that the average Wal-Mart employee earned only $10,950 a year, including profit-sharing; and recounted *Dateline NBC's* investigation of child labor, mislabeled goods, smuggling, and bogus Buy American claims.

Committee members canvassed for volunteers to write to all the area newspapers, which printed dozens of letters-to-the-editor vilifying Wal-Mart as a greedy destroyer of local businesses and the small-town way of life, and as an underhanded plunderer mouthing empty "Made in the USA" promises while taking away American jobs and exploiting children over-seas. Norman staged events meant to energize opponents and garner media publicity, such as a "Main Street New England Walk against Wal-Mart," led by a man dressed as a Revolutionary soldier, and the publication of an open letter to David Glass asking him to find an alternative site.

For their part, Wal-Mart executives in Bentonville, facing opposition in numerous New England towns, already had abandoned the low-key ap-proach they had adopted so long before in Steamboat Springs. Back in March, before the first Greenfield referendum, Tom Seay had authorized spending just under $4,000 for ads placed through the company-funded Citizens for Economic Growth group (whose initial officers, according to state records, were the secretary of the Greenfield attorney whom Wal-Mart had hired and the spouse of another attorney in the same office).

Before the town council's July vote, Wal-Mart had funded a telephone poll in which Greenfield residents were asked such questions as "Do you think that the town council should follow the will of the people in voting along the lines of the [April] referendum, or should they vote against the will of the people?" Anyone saying they favored the zoning change had been urged to phone the town council members.

Wal-Mart ran an even more aggressive version of the poll about the same time in Westford, a northeastern Massachusetts town where it also faced well-organized opposition to a proposed store. There, pollsters asked people to reveal their income, their education level, and their shopping preferences, before popping this question: "Are you prepared to support your town officials in an expensive and losing legal battle if [the proposed store] is denied a permit?"[2]

But such heavy-handed questions irked many Westford residents and seem to have inadvertently boosted opposition to the store. By the end of the month, nearly 5,000 of the 17,000 Westford residents had signed the anti-Wal-Mart petition. Elizabeth Michaud, the leader of the Westford group, organized people to take turns phoning David Glass at home in Bentonville, asking him to cancel the planned store. In September, Shinkle announced that Wal-Mart would withdraw its proposal and conceded the opposition was responsible. "We still feel a majority of the citizens are desirous of a store in Westford," he said, before echoing his comments in Steamboat years earlier that, nevertheless, "Wal-Mart does not want to be divisive in any community."[3]

Unsurprisingly, Norman immediately seized on the comment to tell local newspapers that the issue was just as divisive in Greenfield, and that Wal-Mart should pull out there, too.

In the weeks leading up to Greenfield's October referendum, Wal-Mart spent thousands of dollars on ads that, rather than rebutting Norman's charges, quoted leaders in other towns touting the benefits of having Wal-Mart in their communities. "Who says low prices, big selection and great service are dirty words?" asked one ad. The company also mailed out thousands of unsigned flyers; when Norman promptly charged that unsigned mailings were against state election laws, Wal-Mart initially denied and then belatedly admitted that it had paid for them.

Then, one week before the vote, a county court judge in Arkansas found Wal-Mart guilty of "predatory pricing" and ordered the company to pay $298,407 in damages to the three pharmacists in Conway, Arkansas, who had filed the suit. Though the ruling would be reversed on appeal, the timing of the widely reported decision handed Norman still more ammunition against the company.

Meanwhile, the anti-Wal-Mart committee hired a telemarketing company to conduct its own poll of 4,000 local voters, producing lists of people leaning for or against the store. The weekend before the referendum, volunteers called everyone who'd said they were against the store to remind them to vote.

On the day of the referendum, volunteers sat by the polling booths and ticked the names of known Wal-Mart opponents off their lists as people arrived to vote. In late afternoon, they telephoned everyone who hadn't shown up yet and asked them to vote.

The effort paid off. Greenfield rejected the rezoning by 9 votes—2,854 to 2,845. For Wal-Mart, the defeat, which made headlines and network newscasts across the country, was profoundly embarrassing. It was one thing to walk away from a site, as in Westford. This public repudiation was another matter.

Wal-Mart reported spending $30,500 on the election campaign, including nearly $25,000 for a public relations consulting firm that had designed the advertising, flyers, and polling effort. We're Against the Wal had spent $17,000.

But far beyond Greenfield, the trends were frustrating—and infuriating—to Tom Seay and the other executives. Three years of effort to open stores in Williston and St. Albans, Vermont, had so far gone nowhere—even though, in St. Albans, 1,000 people had signed petitions favoring Wal-Mart. In June, the National Trust for Historic Preservation, which annually published the list "America's 11 Most Endangered Historic Places," had taken a swipe at Wal-Mart by declaring the entire state of Vermont to be endangered by superstore sprawl. That same month, in Saugus, Massachusetts, a town already chock-full of competing discounters, chain restaurants, and billboards, the planning board voted unanimously to keep Wal-Mart out. In Bath, Maine, opponents had thrown up one roadblock after another, forcing Seay to opt for a fall-back site in the town of Brunswick, instead. Wal-Mart had been forced to give up plans in North Olmstead, Ohio, too, and in Paramus, New Jersey. And, of course, in Westford.

Less than a month after the Greenfield referendum, Shinkle would announce that Wal-Mart was putting on hold its plans in two more Massachusetts towns: Framingham and Northboro.

In other parts of the country, up until the early '90s, it had taken Wal-Mart an average of six to nine months to acquire land, get the necessary permits, and build a store; in New England, it was taking an average of thirty months—as the company admitted at a meeting in Bentonville for Wall Street analysts. Six of the first 30 stores Wal-Mart proposed in the region had sparked heated fights. Even where opposition was minimal, state and local land-use laws, conservation regulations, and historical preservation codes were proving far more stringent and troublesome than in the South or the Midwest.

Don Shinkle argued, and sometimes with justification, that the opponents were "a vocal minority." And every time the question came up, he said that none of these fights were affecting the company's bottom line; but putting that spin over convincingly was becoming tougher with every new headline.

It wasn't much comfort that other retailers, many of them imitators spawned by Wal-Mart's success, also were running into barricades. Atlanta-based Home Depot, for example, was embroiled in litigation over proposed stores in the Boston suburb of West Roxbury and in Ozone Park, in Queens, New York, among others.

In large part, it was the explosion of the "big box" retail chains—so called because the usually windowless stores looked like big boxes—that was giving rise to all this community activism. Home Depot, a building-supplies chain, was one member of a whole new type of big-box retailers that had sprung up in the '80s: the category killer. Toys "R" Us was one of the earliest examples, a chain of very large stores that tried to dominate one narrow retail category by offering the best selection and lowest prices. Its chairman, Charles Lazarus, whom Walton had appointed to Wal-Mart's board of directors (over Jack Shewmaker's objections) from 1984 to 1989, had proven an apt disciple of Walton. But there were dozens of others—including all those specialty chains Antonini had bought for Kmart—specializing in office supplies, sporting goods, home improvement, electronics, and more.

The chains extended the low-price, high-volume strategy into more specialized niches, but like Wal-Mart, most avoided existing commercial centers, opting for cheaper, undeveloped land on the edges of suburbs or in outlying areas of small towns. The stores might stand alone or be grouped with other category killers in so-called power centers, but, like Wal-Marts, they always were surrounded by acres of parking and were usually plopped down near highways, for easy access by trucks bringing in goods.

Then, too, the warehouse-club industry had exploded with the rivalry between Sam's Club, Pace, Price Club, and Costco, as each raced to establish itself in as many markets as possible ahead of its rivals. As all these new chains sprawled across the country, they were competing for real estate and market share in the same suburbs and sleepy towns. Adding to the pressure was a new retailing concept, the factory-outlet mall, which featured cutprice stores where apparel makers and other manufacturers sold their old inventory. From 1988 to 1993, the number of such outlet malls more than doubled, to 275.

Everybody building big stores and malls knew there were already too many out there; but everybody seemed convinced that they could be the one to snatch someone else's business away, rather than being the victim. It got to the point that few commercial developers could get money to build shopping space—not that this slowed the retail frenzy. And, in a deposition for a lawsuit, Tom Seay described why: "We have more shopping space in the U.S. than is needed. We're in an overbuilt situation. So most people cannot get financing to build a center. And so if we want to continue our program of expanding stores, relocating stores, building new stores, [continuing] our growth and serving the customer and taking care of that customer, then in today's financial environment we have to fund it ourselves."[4] And that's just what Wal-Mart and many other big retailers did.

To many preservationists, new commercial developments seemed to spring up willy-nilly, practically overnight. In 1992, major retailers spent more than $11 billion building stores, on top of $9 billion the year before.

Wal-Mart itself, in 1992, built 161 new discount stores, relocated or expanded 170 more, added 48 new Sam's Clubs, and relocated or expanded 40 others.

That "the protests have grown in proportion to the relentless, expansionary march of behemoth retailers," as *Time* magazine's Sophronia Scott Gregory so aptly put it, should not have been surprising.[5] And, as the biggest retailer in the world, the one building the most new stores, and the archetype for imitators, Wal-Mart became the obvious choice for chief villain.

As he had worked on the Greenfield campaign, Al Norman had tracked groups in other towns fighting Wal-Mart and had swapped information and suggestions with some of them. Now, with the win in Greenfield, Norman's bearded visage popped up everywhere from the *New York Times* to network newscasts—and he found himself in high demand. Groups opposing Wal-Mart stores elsewhere in New England, and farther afield, phoned and faxed him begging for help. Could he come and speak? Could he help them organize? Did he have research they could use?

Could they, too, succeed by portraying Wal-Mart as a Frankenstein's monster run amok?

The defeat in Greenfield began to cast a looming shadow over scores of other places the company planned new stores. The march of Wal-Mart and rival retailers already had created a cottage industry of doomsayers; but most, like Ken Stone, counseled small towns and small businesses on how to adapt to the inevitable, on how to minimize their losses, on how to change their ways of doing business in order to survive.

Norman, on the other hand, had people all but hoisting pitchforks and torches against the company. On his weekends, he started traveling to visit groups that had phoned him in such towns as Lake Placid and East Aurora, New York; Quincy, Massachusetts; Lancaster, Pennsylvania; and Williston, Vermont. Some groups were battling other big-box retailers, but the vast majority were opposing Wal-Marts. Norman designed a campaign package he could send to any group that called. It included newspaper clippings about the Greenfield fight; other clippings critical of Wal-Mart on various fronts; copies of his campaign materials—ads, letters to the editor, even the phone survey forms—and copies of Wal-Mart's responses. It was a blueprint for how to fight.

Several of the groups, he found, already had begun amassing names, phone numbers, and addresses of their counterparts. Anti-Wal-Mart activists were beginning to form a network.

That December, the National Trust for Historic Preservation organized a two-day conference at Boston's Museum of Science on what it called "superstore sprawl." Norman sat on one panel; so did Elizabeth Michaud, who had led the fight against Wal-Mart in Westford. The conference, meant to encourage development in town and city centers, rather than at the edges, was filled with conservationists, land-use attorneys, developers, union activists, and community activists. But Wal-Mart and the other big-box retailers were not invited. Constance Beaumont, one of the organizers of the conference, said, "The idea was to help citizens' groups who felt isolated and beleaguered, to let them see they weren't alone."

Some of the 150-odd attendees spoke excitedly about creating an Internet-based "sprawl-net," linking opposition groups. Norman thought the idea to be overly optimistic; few of the activists he'd visited seemed particularly computer-savvy. He thought more effective work could be done on the ground.

Norman seemed to take particular delight in finding ways to get under the company's skin. Wal-Mart sold more underwear than any other retailer. In speeches, Norman took to saying that "Wal-Mart is like a cheap pair of underwear—it just keeps creeping up on you." Such comments inevitably made their way back to Bentonville, where Glass, Seay, and other Wal-Mart executives agreed to ramp up their response to the opposition.

First, they beefed up the company's modest public relations division, authorizing Don Shinkle to hire more people. Shinkle also hired a Florida consultant, ADI PressTrac, to monitor all news coverage of Wal-Mart, whether print, television, or radio. The coverage was broken down by specific market areas and included news stories, editorials, letters to the editor, and opinion pieces. These were measured and analyzed not only by quantity but by how favorable or unfavorable they seemed. As Shinkle put it, with this information, "they knew" precisely where to focus special attention next month, based on last month's report.

"We also know, through this database, which reporters are more balanced and which ones need special stroking based on previous reporting," he said.[6] The data, Shinkle added, helped the company decide where to spend money and how to get its side of any story out not only to the public, but to its own workers and shareholders.

Second, Shinkle persuaded executives to try a rapprochement with such groups as the National Trust. The month after the last Greenfield referendum, company executives agreed to meet with trust leaders, including Beaumont and trust president Richard Moe, who both flew down to Bentonville. Glass, Rob Walton, Don Soderquist, Seay, and Shinkle sat in on the meeting. Moe did most of the talking.

He said the trust didn't oppose Wal-Mart or the opening of more Wal-Mart stores; but he hoped to convince the company to develop a new prototype that would be more community friendly: designed for pedestrians and mass transit instead of for cars and, at 50,000 square feet, easier to find space for in existing town centers. He tried to make the case for stores with more than one floor, so that Wal-Mart could move into empty downtown spaces more easily. He wanted, he said, to encourage the company to be more responsive to community concerns.

The Wal-Mart men listened politely, and Walton and Soderquist asked many questions. But they demurred from making any promises. They knew retailing, and from a retail standpoint, their formula worked. Big stores drew more people; since early on, most Wal-Mart customers always drove to the store; and stores on one level were easier and cheaper to build, maintain, and restock. From their perspective, every one of Moe's ideas carried a hefty price tag without any promise of a bottom-line return.

But neither side had expected too much. Moe and Beaumont had simply wanted, for now, to have their ideas heard; the Wal-Mart men had hoped to defuse, a little, opposition from a group that seemed particularly likely to stir up resistance to more proposed stores.

After an hour, everyone shook hands, and Moe promised to write and flesh out his proposals. And that, pretty much, was that.

Wal-Mart's other initiative was to hire more public relations pros and have them design more effective counterattacks. Among the public relations companies the retailer now brought on board was National Grassroots & Communications, a firm based in Washington, D.C., that, in the words of its chief executive, Pamela Whitney, was supposed to "take on the NIMBYs and environmentalists."[7] NIMBY, short for "Not In My Back Yard," was the public relations industry's dismissive acronym for community activists.

National Grassroots specialized in fighting grassroots efforts through what have come to be known as "AstroTurf" operations: creating the appearance of grassroots support for a project, irrespective of whether any exists or not, and then cultivating local community leaders to come on board. That had been one strategy in Greenfield, where early ads favoring the Wal-Mart store had been signed as paid for by Citizens for Economic Growth, even though the funding actually came from Wal-Mart. Eventually, local spokesmen had been recruited by a public relations agency to front the effort.

Whitney explained the approach at a public relations industry conference in Chicago. "One of the things we don't like to do is hire a local PR firm," she said. "They are not part of the community.

"We hire local ambassadors who know the community inside and out to be our advocates, and then we work with them. They report to us. They are on our payroll, but it's for a very small amount of money," she said. These local representatives would be managed by professional campaign organizers—counterparts to Norman, in effect. Emphasizing her strategy, Whitney said, "It's important not to look like a Washington lobbyist. When I go to a zoning board meeting, I wear absolutely no makeup, I comb my hair straight back in a ponytail, and I wear my kids' old clothes. You don't want to look like someone from Washington, or someone from a corporation. . . .[that] is how you fit in, that's how you're one of them instead of somebody from the outside coming in."[8]

All these stratagems sounded pretty slick. But Wal-Mart and its hired operatives at National Grassroots and similar outfits were surprisingly clumsy in practice.

For example, in the fall of 1992, Wal-Mart invaded New York in force. Ithaca, a scenic Ivy League college town (home of Cornell University) at the lower end of Lake Cayuga, seemed like a natural target: good trade area, reasonably high disposable income, and competition that consisted only of an ancient Woolworth store and an equally musty Kmart, one of Dewar's downsized stores from the '70s. Easy pickings.

Through a front company, Wal-Mart floated a proposal to the town in October 1992 for a 155,000-square-foot supercenter at the south end of Ithaca, directly across from the Buttermilk Falls State Park. But, tied up with other struggles and with meeting New York's fairly stringent environmental regulations, Wal-Mart poked along on getting its permits.

At first, there didn't seem to be any opposition; but it gradually coalesced as Wal-Mart dawdled. By the spring of 1994, as Ithaca's planning board began its review, opponents, calling themselves Stop Wal-Mart, were in high gear. This time, though, the leaders weren't local business owners but a hodge-podge of old hippies, economists, environmentalists, and folks who lived by the maxim that small is beautiful. Many were worried that Wal-Mart would kill the town's Commons, a downtown pedestrian mall and local gathering place. In a sort of tag-team effort, they divided up into groups to attack every potential weak spot in Wal-Mart's draft environmental statement, looking at everything from traffic to the impact on the local economy to wetlands to how the view from the trail to Buttermilk Falls would be spoiled.

And here, Wal-Mart's "AstroTurf" counterattack began. One day, Michael Robinson, a local business consultant, former Marine and erstwhile town alderman, got an unexpected call from the owner of the property where the Wal-Mart would go, asking him to come to a meeting. The owner, Reubin Weiner, said he'd seen a letter Robinson had written to the local paper saying a Wal-Mart store would bring jobs and push local prices down.

About a dozen people showed up for the get-together at a trailer park Weiner owned. He explained that this was the start of Ithaca For Wal-Mart. "Reubin said, 'I'll get money from Wal-Mart and give it to you to do the things that need to be done,' " Robinson said. Robinson felt a little unsure about the arrangement, but he agreed and became, almost by default, chairman of a committee that included Weiner and his fiancée, and two other people from the meeting.

Wal-Mart secretly paid for ads, and it funded a phone line and answering service. The phone line, purporting to be a way to reach the "grassroots" group, connected to the office of the developer's lawyer in Syracuse, almost an hour away. Naturally, when one of Stop Wal-Mart's members discovered this, they were able to make great hay out of it. Wal-Mart also provided buttons that read I'M FOR WAL-MART, ALWAYS that most supporters were too embarrassed to wear.

As the fight heated up, Wal-Mart decided to host a get-together for supporters—but didn't bother to tell its citizens' group until three days beforehand. "They scheduled it at the Ramada Inn, which isn't even in Ithaca—it's in the town of Lansing," Robinson said later, rolling his eyes. He tried to convince them at least to move the meeting to Ithaca, to no avail. Wal-Mart provided boxes of handouts Robinson remembered as "ten pages of tripe . . . letters from people Wal-Mart had given money to—nothing that said Wal-Mart means jobs, or more money for Ithaca."

Before the Ramada meeting, Robinson had gotten a phone call from a Bob Stuart, who was trying to do a documentary on the Wal-Mart fight. Stuart asked to come and film the meeting, and Robinson readily agreed. But when he got to the Ramada, he found Stuart and a couple of his helpers lounging outside. He said the Wal-Mart people had thrown him out.

Robinson marched in and found Betsy Reithemeyer, one of Shinkle's assistants. He asked if it was true they'd tossed out Stuart and the others, and she said yes.

"What moron did that?" Robinson demanded. "I did," said Reithemeyer, surprised.

"It won't do us any good to have them go and tell the Ithaca *Journal* or *Times* that we apparently have something to hide," said Robinson, exasperated. "If they aren't in this room in five minutes, I'll bet I can talk to every-one we have here from Ithaca for Wal-Mart and get them to come with me and leave."

Reithemeyer agreed to let them film.

The more he dealt with the Wal-Mart people, the more disheartened Robinson became. It bothered him that they referred to the planning board members, people he knew, as sons of bitches. It bothered him, too, that Wal-Mart made an issue out of even the most picayune accommoda-tions that planning board members suggested—such as planting more trees in the parking lot. "I very rapidly developed a distaste for the way they do business," he said.

> I ended up on several occasions in an adversarial situation with repre-sentatives of Wal-Mart or East Coast Developers because they'd say, "We're gonna do this," and I'd say, "Wait a minute, who's 'we'?" and they'd say, "Your organization," and I'd say, "You can't tell us what to do—all you've done is cause us problems. . . . If you say something that makes sense to us, we'll work with you. If it doesn't, we won't—and if that isn't good enough, you can disassociate yourselves from us publicly and go hire your own people."

Members of the Stop Wal-Mart group mercilessly spotlighted short-comings in Wal-Mart's filings and studies. Though not guided by Al Nor-man, they'd picked up one of his packets and had taken to heart his admonition to do their research. When a consultant hired by the city to study Wal-Mart's impact came back with a glowing report, Stop Wal-Mart delivered a withering critique describing in exquisite detail how the con-sultant had used misleading, incomplete, and inaccurate data to reach skewed conclusions. The group also pointed out that the consultant not only worked for Wal-Mart in other towns, but had written newspaper edi-torials praising the company.*

At a public hearing, when opponents complained about the store hurt-ing the view from the state park, a Wal-Mart spokesman replied, "It's not like it's the Grand Canyon"—which might be true, but was hardly likely to win the company friends.

In the end, said Robinson, "Wal-Mart did everything it could to shoot itself in the foot." Planning board member David Kay said the company simply never answered environmental questions about the site, which sits

---

* Planning board members said they'd known that the consultant, RKG Associates, had done work for Wal-Mart, and had taken that into consideration.

in a floodplain. After a four-year fight and a losing lawsuit by its developer, Wal-Mart walked away in 1996.

Robinson was disappointed—he didn't like the people, but he wanted the store—and a bit puzzled. He'd met Sam Walton seventeen years earlier at a store opening when he lived in Texas. He'd found it weird that workers called him Mr. Sam; to Robinson, that smacked of the way slaves on Southern plantations addressed their masters. But he'd been impressed by Walton's affability, his feeling for people. That, it seemed to him, was gone. "All they needed to do was come in with a little humility," he said, "but they were their own worst enemy."

What Wal-Mart was running into was something that nobody from David Glass and Tom Seay on down to its local real estate people and hired public relations guns seemed to know how to deal with: opponents who felt that Wal-Mart threatened their sense of community. There were a hundred Ithacas. And in the Northeast, Northwest, and Western communities Wal-Mart was now trying to move into, it was finding far more community activists who knew how to work the system—people who, like Al Norman, had past experience from organizing protests against Vietnam or nuclear power, or who had been involved in community activism in other ways. The popular take on these NIMBYs—in the media, anyway—was that as they reached middle age, the former hippies and protesters were trying to preserve their neighborhoods rather than save the world. There was a grain of truth to it. "It's not as death-threatening as nuclear power," said Carol Rettew, an activist in Lancaster, Pennsylvania, who'd protested years earlier against the nuclear reactors at Three Mile Island. "You'd think you'd be fighting something more world-devastating than Wal-Mart."

But at heart, the issue here was one of enormous national importance: Many Americans felt their communities crumbling around them. And Wal-Mart, with its size and aggressiveness, was now becoming the symbol of some of the most endemic and dismaying aspects of American society: mindless consumerism, paved landscapes, and homogenization. Wal-Mart's new public identity as a blanderizing steamroller received the ultimate pop-cultural seal when community opposition to the company became the subject of two weeks' worth of Garry Trudeau's comic strip "Doonesbury" in 1994.

Across the country, there was a commonality to the explanations company foes gave for their opposition to the giant retailer.

"We've lost a sense of taste, of refinement—we're destroying our culture and replacing it with . . . Wal-Mart," said Alan Wolf, a Kent State alumnus trying to keep Wal-Mart out of Cleveland Heights, Ohio.

"We'd never have fought another business as hard as we've fought Wal-Mart," said Alice Doyle, a Cottage Grove, Oregon, community organizer who called the retailer "the ultimate predator."

In Fort Collins, Colorado, Shelby Robinson, a self-employed clothing designer who'd remained an activist since her days working for the George McGovern presidential campaign two decades earlier, said, "I really hate Wal-Mart.

"Everything's starting to look the same, everybody buys all the same things—a lot of small-town character is being lost. They disrupt local communities, they hurt small businesses, they add to our sprawl and pollution because everybody drives farther, they don't pay a living wage, and visually, they're atrocious," she said.

Another Wal-Mart foe, James Howard Kunstler, a former editor at *Rolling Stone*, liked to discuss what he called the $7 hair-dryer fallacy. This holds that people who shop a giant discounter to save $7 on a hair dryer don't realize that they pay a hidden price by taking that business from local merchants, because those merchants are the people who sit on school boards, sponsor Little League teams, and support the civic institutions that create a community. He described Wal-Mart as "the exemplar of a form of corporate colonialism, which is to say, organizations from one place going into distant places and strip-mining them culturally and economically."

Of course, convincing most Americans that it's worth paying more for a hair dryer or anything else to support local businesses was an uphill battle. Wal-Mart's success in offering the lowest price fed off more than a hundred years of relentless training in consumerism, desire for goods, and desire to buy the most goods you can for your dollar.

"In a way, Wal-Mart is a metaphor for the American dream run amok," said Peter Calthorpe, an urban designer from San Francisco. "It's the fall guy, one piece of a system in which everywhere you go, the end destination is a parking lot."

And really, Wal-Mart was both cause and effect—the product, as much as Kmart and the other big-box retailers, of eighty years of an increasingly car-based culture, of forty years of federal policies that subsidize single-family homes in ever-farther suburbs and that subsidize highways to reach those suburbs. Americans have been well trained not to notice or consider how much they pay for the infrastructure that makes big-box stores cheap, how much they spend for cars, gas, repairs, insurance, parking, taxes for roads—never mind the costs in time, stress, and air pollution. The average

American family spent, in 1995, almost 20 cents out of every dollar on transportation—three times as much as the average family in Europe. "It's a false microeconomics," argues Calthorpe. "For my pocketbook, it's cheaper to go to Wal-Mart, but for the society it's more expensive to build and operate within that framework."

The counterargument, of course, is that Americans love their cars and that this country has the transportation and urban-suburban layout and retailing system that people want.

In the opposition to Wal-Mart that swelled in the '90s, Calthorpe read the germ of a new direction. "People no longer love the environments they're creating—and that's why they oppose developments all the time," he said. "People's intuitions tell them this is not what they want. They understand that having a human-scale community is important, and they don't want to lose it. Those places that don't have that don't understand what they're missing.

"I think people are saying Wal-Mart is not particularly good for the collective well-being. It's like the loose thread in the sweater: You pull on it and the whole fabric comes apart," he said.

And certainly some of Wal-Mart's foes in Ithaca articulated a similar philosophy and came from a tradition of fighting for a community. The Stop Wal-Mart group included people such as Clare Grady, who ten years earlier was jailed as a member of the Plowshares group for pounding dents on the bomb-bay doors of a B-52 bomber with a hammer. One of the early organizers was Paul Glover, a self-professed former hippie and anarchist who had settled in Ithaca to run a community newspaper and who worked closely with small-business owners to develop a legal alternative local currency—Ithaca Hours—that dozens of shops accepted in lieu of cash, and which, of course, could only be recirculated in that community.°

Glover, like Calthorpe, saw the seeds of change. Told that Wal-Mart dismissed its opponents in Ithaca and elsewhere as a vocal minority, Glover grinned. "Every large social change has begun with a small minority, from women's suffrage to stopping the Vietnam War," he said. "It's the cycle of history."

° Hours were valued at $10, the area's average hourly wage.

18

The Land of
Milk and Honey

To visit Lancaster County, Pennsylvania, in late August is to understand what a farmer means when he talks of God's country—towering thick stalks of corn, broad glossy leaves, ears plump to near bursting. At the farmers' markets, baskets overflow with fat, ripe tomatoes, juicy and flavorful enough to devour on the spot like a fine peach, even without a pinch of salt. Beside them sit stacks of gorgeous, delicately-scented squash and zucchinis as big as a man's forearm, the products not of genetic engineering or growth hormones but of the stunning fecundity of the richest rain-fed top-soil in North America.

It isn't hard to see why this land, in the mid-1700s, attracted Amish and Mennonite settlers fleeing religious persecution in Europe. Its abundance allowed their close-knit society, emphasizing simplicity, thrift, and steward-ship of the land, to thrive, enough so that today many of their descendants, on the more than 4,700 family farms in the county, still shun modern ma-chinery and chemicals, relying on horse-drawn plows and manual labor to sow and reap their crops. If ever a land seemed intended by nature or deity to be farmed, surely it was this one.

As the county prospered, so did its seat, the city of Lancaster, which gradually became a major commercial center. But through the centuries, farming continued to dominate the local economy—at least, until the early post–World War II years. That's when tourism became a leading industry, as fascinated visitors increasingly were drawn to see the nineteenth-century lifestyles of the horse-and-buggy driving Plain Sects, as the Amish and Old Mennonites were known.°

But Lancaster County was near enough to Philadelphia and Harrisburg that, by the 1980s, the lush farmlands began sprouting a different and more profitable crop: subdivisions.†

Between 1980 and 1990 Lancaster County became the fastest-growing area in Pennsylvania. Its population jumped by nearly 20 percent, to more than 420,000. Farm after farm was sold and rezoned to make way for new subdivisions, strip malls, hotels, chain restaurants, and chain stores such as Kmart, that sprang up bit by bit at the edges of the county's various townships. Outlet malls and amusement parks arrived, too, especially along what became the sprawling commercial strip east of town, on Route 30, the old Lincoln Highway. Land prices soared, and Amish and Old Mennonite farming families began to leave for more rural farming areas in the Midwest where there was less traffic, and the land was far cheaper, if not as fertile.‡

At first, few people noticed. Most proposed projects sailed through the local planning and zoning reviews unopposed. To draw any fire, a project had to be truly noxious, such as a proposed giant incinerator near the township of Ephrata, beaten back in a rare flurry of public resistance. The development was haphazard: Under Pennsylvania's legal system, each of the 60 townships in Lancaster County enjoyed exclusive control over planning and zoning on its turf; few townships worked together on any planning, and county officials had little power—and little interest in trying—to impose any kind of order.

But, at the same time, countercurrents were building. Some of the new arrivals who'd fled suburban sprawl fretted anxiously about the development that followed them. Small groups, such as Lancaster's Historic Preservation Trust, turned their attention from saving individual buildings to discussing how to preserve the character of the whole region. Even some of the Plain Folks—who normally avoided politics or public controversy—

° Over the centuries the Mennonites split into a dizzying array of sects varying greatly in their strictness. The most traditional groups often were lumped together as the "Old" Mennonites, to distinguish them from others who embraced more mainstream, modern ways.

† Philadelphia's suburban sprawl was such that even though the metro area's population fell by 3 percent during the '70s, the land area gobbled up by development climbed by 32 percent.

‡ During the 1980s, 68 square miles of farmland in the county were rezoned and developed. By the early '90s, Lancaster-area developers were routinely paying $20,000 an acre or more for farmland. By selling a typical 50-acre farm, a landowner could often buy four times as much acreage in, say, Iowa, and still have money left over. Farms on major roads near townships commanded even higher prices.

began quietly urging their brethren to do *something* to stem the tide of development, arguing that there was nothing sinful about voting in local elections.

And then Wal-Mart launched its great invasion.

It began in late 1993, and in less than a year, Wal-Mart announced plans to build five huge 200,000-square-foot supercenters and one Sam's Club in the county, all within about 20 miles of each other. From the viewpoint of David Glass, Tom Seay, and Wal-Mart's local real estate man, Michael Gardner, there was certainly an enticing enough market to justify each and every one of those stores. But given the degree of opposition Wal-Mart was running into in the Northeast, and the way the company had become a symbol of unchecked sprawl, perhaps they should have anticipated the reaction such a blitzkrieg would provoke.

The first skirmish was over in the relative blink of an eye. Word leaked in the fall of 1993 that Wal-Mart planned to build a supercenter in West Hempfield, a small township about six miles west of the city of Lancaster. An opposition group, calling itself "Up Against the Wal," formed almost immediately, launching its fight with a protest march one icy night in December. To arrange a countershow, Wal-Mart swallowed its usual anti-union stance and approached leaders of an electrical workers' local, dangling the prospect of construction jobs in exchange for public support. Union members showed up for a zoning-board hearing outfitted with placards reading WAL-MART MEANS JOBS, and HONK FOR WAL-MART.

In early May of 1994, after five rancorous hearings, a unanimous zoning board took all of eleven minutes to shoot down Wal-Mart's request for an exception to build the store in an industrial zone.

By the time of this abrupt defeat, though, Wal-Mart had unveiled plans for three other supercenters. Over the following months, it made public plans for a Sam's Club and still another proposed supercenter. One proposed store glided through smoothly: that was for a supercenter in East Lampeter, along the already sprawl-ridden Route 30 corridor on the eastern edge of the city of Lancaster. It was an inarguably appropriate site, and by November, it won all the needed approvals. The store replaced a former "Amish Homestead" tourist attraction.°

Elsewhere, though, the sound of both sides' calls to arms would ring far beyond the county's confines.

° Wal-Mart paid $4.48 million for the 31-acre site, or more than $157,000 an acre.

•   •   •

Like many Plain Sect farmers, Melvin Martin had never lived anywhere but Lancaster County; in fact, he'd barely been outside his local township. A bright, shrewd man who grew feed corn, tobacco, hay, and wheat, and ran a small roadside vegetable stand, he'd had only the most basic academic education. His life's biggest change had come in 1955, when he'd moved a couple of miles from his parents' farm to work a farm of his own, just outside the town of Ephrata, about a dozen miles northwest of the city of Lancaster.

Then, in the early '70s, the state sliced through his 57-acre property to build its new divided highway linking the city of Lancaster to U.S. Interstate 76. The $85,000 he was offered for the whole property wasn't nearly enough to buy another suitable farm in the area. So he stayed on the 40 acres he had left after the road was built. Martin had realized that, sooner or later, developers would consider his farm, at the highway's Ephrata intersection, prime property. Twice over the years he agreed to sell the land to developers, only to have each deal fall through. So he hadn't been terribly surprised when some men from a company called Wal-Mart asked about buying his land, saying they wanted to put up a store there. He knew they'd be willing to pay a lot for the site, far more than any farmer would pay for it.

He had, of course, no idea what he was letting himself in for.

As soon as word got out about the proposed Ephrata Wal-Mart, nearby residents formed an opposition group. It was led by Dawn Rapchinski, an energetic and forceful woman who'd headed the successful grassroots campaign to scuttle the proposed incinerator a few years earlier. Rapchinski had grown up in the area, and she knew how to work the levers, even in the insular Plain Sect communities. Many of the Plain Folks had made and donated quilts to fund the fight against the incinerator. Now, Rapchinski again approached church leaders and elders among both the Amish and Old Mennonites. Well aware of what was happening, many were worried enough to agree immediately to help fund the fight to block the store.

One of the leaders she approached was the bishop of the Pike Mennonite Church, who was Martin's brother-in-law. Within that tightly knit church, where the Martins worshipped, Melvin Martin's decision to sell his farm became an unusually contentious issue. Many of the members made their ire clear, in some cases by avoiding any contact with the Martins. When Dawn Rapchinski and her husband Tom called on the Martins, in hopes of convincing Melvin not to sell his farm, he seemed to them not to want to believe that any harm could come of the sale of his 40 acres. Standing in his front yard, they brought up the danger from thousands more cars on the road. "Traffic's bad already," said Martin, whose own horse had twice been hurt in accidents with cars. Anyway, he added, Wal-Mart had promised to put in horse-and-buggy hitches at the store.

"Who in his right mind would take a horse and buggy into a Wal-Mart parking lot?" Dawn Rapchinski thought to herself. When she pushed Martin on the issue, saying it would hurt local businesses, and that it would make life harder for the Plain Folk, he spread his hands wide, as if to say it was out of his control.

Members of Rapchinski's group called on the Martins twice more over the following few months. By the third visit, Martin was furious, charging out onto his porch and ordering them off his property the moment he saw them arrive. As the three visitors tried to talk to Melvin, Irene Martin came out onto the porch behind him. Millie Eisemann, who'd known Irene for forty-seven years, was shocked at how unhappy and fearful she looked.

There was a community meeting set for that night at a nearby school. "Irene said, 'They're going to throw stones at our house after the meeting, aren't they?'" recalled Eisemann. "I said, 'No, no one's going to hurt you.'"

As Melvin argued with the two men who'd accompanied Eisemann, Irene Martin stood quietly, head downcast, wringing her hands. It quickly became obvious there was no point in arguing. As the three visitors left, Irene Martin raised her head to watch them go. There were tears running down her face.

Among the Plain Folk opposed to the store, the biggest worry was the traffic it would bring. "It's already a problem driving with a horse and buggy" on the road to Ephrata, because there's no room to pull off so automobiles can go by, said Rebecca Huyard, an unusually outspoken young Amish teacher in nearby New Holland, chatting about the battle with a visitor in her trim kitchen. Huyard, in a traditional plain light-blue dress and wearing a white bonnet over her neatly-parted brown hair, spoke from personal experience. She'd been forced off the road by an aggressive driver in a car one day while driving her brother's rig; the horse had fallen, snapping the wooden shaft harnessing him to the buggy. The horse was hurt, she was stranded, and she incurred a debt of obligation to a nearby farmer who helped her out.

"That's the kind of thing that happens on that road now," she said. "I cannot imagine the nightmare of driving on that road when a Wal-Mart is there."

"Many Amish don't know what Wal-Mart is, so they aren't worried. Those of us who live in a fast-developed area like New Holland know it's a real concern, and we're worried. Our people have moved away from here fast in the last few years because of developments like Wal-Mart. There have been new settlements in Indiana, Kentucky, and Wisconsin in the last five years. Hundreds of Plain people have moved out of Lancaster County because of the lack of land. This vast development had created such a rise in the price of land. . . . farms here now cost anywhere from $500,000 to $800,000, which makes no sense. A farmer couldn't pay that off in his life-time unless he already had three or four farms behind him."

Plain Sect farmers who feel the outside world pressing in are supposed to follow the Old Testament example of Isaac: After warring Philistines stopped up the wells of his father, Abraham, Isaac moved to new lands and dug new wells, rather than trying to defend his property.[1]

"You won't get the Amish people to fight," Huyard said, grimacing. "They'll just leave. And what is here when it's all suburbs? Nothing. All the tourists will leave and go to Disney World."

In terms of values, Wal-Mart's ways represented the polar opposite of Amish and Old Mennonite beliefs. To the Plain Sects, large-scale enter-prises are dangerous. Traditionalists avoid using tractors and other ma-chines that would allow them to operate larger farms, because that conflicts with the notion that one has to stay close to the soil to be its steward. Amish scholar and sociologist John Hostetler put it this way: "Amish economic thinking is subjected to a traditional wisdom requiring the restraint of self-ishness, greed, leisure and expansionist thinking."[2]

So perhaps it shouldn't be surprising that Huyard didn't mince words about the idea of one of their own selling his land to Wal-Mart. "I think it's despicable," she said. "I think there are folk with the attitude that Lan-caster County is going down the tubes anyway so they might as well cash in and get out." She bemoaned the fact that many Mennonites had gone into business and no longer worked the farms. Without that connection to the land, many were willing to sell it for development.

"To live in a community, you have no right to feel you belong there un-less you put back into it," Huyard said. "I don't believe Wal-Mart has any concept of community involvement.

"I believe old Sam Walton was an honest man," she said. As for those controlling the company now, "I don't believe that's true, and it's sad. They themselves will destroy their company," she said.

Huyard's sentiments were widely shared among the Plain Folk. Late on an August afternoon, Mahlon and Arlene Stauffer thundered up to their barn on a great wagon with steel-covered wooden wheels, loaded with bales of hay. Mahlon, a battered straw hat above his tanned, deeply seamed and cheerful face, stood loosely, holding in both brawny hands the reins to the four powerful Belgian horses, hitched side-by-side, pulling the clattering wagon. With practiced economy, the Stauffers unhitched the team, and she guided the wagon from one end as he wheeled the team around to the other end and had them push the wagon into the barn.

Cornfields stretched behind their farmhouse. Tall sunflowers, full with seed, arched upward at the house's edge. A peacock strutted in the yard, as a large golden-yellow dog watched idly. The Stauffers, too, lost 13 acres when the new highway, Route 222, went through Ephrata. And they were greatly perturbed about the traffic a Wal-Mart would bring. Speaking of the highway, and of Martin's farm, Mahlon Stauffer said, "I wouldn't want to be in that corner even if Wal-Mart wasn't coming in. . . . Ever since 222 was built, we expected the area to be built up sometime. We never had any idea how it would be built up, but we knew we could expect to get some businesses in there.

"The traffic is difficult as it is," he said. "It's unsafe. . . . it seems like you're in everybody's way, once you're out there on the main road . . . and once Wal-Mart is here it'll be worse, if not impossible. I expect the fast-food places will want to have a place nearby and get a corner here and there," he said. "So we really aren't happy about what looks like is developing here."

As it was, Stauffer said, three of his children already had opted to move to Ohio and Missouri. He seemed resigned, rather than angry, at the changes he saw coming. As for Martin, he said simply, "He realizes there's a lot of unhappy people around." Arlene Stauffer, who'd been painting a rabbit on the side of a milk jug as her husband spoke, looked up from her work. "He didn't realize he was going to have some enemies from this," she said softly.

Meanwhile, as Wal-Mart's proposals for the other sites moved forward, there was the usual sparring at public hearings. Opposition groups sent members to each other's public hearings, in shows of support. Al Norman came down and coached them on strategy and tactics. Drawing on his help and on the research of scores of other Wal-Mart foes around the country, the various Lancaster groups collected and fired enough salvos of facts, figures, and studies to make the hearings the most contentious Wal-Mart had dealt with yet. At one early hearing in the township of Mount Joy, a planning consultant for Wal-Mart, routinely presenting his qualifications, found himself subjected to three hours of grilling by the township counsel before he could even turn to the testimony he planned to deliver.

Wal-Mart hired, as its main local attorney, Mark Stanley, who'd worked the previous five years as the counsel for the Lancaster Farmland Trust, a nonprofit group trying to preserve farmlands. He, too, wasn't cut an inch of slack on anything. Under fire, Stanley felt forced to resign from the trust shortly after signing on to represent the giant retailer. At a hearing in Ephrata, one Wal-Mart foe, John Jarvis, decided that Stanley was dominating the proceedings because he stayed standing throughout the meeting while everyone else sat down after they finished speaking. So Jarvis asked the chairman to order Stanley to sit, too. When Stanley said, "I've been sitting all day and I need to stand up," Jarvis motioned to everyone else there to stand, as well. The meeting continued with everyone on their feet.

Wal-Mart, too, of course, tried to drum up local support, sending letters to its Sam's Clubs members in that part of the state, asking them to write or come to hearings. The company ran full-page ads in Lancaster newspapers with a telephone number folks could call to join a pro-Wal-Mart group. While there undoubtedly were people in Lancaster who wanted Wal-Mart to come, the company's entreaties drew so little response that Wal-Mart never even got an AstroTurf group going. A few weeks after the ads ran, the line was disconnected.

As president of the Historic Preservation Trust of Lancaster County, John Jarvis became a point man in the Wal-Mart fights. A Scotsman, he had emigrated to the United States after serving as a British army officer in India during World War II. He'd spent the past thirty years as the headmaster of the Lancaster Country Day School. His background was thoroughly evident in his bearing.

To Jarvis, Wal-Mart wasn't really the problem. It was just another symptom, along with the malls and subdivisions, that were taking over local farmlands. "We've got to have planning on a larger scale," he would argue, to anyone who would listen. "Unless the townships pull together, Lancaster County will disappear." But even as he beat the drum to get townships to plan jointly, Jarvis did everything he could to stop Wal-Mart.

He called one of his former students, a producer at CBS's *60 Minutes* and said, "Patty, Lancaster needs your help." Camera crews from the show came to Lancaster, and in April 1995, *60 Minutes* aired a rather critical segment about Wal-Mart's impact on small towns, featuring the battle in Lancaster County. David Glass delegated on-camera duties to Tom Seay, who said that Wal-Mart hadn't forgotten its small-town roots, and pitched the company line that its impact on small towns was overstated. There are good business people and bad business people, Seay told correspondent Morley Safer, "and the ones who are not good business people don't stay in business."

Al Norman, of course, was interviewed too, repeating his argument that you can't buy small-town quality of life at a Wal-Mart, and that "once they steal it, you can't buy it back."[3]

Meanwhile, Wal-Mart sent one of its senior public-relations men, Bob Cheyne, up to Lancaster to help make the company's case to the public. Cheyne, a tough but grandfatherly looking figure, went to public hearings and did interviews with local publications, painting Wal-Mart opponents as outsiders who'd moved in from the big city and now wanted to lock the gates behind them.

After a great deal of jawboning, one local TV station convinced the company to let Cheyne and Wal-Mart's local real estate man, Mike Gardner, debate Jarvis and another company foe on air. Jarvis decided, before the program, that he would set aside his usual manners to interrupt and challenge Cheyne at every opportunity.

It was a bizarre debate. Cheyne tried to adopt a friendly, avuncular tone, while Jarvis broke in repeatedly to dispute Cheyne's claims. Jarvis raised charges, aired on the recent *60 Minutes* program, that Wal-Mart had turned the downtown of Donaldsonville, Louisiana, into a ghost town. On the program, Donaldsonville shopkeeper Glenn Falgoust had poured out his personal account of how Wal-Mart had devastated his town. For ten years, while he struggled to keep his auto-parts business afloat, Falgoust had kept track of every bankruptcy and store-closing in Donaldsonville. Then he'd gone back and collected the same figures for the ten years before the Wal-Mart had opened there in 1983. The numbers were startling: Store closures jumped from an average of about four a year in the decade before Wal-Mart opened, to an average of 18 a year over the ten years after Wal-Mart opened.

As the businesses failed, middle-class business owners had moved away, Falgoust said. He had elaborated on that argument in an opinion piece he sent to a local Lancaster newspaper: Falling tax revenues forced the city to close its swimming pool, then to lay off its police force. To save money, Donaldsonville contracted with another local police force to cover their town, too. It contracted out its sanitation department. It sold off city buses.

An outsider might point to other factors at work: Donaldsonville shop-keepers faced growing competition not only from Wal-Mart but from shop-ping malls and outlet centers in neighboring Louisiana parishes. But in Falgoust's own case, there was little doubt Wal-Mart had hammered his business. He simply couldn't match the giant retailer's prices on what had once been his highest-margin items, such as bicycles and lawn mowers. Fi-nally, in December 1994, he closed his dwindling business, and sold about half of his inventory to another business that took over his space.

From that point on, Falgoust became one of Wal-Mart's harshest and most active critics. He fired off columns around the country, warning against letting Wal-Mart come to town. "Fight Wal-Mart," he urged read-ers of one Lancaster newspaper. "Fight it with all your heart and soul. Make them spend their money on legal fees and reworking plans and don't ever give up."[4]

He put together a video and information packet about Wal-Mart to send opponent groups around the country. He denounced Wal-Mart's ways on several daytime talk shows. On the *60 Minutes* program, he'd taken a film crew on a tour of the boarded-up shops in downtown Donaldsonville.

Cheyne was familiar with Falgoust; and as soon as Jarvis brought him up, the Wal-Mart man curtly dismissed his claims. Cheyne painted Fal-goust as a flat-out liar, saying that the former shopkeeper had sold his busi-ness at a profit; that Donaldsonville was healthy, and that the video on *60 Minutes* of the boarded up downtown had been filmed to be intentionally misleading. He waved a sheaf of what he said were letters from the town's mayor and leading citizens countering Falgoust's claims.

Don Scanlin, a print-shop owner and one of the leaders of the Mount Joy fight, sent a tape of the program to Falgoust—who, ironically, had been about to declare a truce with the company. Rumors had begun to float in early 1995 that Wal-Mart would close its Donaldsonville store. Falgoust, worried that if Wal-Mart pulled out now Donaldsonville would have noth-ing, actually had campaigned for Wal-Mart to stay. He had called the com-pany's Don Shinkle, and the local district manager, pleading for assurances they wouldn't close the store. He'd helped set up a meeting between Shin-kle and other Wal-Mart officials and the town's mayor and council mem-bers. At the meeting, the Wal-Mart group said they planned to keep the store open. And Falgoust told Shinkle he was ready to be the company's friend, rather than enemy—if it kept its word.

Then the tape arrived. Falgoust, enraged, phoned the Lancaster televi-sion show's producer, demanding equal time. He called every other day for a month. The producer tried to set up a second debate pitting Falgoust directly against Cheyne, or whoever else Wal-Mart would send. But the company wouldn't bite.

Finally, in July, Falgoust and his wife drove up to Lancaster and were given their time on air to rebut Cheyne's claims.° Falgoust met with various anti-Wal-Mart groups in the county—and then, seeing as he was up north anyway, drove up to Massachusetts to meet with Al Norman. The two did several rallies together at other towns fighting Wal-Marts—including one in Ticonderoga, New York, to which the company bussed in dozens of employees who heckled and catcalled Falgoust's speech.

If Falgoust had considered any kind of rapprochement with Wal-Mart, that was over now. He would make opposing them all but a full-time job.

By the middle of 1995, with the single exception of the victory in East Lampeter, on the busy Route 30 corridor, none of Wal-Mart's campaigns seemed to be getting anywhere.

The company had proposed one supercenter outside the burg of Lititz, north of the city of Lancaster. But Carol Rettew and the other leaders of the "Concerned Lititz Citizens" had collected more than 3,000 signatures against the store, mostly by playing up worries about traffic. "As soon as we heard about it, we knew it wasn't going to work on this road," said Rettew, on a visit to the site, pointing to the two-lane road that would have fronted the proposed store. After a yearlong fight, the township rejected Wal-Mart's plan in March 1995. The day the township said no, Gardner (with Seay's approval) filed four alternative plans for the same site, and Stanley filed suit against the township over the rejection. But filing a slew of alternatives backfired. The township's staff didn't have time to review all the plans, so they sat idle for months.

In February 1996, after a nineteen-month battle, Wal-Mart dropped its planned Sam's Club in East Hempfield after that township's zoning board refused to grant a zoning variance. Meanwhile, the merged PriceCostco Co. began constructing a warehouse club in the city of Lancaster. Its plans had run into no real opposition. Similarly, the BJ's Wholesale Club chain easily won approval that January to build a warehouse club just four miles from the proposed Sam's Club site.

In February, too, Ephrata's planners shot down Wal-Mart's proposal for

---

° Falgoust said he was still paying off his business debts from the losses he incurred. He also cited a state economic study and business failure data to buttress his point that, in fact, Donaldsonville was in an economic decline and that the rate of business failures had jumped after Wal-Mart arrived.

a supercenter at the edge of their town, saying Wal-Mart would have to do much more to accommodate traffic concerns, including meeting the needs of the horse-and-buggy Plain Sects.

By the following August, Wal-Mart gave up on the Lititz site, withdrawing its proposal without saying why. At the same time, Wal-Mart dropped its planned supercenter in Mount Joy. After twenty months of public hearings on that site, at a cost of more than $105,000 to the township in legal and other fees, Wal-Mart gave up when township officials refused the last of its repeated requests for a permit extension.

In all of these places, Wal-Mart's foes had enjoyed a big advantage: their township officials had been none too keen on Wal-Mart. Ephrata, though, was different; planners there were split, and the township's attorney was comparatively timid. In February, when the township said Wal-Mart had to address traffic concerns before getting approval, the company had seemed trapped in a catch-22. To make the road and highway-exit improvements the township demanded, Wal-Mart would have to buy more road-front land from a neighboring farmer; and he refused to sell. But Stanley sued the township, arguing that it couldn't legally force Wal-Mart to make the improvements it was demanding. Worried about the cost of a legal battle, and dubious about the prospect of winning, the township folded in March. Wal-Mart won a permit for its Ephrata store.

Rapchinski was furious. She was sure that Wal-Mart's suit was a bluff, and that if the township had hung tough, Wal-Mart would have pulled out of Ephrata, too. Perhaps so—but she'd never know.

A few months later, Melvin Martin and one of his sons went up onto the property to haul off some farm equipment they needed to clear out. Martin, a beetle-browed, grizzled, gray-haired man in thick black boots, heavily stained work clothes, and an almost shapeless straw hat, wasn't too keen to talk about his dealings with Wal-Mart, or about whether he'd been able to come to terms with his neighbors and fellow church members. Local news coverage had made things a lot worse, he said. He'd gotten letters from folks unhappy about the sale—though he quickly added, "that didn't mean nothing to me."

"Well," he said, all the same, "I'm glad to be out of this corner."

Martin looked terrible, eyes watery and rimmed with red, as if he'd been sleeping poorly for some time. What would he do now? Maybe he'd buy a new farm, and move. To where, he couldn't say. He would soon be able to buy a substantial farm or two just about anywhere. Maybe he'd move to the southern end of the county; it wasn't so developed yet. One way or another, he seemed to be leaning toward leaving the only place, the only community, he'd known his whole life. It just wasn't the same any-more. In August 1997, Wal-Mart agreed to give Martin $2.7 million in other local real estate for his farm.

Despite Wal-Mart's permit, opposition to the Ephrata store dragged on. Two years later, the company still hadn't broken ground on Martin's old farm; resolving disputes before the township over construction details was like wading through molasses.° Out of six stores it had proposed beginning in 1993, five years later Wal-Mart had opened only one, facing relentless opposition even as proposed stores by other big retailers, such as Price-Costco, BJ's, and Kmart, had slid in seemingly nearly unnoticed. But that blitheness toward other developments in the county was changing—and changing because of Wal-Mart.

Despite a few unique features, such as Amish farmers helping Wal-Mart opponents under the table, the battles in Lancaster hadn't differed in their general shape from those in Ithaca, Greenfield, Sturbridge, or a hun-dred other places.

But, by its effort to blitz the county, Wal-Mart wound up encouraging the various groups opposing it to look at what was happening not just in each of their backyards, but across the county as a whole.

The executive director of Lancaster County's planning commission, Ron Bailey, had come to Pennsylvania from Oregon, which had adopted the country's most far-reaching statewide planning laws in 1973. Oregon re-quired municipalities to define growth boundaries and to coordinate plan-ning so that it took into account everything from transportation to retail zoning to schools. Oregon created regional planning authorities to make neighboring municipalities work together instead of competing with each other. Oregon's cities still had strip malls and cloned subdivisions and giant, big-box retailers. But the difference was that in Oregon's cities—Portland, for example—big retailers and malls were zoned along transportation cor-ridors (light-rail and bus routes) giving people alternatives to driving every-where by car. And the existence of growth boundaries encouraged redevelopment of depressed areas in the cities, instead of sending all the growth to suburbs sprawling ever-farther out from the city center. It wasn't perfect; but Oregon's developers had learned to live with the regulations.

Bailey had begun working toward creating similar statewide and re-

---

° In the interim, the old Kmart at the other end of Ephrata easily won approvals and expanded from 40,000 square feet to 70,000.

gional planning for Pennsylvania and Lancaster County. Because of Pennsylvania's fragmented township system, though, the comprehensive plans that Bailey helped develop had been essentially unenforceable.

But now, as a result of the Wal-Mart fights, members of the various opposition groups banded together in new organizations to protect farmlands and create planning on a larger scale. In 1995, Richard Moe and Constance Beaumont, from the National Historic Trust, attended a statewide conference on sprawl. New groups formed, such as Citizens for Responsible Growth (which in 1995, in the midst of the Wal-Mart fights, helped elect several Lancaster city commissioners sympathetic to regional planning) and 1,000 Friends of Pennsylvania, modeled on an Oregon group that led the drive for statewide-planning laws in that state. Research that came out of the fight led Lancaster's historic trust to dust off a little-used state history code that required planners, before approving any development, to take into account how it would affect local historical and cultural resources. Some at the trust began to argue that, legally, the code could apply to the Plain Sect communities as a whole, and so might be used to limit any development that might affect them.

All these efforts were in their early stages by the late 1990s. But by invading Lancaster, it began to look as though Wal-Mart just might have helped save it.

"The good thing about Wal-Mart," Jarvis said, in retrospect, "was that it was big enough, nasty enough, and aggressive enough to make the problem of uncontrolled growth clear."

19

Live with Charlie
and Kathie Lee

It was just a small rectangle of cardboard, a few inches across, with a photo of a pretty, brightly smiling woman on it. The young Honduran girl who'd smuggled it out of the factory had no idea who the woman was or what the writing below her photo said; but the tall *norteamericano* had asked her to bring him anything—labels, hangtags like this one—that would tell him what brands of clothing she and the other assembly-line workers were making.

The face on the picture didn't mean anything to the tall American, either. Charlie Kernaghan had come to Honduras to track down factories making clothes for the Gap, a mid-scale clothing chain he'd been investigating. A grizzled professorial type with a nose that looked like someone had once punched it very hard indeed, Kernaghan was head of the National Labor Committee Education Fund in Support of Worker and Human Rights in Central America—a rather grand name for a tiny three-person outfit working out of a shoe-box office in lower Manhattan and scraping by on donations from sympathetic unions and churches.

When some of the women at this factory, Global Fashion, had heard that he was asking people at other factories about conditions and how workers were treated, they had approached him to complain about their 14-hour days, the forced overtime without pay, the locked bathrooms, the way they were screamed at and hit. Kernaghan had asked how old the workers were and had been intrigued to find some were as young as twelve years old. But—like most apparel workers in Honduras—the women at

Global Fashion had no idea who they made clothes for. Many couldn't read, and few of them ever saw the labels and tags anyway. Kernaghan said he wanted to help improve their conditions, but bluntly added that he couldn't do anything unless they could bring him more information.

Now, standing behind a dusty food stall 100 yards down the road from the barbed-wire-topped walls of the factory, Kernaghan fingered the hang-tag. "A portion of the proceeds from the sale of this garment will be do-nated to various Children's Charities," it said below the photo, in English. He shook his head at that. This wasn't any Gap label, but the irony of chil-dren slaving in sweatshops to make a brand that purported to help children wasn't lost on him. This might be worth following up, he thought. He glanced again at the photo, and the looping swirls of the signature above it, and wondered just who this vaguely familiar woman was, this Kathie Lee.

This Kathie Lee was the seemingly inescapable Kathie Lee Gifford, cohost of one of the country's most broadly syndicated TV talk shows, *Live with Regis and Kathie Lee*. On any given morning, more than 8 million viewers tuned in to watch the interplay between the acerbically avuncular Regis Philbin and the brash, relentlessly upbeat Gifford, whom one critic de-scribed as "the perfect TV cutie, except she's wacked."[1] A wholesome, pop-ular born-again Christian, who was inevitably referred to as perky or spunky, the forty-two-year-old Gifford was beloved by her viewers for seeming to say whatever popped into her head without worrying about its propriety—if in language that was often cloying and precious (e.g., "pee-pee"). In the unscripted chat with Philbin that began each show, she might talk about anything from how she'd spotted talk-show host David Letter-man picking his nose in traffic to how she was combating flab on her thighs, which she referred to as "wuggies." She would talk in excruciating detail about such personal matters as her breast-feeding of her son Cody—but in a self-mocking way. "I am fully aware that there are people out there who look at me and want to throw up," she once said. And while her proud mom–bubbly Pollyanna persona put off some critics (*Washington Post* writer Tom Shales called her "at least as frightening as Godzilla"), her pre-dominantly female, morning viewing audience adored her.

Wife of football great and sports announcer Frank Gifford, Kathie Lee was also a singer, often performing in Las Vegas; and she worked as the spokeswoman for Carnival Cruise Lines, dancing and singing on their TV ads. This was the celebrity that Wal-Mart had picked in 1995 to front its an-swer to Kmart's hugely successful Jaclyn Smith clothing line.

Gifford's combination of fizzy glamour and down-home, clean-cut appeal had seemed to make her the perfect celebrity for Wal-Mart, with its flag-waving, mom-and-apple-pie image. For Wal-Mart, of course, there was the added bonus of effectively getting free advertising every day her show was on the air. And her clothing line had roared off to a phenomenal start—with an estimated $300 million in sales its first year. Gifford's cut was 3 percent, $9 million, of which she gave roughly 10 percent to children's charities.

Gifford's ease in public and her sunny, shoot-from-the-lip personality were what people noticed, but she hadn't gotten where she was by being a bubblehead. Bright, calculating, deeply insecure, and tirelessly hard-working, Gifford was a woman with an insatiable hunger for approval who simultaneously seemed often to feel guilty for being so famous and successful.

She was born Kathie Lee Epstein in Paris in 1953, the second of three children brought up by very conservative, deeply religious parents. Her mother, Joan Cuttell, was a secretary at the Naval Research Laboratories in Washington, D.C., when she met Aaron Leon Epstein, a naval officer, toward the end of World War II. After the war, Epstein's postings took the family to several European countries. When Kathie Lee was four, the family moved back to West Annapolis, Maryland. She grew up there, and later in Bowie, Maryland, where her father worked as a newspaper distributor and insurance agent. The Epsteins also eventually bought a hotel in the beach resort town of Rehobeth Beach, Delaware, where they spent their summers.

While Aaron Epstein was Jewish by descent, he'd been raised as a Christian, and that was the faith the family followed—casually, at first. Then in 1965, while watching Billy Graham on television, Joan Epstein experienced a religious transformation that she said left her feeling at peace for the first time since she'd aborted her fourth pregnancy eight years earlier. The rest of the family, Kathie Lee included, went through similar "born-again" experiences. Kathie Lee's came later that year, when the twelve-year-old was frightened by a Christian film called *The Restless Ones*, about "the tragic consequences of a young girl having sex and doing drugs." After the movie, Kathie Lee said, "a local pastor asked people to come forward and receive Christ" and she did so. "If this was my religious epiphany, it was subtle and simple," she said.[2]

Aaron Epstein, who'd played saxophone on weekends in a jazz combo while in the Navy, encouraged his children to sing and act on stage. By the time Kathie Lee was fifteen, she and her younger sister Michie were performing in a folksinging group in local coffeehouses. In high school, Kathie Lee was a self-described Little Goody Two Shoes and a ham for the spotlight who, at the end of her senior year, won the state's Junior Miss pageant.

At the national pageant, where she sang "Go Down, Moses" as her talent piece, she met Anita Bryant, the Christian singer and orange-juice pitchwoman. Bryant soon adopter her as a protégé—beginning a series of disillusioning experiences that would show the young girl the great hypocrisy that could underlie celebrities' public images. For a year, Kathie Lee lived with and worked for Bryant and her husband in Key Biscayne, Florida, as a secretary, baby-sitter, and fill-in singer at Baptist church events. Bryant's model Christian marriage seemed to Kathie Lee to be a sham, maintained by two unhappy partners solely for the sake of Bryant's career and her standing in the Southern Baptist community. Bryant, knowing Kathie Lee, too, was unhappy, arranged for her to go to televangelist Oral Roberts's university in Tulsa, Oklahoma, in 1972. There, Kathie Lee sang with a chorus on Roberts's television show and at his tent revival meetings throughout the South.

She described this as an Orwellian experience. "I sensed—then and later on throughout the Christian movement of the 1970s—" she said, "an unmistakable worship of money and power."[3] She said it made her sick to watch the revival teams counting up the money after each meeting, to see the manipulation of the poor and the sick, to note the contrast between Roberts's own wealthy lifestyle and his haranguing of the poor to give money.

During her junior year, she dropped out, rented an apartment in Tulsa with what remained of her Junior Miss scholarship money, and spent three weeks writing a spiritually oriented diary that would be issued a few years later by a Christian publishing firm under the title *The Quiet Riot*. Then she moved to Los Angeles, where she worked whatever gigs she could get, including TV commercials, bit parts on the soap opera *Days of Our Lives*, and singing on a Sunday morning faith-healing TV show. She also became involved with a Christian musician and music publisher, Paul Johnson, whom she married in the spring of 1976. She was twenty-two years old. She said she spent her wedding night crying miserably, feeling she'd made the biggest mistake of her life. In her autobiography, this was one of the few areas of her life that she talked about circumspectly, describing her conjugal union simply as an illusion, a union that wasn't consummated. The Johnsons slept in separate rooms.

As one way of avoiding the incompatibilities that eventually ended their marriage, Paul Johnson encouraged Kathie Lee to pursue her own career, and she did so unflaggingly. On the Christian music circuit, she performed on shows such as *The 700 Club* and recorded several pop-gospel albums on her husband's label, Petra. With coaching from a management firm, she put together a nightclub act. She became the singer on the quiz show *Name That Tune*, known as the La La Lady because she sang those syllables instead of the lyrics. Then she won a role on *Hee Haw Honeys*, a short-lived sitcom spin-off of the country-music comedy show *Hee Haw*.

Her growing exposure won her work as an opening act for various comedians (Bill Cosby and Shecky Green, among others) at Nevada casinos. Gambling was at odds with her fundamentalist Christian faith; but in her mind, she disconnected her work from what that work supported. "It would have killed Mom and Dad to think I led people to a casino where they could lose their life savings," she said. "But I went to the casinos to entertain, not to minister, and I had no qualms about accepting those engagements. I didn't enjoy gambling, of course (except when Bill Cosby gave me *his* money!), and I did not encourage it."[4]

She also continued performing on religious programs, until a personal snub led her to break with the whole televangelist world. Kathie Lee and her sister Michie had agreed to appear on Jim and Tammy Faye Bakker's *PTL Club,* even though to make the engagement, Michie had to leave home the day after her infant daughter had open-heart surgery. Kathie Lee said she and her sister felt a calling to "discuss how a disease or loss doesn't nullify God's power, but glorifies it."[5] At the show, though, they weren't allowed to talk on air; and when Tammy Faye Bakker walked off in mid-sentence while Michie was telling her about the operation, Kathie Lee became infuriated.

> At that moment I said to myself, I will never be a part of this again as long as I live. I know this sounds self-righteous of me, but the truth is, I didn't want to make one more dollar in the name of God after that. I did not want to buy a dress, buy mascara, pay my mortgage with one dollar made from God. I did not want to have anything to do with that world again. . . . It was a world of people seeking power, ego gratification, and monetary and material wealth in the name of serving God. . . . I can't explain how much it bothered me that they could get the poor and vulnerable to fork over their fixed incomes and pensions and Social Security payments as a way of praising the Lord, when in fact the money wasn't going to much of God's work at all. If I raised a penny for them, then I too would be responsible for what they were doing.[6]

She performed at scores of conventions and trade shows, and became a spokeswoman for Coca-Cola. Meanwhile, her husband—though emotionally and physically distant—became increasingly resentful of the time and energy she devoted to her career. Then, in 1981, she got her biggest break yet when Regis Philbin, then the host of the local TV show *A.M. Los Angeles,* moved to New York. Kathie Lee was one of a succession of temporary replacement hosts. On one of the two days she filled in, she was spotted by the executive producer for *Good Morning America,* ABC's national morning show, who offered her a job as a reporter, with occasional duties filling in for cohost Joan Lunden. Simultaneously, her husband left her. She moved to New York in 1982.

Never having been a reporter, she worked entirely from scripts written for her by producers; but gradually she gained experience in doing live, unscripted interviews. After three years on *Good Morning America,* she was offered a job cohosting with Regis Philbin on WABC's *The Morning Show,* in June 1985. Then, in 1988, the Disney Co. agreed to syndicate the program nationally, under the proposed title *The Regis Philbin Show.* Gifford threatened to walk unless her name was on the program title, too. They renamed it *Live with Regis and Kathie Lee.*

Meanwhile, after two years of a single, high-profile society lifestyle, which she described as hectic, depressing, and painful—involving her with people whom she felt lived in a moral and ethical void, desensitized by their power and success—she became romantically involved with Frank Gifford, whom she'd been friends with since they'd met years earlier on *Good Morning America.* Frank Gifford, who was the same age as her mother, was embroiled in a troubled marriage. No matter. Gifford soon divorced his second wife. She accused him and Kathie Lee of having an affair that broke up the marriage, an accusation both Gifford and Kathie Lee denied. "Anyone who knew Frank considered him divorced months and months earlier," Kathie Lee said later.[7] The two married in the fall of 1986.

As her television show steadily gained a bigger audience, Kathie Lee Gifford continued to perform in other arenas. In 1991, she and Philbin began hosting the annual Miss America pageant. The next year she published an as-told-to autobiography. She did shows in Atlantic City—with Frank Gifford chartering a helicopter to fly her back and forth from New York. By 1992, *Live with Regis and Kathie Lee* was syndicated on over 200 stations. That year, she signed a licensing agreement with Halmode, an apparel maker, for a Kathie Lee line of clothing to be sold in department stores. The line was modestly successful; but it was too upscale and expensive for many of her devoted watchers. It wouldn't really take off until 1995, when it was redesigned and licensed to Wal-Mart.

The Kathie Lee Gifford whose picture Charles Kernaghan perused on a dusty Honduran roadside was a woman who could be—more than most people—both astonishingly selfless and stunningly self-absorbed. She could disapprove of gambling, but profit from it; she could see televangelists' flimflams, but perform on their shows, until their behavior touched her personally. When, in her autobiography, she described two harrowing illnesses that her sister Michie and Michie's daughter Shannie faced, Gifford seemed to see their ordeals mostly as God's way of testing *her own* faith. She was obsessed with her looks and popularity—once feverishly campaigning, mostly but not entirely in jest, for viewers to vote for her as *TV Guide*'s Most Beautiful Woman on Television. (She won, with five times as many votes as the second-place finisher, Jaclyn Smith.)

On another occasion, asked by a *TV Guide* writer whether her son Cody was ever embarrassed by how much she talked about him on the show, she said that she told him, "I won't talk about you on the show if it's not okay with you. But then Mommy's going to have to find a new job and you might not be able to go to that private school anymore, or Disneyland."*

But this was also the woman who, shortly before Thanksgiving in 1981, while living alone in Los Angeles, picked up a homeless couple hitchhiking with their three-year-old daughter, fed them, took them to her home, washed their clothes, put them up for the night, and got them in touch with a shelter the next day. She was someone who worked with a wide variety of charities, including AIDS groups and homeless shelters, quoting from scripture to say that from those to whom much is given, much is required. From the beginning, Gifford had given a tithe of her earnings from the clothing line to the Variety Club Children's Charity.

Could it be possible she had any idea how her clothing for Wal-Mart was being made? How would her conscience respond when she found out?

As for Charlie Kernaghan, well, in some ways he was very like Kathie Lee Gifford—bright, glib, disciplined, with an enormous capacity for work. Like her, he was the second of three children, brought up by parents with strong Christian convictions. But he could scarcely have had a more different world view.

---

* Asked if that wasn't just a bit manipulative, she said, "I know I'm a good mother." (Quotes from "Kathie Lee Gets Mad," by Ileane Rudolph, *TV Guide,* Dec. 16, 1995, p. 16.)

Five years older than Gifford, Kernaghan grew up in Brooklyn, New York. His father was an immigrant machinist from Scotland, his mother of Czechoslovak descent. Both devout Catholics, they believed in an active definition of Christian charity and took in a series of foster children with health problems. They imbued their children with their beliefs. Kernaghan's older brother became a Jesuit priest.[*] And Kernaghan himself would say that his own ideology sprang out of his parents' teachings.

Kernaghan went to a Marionite high school on Long Island, then to the Jesuit-run Loyola University in Chicago, and finally got a master's degree in psychology from the New School for Social Research in New York. A loner who spent much of his time reading novels, he lived without a telephone or television. His direction in life seemed anything but constant. He taught, briefly, but then he decided he wanted to be a photographer. While working to that end, he labored at odd jobs: moving furniture, working construction, driving a taxicab.

He had the notion that artists don't often capture or honor what is precious in everyday life. So he came up with the idea of traveling cross-country to Duluth, Minnesota, where he'd just pick a street corner and photograph whatever happened there over the course of two or three days. As he prepared to do this, in mid-1985—just as Kathie Lee was joining Regis Philbin's show—a missionary friend called him from California and asked him to come along on a peace march to El Salvador and Honduras. Like his friend, Kernaghan was strongly opposed to the Reagan administration's covert war in Central America; so he abruptly decided that Duluth could wait.

He wound up in the city of San Salvador, joining a group of peasants who occupied the city's cathedral for three days. Sleeping on the stone floor, he talked long into the nights with workers who told him of union leaders being assassinated by right-wing death squads, of teenage workers imprisoned for trying to organize.

Like most Americans, Kernaghan had had little idea of the social and labor conditions there; when he came back to New York, he decided that people needed to know what was happening. He began writing letters and hooked up first with Barbara Briggs, a union activist he'd met in El Salvador, and then, too, with the Reverend David Dyson, a Presbyterian minister and one-time labor organizer who'd founded the National Labor Committee a few years earlier to protect Central American trade unionists whose lives were in danger. By 1990, as the fighting in Central America

---

[*] Gifford's older brother, too, became a minister.

wound down, Dyson moved on to found a new group, and Kernaghan became the committee's director. He began to focus more and more on improving labor conditions for workers making U.S.-bound goods, and on how U.S. tax dollars were helping companies move to foreign factories.

Kernaghan was driven, often skipping meals during the day and working until nine or ten at night, then gorging at home while watching *Nightline* or other news programs. Weekends, too, he often spent at his office, trying any tack he could to attract the public spotlight to his issues. He hit on the idea of bringing young workers to the United States, so people could see and hear directly from them what was happening. But it wasn't easy; the poorly educated Honduran workers had no idea of the broader world and were suspicious of the Americans' motives. When he first proposed bringing up a young girl worker in 1994, neighbors of the girl's mother warned her that the Americans were only taking her away to harvest her organs.

And there was the issue of what would happen to the girls after they went back home. Kernaghan and Briggs took it as a given that any worker they brought up would be blacklisted from ever working in a factory again. So they raised funds to put the girls through school.

The Labor Committee's budget didn't stretch to afford hotels, so the Hondurans stayed with Kernaghan and Briggs in the tiny rent-controlled railroad flat they shared on East 6th Street. The pair of them would interview the young workers, have them outline their life and their work, and coach them on sticking to the main points. "They might go on at great length about how, say, they were cheated of ten cents in social security, and we'd say, that's not a big issue," Kernaghan explained.

In Honduras, to break down the labor costs, Kernaghan would tell the workers not only to get labels, but to study the production line. How many workers were on a line? How many garments did they produce an hour or a day? Answering these questions was the key to figuring out the labor cost of the apparel, and how that cost compared with the retail price. Kernaghan knew that those numbers would give him a solid, easy-to-grasp argument. It was one thing to say workers weren't paid well; it was another to be able to say that the Gap paid workers 16 cents a shirt and to compare that cost with the shirt's $20 retail price—to be able to say that the labor made up less than one percent of the shirt's cost. That made it far tougher for a company to argue that they couldn't afford to pay anything more.

It was a tactic that first fully paid off with the campaign aimed at the Gap. In early 1995, workers tried to organize at a Honduran factory, called Mandarin, making clothing for the Gap and Eddie Bauer. Judith Viera, a fifteen-year-old who'd worked there for two years, was one of 350 union members illegally fired, and one of two teen workers Kernaghan brought to the United States. She made a substantial impact. Though getting press coverage proved tough, Kernaghan did gain an ally in the syndicated *New York Times* columnist Bob Herbert, who wrote one scathing piece after another denouncing the sweatshops and the Gap's exploitation of children.

In one of his pieces, Herbert described a glossy full-page color ad that a U.S. AID–funded group ran in an apparel trade magazine in 1990. It showed a young woman sitting at a sewing machine. The text read "Rosa Martinez produces apparel for U.S. markets on her sewing machine in El Salvador. *You* can hire her for 57 cents an hour." The ad assured that "she and her co-workers are known for their industriousness, reliability and quick learning."

The following year, Herbert noted, the same ad ran in the same magazine, except that this time, it read *"You* can hire her for 33 cents an hour."[8] It was a perfect illustration of what Kernaghan liked to call the race to the bottom, of how pressure from big American retailers for suppliers to offer the lowest possible cost was driving down wages that often already were below subsistence level.

Still more important for the campaign, though, was the pressure that schools, colleges, and church congregations put on the Gap. The Reverend Dyson's group, People Of Faith Network, organized letter-writing efforts and informational picketing, contacting a loose network of progressive churches that had actively opposed U.S. intervention in Central America back during the Reagan years. Typical was a letter to Gap chief executive Donald Gisher, from two rabbis at Congregation B'nai Jeshurun, on Manhattan's Upper West Side. "Before we publicly announce to our congregation that shopping at the Gap and the Banana Republic is a violation of Jewish ethical laws," they wrote, "we would like to hear from you if there are any plans to immediately correct these violations."[9]

Like most retailers by 1995, the Gap had a code of conduct. And, again like most others, its code was far more impressive on paper than in practice. For months during the campaign, executives at the Gap denied that there were any problems, or that Mandarin workers had been mistreated. They talked about canceling the contracts and walking away from the Mandarin factory—which Kernaghan opposed, knowing it would do nothing but harm the workers.

But the pressure on the Gap was unrelenting; and on December 15, 1995, the company capitulated. It signed an agreement with the National Labor Committee to let human rights ombudsmen in El Salvador and other Central American countries monitor whether factories were following its code of conduct. As part of the agreement, too, the Mandarin factory's owners agreed to meet with its fired workers and reach a fair settlement—with the understanding that lack of a settlement meant no more work for the Gap.

It was an unprecedented victory—the first time any U.S. retailer or apparel maker had agreed to let outsiders make sure its code was enforced.

During the Gap campaign, Kernaghan had been too busy to do anything with the Kathie Lee tag or any of the other information given to him by the workers at Global Fashion. But when he'd shown the tag to David Dyson, the minister had recognized Kathie Lee Gifford immediately and had seen instantly that they had dynamite in their hands.

By the time they got back in touch with the factory, though, it was too late. They discovered that in November 1995 Wal-Mart had left Global Fashion, moving its production to an even cheaper factory in Nicaragua. They decided to interview workers there anyway, by phone, through a human rights group they'd been in touch with. Kernaghan later said it took until early March 1996 to be sure of all the details of Global Fashion's production—but it may be, too, that he took his time because he didn't expect much to happen, with the Kathie Lee line already gone.

Still, on March 15, a Friday, he hand-delivered a letter to the offices of the *Live with Regis and Kathie Lee* show at ABC. The letter opened by asking Gifford for her help. It described the fact that the Global Fashion plant had employed children to make her clothes and detailed the long hours, forced overtime, humiliating treatment, low pay, illegal firings, and other problems at the plant. "The solution is not in taking Kathie Lee work out of Honduras," he wrote. "These young women need jobs, just as the U.S. people do. But these jobs must respect basic internationally recognized human and workers' rights."

> Perhaps no other person in the U.S. could have so important an impact, or make such a difference in cleaning up these sweatshop conditions as you could. What a profound difference it would make in the lives of tens of thousands of poor families if you made it public policy that Kathie Lee garments will never be made by children or by women whose basic rights are violated. You could move the entire industry to set new human rights standards, if you would announce that indepen-

dent human rights monitors will have access to all plants which produce clothing for Kathie Lee.

I am anxious to work with you on this in any way I can be of assistance. The lives of these women and children in Honduras, and elsewhere, cannot wait. They deserve our attention.

Kernaghan closed by telling her how to reach him.

On Monday, not having heard anything, he called ABC to see if she'd gotten the letter; but no one could tell him. Nor would anyone he could reach at ABC give him a fax number to which he could send the letter. So Kernaghan wrote again, this time to Michael Gelman, the show's producer, enclosing another copy of his letter to Gifford and asking Gelman to make sure it reached her.

Gifford, meanwhile, had gotten the letter. She'd called Wal-Mart and Halmode, the clothing company making the line, and sent them both copies, asking whether there was anything to what Kernaghan was saying. Wal-Mart assured her that they'd left the plant.

The first Kernaghan heard back was on March 27, when he got a call from Halmode's Mickey Kaufman. As he recalls the conversation, she yelled at him for being so naive as to send a letter to Gifford. Didn't he realize she got thousands of letters? He asked Kaufman where the Kathie Lee line was now being made; she told him there were 27 subcontractors, and that she didn't know where they sub-subcontracted in turn. Talk to Wal-Mart, she said.

The next day, Kernaghan wrote to Gifford again, outlining the conversation and asking Gifford again for her help. "Given the urgency of these issues," he wrote, "if I have not heard from you by Wednesday, April 3, I will have to begin approaching human rights organizations for their assistance."

This time he heard back faster—but not from Gifford. On April 4, Kaufman called him again. As he recalls, she asked him sneeringly if he was trying to save the world. He hung up on her. Kaufman also spoke with John Lupo, a Wal-Mart divisional senior vice president, who became the point man on the crisis. The men differ sharply on some details: Kernaghan says they first spoke within a day of Kaufman's call; Lupo says it wasn't until mid-July. Both remember Lupo saying Wal-Mart had conducted an unannounced inspection of Global Fashion on April 1. As Kernaghan recalls, Lupo said they'd confirmed his allegations. Lupo says that while Wal-Mart did indeed find children there at a second, later inspection, on the April 1 visit the factory was "clean." Lupo also said the plant had been inspected before and during the production of Kathie Lee's clothes there. (The earlier inspectors hadn't been from Wal-Mart but from Halmode's subcontractor. Like many retailers, Wal-Mart relied on its vendors and subcontractors to police themselves. The April 1 and follow-up inspectors also weren't from Wal-Mart but from a buying agent for Wal-Mart.) Kernaghan remembers Lupo noting that Wal-Mart had left the plant months ago, and suggesting they just forget the whole thing. Lupo says he likely did say that, though not in early April. Within days of Kaufman's call, Kernaghan also heard from an attorney for Global Fashion, demanding a retraction.

This wasn't the progress he'd had in mind. It was time to go public. On April 29, Kernaghan testified at a hearing on Capitol Hill about child labor and work conditions in overseas factories. At first, Kernaghan was surprised to see that there were lots of reporters on hand—but then he found out they weren't there to hear him, but to report on a young Canadian boy who'd founded an anti-child-labor group. When his turn came, Kernaghan, spitting out his words in his usual rapid-fire, machine-gun bursts, described his work over the last year or so, and showed the labels he'd collected from the Gap and Eddie Bauer and others. Then he held up a pair of Kathie Lee pants, sold at Wal-Mart for $9.96, and said he'd visited one plant in Honduras where these were made and found more than 100 children working 13-hour weekdays and 9-hour Saturdays. They earned less than 10 cents a pair, he said, less than one percent of the price of the pants.

After the hearings, the reporters there didn't seem that interested; only a few of them asked him any questions, and Kernaghan headed back to New York convinced his Kathie Lee broadside was being ignored. But in fact, several TV shows—such as the fluffy *Entertainment Tonight* and tabloid *Inside Edition*—aired his accusations that night, after calling Gifford for comment. She had her attorney issue a statement saying she'd contacted Wal-Mart as soon as she learned about the problems, that she'd been told Wal-Mart had left the plant, and that she would never condone or accept the exploitation of children.

But Gifford was far too high-profile for that to be the end of it. All the next day, calls kept coming in. Then the following morning, on her show, Gifford—wearing an outfit from her own collection—launched into a defense on air, saying indignantly, "I started my clothing line to benefit children. Millions of dollars have gone to help children, and I truly resent this man impugning my integrity." Then her mouth twisted. Her lips quivered and she began to cry. "You can say I'm ugly," she blubbered. "You can say I'm not talented. But when you say that I don't care about children and I will exploit them for some kind of monetary gain, for once, mister, you better answer your phone because my attorney is calling you today."*

"How dare you!" she raged, dramatically flinging down a handful of papers (presumably letters) to cheers from her studio audience.

As Philbin visibly flinched, seemingly utterly at a loss, she added that the moment she'd heard about the factory, "I immediately called Wal-Mart and said, 'This is obscene if this is happening.' They said, 'That happened months ago; we found out about it and took care of it.'" She railed against Kernaghan and what she called his vicious attack, calling him a nobody. "I'm supposed to be personally responsible for everything that happens around the world? In Honduras?" she asked, adding, "They're not going to stop me. They can kick me all they want."

Kernaghan, of course, missed this performance (which *Time* magazine called her "it's-not-my-fault, TV hissy fit"); but from his viewpoint, it was priceless. Her reaction was replayed on dozens of news and entertainment shows; and it seemed as though every newspaper in America had a story about it the next day. Kernaghan finally had gotten the spotlight on his issue. He was inundated with calls from reporters begging him to comment; camera crews literally lined up outside of his office. Producers begged him for footage of the sweatshops, which he was only too happy to provide. On camera, he said, "I ask Kathie Lee to come with us and take a look with her own eyes, see the kids in factories and let her talk to them."[10]

Determined to take advantage while they could, Kernaghan and his allies ramped up the crusade. Dyson wrote Gifford a letter May 7 on behalf of 10 religious groups, asking her to help get Wal-Mart to go back to Global Fashion and clean it up. "Pulling out of Honduras is not a just solution," he wrote. "Why not send the kids to school and hire their parents?" He asked her to push Wal-Mart to agree to independent human rights monitoring of the plant. The implicit threat of more publicity if she failed to act was left unstated.

For Gifford, of course, it was a nightmare. Her self-righteous salvo had only magnified the matter. Overnight, she became the sweatshop queen, the butt of countless late-night talk-show jokes and editorial cartoons. Quickly, she realized she needed to do something before her public image—on which her whole living was based—crumbled completely. So

---

* Dyson said an attorney for Gifford did call, threatening a suit. "We said we'd file for discovery of her financial records to find out how much she made, how much she kept, and how much she gave to charity. They called us back the next day and said Mrs. Gifford elected not to litigate."

she did what any millionaire celebrity would do in such a mess: She hired the best public relations man she could afford. In her case, it was Howard Rubenstein, who'd helped rehabilitate the public images of such personalities as New York Yankees owner George Steinbrenner and Sarah Ferguson, the Duchess of York.

As Rubenstein worked out a strategy, Gifford educated herself on the sweatshop situation. She came to realize that, in fact, sweatshops were rampant and that Wal-Mart's code was no guarantee—that children very well might be making her clothes.

Soon, Gifford was singing a different tune. Her rehabilitation would begin, naturally enough, on TV. An interview on tape was quickly arranged on friendly turf, ABC's *Prime Time Live*, which, like Gifford's own syndicated show, was owned by Disney Co. During a softball interview by Diane Sawyer, a tearfully innocent Gifford announced that she would hire inspectors to keep an eye on every factory making her clothing. The night the show aired, May 22, she and Frank Gifford were relaxing at home. She was over the hump, it seemed. But then the phone rang. It was a columnist from the *New York Daily News,* the splashy tabloid. He had a horrifying surprise for them.

Barely a week earlier, a terrifically juicy tidbit had come the way of organizers at UNITE, the Union of Needle-trades, Industrial and Textile Employees.° The union maintained a "justice center" in Manhattan's garment district, where the mostly nonunion workers from the many nearby sweatshops could bring their complaints. One day the week before, a group of workers from a sewing shop called Seo Fashions had brought in a drearily predictable set of gripes: They hadn't been paid in weeks; they weren't being paid for overtime; they were getting less than minimum wage. All numbingly routine, until the workers fished out the tags from the clothing they'd been making—tags with Kathie Lee's smiling face on them.

It was too rich. These workers had been toiling just a couple of subway stops from the TV studio where Kathie Lee and Regis Philbin held court. For days, union leaders debated whether to offer the story to the staid *New York Times* or the bombastic *Daily News*. At the same time, they had to convince the Seo workers to go public, and that wasn't easy. Many were illegal immigrants from Latin America; the last thing they wanted was pub-

---

° UNITE was formed in July 1995, when the International Ladies Garment Workers Union merged with the Amalgamated Clothing and Textile Workers Union.

lic attention. Union members pushed them for days, translating news stories into Spanish, talking about the worldwide sweatshop problem, playing
videos for them, and arguing that here was the chance to make a difference.
Finally, the workers agreed. Union leaders, meanwhile, decided they were
likely to get the best play from the tabloid.

And so, the night of the *Prime Time Live* show, columnist Jim Dwyer
stunned the Giffords by telling them about the story he'd be running the
next day.

"Are you sure of this?" Frank Gifford asked. Almost immediately, he
said, "We will pay them ourselves—pay them in full, with Social Security
taxes and everything else done properly that's not being done. And you will
have that in writing." Kathie Lee Gifford echoed his comments, saying "We
don't want any human being degraded in any way in the manufacture of any
product with my name on it, or any product, period."[11]

And so, the next day, after the screaming headlines in the *New York
Daily News*, there was the next enthralling installment: Frank Gifford, surrounded by television camera crews and photographers, marching sternly
into an unfriendly throng on West 38th Street. With Rubenstein at his side
and workers shouting, "Kathie, where's our money?" the square-jawed Gifford went into the Seo factory and began handing out white envelopes,
each with three $100 bills, to the workers there. (He'd brought $9,000 in
cash with him; Kathie Lee, he said, became too physically ill after hearing
the news to be able to come and deliver the money herself.)

The *Los Angeles Times*, comparing Gifford to a sheriff parting his way
through a lynch mob, rhapsodized that the scene was pure adrenaline:
"This was no longer a Frank Gifford tamed by the years and caged by a
broadcast booth. This was No. 16, again, son of a California oil roughneck,
All-American at USC, the most dependable of go-to guys."[12]

The made-for-TV drama of the moment let the Giffords seize back the
public relations initiative. Unfortunately for most of the Seo workers, the
sweatshop had shut down a few days earlier; so only 13 of the 45 workers
were around when Gifford arrived. However, thanks to the high profile
their case now assumed, two months later the Labor Department was able
to pressure the company that had sub-subcontracted with Seo to pay all the
workers a total of $19,623 in back wages.

Meanwhile, though, Kernaghan moved on to the next step in his campaign.
He fired salvos against other retailers and apparel makers he'd identified;
but keeping the pressure on Gifford was his top priority. In his office, he

perused the photos he'd taken at Global Fashion in Honduras. In one picture of a group of workers, there was a strikingly somber but pretty girl in the middle whose piercing gaze burned right out of the surface of the photo. Kernaghan had no idea who she was, but he faxed a copy of the photo to a friend of his, a human rights worker in Honduras, and asked her to find that girl. That was the girl he wanted to bring to the United States to talk about how workers were treated. He had the perfect forum in mind: an upcoming press conference at which Representative George Miller, of California, would call for a voluntary labeling program for apparel and independent monitoring to verify that clothes were made by adults under humane conditions.

It took Kernaghan's friend, Esperanza Reyes, three days to track down the girl, fifteen-year-old Wendy Diaz. And when she found her, Reyes wasn't sure Diaz would be any good. An orphan, living in a one-room shack with 11 other people, she was shy, ill-educated, and as quiet as a mouse. She'd never traveled anywhere outside of her town. Reyes told Kernaghan the girl seemed too naive, too innocent, and not brave enough to make a decent public speaker. As far as Kernaghan was concerned, though, the more innocent and naive she was, the better.

After a brief tussle with the U.S. Embassy in Honduras, in which several sympathetic congressmen intervened to get Diaz a visa, she arrived in New York, to spend a few days with Kernaghan and Briggs before heading down to Washington. Imagine, from her perspective, what this trip must have been like, to go from living in a shack in a small rural village and working hunched over a sewing machine 70 or more hours a week, to flying by jet to an alien land and a city of incomprehensible immensity. She was explosively curious, fascinated by nearly everything she saw—especially the Labor Committee's computers.

In Washington, before the national press corps, the tiny girl (4 feet 9 inches tall) was utterly and unaffectedly pitiable. Matter-of-factly, through a translator, she spoke of her life supporting three younger brothers on her pay of less than $22 a week, and how she'd begun to work at the factory when she was thirteen years old, along with scores of other minors. She described her 70-hour workweeks, the nights of forced overtime when, to make quotas, they'd have to work until 6:30 in the morning.

> The supervisors insult us and yell at us to work faster. Sometimes they throw the garment in your face, or grab and shove you. They make you work very fast, and if you make the production quota one day then they just increase it the next.

> The plant is hot, like an oven. They keep the bathrooms locked . . .
> even the pregnant women they abuse. They send them to the pressing
> department where they have to work on their feet 12 or 13 hours a day
> in tremendous heat, ironing.

The company did this to make them quit so it could avoid paying maternity benefits, she said. She described physical abuse by the managers.

"North Americans from a U.S. company visited the plant several times, but they never spoke with the workers," she said. She told of how many of the workers had been fired after they met with Kernaghan. "If I could talk with Kathie Lee, I would ask her to help us," she said, "so that they would stop yelling at us and hitting us, and so they would let us go to night school and let us organize to protect our rights. We would like Kathie Lee to return her work to our factory, only under better conditions. We also need a just wage. Please help us."

Reporters wanted to know how she felt about Gifford, if she knew anything about her. "Maybe her heart is black," Diaz answered. "I wish I could talk to her. If she's good, she will help us."

While all this was going on, Secretary of Labor Robert Reich had entered the picture. Reich, a former Yale professor and a fellow Rhodes Scholar with Bill Clinton, had been trying for several years to attack sweatshops by going after the manufacturers as well as the subcontractors, threatening to use old laws from the Depression days to seize goods made under illegal conditions. He had to take a novel approach, since neither Clinton nor Congress was willing to pay to rebuild the ranks of labor inspectors that had been so severely cut back under the Reagan and Bush administrations.*

As always, apparel makers and retailers had argued that whatever sweatshops the scraggly little band of federal inspectors turned up were just a few bad apples, the rare exceptions. But a couple of vigorous investigations in California had shown that up to three-fourths of *registered* garment factories weren't paying overtime or were breaking some other wage law. And then in August of 1995, Labor investigators raided a factory in El Monte, a suburb of Los Angeles, where they found dozens of Thai and Mexican workers held in virtual slavery in a compound surrounded by razor wire. Reich decided to publicize the names of the retailers for whom the

---

* In 1996, the Labor Department had about 820 inspectors to keep an eye on more than 22,000 apparel contractors and 6 million workplaces in the United States. Twenty years earlier, under President Carter, there had been more than 1,600 inspectors. Under Reagan, the number dropped below 700.

clothes were being made. Executives at the retailers—Neiman Marcus, Macy's, Sears, Dayton-Hudson's Mervyn's division, Montgomery Ward, and 13 others—went ballistic. But most, along with other retailers not named this time, also agreed to meet with Reich's assistants to try to figure out ways to protect themselves.

"Wal-Mart's reaction, though, was 'We're not interested. Don't call us. Don't write us. This has nothing to do with us,' " recalls one of Reich's aides. The retailers who did show up for Reich's "sweatshop summit" had resisted any moves to make them take some responsibility for how the clothes they sold were made. But Reich had tried to keep up the pressure through a carrot-and-stick approach, publicly naming the good retailers (such as the post–Kernaghan Gap and Levi Strauss) as well as the bad. So when the second Kathie Lee sweatshop flap hit the news, he too saw the opportunity it offered.

He had a staffer call both Rubenstein and Gifford's attorney, Ron Konecky, to say that he would love to have Kathie Lee work with him to clean things up. Rubenstein was intrigued. What better way to rescue Gifford's image than to have her leading the fight against sweatshops?

On May 30, the day after Wendy Diaz appeared in Washington, Reich and one of his aides met the Giffords, Rubenstein, his assistant, and Konecky for dinner at a cozy Italian restaurant on the Upper East Side of Manhattan, off Lexington Avenue. The Giffords were full of questions: How big was this problem? What could they do to avoid sweatshops? Reich talked about the huge numbers of sweatshops, about his efforts to involve big retailers such as Wal-Mart, and how he believed that only if the industry helped police itself could any real change take place.

Gifford was ready to listen. She said she'd had no idea that Wal-Mart let such things happen. (Later, she claimed she hadn't seen or heard about the *Dateline NBC* story or any of the other coverage of Wal-Mart's previous sweatshop scandals.) She'd been furious with Wal-Mart, having trusted them with her name and image; and she thought they certainly ought to know the conditions under which their clothes were made. And, as Reich's assistant pointed out, they had people going to the factories to check on production anyway, right? The Giffords said they already were negotiating with Wal-Mart about what the company should do to make sure her clothes were made by properly paid adults. (Wal-Mart executives adamantly opposed any kind of independent monitoring, claiming it would offer an excuse to organize at the factories; if Gifford wanted her own monitoring, it would be better to set it up under their control, they argued.)

By the end of the three-hour dinner meeting, Gifford agreed to help.

The next day, she appeared at a press conference with Reich, at which she claimed she'd thought about dropping her clothing line entirely. "You say to yourself, 'Who needs this?' " she said. But, she added, "the problem is not going to go away until we combat it. If I feel like I can do something, I should stay; it's my responsibility."[13] She appealed to other celebrities, such as Michael Jordan and Jaclyn Smith, to make sure that clothing with their name on it was being made properly.

Jordan, who endorsed Nike products, typified the celebrities' reactions. Evidence that Nike used sweatshops had popped up repeatedly for years. But Jordan, offered the opportunity to take a stand, made it clear he couldn't care less. "I don't know the complete situation," he said. "Why should I? I'm trying to do my job. Hopefully, Nike will do the right thing, whatever that might be."[14] Within days of Jordan's response, *USA Today* publicized charges that eleven-year-olds were making Air Jordan sneakers in Indonesia, for 14 cents an hour.

Smith, meanwhile, out of either naiveté or complacency, said Kmart's code of conduct didn't allow child labor. Kernaghan promptly offered up a factory in Honduras where thirteen-year-old girls were making Smith's clothes under conditions similar to those at Global Fashion.

A few other celebrities contacted by the Giffords—including model Cheryl Tiegs and fitness guru Richard Simmons—did jump on board, agreeing to appear with Gifford at a Labor-sponsored "fashion forum" on how to make codes of conduct stick.*

When Wendy Diaz had said in Washington that she hoped to talk to Kathie Lee Gifford, reporters naturally had called Gifford for comment, and Rubenstein had said Kathie Lee would be happy to meet with her. It wasn't quite that simple, though; Rubenstein and Kernaghan first had to engage in a tug-of-war over where and under what circumstances the meeting would take place, and who else would sit in. Jay Mazur, the head of UNITE, acted as Kernaghan's intermediary. Rubenstein wanted to meet at a fancy uptown club; Kernaghan insisted on Reverend Dyson's church. They compromised on meeting at the mansion of Archbishop Cardinal O'Connor, whom Rubenstein knew professionally.

On June 6, they gathered in a large, lavish salon. One team consisted of Kathie Lee; her attorney Konecky; Rubenstein's assistant, Gary Lewi; and

---

* Simmons said that he personally visited factories where his seventeen licensed products were made to make sure they weren't sweatshops.

Mickey Kaufman, the woman from Halmode who'd torn into Kernaghan on the phone a few weeks earlier. Kaufman, to Kernaghan's surprise, looked grandmotherly—not at all as he'd pictured her over the phone. Diaz, Kernaghan, and Briggs were accompanied by Dyson, Mazur and an assistant, and Esperanza Reyes, who'd flown up from Honduras.

Through a translator, Gifford asked Diaz what her life and workdays were like, and Diaz told her. It was like her testimony in Washington. She talked about how she and the other young girls would group together and run home when they got out late at night, because they were scared to go home by themselves, and about her struggle to provide for her three little brothers on her meager salary.

Gifford seemed to listen attentively—but as Diaz finished, she jumped in to tell the girl how hard all this had been on her, too. As if seeking her sympathy, Gifford told her a story she'd already repeated several times to reporters, about how terrible she'd felt when the newscasts had talked about her on TV, and her little boy Cody had asked her, "Mommy, why are people saying that you're such a bad lady?" Diaz just looked at her without saying a word.

After a brief silence, Gifford apologized to her. "Please believe me," she said. "I didn't know—and now that I know, it'll never happen again. I want to make sure it'll never happen again."

Lewi and Konecky asked Diaz what she considered a living wage. Then Lewi told the girl that Gifford planned to work with Wal-Mart to set up her own monitors. That was fine, Diaz said, but the workers were interested in having any monitoring done by a human rights group they knew and trusted, such as the one Reyes worked for. A long discussion followed between both sides on what monitoring should consist of, on getting Wal-Mart back to Honduras.

In the end, the groups settled on a loose joint statement. Gifford said that she acknowledged "the reality of labor abuse in the apparel industry"; that she supported independent monitoring for this factory, for Wal-Mart, and for the whole apparel industry; and that she would encourage Wal-Mart to go back to Global Fashion as soon as conditions improved enough.

Kernaghan, in return, said that "Kathie Lee Gifford deserves tremendous credit and support for the major step she has taken to defend worker and human rights by calling upon Wal-Mart to return to the Global Fashion plant in Honduras and establish independent monitoring." Then he added an apology: "In our efforts to defend the rights of children and women working in the assembly plants in Central America, we never intended to hurt anyone personally and are truly sorry for any pain caused to Kathie Lee Gifford and her family by this work."

Wal-Mart, in a carefully worded statement, didn't quite agree to go back to the plant as soon as it was "certified under our strict standards," but rather "to put them back on our approved vendor list" and give them opportunities along with all their other approved factories.

Still, it seemed like tremendous progress. Gifford, in her statement, said, "Wendy Diaz has a message that compels every American consumer, every American manufacturer, and every American citizen to ask, Under what conditions are the products we buy being manufactured?" And Gifford repeated that now that she knew what was happening, she would do everything she could to help. Kernaghan left the meeting touched by her sincerity, impressed with how she seemed to genuinely understand and care about what was happening, and convinced that he'd gained an ally.

What, then, to make of what happened the next day?

It was June 7, and more than 17,000 Wal-Mart shareholders and workers flocked into the huge Bud Walton Arena on the University of Arkansas campus in Fayetteville for the company's annual meeting and pep rally. Halfway through the morning, Kathie Lee and Frank Gifford were introduced, striding out onto the huge octagonal stage to the cheers of the audience.

Did Kathie Lee Gifford talk about her new commitment to fight sweatshops? No. Instead, in a rambling, self-pitying monologue, she complained about the hard time she'd had lately, somehow linking recent events to the fact she had been booed a year and a half earlier when she was introduced to lip-synch the national anthem at the Super Bowl in Miami.

"I've done some bad things," she said of the sweatshop scandal, "but this ain't one of them." She complained that people were out to get her. "When all this happened, it wasn't entirely unexpected, but the viciousness of it was appalling. . . . The minute I realized the line would be successful, I knew the honeymoon was over.

"We didn't do anything wrong. That's the important thing," she said. "We live in a weird world. This country will forgive you rape, will forgive you murder, will forgive you anything but success." That was why she and Wal-Mart were being attacked, she said—because they were successful. "We have to look at it as a compliment," she told the crowd, "and we can be proud of ourselves as human beings."

Was this the real Kathie Lee Gifford? Was her apology to Diaz just an act, a case of playing to her audience? It would seem so—but this is probably too simplistic a conclusion. Certainly, Gifford was repeatedly disingenuous about her clothing line, insisting that she'd only done it to raise money for charity, when in fact she took in far more money from her licensing deal than from her TV show. Still, she *did* give millions to charity. And for all that Gifford felt like lashing out, and for all that her tendency to be self-absorbed often won out, she did, ultimately, take more responsibility for her label than many other celebrities would do—or than Wal-Mart's executives were inclined to do.

The Wal-Mart men who followed her onstage made what they considered the most important point: Sales of the line hadn't been hurt.* A little later in the meeting, Don Soderquist, the vice chairman, lumped together the Kathie Lee fracas with claims of Wal-Mart hurting small towns and other criticism. "When you become number one, you become the target," he told the crowd.

"I've heard we're not the same company as when Sam was here," he said. "We haven't changed, folks. Our principles are the same as when Sam was here." This was certainly true, if not in the sense he meant to convey.

To the shareholders, Wal-Mart executives claimed they were already doing everything possible to make sure that people making their products were being treated properly. But Jay Allen, who'd succeeded Don Shinkle as the company's chief spokesman, said privately later that Wal-Mart would now begin training its buyers, who visited factories to check on production, on the labor standards in Wal-Mart's code of conduct.

Behind the scenes, Gifford, Wal-Mart, and Kernaghan continued negotiating, even as Kernaghan publicly went after the Disney Co. for goods he charged were being made under even worse conditions in Haiti. In late June, Gifford announced that she'd hired a nonprofit group to do her monitoring. The outfit, run by a former buying agent, would train apparel makers' quality-control inspectors on how to look for labor, health, and safety problems, and could, if asked, train local human rights groups to do inspections too. Gifford wouldn't say who would inspect the factories making her clothing—leading Kernaghan to question just how independent these inspections would be.

On July 15, testifying before a House subcommittee on human rights, in a room jam-packed with reporters, Kathie Lee, with Frank at her side, said, "I think I was the right person to pick on" and that "everything changed for me after I met with . . . Miss Diaz." But she also said that putting together an inspection program wasn't as simple as she had thought. "You have to identify local human rights agencies where there's

---

* Wal-Mart didn't release actual sales numbers, and declined to do so later.

only one agenda," she said, apparently referring to Wal-Mart's argument that human rights groups were just fronts for would-be union organizers.

The next day, she took part in Reich's fashion forum, at which hundreds of retailers, apparel makers, and union leaders, and a few celebrities met to discuss how to improve sweatshop conditions. Out of that forum, President Clinton would appoint a task force to craft a voluntary, industrywide code meant to banish sweatshops in the United States and abroad. Kernaghan was there; and just after he finished giving an interview to a TV crew, a man who'd been watching came up and introduced himself: John Lupo, Wal-Mart's vice president in charge of international merchandising. Lupo wanted to meet; they agreed to get together at a church in New York about a week later.

"What do you want?" was Lupo's first question, at that meeting. Kernaghan laid out his usual demands, starting with having Wal-Mart go back to Global Fashion. But Lupo said Wal-Mart's inspectors had just been there and that the factory was too far gone. Kernaghan, of course, said that not going back would punish the workers for raising problems. Lupo offered to have Wal-Mart bring work to some other factory in Honduras instead. He also told Kernaghan that he'd been talking with his counterparts at The Gap about their independent monitoring program, and that Wal-Mart was open to that possibility. But he wouldn't sign anything to that effect, saying he couldn't make that commitment on the spot. "Are you trying to organize these workers?" he asked. Kernaghan demurred, saying he was just trying to get them decent conditions.* Lupo was as skeptical of him as Kernaghan was a few minutes later, when Lupo said, "It's too bad you didn't come straight to us earlier; we'd be so much farther along."

"I snickered under my breath," Kernaghan said later. "If we'd followed their scenario, nothing would have changed. There's only one thing companies respond to, and that's pressure."

And, in fact, by pointing the finger at Gifford, Kernaghan had brought enormous pressure to bear—and not just against Wal-Mart. "There's little doubt that Charles Kernaghan and his anti-sweatshop battle have been shaking up the issue of labor abuses in the apparel industry like nothing since the Triangle Shirtwaist fire," said two writers for *Women's Wear Daily*.[15] The fear and loathing he engendered was incomparable: He was attacked by apparel industry executives as a devious fanatic, a charlatan, a vicious, irresponsible, duplicitous front man for organized labor who didn't play fair. When he was accused of exaggerating or misrepresenting situa-

----
* Lupo didn't recall asking Kernaghan about organizing but said he might have done so.

tions, Kernaghan would unapologetically cite example after example of times when the companies had lied, fudged, or twisted the truth.

But—in league with Reich's campaign and various union efforts—he got results, inch by inch: J.C. Penney said any supplier caught violating its code would lose all future contracts unless they put independent monitoring in place. Disney—which had to be as hypervigilant about its Snow-White image as did Gifford about hers—quietly investigated his accusations against it in Haiti, even as it denied everything, and then said it would appoint monitors to look over its factories. So did Kmart. So did Eddie Bauer. Kernaghan's main goal remained getting *independent* monitors to keep an eye on factories, as he'd done with The Gap. And, bit by bit, he kept pushing the industry in that direction.

Kernaghan repeatedly argued that retailers were pitting U.S. workers against poor teenagers in Third World countries in a race to the bottom, forcing them to compete over who would accept the lowest pay and most miserable conditions. He blamed the presence of U.S. sweatshops on retailers' demands "that their U.S. contractors meet the same production prices they get off shore, which is impossible to do legally.

"The corporations tell us that they go off shore to provide the U.S. consumer with lower prices. What they conveniently leave out is that the traditional 100 percent markup when a product goes from a U.S. manufacturer to the retailer becomes a 500 percent to 600 percent markup when the production goes off-shore," he said.[16]

Kernaghan was exaggerating a bit—the typical markup on imports was closer to 400 percent. But his basic point was true: At the same time that retailers—Wal-Mart included—were complaining that they had to go wherever they could get the cheapest production to compete, they were tripling and quadrupling their markup by importing goods. And there was no question about the race to the bottom: By 1997, many of the 28-cent-an-hour jobs Kernaghan complained about in Honduras would have moved to Nicaragua, where workers made as little as 14 cents an hour, or to Indonesia or Burma, where wages were as low as 11 cents an hour.

This wouldn't be a struggle with a clean-cut ending. In April 1997, the White House anti-sweatshop task force announced a watered-down agreement for companies to put "No Sweat" tags on their goods. The code of conduct called for workweeks of no more than 60 hours, for paying at least the local minimum wage, for recognizing workers' right to organize, for a ban on child labor (with a minimum age of fourteen)—and for independent monitoring. Left unsettled was who would do that monitoring: accounting firms and private security firms reporting to the companies, as the retailers and apparel makers wanted, or human rights groups, as some labor and watchdog organizations proposed.

Meanwhile, Gifford's rehabilitation, steered by Rubenstein, continued. Over the fall of 1996 and the following winter, he negotiated flattering cover stories about her in various women's magazines. *Good Housekeeping* described her on its cover as "Betrayed, attacked, and now fighting back." *McCall's* promised its readers the inside scoop on "How she made it through."

A more significant accolade came from one of Reich's aides, who said, "Personally, I can't stand Kathie Lee, but I have to give her credit. If she'd given us the same reaction as the retailers, of 'It's not my problem; I just put my name on it,' nothing would have happened. . . . The retailers don't want to admit they're doing anything different from before, but they are. They're being far more careful—and putting more pressure on the manufacturers."

But it was a slow process. Kernaghan, too, kept at it. In November 1997, the tabloid TV show *Hard Copy* aired a sensationalistic three-part report on workers in Nicaragua making clothes for Wal-Mart for as little as 10 cents an hour (the legal minimum wage was 14 cents an hour). The workers complained of being physically and sexually abused. The cameras lingered on the tired, pathetic-looking workers and the dirt-floored, ramshackle wood and cardboard shacks in which they lived. And there, on camera, was the man who'd handed *Hard Copy* the story: Charlie Kernaghan, blasting away again at Wal-Mart—and at Kmart and Penney, which also had clothes being made there. Wal-Mart said its monitors had been there but hadn't found any violations; the other two promised, as usual, to investigate.

Francisco Aguirre-Sacasa, Nicaragua's ambassador to the United States, denied *Hard Copy*'s charges. He said that the workers earned well above minimum wage, and that the factories didn't knowingly employ anyone under eighteen. Wal-Mart, for its part, distributed copies of a *Miami Herald* story, following up on the scandal. The *Herald*'s reporter reasonably questioned whether factory conditions were as bad as *Hard Copy* and Kernaghan had painted them. But the *Herald* then cast the debate in terms of the false choice between bad jobs or no jobs at all, rather than considering whether it was reasonable to fight for better conditions. "This job is important to me," factory worker Fatima Estrada was quoted as saying. "If I don't work, we don't eat. . . . If the factories close, it would be a crisis."[17] Overlooked in this was the fact that Kernaghan wasn't calling for closing any factories. The story also wrongly accused Kernaghan of costing several hundred factory workers their jobs in Honduras after the earlier Kathie Lee flap.

But at the same time, Wal-Mart's Jay Allen announced a new toll-free number through which workers at its manufacturers, or other people, could report to Wal-Mart any violations of its code of conduct. Allen also said the company would produce a poster, to be put in its factories, describing its standards in English, Spanish, and Mandarin Chinese, and telling workers how to contact the company.

Apparently, those posters weren't in place very quickly. Less than a month later, New York labor inspectors raided three sweatshops making Kathie Lee clothes in lower Manhattan. They found Chinese immigrants working up to 80 hours a week, many for under minimum wage; some workers had been stiffed for as much as 10 weeks' pay. Gifford's inspectors had been in the factories several times, and had found some problems, which they'd warned the factories to correct, Rubenstein said. But none of the inspectors spoke Chinese, so they hadn't talked to any of the workers— and hadn't had a clue about just how bad things were. Gifford promised to cooperate with the state attorney general on an investigation and put up $50,000 toward the $300,000 in back wages the workers were owed. "We've learned a lesson," said her spokesman, Gary Lewi. "We must go in with translators," as state labor inspectors had, he said.[18]

But then in March 1998, Kernaghan reported finding young women working at a factory in China making Kathie Lee handbags for 13 cents an hour, while working 10 hours a day, seven days a week.° Such conditions clearly violated Wal-Mart's code of conduct, which mandated days off, no forced overtime, and a living wage (estimated at 60 to 80 cents a day in China). Again, a spokesman for Kathie Lee promised to investigate. Wal-Mart, without denying Kernaghan's charges, issued a press release reiterating that it has a code of conduct for vendors and saying, "The problems outlined by the National Labor Committee transcend Wal-Mart, Kathie Lee, and the modern garment industry."

Insisting that Wal-Mart did enforce decent work conditions at the factories, the company's Jay Allen complained, "If Kernaghan is really worried about factory conditions, why doesn't he report the problems directly to us?"

° Kernaghan's report named 18 U.S. companies having goods made at 21 Chinese factories, with work weeks of up to 96 hours. The companies included Dayton-Hudson, Disney, Esprit, Federated Department Stores, Kmart, The Limited, May Co., J.C. Penney, Nike, Ralph Lauren, Reebok, and Sears, among others. The various retailers denied exploiting workers or violating China's labor laws.

A cynic might look at all this and conclude that nothing really had changed. But just as once the workers being profiled in exposés were eight and nine years old, then eleven and twelve, it was notable that none of the Nicaraguan workers Kernaghan had spotlighted were any younger than fifteen. Too, each time someone else was caught, the pressure ratcheted up a bit more to do a better job of inspecting. Critics of the whole process—editorial writers at the *Wall Street Journal,* for instance—trotted out the reliable sweatshops-are-better-than-no-shops argument and dismissed efforts to better conditions as labor inching "its anti-import agenda one step farther up a big, hopeless hill."[19]

Retailers, meanwhile, even as they scrambled to protect their image whenever they got caught in a compromising situation, insisted that American shoppers really didn't care about anything other than getting the lowest price.

But for his part, Charlie Kernaghan insisted that "the American people are too decent for that. . . . That's why we've been effective with such a tiny staff and small budget." Sure, he said, not everybody cares if the stuff they buy exploits someone. But enough do. "Maybe it's 20 percent, 30 percent, 40 percent who care about these issues," he said. That would be more than enough to make a difference. "I don't think we've begun to tap the number of people out there who are decent," he said.

The future of thousands upon thousands of workers around the world would rest on whether Kernaghan's assessment was correct.

20

Bleak House

On a stage in front of more than 14,000 shareholders, a loose, relaxed Bud Walton joked and laughed and waved at people squeezing onto the floor of the University of Arkansas's Barnhill Arena to take their seats for Wal-Mart's 1993 annual meeting.

He'd been designated as the company's substitute for his late brother Sam for the event. The seventy-one-year-old, wireless microphone in hand, urged people not to stand on ceremony. "There's no breaks," he warned, "so if you have that urge, go."

Behind him, David Glass, Don Soderquist, and all the Wal-Mart directors took their seats as the carefully choreographed show got underway. But then Bud Walton unexpectedly veered from the agenda to say he wanted to talk about something he hadn't mentioned to the board or other executives. "I probably shouldn't even bring this up," he said. But sales at stores open more than a year had stagnated in recent months, he noted, so Wal-Mart was cutting payroll, cutting back on people's hours to cut expenses.

"I think that's wrong," he said, to shouts of approval from the several thousand employees in the arena. "Does that tell you guys anything?" he asked, turning to look at the directors lining a long table behind him as the cheers continued. "I know we got to cut expenses, but we can find another way," he said, to another ovation.

"It affects customer service," someone shouted from the crowd.

Walton added that Sam always said he learned so much from the folks in the stores and that they were the company's most important asset. "It's difficult for people to manage on paychecks for only 30 or 32 hours," he said to the directors, before turning back to the crowd. "I'm sticking my neck out for you. They didn't have any idea I was going to bring this up. . . . I want you to go back and tell your people I'm behind them 100 percent.

"This is a company problem, and I don't think we've faced it," he said, to more applause.

"I'd suggest maybe the executives should take a pay cut," Walton added loudly, to a thunderous cheer from the crowd, as the other directors and executives sat stone-faced behind him. "I'm sure we're getting through to them today," he said to the audience, gesturing behind him.

He paused and looked over the throng. "I'm still with you," he said. "I'll always be with you. Any way I can help you, you let me know."

Walton then relinquished the stage to country singer Reba McEntire, who kicked off the official meeting by singing the national anthem.

If Bud Walton tossed a bucket of cold water on Wal-Mart's executives, it was how they responded that really signaled how dramatically Wal-Mart's culture already had changed in the year since Sam Walton had died: They completely ignored what he'd said, pretending it had never happened. Not Glass, not Soderquist, not one of the other executives who bounded up onto the stage over the next few hours said one word about the issue Walton had raised. Such a wall of silence would have been unthinkable to Sam Walton; but it was the way things were done now.

Afterward, in a private conversation, Walton said he hadn't really liked bringing the matter up the way he did, but he hadn't seen any alternative. He'd been hearing complaints from workers, and it was obviously a hardship for them. "With Sam being gone, it's different," he said. "In size, it's different—and I want the people in operations to understand how these people feel."

Glass, caught hurrying off to meet with a group of Wall Street analysts, was curt, obviously annoyed at Walton's indiscretion. "When you run below plan, you reduce hours," he said. "Unless you react, you're not going to be very successful." Then he added, pointedly, "You know, Bud spends most of his time fishing and hunting these days."

This was true. Walton himself readily admitted that he wasn't as close to the business as he'd once been. Hell, it was no secret he'd rather be fishing than doing just about anything else, and that he traveled from Alaska to Tierra del Fuego to cast his lines, as he had for years. But unlike any of the rest of them, Bud Walton remembered when the business had been one small variety store on the main drag of one small town, when he'd had to clean out the damned soft-serve ice-cream machine himself. Even though

Wal-Mart now had some 450,000 employees working in more than 2,200 stores, Walton hadn't lost sight of the personal element, of the fact that the decisions the executives made affected these people's lives in significant ways.

But to the extent that he, along with Helen Walton, once acted as Sam Walton's conscience, pushing him to show more consideration for the sales clerks and other hourly workers, that role had been buried along with Sam Walton himself. Glass and the other managers weren't all that interested in what Bud had to say—and they were livid about the way he'd raised the issue. There was no change in policy.

At the next annual meeting, Bud Walton sat on stage with all the other directors and top executives; but he wasn't invited to speak.

In other ways, too, the culture began fraying—especially when Wal-Mart's stock stalled out. Sam Walton's death in 1992 hadn't hurt Wal-Mart's stock price, which climbed upward the rest of that year just as it always had. By February of 1993, the price soared above $64 a share, and the directors approved yet another stock split. After that split, someone who'd paid $1,650 for 100 Wal-Mart shares back in the original public offering would have had stock worth $3.5 million.

But then the price of Wal-Mart shares began to slip, bit by bit. From a peak of $34.125 a share just after the split, by that fall they'd fallen to below $24 a share. A few brief rallies flagged. By early 1995, the price fell below $21 a share. Then below $20. For more than four years, Wal-Mart shares would scrape along far below that 1993 post-split high.

Within Wal-Mart, these long doldrums seemed as inexplicable as if the sun had decided not to rise. It wasn't just a question of unhappy shareholders; at Wal-Mart, it was a basic tenet of the faith that, even if you were only paid $5 or $6 an hour, you would eventually be lifted into a comfortable retirement by the ever-rising tide of Wal-Mart's share price.

Store managers long had recruited workers to buy shares through a payroll-deduction plan (at a 15 percent discount); and stores competed to get the highest percentage of employee shareholders.

"In management terms, it was our job to convince the associates that their performance and our performance is directly reflected in the stock," said Phillip Sanders, an assistant store manager in Liberty, Missouri. And that policy had worked pretty well. Though, by 1995, fewer than half of Wal-Mart's 600,000 employees had been with the company as long as three years, more than 55 percent joined the payroll-deduction program. The recruiting was aggressive. "They said to take it out of your paycheck until it hurts, to buy as much stock as you can because eventually you'll have tremendous amounts of money," remembers Denise Botelho, who hired on as a sales clerk at a Wal-Mart store in Fairhaven, Connecticut, in mid-1992.

Then there was the company's pension plan. This was not like a traditional pension plan, in which a retiring worker is guaranteed a certain minimum payout every year. Instead, it took the form of an employee stock ownership plan, or ESOP, with 89 percent of its holdings in Wal-Mart stock. Each year, Wal-Mart would contribute a certain amount of its profits to the plan; that money, along with any gains earned by the plan's investments, was divided up among the plan's members in proportion to their pay. As an ESOP, the pension plan was unusually dependent on how Wal-Mart's stock performed. (In a 1994 study of the pension plans of 262 major companies, Rutgers University economist Douglas Lynn Kruse found only eight that relied on their own stock as heavily as Wal-Mart did.)

The original appeal to Sam Walton of rewarding workers with shares of stock had been that it was relatively cheap; it gave the workers a sense of ownership; and it motivated workers because they could expect hefty gains as the fast-growing company's stock price soared. And, since Wal-Mart's executives appointed the pension plan's trustees, it had the added advantage of keeping another hefty chunk of stock under management's control. The idea worked so well that scores of other companies had followed Wal-Mart's example (Home Depot, MCI Telecommunications, Federal Express, and Southwest Airlines, to name a few).

In actuality, even at the peak of the good years, few rank-and-file workers really cashed in big. Partly because of high turnover, fewer than 1 in 50 Wal-Mart workers ever accumulated as much as $50,000 in stock. But those few were showcased endlessly at meetings and in newsletters, to give workers a very different impression.

That promise of cashing in big had been—along with the personal loyalty Sam Walton inspired—the glue that made the company culture stick. But Sam, of course, was gone.

And now Wal-Mart executives discovered the risk of having a profit-sharing plan—and a company culture—so reliant on Wal-Mart stock. Those risks had been easy to ignore while Wal-Mart shares kept rising—but now that they were slipping, employees saw their pensions slipping away too. By early 1994, the Wal-Mart shares that made up so much of the profit-sharing plan's assets had lost more than $350 million in value from the year before, cutting the plan's assets to $2.1 billion. By the end of that year, they fell nearly $250 million more. One pair of married employees canceled their plan to retire in 1995, when they both turned seventy, after the drop in Wal-Mart's stock price lopped their combined profit-sharing by $50,000, more than a third of its value—money they'd hoped to use to pay off their mortgage. "Under Wal-Mart's rules, we had to take our profit-sharing out once we were seventy," rather than wait in hopes of a rebound, said the wife.

At first, though, most workers kept the faith. After all, there had been dips before—often just after stock splits—and always, the stock had bounced back quickly. But with every passing month, that faith was tested more and more sorely. By the spring of 1994, nearly every time he walked into a store Glass was asked the same questions: When was the stock price going to go back up?

At the 1994 annual meeting, Glass and Soderquist devoted some 40 minutes to discussing just that question. Glass reassured workers that there were plenty of opportunities ahead and that "if sales keep going up, and profits keep going up, then the stock will go up long term—it absolutely will happen."

Privately, Glass said that Wal-Mart's stock had been overvalued. As for getting it back up, Glass and his cohorts found that satisfying Wall Street wasn't simply a matter of pointing to rising sales and profits.

Take L. Wayne Hood, a perceptive analyst at Prudential Securities. In early 1995, he predicted that Wal-Mart would boost its earnings by 19 percent a year through the end of the decade, a spectacular performance for what was then a company with $67 billion a year in sales. But that didn't mean Hood was recommending anyone rush out to buy the stock. To the contrary, reminiscing about the days when Wal-Mart sales jumped 30 percent and 40 percent a year, Hood blamed the sagging stock price in part on a lot of investors taking money out of Wal-Mart to invest it in smaller companies that were growing faster—a strategy that he felt made perfect sense.* Other Wall Street analysts fretted about the sagging Sam's Club division, still reeling from the warehouse-club wars of the early '90s. And, too, Wal-Mart was struggling with digesting and converting 122 Woolco stores in Canada, which it had bought from Woolworth for $335 million in early 1994.

Workers had other worries besides the stock price. Even as they saw their pensions slipping, they found themselves paying more out of their

---

* Wal-Mart paid relatively low quarterly dividends, so the stock's primary appeal for investors was in its growth prospects.

own pocket for health benefits. By 1994, the average Wal-Mart worker paid $1,900 a year to provide his or her family with health insurance. Wal-Mart workers paid 35 percent of their insurance premiums (compared to a national average of 20 percent), plus deductibles and 20 percent of any medical costs that were covered. Less than half the company's workers opted for health insurance coverage; after all, for a typical worker making between $12,000 and $20,000 a year before taxes, that premium took a big bite out of every paycheck. And nearly a third weren't eligible anyway, because they were part-timers.°

The biggest worry, of course, was holding on to one's job and getting enough hours in the first place—the issue Bud Walton had raised. Glass was a big believer in maximum efficiency, and he centralized and computerized scheduling to match the number of workers on duty at any store with the expected flow of customers. "It's done just like we order merchandise," he said.

For the workers, though, this efficient approach had the disadvantage that many of them couldn't count on the same schedule and same number of hours from week to week; nor could they count on getting 40 hours every week. Wal-Mart executives recognized that concern in part by granting benefits to workers putting in 28 hours a week or more. The shorter workweek let Wal-Mart raise a worker's hours during busy times without having to pay overtime (unless workers went above 40 hours).† But the company also—logically—hired and laid off workers throughout the year as demand varied. Needless to say, this didn't delight the employees.

Denise Botelho, for example, was laid off in early 1994, in the post-Christmas sales droop—and hit with a double whammy. Like many workers who'd hired on and signed up for the payroll-deduction stock plan in the previous year, her shares, at the time she was let go, were worth less than she had paid for them, even with her 15 percent discount.

"All the temporary Christmas help had been laid off," she said. "Then all the part-timers, over a period of about two weeks. I asked the manager

---

° Not that Wal-Mart was unique in this regard. At Kmart, 40 percent of workers in 1994 were part-timers and ineligible for health benefits. Part-timers at Wal-Mart could become eligible for health insurance after two years of employment.

† In 1996, 150 Wal-Mart pharmacists filed two suits seeking class action status and trying to force the company to pay all its pharmacists millions of dollars in overtime back pay. Wal-Mart considered the pharmacists to be on salary (meaning no overtime pay); but at the same time, it sent the pharmacists home during slow periods and docked their pay. The suit argued, essentially, that Wal-Mart shouldn't be able to have it both ways: Either it should have paid overtime, or it shouldn't have docked the pay of "salaried" workers during slow periods. The suits were still pending in mid-1998.

if my department would get any layoffs, and he told me all the jobs were safe. The next day, an assistant manager told me I was laid off. . . . when I went to Chris, our store manager, he said, 'I couldn't tell anybody.' "

Hired at $5.50 an hour, she'd gone from working 45 to 48 hours a week setting up the store before it opened, to 40 hours a week after it opened, then down to 28 hours a week. After a few months, she got a raise—the biggest allowed—of 35 cents an hour. The meagerness of the raise irked her a bit, but Botelho liked working at Wal-Mart; she liked the people around her, and she bought solidly into the company philosophy. Underlying her views, though, was a pragmatism that was becoming increasingly common as Wal-Mart expanded into new territories.

"It was a fun place to work," she said.

> There were lots of things. On Fridays, we'd run silly contests, or have themes for employees to dress up. They tried to keep the morale up the best they could—knowing they couldn't or wouldn't compensate you with more money. But as much as I really loved the environment, financially, I felt I was really wasting my time.
>
> They talked to me about becoming an assistant manager. But the first thing you have to do is relocate, and I didn't want to do that. They promote from within the company, but you have to hit the road. They can move you as often as every six months—uproot you to a different state—or at most every two years. You have to have a certain attitude to be able to deal with that.
>
> They talk about how much money they match to give away for charity. There's always bake sales, and on Friday you could pay a buck to dress down, and the money went to whatever cause people voted in. If you raised $200, the company would match it. We gave money to a women's center and to a family burned out of their home. . . . That's great.
>
> But when you're a single parent, with a two-year-old son, $6 an hour doesn't get you very far.

Botelho said she wouldn't reapply there. "The people laid off were all told that, at a future date, we should reapply. But you have to go through the drug test again, and start out at base pay again." She figured there had to be better jobs out there somewhere.

This was the problem Wal-Mart executives faced: It wasn't that it was hard to find workers; economic times were tough enough through much of the early '90s that anytime a Wal-Mart opened, far more people lined up to apply than there were jobs available. But, games and stunts and silliness aside, once the promise faded that by sticking around and buying stock a worker could cash in big, all that was left was another near-minimum-wage job with no long-term security.

In such an environment, there were, of course, individual managers who through force of personality could inspire enough devotion—or fear—to make their store hum. But then, many couldn't. And managers moved so often that it was hard for even the best of them to establish any kind of legacy.

One Wal-Mart director, a long-time confidante of Sam Walton's, noted with distress that the company culture didn't seem to be taking hold as strongly among new hires. On regular trips to stores around the country, he noticed more and more restrooms that hadn't been properly cleaned. He watched employees walking repeatedly past spilled merchandise without picking it up. Sam Walton's rule that associates should smile and greet any customer who came within 10 feet—So help me Sam—seemed to have been forgotten. This was true even at the shiny new Wal-Mart supercenter in Bentonville itself, just a few hundred yards from headquarters. "These may seem like minor things, but they all relate to whether customers come back," he said. He fired off memos to Glass, as he once had to Walton. But the problems seemed to keep recurring.

It wasn't that easy. Obsessed with getting enough growth to get the stock price back up, Glass and Soderquist and the other executives were focused on pushing hard to roll out the supercenters as fast as possible, in most cases by going back and expanding or replacing existing Wal-Mart stores. Glass also turned increasingly beyond the United States, convinced that within a few years, Wal-Mart would have to look for most of its growth overseas. Glass had his own ambitious long-term goal for Wal-Mart: $300 billion a year in sales. The only way to get there would be to dominate the grocery business the way Wal-Mart dominated discount retailing and to make Wal-Mart's formula work abroad.

Wal-Mart had invaded Mexico in late 1991, in a joint venture with a big Mexican retailer, Cifra S.A. It went into Puerto Rico in 1992 and into Canada in early 1994. It then opened a short-lived joint venture in Hong Kong that fall and opened its first stores in Argentina and Brazil in 1995. In 1996, it opened its first stores in Indonesia and in mainland China, in Shenzen. Glass had his highest hopes for the Chinese market, where, despite the treacherous political currents, economic development was picking up and there were a billion potential customers waiting to be plucked.

By 1996, Wal-Mart's sales outside the United States reached $3 billion a year; but profits were still a dream. Wal-Mart was engaged in ruthless price wars against the venerable Hudson's Bay Co. in Canada, against the French giant Carrefour in Argentina and Brazil, and against a slew of rival Mexican and American retailers in Mexico. Except in Canada, Wal-Mart abroad didn't have the mighty distribution muscle and efficiency that made it so fearsome in the United States. Shortly after it went into Argentina, for instance, it was abandoned by 11 major suppliers there, under pressure from their biggest customer, Carrefour. This wasn't like waltzing into small towns in Tennessee or Texas: Cultivating customers and building distribution networks abroad turned out to be a tough, slow job. There were thousands of tiny details to master—most Mexicans, for example, won't buy cuts of meat pre-wrapped, as Americans do; they prefer having a butcher cut it on the spot—and Wal-Mart executives parachuting into these operations didn't always listen to their local partners until they had learned the hard way that, for example, having no butcher on staff meant no meat sales. Glass, though, put up with the losses, because he believed that eventually Wal-Mart would prevail—and, after all, where else could he find big new markets?

He was confident enough to spend $1.2 billion in mid-1997 to buy a majority stake in Cifra, Wal-Mart's partner in Mexico, and to move into Germany at the end of that year by buying a 21-store hypermart chain there, Wertkauf GmbH. By then, sales from Wal-Mart's international operations topped $5 billion a year and were beginning to turn a small profit.

In another effort to boost the stock price, Wal-Mart executives spent more than $2 billion to buy back shares of its stock; the board also sweetened the dividend, a tacit admission that they had to make some concessions to attract shareholders now that growth was slowing down.

Meanwhile, in Wal-Mart's U.S. stores, worker discontent was building. In 1994, the company faced organizing efforts at four stores—in all cases, not because of any effort on the part of unions but because unhappy workers tried to take matters into their own hands.

Four out of some 2,600 stores and warehouse clubs may seem paltry; but consider the degree of discontent it takes to push workers to risk their jobs by organizing—and the fact that this was more organizing efforts than Wal-Mart had faced in the previous five years put together. At how many other stores were workers gradually reaching a slow simmer?

Some of these new workers weren't as scared of the consequences as in years past. Ann Bertelli, a thirty-five-year-old photo-finishing clerk at a

Wal-Mart store in Walpole, Massachusetts, didn't hesitate to contact the UFCW after she was harassed by a supervisor. "We're going to unionize this store if it kills us," she declared in late 1994, to the *Wall Street Journal.* Asked if she wasn't worried about losing her job, she laughed. "If they fire me, I don't care," she said. "They only pay me $6 an hour. I can get a job anywhere for that money." Once she was fired, Bertelli immediately filed a complaint with the National Labor Relations Board and then took the company to court.*

Wal-Mart managers were still as determined as ever to keep unions at bay—and as heavy-handed as ever about how they did it, as Linda Regalado, a sales clerk at the company's Hinsdale, New Hampshire, store discovered. Regalado, thirty-four, had grown up in Brooklyn and Miami, the oldest of four children. Her father had owned his own small business, a print shop. When she began working for Wal-Mart in 1991, in Florida, she was on her second marriage and had five children. Before Wal-Mart, she'd been working as a secretary at a school for handicapped adults, where her husband Gilbert was a teacher.

When a Wal-Mart store opened nearby, she decided to try it. Hired on as a sales clerk, she did well enough to be promoted to department manager in little more than a month. When her manager told her she'd have a better chance at further promotions if she was willing to move to New England, she convinced the family to pull up stakes and head north. She had to pay her own moving costs, though Wal-Mart did provide her with a hotel room until the family was settled.

Her new job called for her to help with training in various stores, so she spent weeks at a time on the road in her 1985 Dodge Colt, putting in lots of overtime. She didn't mind too much, figuring it was just a temporary arrangement until the right position opened up in a store. The overtime pay was helpful anyway, what with the large family to support. And soon, in fact, both she and her husband were able to get jobs working in the same store, in Hinsdale.

That's where her troubles began. A small group of workers at the store began talking about organizing. But most of them were too scared of losing their jobs to take the step of actually contacting the union—so Regalado, who was sympathetic to the idea, phoned a local UFCW chapter herself. Dan Clifford, the union agent who took the call, actually tried to talk Regalado out of trying to organize the store. Clifford knew how tough it would

---

* After three years in court, Bertelli decided to drop the case in late 1997.

be, and after chatting with Regalado, wasn't at all convinced there was a big enough core of workers committed to organizing to make a push worthwhile.

Still, Regalado was insistent, so he agreed to help. Wal-Mart disputes what happened next. However, according to a petition filed by the National Labor Relations Board seeking a federal court injunction against Wal-Mart, and according to Regalado: Soon word got around the store; and one day in late February 1994 an assistant store manager, Michelle Devoe, asked Regalado to go for a ride with her. "We know what you're doing," Devoe said, with little preamble. She said that she'd heard about the organizing effort. If Regalado would agree to drop the union push, they'd give her a promotion and a raise, Devoe said.[1] Regalado said no.

A few days later, Wal-Mart's district manager came to the store and pulled Regalado aside for a meeting. He, too, promised her a promotion if she'd stop trying to organize, but again she refused. So the store's manager, Erick Wickland, tried the stick instead of the carrot. Confronting her in the parking lot a few days later, apparently convinced she was loitering there to hand out union information or meet with other workers, Wickland ordered her to leave and threatened to fire her if she had any more contact with the UFCW. The next day, unsure if she'd been fired or not, Regalado talked to the district manager, Joe Woods; when she brought up the possibility of complaining to the National Labor Relations Board, Woods told her that if she even mentioned the NLRB or the union again, she'd be canned.

Still, Regalado stuck it out through a series of harassments. Wickland ordered her to sign a statement saying she wouldn't talk with other workers, on or off the clock, about Wal-Mart's policies or benefits or any other work-related issues. Other workers at the store were ordered not to socialize with Regalado, and she was ordered not to talk to or socialize with them. Another new rule: She couldn't receive any personal phone calls at work. She was transferred to a new job, file clerk, where she would have fewer opportunities to talk to other workers—and then she was told that either she or her husband would have to be demoted or transferred again so that they wouldn't be in the same department. Finally, when she still wouldn't give in, she was fired.

When Regalado applied for unemployment benefits, Wal-Mart attorneys contested her claim, saying she'd been fired not for organizing, but for using foul language. Wal-Mart denied any mistreatment of Regalado. At the same time, they demanded she turn over the names of any other workers who'd been involved in organizing. She refused. Wal-Mart also subpoenaed the UFCW to get the names, again without any luck. The union filed an NLRB complaint on her behalf. "They put her through almost a week of depositions," remembered Clifford, speaking of Wal-Mart's attorneys. After months of wrangling, the NLRB went to federal court that September to get an order forcing Wal-Mart to stop breaking the law, to rehire Regalado, and to pay her back wages. Under the weak federal labor laws, this was about as tough an action as the board could take.

Wal-Mart's attorneys made an offer: Without admitting any wrongdoing, Wal-Mart would pay Regalado $15,000, about one and a half times her back pay from the time she was fired. And the company would put up a notice in the Hinsdale store acknowledging that workers have the right to organize. Regalado, who by this point didn't want in the least to go back to the store, agreed.

The notice went up in the employee lounge, behind two artificial trees that completely blocked it from view. Gilbert Regalado, who was still working there, took pictures and showed them to Clifford, who got an order to move the plants. With that, the Hinsdale organizing campaign, such as it was, died.

Regalado soon discovered that getting another job wasn't that easy. The contretemps had been covered in the local press, and she was tagged as a troublemaker. She certainly couldn't use her managers at Wal-Mart for job references. Meanwhile, Gilbert Regalado was injured while moving a pallet of cardboard in the stockroom; managers tried to talk him out of filing a worker's compensation claim, saying it would push the store over a claims limit and cost the entire staff their safety bonuses for the year, Linda remembers. At first, he waited, but his doctor said he needed surgery on the injured leg to avoid further damage. Wal-Mart contested his claim; the Regalados hired an attorney and again got a settlement, this time to cover Gilbert's medical costs. At that point, he quit.

"We figured maybe it was time to go someplace no one knew who I was," said Linda Regalado, at the time. "I'm just trying to put it all behind me." Through a sympathetic stranger, who'd heard about their case, they found work caretaking a rural estate in northern Minnesota, near the Canadian border.

What's notable about Regalado's case is that she was offered a carrot at all. More commonly, Wal-Mart was much more abrupt. In September of 1993, for example, Wal-Mart raised the wages in its Minneapolis-area stores to attract more job applicants—except for one store in the suburb of Hastings. Workers there were miffed—not understanding why every other store in town but theirs was getting a pay hike. So when workers there decided to ask for raises, too, one department manager, Kathleen Baker, drafted a letter on her own time, which 80 workers at the store signed. When the store manager heard about it, Baker was fired on the spot. The store manager wrote on her termination papers that she was fired for "negatively affecting team concept and store performance . . . misuse of Company Payroll (gathering signatures while clocked) . . . and use [of] Company Assets (typewriter) for personal use." "I'd worked there three years," she said. "They told me I was violating the 'open-door' policy and undermining management's authority—how, I don't know.

"I was escorted out the door like I was a common criminal. . . . I didn't know how I was going to tell my husband I'd been fired. I was so upset I had to send him back to empty out my locker."

When she filed for unemployment benefits, Wal-Mart contested her claim, too, saying she'd been fired for misconduct. Baker, too, went to the NLRB, settling, after months of wrangling, for $8,000 in back pay and a clean record.

"I see a big difference in the way we're treated since Sam died," she said, at the time. "They seem to care less about you as an individual and more about the almighty dollar."

Of course, the almighty dollar was exactly why Wal-Mart had become such a retailing juggernaut. Despite everything, Baker went back to the store not long afterward to get her daughter's ears pierced and buy her some earrings. "After all," she said, "they do have the cheapest prices."

From 1994 on, there was a spreading trickle of organizing efforts at stores and clubs in Maryland, California, Massachusetts, Alabama, Wisconsin, and elsewhere. Again and again, taking its usual tough stance, Wal-Mart was able to defeat each unionizing drive.

When Wal-Mart finally got its first unionized store, in 1997, after John Tate had retired, it was in Canada, where labor laws had more teeth. The United Steel Workers of America tried to organize a store in Windsor, Ontario; but, facing the usual stiff countercampaign, including the threat of losing their jobs, most workers voted not to unionize. This time, though, an Ontario court ruled that Wal-Mart had illegally intimidated workers in the days leading up to the vote and ordered the company to recognize the United Steel Workers as representing the workers. Wal-Mart immediately set about organizing a drive to decertify the union,* but in late December, by a nearly three-to-one margin, Windsor workers approved a two-year

---

* That is, to get workers to vote *not* to be represented by the union.

contract—legally forcing Wal-Mart to put off any decertification drive until at least July 1999. Other drives soon began in other Canadian stores.

That same month, as a condition for buying the German hypermart chain Wertkauf, Wal-Mart agreed to keep on board that chain's 4,900 unionized workers. Increasingly, it began to seem only a matter of time before, at some U.S. store, the number of workers willing to vote for a union would reach critical mass.

The further Wal-Mart moved from its small-town, Southern roots, the more workers it ran across who were willing to challenge its paternalistic ways. The workers usually lost, of course; but, like exploding flashbulbs, each successive clash exposed the growing gap between the company's self-described family-like atmosphere and a rather less appealing reality.

One such case was that of Laural Allen and Sam Johnson, two clerks at a Wal-Mart store in Johnstown, New York, who were fired in early 1993 for breaking a company policy that banned married employees from dating. The twenty-three-year-old Allen was indeed married when she and Johnson began going out—though she already had separated from her husband and was in the process of getting a divorce.

New York's attorney general sued Wal-Mart on behalf of the couple, arguing, in essence, that the company couldn't order its employees not to do something perfectly legal—see each other—on their own time. In this kind of situation, one might reasonably argue that Wal-Mart executives were simply upholding traditional family values and trying to protect the sanctity of marriage—as, in fact, some conservative commentators claimed in applauding the company. But that argument became much less persuasive if one looked at the double standard that had long been at work.

Sam Walton himself, of course, had instituted dating rules, perhaps in reaction to his own experience after he broke J.C.Penney's employee-dating ban back in 1941. And he apparently had felt strongly enough about the rules that even Bud Walton had felt obligated to sneak around when he began an affair with a Wal-Mart office worker in the late '70s that eventually led to his divorce from his wife, Audrey.

But even as Wal-Mart was firing Allen and Johnson for their sins, Robert Rhoads, Wal-Mart's general counsel—its chief upholder of the law—was divorcing his pregnant wife, Johnnie, to continue an affair of his own. In an affidavit she filed with the Benton County Chancery Court, Johnnie Rhoads said, "Seven days after our daughter's birth, I discovered that my husband was having an affair and had been having an affair with Lauren Beaman since before he left the marital home. When I confronted him with this fact, he admitted it. I agreed to keep this information secret because he is general counsel with Wal-Mart Stores, Inc., and she was a file clerk in his department when the affair began and . . . it could adversely affect him in his job."

While the New York lawsuit was pending, Wal-Mart changed its dating rule to forbid only supervisors from dating their direct employees. Subsequently, a New York State Supreme Court justice found that Wal-Mart's revised rule was legal. By then, neither Johnson nor Allen wanted to go back to Wal-Mart anyway. Rhoads, who subsequently married Beaman, of course, wasn't fired. Wal-Mart said an outside attorney brought in to investigate "found that there was no violation of Wal-Mart's fraternization policy."*

It wasn't an isolated instance: Court rulings and findings by the Equal Employment Opportunity Commission and various state commissions listed case after case of lower-level workers fired or punished for behavior that managers were allowed to get away with, of women fired or rebuffed after complaining of being sexually harassed by their supervisors, of interracial couples fired for dating when couples of the same race were allowed to break the rules. In one Kentucky case in which Wal-Mart was found guilty of racial discrimination, the state human rights commission found that Wal-Mart had encouraged other employees to spy on a black man and white woman who were dating each other, and that the fired workers were told that customers wouldn't approve of interracial dating. In a Texas case, a white woman was warned by her manager she'd have no future at the company if she continued to date a black man; shortly after she married the man, she was fired. Of course, at any company Wal-Mart's size, there are bound to be some crude, ignorant, or abusive employees that make it into the management ranks. And, like any other large corporation in the '90s, Wal-Mart had stringent written policies against discrimination and sexual harassment. What's more interesting about these cases is the behavior of higher-ups at Wal-Mart once they became aware of the situations—how they often ignored the complaints, how they often acted not to correct the problems, not to oust these troublesome managers and restore the aggrieved employees, but rather to cover up and defend fundamentally indefensible actions, to claim the workers were fired or had left for other reasons, claims that courts and commissions found time and again simply were not credible.†

---

*Neither Rhoads nor other executives would answer questions about Rhoads's affair. The quote is from a May 6, 1998, letter from Martin London, an attorney representing Wal-Mart.
† In some cases, the offending managers eventually were let go; in some others, they were transferred and or demoted.

• • •

By 1997, Wal-Mart, with 728,000 workers, had long since passed General Motors Corp. to become the country's biggest private employer. More significantly, the kind of work offered by Wal-Mart and other discount and category-killer chains—Kmart, Target, Home Depot, Toys "R" Us, and so on—had replaced manufacturing to become the dominant new blue-collar job in the United States.

These were jobs that offered far lower wages, fewer benefits, and less job security than the old manufacturing jobs they replaced. The *Wall Street Journal* offered an instructive comparison by contrasting, in 1997, the typical old unionized GM assembly-line job with the new Wal-Mart service-industry job. The average wage at GM was $19 an hour; at Wal-Mart, $7.50 an hour. With benefits included, the GM worker's compensation jumped to $44 an hour; the Wal-Mart worker's, $10 an hour. Workers at GM didn't have to pay any premium or deductible for their health care plan; workers at Wal-Mart paid a third of their plan's premium out of their own pocket, along with a $250 deductible.[2]

The point of this comparison isn't to suggest that Wal-Mart should have been paying its workers $44 an hour (with benefits), but to note what kind of jobs the new service economy offered. At 40 hours a week (which would be on the high end for most Wal-Mart workers), that $7.50 average hourly wage worked out to $15,600 a year—coincidentally, the government's poverty level for a family of four.[3]

Wal-Mart had become a mirror for the new American workplace: By Wal-Mart's "full-time" worker standard of 28 hours a week, roughly a third of its employees were part-timers, about average for the retail industry. Federal employment figures—using the traditional 40-hour week—showed that more than 30 percent of American workers held only part-time or temporary jobs.

Wal-Mart and other discount chains still offered workers without a college education or post-graduate degree the chance to advance in business. In 1997, 60 percent of Wal-Mart's 30,000 managers and assistant managers had once been hourly workers, the company said. One of these ladder-climbers was Michael Quinn, who began working at a Wal-Mart store part-time, while he was in high school, as a clerk and bathroom cleaner. He dropped out of college to work full-time, became an assistant manager at nineteen, and was given his own store to manage at twenty-three. By the time he was twenty-five, still with no college degree, he was making about

$75,000 a year managing a store in Greenwood, Mississippi, with more than 200 employees and $22 million a year in sales.

"My parents used to say I made a big mistake dropping out of college. They don't say that anymore," he said.[4]

Of course, Wal-Mart and other chains also recruited at colleges and graduate schools with great success. Randy Rients stunned his friends when, after getting a master's degree in economics from Cambridge University, he turned down an offer from an investment-banking firm to become an assistant manager at a Target store. But by the time he was twenty-nine, he was making more than $100,000 a year managing a supercenter store with more than 400 employees. Target gave its management college-recruit trainees their own stores to manage in as little as three years, about par for discounters. All the chains raided each other for managers, too, adding to the opportunities. Rients, for example, said he'd been called at home by Wal-Mart and two other chains trolling for recruits.

Back when Sam Walton began as a Ben Franklin franchisee just after World War II, he'd followed all the dictums from headquarters—what to carry, how to display it, how to keep track of sales, etc.—that had enabled him, with little experience, to run a retailing business successfully. By the 1990s, store-management jobs were infinitely more specialized, but the principle was the same: Headquarters kept the books, did the buying, set the prices, created the advertising, sent orders as to how to display the goods, and so on. The job was considerably simpler than running an equivalent business on one's own, which was why such young and relatively inexperienced managers could do so well. They simply had to be smart, ready to learn, and willing to work the long hours that always had characterized retail—anywhere from 60 to 80 hours a week. And they had to be willing to pick up and move at the company's whim. Quinn, for example, moved seven times in eight years, a pretty common track record.

Delivering the numbers meant everything. In a typical televised broadcast from Bentonville one day in August of 1995, Don Bland, a regional vice president, announced that any Wal-Mart store manager who didn't rack up double-digit sales gains for that year was a major-league wimp—an announcement that, doubtless as intended, set Quinn to worrying about whether he was keeping pace. That was one reason there were always opportunities in management: Those who couldn't boost sales and profit would be busted down—as Quinn said happened to two friends of his who were promoted to manager about the same time as him. "The bottom line is, if you don't keep performing, you don't last," he said.[5]

•   •   •

Of course, that managers had to make it count on the bottom line to advance should hardly be surprising. But there were signs, too, that the farther in time Sam Walton's death receded, the less his bottom-line approach was tempered by broader considerations. At any corporation, the subtler nuances of a corporate ideology can be lost after a founder passes on. The ideology can become less adaptable, less flexible. "Companies that succeed by shaving costs can become miserly, and lose their focus," said Danny Miller, a professor of business studies at the École des Hautes Études Commerciales in Montreal. "On the death of the founder, a corporate culture starts to codify that founder's values."

"Rightly or wrongly," he said, there's a tendency for "the repertoire of corporate behavior to narrow."

Walton had tried to prevent that by making openness to change part of Wal-Mart's ideology. But underlying everything else was the fundamental creed of doing whatever it took to cut costs. And that now expressed itself in ways that could be funny, stupefying, or appalling, in the company's treatment both of its employees and of its supposedly sacred customers.

Early one morning in 1992, while restocking shelves on the night shift at a Wal-Mart in Savannah, Georgia, thirty-eight-year-old Annette Bryant, a single mother, collapsed. Neither her co-workers nor the paramedics they called could open the store's locked doors until police drove to an assistant manager's home to get a key. By then it was too late. Bryant died. During the lawsuit brought by her family, it was discovered that Wal-Mart's operating manual called for locking in night-shift workers and for padlocking the fire doors—to prevent "shrinkage." After a federal health and safety investigation, Wal-Mart agreed to change its policy and paid a modest $6,600 fine. A state appeals court ruled that, under workers' compensation laws, Bryant's family couldn't recover any punitive damages beyond the $6,000 in benefits to which she was legally entitled.

One day in 1995, Carla Jones, a twenty-year-old newlywed, was walking to her car in the parking lot of a Wal-Mart store in Searcy, Arkansas, when two men grabbed her, forced her into her own car, drove her off, and then

raped and murdered her. When Jones's family sued Wal-Mart for negli-
gence, it turned out that Wal-Mart had done a study, a few years earlier, of
how to make its lots safer.[6] In an article for *Security Management*, a trade
journal, Wal-Mart vice president David Gorman noted that in 1994 tests,
having uniformed employees in golf carts patrol the parking lots of several
stores had eliminated crime dramatically. At a Tampa, Florida, store with
226 car thefts, 25 purse snatchings, 32 burglaries, and 14 armed robberies
in its parking lot in one year, a golf-cart patrol the following year cut crime
to zero. Gorman said the patrols, made in golf carts with flashing lights and
two-way radios, cost as much as $45,000 a year per store, but helped busi-
ness by encouraging people to shop at night.

By the late '90s, parking-lot safety was becoming more of an issue as
Wal-Mart switched more of its stores to being open 24 hours a day. But, apparently because of the costs, Wal-Mart limited golf-cart patrols to one
store in 11 in 1996.

As far as legal liability, that was a toss-up. Different courts had come to
opposite conclusions as to whether Wal-Mart and other retailers had any
legal duty to protect customers on their properties from crime. A federal
court in Arkansas dismissed the Jones family's suit, for example, while a
Florida state court awarded $1.5 million to a man shot during a 1993 armed
robbery in the parking lot of a Wal-Mart in Jacksonville.* State courts in
West Virginia and Tennessee also found Wal-Mart could be held liable, in
similar suits.

More revealing was the company's bolt-the-barn-doors-after-the-
horses-have-escaped response. *After* the major crimes, it began golf-cart
patrols at the Searcy and Jacksonville stores. At the same time, in depositions for the Jones case and two others, Wal-Mart managers testified that
they had never asked local police for crime reports or otherwise looked into
how much crime took place on their lots.

One day in 1995, Eric Matthys, a software salesman in St. Charles, Illinois,
bought four new tires at the local Sam's Club for his pickup truck. While
the tires were being put on the truck in the club's service area, he did some
shopping. When he went back to pick up his truck, it turned out that a
Sam's Club employee, who happened to be a heroin addict, had stolen the
truck to strip it for parts he could sell for drugs. By the time police recovered the truck, Matthys's leather jacket, his wife's coat, and his tool box

---

* Both cases were under appeal in early 1998.

were gone, along with the truck's stereo, mirrors, and most of its insides. Matthys had to pay $220 to get what was left towed back.

Matthys, reasonably enough, felt that Wal-Mart should make him whole. One might justifiably suspect that Sam Walton—who advocated tossing in something extra, say a free pair of socks, whenever a customer had to return so much as a defective pair of shoes—wouldn't have balked for a moment at making restitution. But when Matthys called Bentonville, officials there told him Wal-Mart wasn't responsible and refused to give him any compensation—until *Chicago Tribune* columnist Mike Royko etched a scathing account of the whole affair in one of his nationally syndicated columns. At that point, Wal-Mart officials abruptly decided they could compensate Matthys after all.

What linked all these anecdotes was an attitude of penny-pinching myopia that—even aside from any question of right or wrong—led Wal-Mart executives and managers to behave in ways that also hurt the company and its carefully crafted public image.

The obsession of Wal-Mart and Wal-Mart executives with what Kathleen Baker called the almighty dollar posed another problem for David Glass, too—and that was figuring out who to hand the reins to next.

Shortly before he died, Sam Walton had bragged in his autobiography about the terrific generation of hard-charging young Wal-Mart executives poised to succeed Glass and Soderquist. "I know one day they'll put us all to shame," Walton said, naming such burgeoning stars as Bill Fields, Dean Sanders, and Joe Hardin, three young executive vice presidents.[7] But by 1997 when Glass turned sixty-two, all three of them were gone. Sanders had been burned out by all those weekdays on the road, those evenings and weekends away from home, the endless work and pressure. He simply opted to retire comfortably in 1995 at the age of forty-five, to spend more time with his family. The other two men made logical, bottom-line moves, and left for more money elsewhere.

Wal-Mart always had paid its executives relatively modest salaries, but that was especially true in the 1990s, given the vast size of the company. When *Discount Store News,* a trade publication, listed the 50 highest-paid executives in discount retailing for 1996, only two Wal-Mart executives made the cut: Glass, at nineteenth, and Soderquist, at thirty-fifth. Glass's compensation barely topped $1 million, which, by the lofty standards of Fortune 500 companies, was a pittance for a chief executive. Of course, both he and Soderquist had socked away fat nest eggs stuffed with Wal-

Mart stock. And they had held fast to Sam Walton's policy of rewarding executives mostly with stock.

The problem, of course, was that the years-long slump made the stock options being granted to all those mid-level executives a lot less appealing. When Joe Hardin left in 1997, jumping ship to become president and chief executive of Kinko's Inc., the copy-center chain, friends said that the higher pay and potential stock options were as much a factor as the chance to run his own company.

But the one that stunned many at the company was the defection of Bill Fields, who had been Walton's favored protégé among the younger executives, and who had been widely seen as the obvious successor to Glass among the younger generation. Both within Wal-Mart and at its rivals, Fields was considered as perhaps the company's most brilliant merchant since at least Shewmaker.

But when Viacom Corp.'s Blockbuster video division dangled several million dollars and juicy stock options in front of him in 1996, Fields jumped. "He had such a financial package offered he just couldn't refuse it," remembered Nick White, another executive vice president who'd worked with Fields since the early '70s.

When Fields first told Glass he was leaving, Glass thought it was a joke and didn't believe him. Even when Fields told him a second time, Glass seemed to have trouble absorbing what he was hearing.

As it turned out, Fields had about as much impact at Blockbuster as Ron Mayer had had at Ayr-Way two decades earlier. After a shockingly brief stint, he was ousted, shortly landing as chief executive of Hudson's Bay Co., in Canada.

Other executives besides Fields, Hardin, and Sanders also left for bigger opportunities. Of course, there were plenty of other managers ready to move up the ranks to replace them. And, just as Walton had done, Glass hired plenty of talented outsiders, even at the highest levels of the company. From an operational standpoint, Wal-Mart was stronger than ever. Glass and Soderquist hadn't stinted on spending to improve the company's state-of-the-art distribution, information, and communications systems.

The Wal-Mart stores, supercenters, and Sam's Clubs all were racking up solid gains in sales and profits. By 1999, its 730-odd stores in the international division were making a modest profit too, of $551 million on $12.25 billion in sales for the year ended January 31. The company continued spending about $4 billion annually to build, expand or relocate more than 330 stores a year in the United States, mostly supercenters, and to add 50 to 60 new stores a year, of various sorts, overseas.

But increasingly, Wal-Mart focused on growing overseas by snapping up existing retailers that fit into its mold, such as Germany's 21-store Wertkauf hypermarket chain in 1997 and Germany's 74-store Spar Handels chain in 1998. Then, in June 1997, even as fearful European retailers scrambled to consolidate so they could compete with the invading American colossus, Wal-Mart struck again. It foiled the planned merger of two of the largest British retailers, outbidding Kingfisher to snatch away the 229-store British supermarket chain, Asda for $10.8 billion.

Meanwhile, in the United States, Glass had become convinced by mid-1998 that, after years of practice selling perishable food through its supercenters, Wal-Mart and its distribution system were ready to handle an even more direct assault on the $436 billion grocery industry. So he had the company begin testing a new idea: 40,000-square-foot mini-Wal-Mart supermarkets with delis and drive-through pharmacies. Tentatively called "Wal-Mart Food and Drug Express" stores—and quickly dubbed "Small-Marts" by wags—these would be Wal-Mart's version of convenience stores, a way to take on the supermarkets and high-priced convenience stores in places where the company didn't want to build full-sized supercenters. They would be part of Glass's plan to make Wal-Mart the country's biggest grocer, as well as retailer. Even as the test got underway, company revenues continued to expand at a rate that would have Wal-Mart topping $150 billion in sales by the year 2000.

By 1999 Glass—though working hard as ever—increasingly seemed ready to retire. Fulfilling a childhood fantasy of becoming involved in Major League Baseball, he had become interim chairman of the Kansas City Royals after the death of his friend and team owner Ewing Kauffman in 1993.* Widely seen as a potential buyer of the team, Glass had hinted occasionally at his interest in owning the Royals; but in April 1998, on the season's opening day, he reluctantly said he wouldn't buy the team. Though he didn't say so, Glass seemed preoccupied with his one unfinished task at Wal-Mart: finding the right team to carry on and transmit his own version of Sam Walton's legacy.

---

* In 1994 Glass and Wal-Mart director Drayton McClane, owner of the Houston Astros, helped force that year's big-league baseball strike that scrapped the World Series for the first time in more than 90 years. The two men led a contingent of anti-union owners whose hard-line stance on labor costs scuttled efforts to settle a dispute with the players' union. John Helyar gave a vivid account of the events in "Fat Lady Sings: How Fear and Loathing in Baseball Standoff Wrecked the Season" (*Wall Street Journal*, Sept. 15, 1994), p. A1.

Conclusion

What is Sam Walton's legacy?

At Wal-Mart's 1997 annual meeting, Don Soderquist told the multitudes that he believed "Sam is looking down here, and he's very proud."

"We're different from any other company in the world," Soderquist declared to the 17,000 shareholders in the Bud Walton Arena. He spoke longingly of his faith that the company would reach $200 billion a year in sales and become the largest corporation in the United States (at that point, Wal-Mart trailed only General Motors and Exxon in revenue). He waxed ecstatic about the possibilities of retailing over the Internet, and of Wal-Mart's potential to dominate that field, too.

Then he paused, and before launching into a paean to Wal-Mart's charitable giving (lumping in, as usual, "voluntary" contributions from Wal-Mart's vendors), he told the gathering:

"Our company does have a soul."

Only at a company such as Wal-Mart, and only at a gathering such as its annual meeting, with its tent-revival atmosphere, could someone make such a statement with a straight face. And from the applause that greeted Soderquist's claim, it would seem many of the shareholders and workers too would like to believe that Wal-Mart is something more than a money-making machine.

It's an appealing fairy tale. But if anything, the history of the company, especially since Walton's death, provides ample evidence that Wal-Mart, like any corporation, is merely a machine, an amoral construct with one imperative: the profit motive. That pursuing that motive to the utmost may have a corrosive effect on communities or individuals—including people within the corporation—never enters into the equation. The economist Milton Friedman implicitly recognized this inherent problem. Even as he declared that a business's only responsibility is to increase its profits, he said that those profits have to be *justly* obtained. That is to say: Corporations must follow the laws and rules that a society sets up. Of course, societies must act to keep corporate rapacity in check.

Social critic Jerry Mander argues that, like assembly-line workers who must adjust their own pace to the speed of the machine, corporate executives inevitably wind up accommodating their behavior to the corporate profit imperative, regardless of their own moral or ethical beliefs. Those who won't, don't succeed. He offers the example of Warren M. Anderson, the chairman of Union Carbide Corp. In 1986, after the company's chemical plant in Bhopal, India, accidentally released toxic gases that killed more than 2,000 people, Anderson told reporters he would spend the rest of his life trying to make amends and to correct the problems his company had caused. Within a year, though, Anderson was telling *Business Week* that he had overreacted, and was ready to lead the legal fight to minimize the damages or reparations Union Carbide would have to pay. Mander suggests that Anderson—if he wanted to remain chairman—had to set aside his initial reaction and realize that his first obligation wasn't to the victims in Bhopal, but to Union Carbide's shareholders.

On a completely different scale, this argument may help explain how men such as Soderquist, David Glass, and Rob Walton could seem to discount repeated evidence that they sell clothes made by child labor. It might also explain why, at the height of the Kathie Lee flap, executives seemed less focused on countering the child labor charges, or correcting any problems, than on insisting that sales of her lines hadn't dropped.*

A corporation's founder can, by virtue of a certain vision or by force of personality, behave in ways that buck the corporate structure. But it seems exceptionally difficult to institutionalize parts of that vision or those values that conflict with the corporation's primary purpose for being: making profit. James Cash Penney, back in 1913, established as one of what he called his company's golden rules, "To test our every policy, method, and act in this wise: Does it square with what is right and just?" In the 1990s, his photo, and his rules, hung on the walls of Penney offices everywhere—including Penney's buying office in Guatemala, through which goods made by children were being ordered for shipment to Penney stores in the

---

* Wal-Mart declined to provide any actual sales figures to bolster that claim.

United States and elsewhere. Would Penney have thought that selling such goods squared with what is right and just? It didn't matter. His successors' vision was more mundane: to protect the bottom line.

In Walton's case, Wal-Mart seems perfectly to reflect his ultimate intent, which was to create an unparalleled and self-perpetuating retailing machine. Partly by intent, Walton created a company and a corporate culture that mirrored his own nature, building an implacable, driven, and manipulative business that uses cutthroat tactics while operating behind a disarmingly folksy facade.

Early on, Walton set on a course of making Wal-Mart as big as he possibly could, offering the lowest price, and selling more. As his successors navigate that course to its logical conclusion, they only follow Walton's lead in focusing so narrowly on obtaining profits that any other stricture—such as obtaining those profits "justly"—evaporates into the ether.

Back in 1635, in Boston, the General Court of the Commonwealth convicted a Puritan merchant of greed and of defaming God's name, because he sold his goods at a higher profit than the 2 percent maximum allowed by law. The Puritans subscribed to theologian John Calvin's belief that running a profitable business was an honorable way of life and that one's success was an indication of his or her salvation. But, in those days before consumer capitalism, they considered it unseemly to make too much profit.

That changed, of course. And over the next few hundred years, religion became as entwined in the marketplace as every other aspect of American life. Devout Christians such as department store pioneer John Wanamaker (the son of a minister) commercialized holidays such as Christmas and Easter, and borrowed the tools and techniques of religion to evangelize for what became the modern consumer culture.

"Whoever has the power to project a vision of the good life and make it prevail, has the most decisive power of all," says historian William Leach. "In its sheer quest to produce and sell goods cheaply in constantly growing volume and at higher profit levels, American business, after 1890, acquired such power and . . . has kept it ever since."[1]

Perhaps the ultimate value of consumerism as a way of life is choice. Typical general stores of the early and mid-nineteenth century offered a selection of a few hundred goods. By the 1890s, Marshall Field offered Chicago shoppers a choice of 6,000 items. By the 1990s, Wal-Mart supercenters offered shoppers across North America some 100,000 items per store, including different sizes and style of items.

Columnist Richard Reeves a few years ago characterized shopping malls as America's equivalent to churches in Italian villages: the local show-place. "When I was an eastern, elitist reporter on the *New York Times*," he said, "we never stooped to dignify such commercial news as mall-build-ing—only years later did any of us realize we had missed the evolution of a new kind of society defined not by skyscrapers but by parking spaces."[2]

But by making the comparison to churches, Reeves also implies that consumerism displaces other faiths. Wal-Mart is at the heart of that society, the ultimate temple of consumer choice at bargain prices. It is the heir of the earlier giant retailers; and as with its predecessors, it both propels and is carried by consumerism. It would be impossible to separate Sam Wal-ton's influence on our culture from that of retailers such as Penney, Wana-maker, Sears, Wood, Cunningham, and others. But Walton clearly was instrumental in bringing mass retailing to smaller towns on a bigger scale than anyone else. His relentless insistence on efficiency and cost cutting not only brought cheaper goods, but helped drive retailers to seek more and more of those goods overseas. His success with bigger and bigger boxes spawned the category-killer chains that continue to crush smaller busi-nesses and to ensure that every town eventually will have exactly the same selection of books, videos, records, magazines, clothing, food, toys, hard-ware, and everything else, not only from New York to California, but from the Yukon to Tierra del Fuego. He helped create a society in which part-time and temporary jobs are the norm for ever-more workers.

Walton's way of thinking is permeating every part of society. It's there as independent booksellers give way to chain superstores. It's there as giant hospital chains such as Columbia/HCA try to limit medical treatments and push patients out of the hospital sooner in the name of efficiency and cut-ting costs. (Columbia/HCA chairman Richard Scott said he avidly studied Wal-Mart's methods in building what has become the country's largest hos-pital chain.) It's there when a company such as Sara Lee Corp. announces that it is closing or selling most of its factories across the United States so it can save money by contracting out to have its packaged foods and con-sumer goods made overseas.

Walton's way of thinking is so widespread because it makes perfect sense—if one's values are aligned with those of Sam Walton.

But there are alternatives. In Rutland, Vermont, Wal-Mart settled a battle by agreeing not to build a big box on the edge of town but rather to move into the site of a former Kmart store downtown; the store is prof-itable, and Rutland's downtown is thriving. Other communities with strong local planning or zoning laws, too, have managed to ensure that development by Wal-Mart and other giant retailers takes place on the town's terms. By mid-1999, the company began rolling out its smaller 40,000 square-foot stores, redubbed 'Wal-Mart Neighborhood Markets' to get into markets where its giant regular stores and supercenters wouldn't work: metropolitan areas, where land is tight, or very small towns. Of course, the mini-Wal-Mart concept also could be seen as proof that the company was finally coming up with an alternative because so many towns were balking at its sprawl-inducing standard model.

Meanwhile, apparel makers such as The Gap have shown that it's possible to make a good profit while allowing independent inspectors to make sure that clothing is being made by adults under humane conditions in overseas factories. Churches, student groups, and others who campaigned for The Gap to agree to monitoring showed that, just as Charlie Kernaghan insisted, when enough decent people care about such issues, they can make a difference.

In 1990, David Glass told a gathering of retailers in New York City that he expected half of all the retail companies then in existence to be out of business by the year 2000. In the years since, he, Wal-Mart, and similar giant chains have worked hard to make that prediction come true. By 1999, Wal-Mart had more than 3,600 stores on four continents, and there was every reason to believe that it would continue to expand rapidly, both in the United States and abroad. Even at a gradually slowing growth rate. Wal-Mart was on track to become the largest corporation of any kind in the world within another five to ten years. By their very nature as corporate entities, Wal-Mart and its imitators don't consider their impact on small towns or businesses, don't consider questions of social responsibility, or under what conditions the goods they sell are made, except to the extent that they are forced to by outside pressure—by their customers.

When one considers the mind-boggling number of advertisements we are bombarded with from infancy on—how unceasingly we're trained to seek satisfaction through buying more goods and buying them for the best price—it isn't surprising that the average person rarely looks beyond the price tag to ask anything more about what's behind that price. But surely it is worth knowing how that pair of Nike basketball shoes, that Kathie Lee blouse, or that T-shirt from Bangladesh was made.

Sam Walton noted more than once that a shopkeeper's success is entirely up to the customer. That's equally true of a single, small shop on a town square and of a multinational chain with thousands of stores. Whatever the issue—buying American; allowing independent monitors into factories; ending sweatshop conditions and forced and child labor; treating its own workers with dignity and respect; building stores that help rather than hurt a town's sense of community—Wal-Mart, just like that small shop-keeper, ultimately will respond to what the public demands from it. That is to say, to what you demand from it.

It's up to you.

Author's Note

When I first told executives at Wal-Mart that I was writing this book, and asked whether they would be willing to cooperate, they quickly said no. Jay Allen, a vice president, explained that they assumed that any book written about them must be negative. Even putting that aside, he asked, "Why should our busy executives take time away from their work for interviews, unless we have some reason to believe the book will either make our stock price or our sales go up?"

I said I couldn't give them any reason to believe the book would help the company financially.

Although eventually executives at Wal-Mart did cooperate to a limited degree, I could understand their initial reluctance. They had made it quite clear in the past that they were unhappy with some of the stories about Wal-Mart that I had written for the *Wall Street Journal.* And by the time of this conversation, I was familiar enough with Wal-Mart not to be surprised that their response would focus on the bottom line.

I had never been in a Wal-Mart store before I began covering the retail industry for the *Journal* in 1992. Wal-Mart hadn't yet reached the places I'd lived over the previous ten years: New York City, Alaska, and Seattle. Other than having a vague idea that Sam Walton was the richest man in the country, I knew next to nothing about the company, its founder, or Wal-Mart's way of doing business.

But the more I learned about the company, the more convinced I became that there were stories here worth telling. Every generation in this country has had its icon of America Inc., some corporate titan that has dominated the business landscape, woven itself into and then warped the cultural fabric of the nation: Standard Oil, General Motors, Coca-Cola, Microsoft.

And now, Wal-Mart.

As I traveled around the country, and abroad, to report on the company, I kept finding another world behind Wal-Mart's carefully cultivated All-American image. And I kept meeting people for whom Wal-Mart meant something other than bargain prices on underwear and toothpaste.

Some of them were people such as Don Soderquist, Wal-Mart's vice chairman, or Denise Botelho, a clerk at a Wal-Mart in Massachusetts, who both loved working at the company and genuinely felt themselves to be part of the Wal-Mart family.

But they also included workers such as Kathleen Baker of Hastings, Minnesota, who was fired after talking to other workers about asking for a pay raise, and then accused of "misuse" of company time and property for writing a letter on a Wal-Mart typewriter.

These were people such as Mike and Paula Ianuzzo, of Cottage Grove, Oregon, who blamed Wal-Mart for wiping out their photo-shop business in one small town, and were now trying to convince others in their new home to block a proposed Wal-Mart store there.

There were small-business owners such as Rita DeVaney and Linda Brackin of Indianapolis, who won a $7.1-million federal court judgment against Wal-Mart after a jury found that company executives committed civil fraud against the women. Brackin and DeVaney ran a business conducting food demonstrations at stores; Wal-Mart's Sam's Club was a client. But when Wal-Mart executives decided to switch to a rival firm, they first tricked the women into turning over their business records, then gave those records to the other firm and canceled the contract with Brackin and DeVaney. The rival used their records to take over the women's schedules and workers, the jury found. "When I called and asked why they were doing this, they said, 'That's the way Sam's does business.' " DeVaney said.

In Guatemala, there were women such as Flor de Maria Salguedo, a union organizer who spent weeks helping me get into factories and talk to child workers making clothes for Wal-Mart, Kmart, Target, and J.C. Penney. Salguedo, whose husband was murdered years earlier during an organizing drive at a factory in Guatemala City, was herself kidnapped, beaten, and raped shortly after I left Guatemala. It's impossible to know whether, as Salguedo believes, the attack had any connection to the work she was doing. But Salguedo said that as her attackers left, one of them told her, "This is what you get for messing about with foreigners."

After one Wal-Mart annual meeting, in Fayetteville, Arkansas, I had the chance to chat with Bud Walton, Sam's younger brother, about how the company had changed since Sam's death in 1992. Bud worried that the executives were losing sight of how their decisions affected the hundreds of thousands of sales clerks and other frontline workers. But Bud knew exactly how the workers felt, because many of them—even workers who'd never met him—felt comfortable calling him to complain or ask for help. They felt that, like Sam, he would listen, and take care of them.

Encounters such as these led to the book you now hold in your hands.

I never met Sam Walton. As it happens, my experiences with Wal-Mart didn't begin until several months after his death. But everywhere at the company, and far beyond, his presence could be felt even years later.

A Tibetan Buddhist friend of mine, describing his faith's belief in karma and reincarnation, once told me how Tibetans believe that, depending on their past actions, people can come back to other realms besides this one. Some of these realms are more pleasant than ours, some far worse. Among the worst is the realm of the hungry ghosts—a place reminiscent of certain neighborhoods in Dante's Inferno. The hungry ghosts are the reincarnations of people who were covetous or greedy in this life. In the realm of the hungry ghosts, they are constantly ravenous, but can never be satisfied. They despoil and devour everything around them. They consume and consume endlessly and insatiably. It struck me immediately as a metaphor for our own mass consumer culture.

I don't presume to know where Sam Walton wound up after he passed on. But I can't help but think, at times, that his hungry ghost is still with us, in the form of Wal-Mart itself.

Resource List

I invite interested readers to seek current information about the conditions under which the goods they buy are made, and to become involved in efforts to improve working conditions in overseas factories. One of the most effective tools is to contact retailers directly regarding such issues—for example, demanding that to get your business they must allow independent monitoring of factory conditions. For those readers, and for any wishing to becoming involved in controlling development in their areas, here are addresses and contact numbers that should prove useful:

United States

Laogai Research Foundation
Box 361375
Milpitas, CA 95036
(408) 262-0219
Founded by Harry Wu, this group seeks to expose Chinese imports made using forced labor, and to uncover prison factories in China.

National Consumers League
1701 K Street NW
Suite 1200
Washington, DC 20006
(202) 835-3323
A nonprofit consumers organization that runs the Child Labor Coalition, which focuses on domestic and international child-labor issues.

National Labor Committee
275 Seventh Avenue
15th Floor
New York, NY 10001
(212) 242-3002
A nonprofit group that addresses child-labor issues and leads campaigns to
    encourage retailers to allow independent monitoring of factory condi-
    tions.

National Trust for Historic Preservation
1785 Massachusetts Avenue NW
Washington, DC 20036
(202) 673-4000
Addresses community preservation and, through its Main Street Center,
    revitalization of downtown areas.

People of Faith Network
c/o Lafayette Avenue Presbyterian Church
85 South Oxford Street
Brooklyn, NY 11217
(718) 625-2819
A multidenominational network of congregations involved in improving
    labor conditions in sweatshops, among other issues.

Sprawl-Busters Alert
distributed by:
Conservation Law Foundation
62 Summer Street
Boston, MA 02110-1008
(617) 350-0990
A newsletter on sprawl and superstore development, edited by Al Norman.
    Also can provide information and contacts with local groups in and out-
    side of the United States involved in such issues.

U.S./Guatemala Labor Project
333 S. Ashland
Chicago, IL 60607
(312) 262-6502
E-mail: usglep@igc.apc.org
A union-funded project that seeks to improve working conditions and pro-
    tect workers' rights in Guatemala.

Canada

Development & Peace
5633 Rue Cherbrooke Est
Montreal, Quebec H1N 1A3
Canada
(514) 257-8711
A nonprofit group concerned with child labor and related issues.

Corporate Offices

Wal-Mart Stores Inc.
Bentonville, AR 72716-8611
(501) 273-4000
http://www.wal-mart.com
David Glass, president and chief executive officer.

Dayton-Hudson Corp.
777 Nicollet Mall
Minneapolis, MN 55402-2055
(612) 304-0700
Operates Target Stores, Dayton's, Hudson's, Marshall Field, and Mervyn's
    California chains.
Bob Ulrich, chairman and chief executive officer.

Kmart Corp.
3100 West Big Beaver
Troy, MI 48084-3163
(810) 643-1000
http://www.kmart.com
Floyd Hall, chairman, president, and chief executive officer.

Nike Inc.
One Bowerman Drive
Beavertown, OR 97005-6453
(503) 671-6453
Phil Knight, chairman and chief executive officer.

J.C. Penney Co.
PO Box 1001
Dallas, TX 75301-0001
(972) 431-1329
http://www.jcpenney.com
James E. Oesterreicher, chairman and chief executive officer.

Sears, Roebuck & Co.
3333 Beverly Road
Hoffman Estates, IL 60179
(847) 286-2500
Arthur C. Martinez, chairman, president, and chief executive officer.

Acknowledgments

This book would not have been possible without the help of hundreds of people who graciously contributed their time, knowledge, insights, and experiences. To all of them, named and unnamed, I am grateful.

Some individuals central to the story of Wal-Mart and its rivals declined to be interviewed for this book, including Helen, Rob, Jim, John, and Alice Walton; David Glass and Jack Shewmaker at Wal-Mart. Joe Antonini at Kmart declined to be interviewed but answered several questions in writing. Most current executives and directors at Wal-Mart also declined to speak on the record, though many current and former Wal-Mart employees agreed to interviews on the condition they not be named.

I did use material from several interviews with David Glass originally conducted for stories that appeared in the *Wall Street Journal*. Over the course of my research (including research originally done for *Journal* articles), other past and present Wal-Mart employees who agreed to be interviewed on the record include Bud Walton, Donald Soderquist, Nick White, Tom Seay, John Tate, Jay Fitzsimmons, Jay Allen, Don Shinkle, Becky Elliott, Randy Laney, John Lupo, Jane Arend, Dale Ingram, Thomas Jefferson, Claude Harris, Robert E. Thornton, Bob Bogle, Wesley Wright, and Tom L. Harrison, all in Arkansas; and, in other parts of the Wal-Mart empire, Jimmy Wright, Sam Dunn, David Montoya, Larry Havener, Lannie Lee Leavell, Jack Allison, Julia Brown, Gary Benton, Edith Cossey, Connie Burkhead, Kathleen Baker, Thom Starbuck, Dorothy Rudy, Linda Regalado, Sam Johnson, Austin Teutsch, Rosemary Robinson, Denise Botelho, Margaret Rezende, Anne Bertelli, Dora Cook, Cory Constantino, Sonita Gray, Bill Golden, Nancy Ploppert, Phillip Sanders, Rhonda Ericksen, and Jim Peterec.

Former Wal-Mart directors Robert Kahn and James H. Jones also generously shared their experiences and views.

Other friends and associates of Sam Walton or the Walton family who kindly agreed to interviews include George Billingsley, William Enfield, Dean Cannon, Adrian Williamson Jr., Elizabeth Robertson, and architect E. Fay Jones in Arkansas; Burt Stacy and Janna Jae in Oklahoma; Lou Pritchett in South Carolina; and, in Texas, Royce Beall and Dr. Jorge Quesada, Sam Walton's oncologist. Many other friends of various Walton family members spoke on the condition they not be identified.

Harold Hardin and Randall Reid shared their encounters with Alice Walton. Jeanne Remmel Little, in New York, helped fill in details of Wal-Mart's initial public offering.

David Glass's mother, Myrtle Glass, brothers, Richard and Gerald Glass, and sister, Marvalene Gustafson, shared their recollections. Other friends of David Glass who agreed to be interviewed include Joe Duncan and Don Brotherton.

Several people who previously have done research on Sam Walton and Wal-Mart generously shared their insights, including former *Wall Street Journal* reporter Eric Morgenthaler, historian Sandra Vance at Hinds Community College, Danny Miller at the École des Hautes Études Commerciales, in Montreal, Edward Shils at Wharton, and Kurt Petersen at the Orville H. Schell Jr. Center for International Human Rights at Yale Law School. Author Vance Trimble also spoke with me about his research.

Professors Joseph Blasi and Doug Kruse at Rutgers University were extremely helpful in steering me through the complexities of employee stock ownership plans. Stephen Hester, at American Capital Strategies Ltd., also provided aid.

Wall Street analyst Walter Loeb, at Loeb Associates, who has covered Wal-Mart throughout its history as a public company, was particularly helpful. Other analysts and consultants interviewed include Janet Mangano, Donald Spindel, L. Wayne Hood, Jeffrey Edelman, Burt R. Flickinger III, Michael Exstein, and Gaspar Quijano Paredes.

Discount pioneer Sol Price, in San Diego, shared his encounters with Sam Walton. Others in the industry interviewed on various retailing practices include Jim Davine and Gail Dorn at Target, Ken Russo and Barbara Bierman at Penney, and Guy Epstein at Third Generation Inc. Tom Quinn, from Procter & Gamble, also was helpful, as was William Buettner, at Antonoff Miller Properties.

On the subject of their lawsuit against Wal-Mart, I spoke with Rita DeVaney and Linda Brackin, attorneys Lee McNeely and George W. Hopper, and several of the jurors on the case.

Many people inside Wal-Mart were helpful on the subject of Wal-Mart's relations with workers, and its efforts to fend off unionization. From the union side, I am particularly indebted to Jeffrey Fiedler at the AFL/CIO and others at FAST who asked not to be named. Other people who were helpful on this topic include Jeff Hermanson and the Reverend Tim Wagner at the International Ladies Garment Workers Union; Teamsters Ron Heath, in Little Rock, Arkansas, and Patrick D. Kelly, in St. Louis, Missouri; Wendell Young III, Nick J. Torpea, Dan Clifford, and Greg Denier at the United Food & Commercial Workers; Liza McBride and Katie D'Urso, at the National Labor Relations Board; and attorney Michael Smrtic, in New York. Traci Angel at the *Mexico Ledger,* Mexico, Missouri, kindly provided historical material on the Wal-Mart store in that town.

On the subject of Wal-Mart's impact on towns, suburbs, and small businesses, I would like to thank Al Norman; Kenneth Stone, at Iowa State University; John Stauber at PR Watch; John Rector at the National Association of Retail Druggists; attorney Matt Adlong, in Conway, Arkansas; developer Deborah George, in Los Angeles; Richard Moe, Constance Beaumont and Kennedy Smith, at the National Historic Trust; and Edward Robb, at the University of Missouri.

Regarding the fight in Ithaca, New York, those interviewed include Paul Glover, Stephanie Marx, Joe Wetmore, Tim Allen, Elizabeth Dissin, Bob Stewart, John Schroeder, Daniel Hoffman, Erica Van Etten, Michael Robinson, Reubin Weiner, and David Kay, among others.

In Steamboat Springs, Colorado, I spoke with Anne Muhme, Charla Palmer, Richard Tremaine, Tom Ross, Anthony B. Letturnich, Robert G. Weiss, Nancy Clapsaddle, Joan Hoffman, Roy Struble, Ken Stratton, and Julie Schwall, among others. Dan Strammiello, in Denver, also provided information.

Glenn Falgoust shared his experiences, starting with the arrival of Wal-Mart in Donaldsonville, Louisiana. In Donaldsonville, Joe Acosta, James E. Abadie, and Charles J. Lemman Jr., also were helpful, as was economist Loren C. Scott at Louisiana State University.

In Lancaster, Pennsylvania, I would like particularly to thank Dawn Rapchin-ski, Don Scanlin, Carol Rettew, Ron Ettelman, Jim and Margie Pape, Mark Hem-lick, Randolph Harris, John Jarvis, and Ron Bailey. Others interviewed include John Blowers, William Crosswell, Mark Stanley, Chris Fortna, Linda McNell, Melvin Martin, Rebecca Huyard, Mahlon and Arlene Stauffer, Tom Rapchinski, John Sprecher, Nancy Hurst, and Clark Stauffer.

In Greenfield, Massachusetts, Wendy Sibbison, Kevin J. O'Neill, and David L. Bete were especially helpful. People interviewed regarding other fights over pro-posed Wal-Mart stores included Spencer Havlick, Carol Goodwin, Linda Convis-sor, Ann Cousins, Bob Trostle, Jordan Yin, Cynthia Heslen, Steve Bradish, Ann Leary, Sylvia Mignon, Arthur Frommer, Shelby Robinson, Alan Wolf, and Alice Doyle, among others. Peter Calthorpe shared his insights on urban design.

On the subject of corporate codes of conduct, child labor, and forced prison labor, I'd like to thank Jeff Fiedler at the AFL/CIO, Charlie Kernaghan and Bar-bara Briggs at the National Labor Committee, Harry Wu at the Laogai Founda-tion, and Stephen Coats and Rhett Doumitt at the U.S./Guatemala Labor Education Project for their unstinting help. Simon Billenness and Stephanie Leighton at Franklin Research & Development, and the Reverend David Dyson, of Lafayette Avenue Presbyterian Church, in Brooklyn, also were helpful.

Kathie Lee Gifford declined to be interviewed, though I did speak to her spokesman, Gary Lewi, at Howard Rubinstein Associates. Others helpful on this subject included Heather Wiley at Amnesty International, Kenneth Klothen at Defense for Children International, Per Engebak at UNICEF, and Sonia Rosen at the Department of Labor, along with others at Labor who asked not to be named. I also spoke with Brian Ross and Rhonda Schwartz at NBC, and former NBC News president Michael Gartner.

Others interviewed included Joe Allen, an activist in Texas, and Ken Wolfe, press secretary for Representative Christopher Smith, along with others who asked not to be identified.

In Guatemala, I received tireless and cheerful assistance from Flor de Maria Salguedo and Rhett Doumitt. I'd like to thank workers Ana Par, Alicia Perez, Blanca Alvarez, Matilda Pop, Leti Iscajoc, Luz Amelda Chimilio, Adela Agustin, Claudia Villanueva, and many others who asked not to be named. Labor leaders interviewed include Pauline Cifuentes, Luis Merida, Byron Morales, Vinicio Hernandez, Sylvia Lilia Escobar, and Rodolfo Robles. José Asencio at J.C. Penney, and economist Werner Ramirez also were helpful.

At Guatemala's Labor Ministry, I spoke with Gladys Annabela Morfin, Mariano Santizo Diaz, Ana Mendoza de Rivera, and Juan Castillo Rodriguez.

Factory owners and managers who agreed to be interviewed include Carlos Arias Macelli, Fernando Kim, Doong Joon Kim, Daniel Triolo, and Michael Patillo. I also spoke with Robert H. Rahn at GHR Industries, Kathryn Connors at Leslie Fay Cos., Jerry Pomar at Next Day, Luisa Fernanda Migoya at Vestex, and Kim Delaney at U.S. AID, among others.

At Kmart, too, many current and former employees and other people associated with the company asked not to be identified. Those who agreed to speak on the record include Marjorie Alfus, Barbara Loren, Larry Parkin, Robert Dewar, Jeanne Golly, David Carlson, Gene D. Hoffman, Michael Wellman, Charles Steinbrueck, Carol Farmer, Reno S. J. Cyr, Thomas Vander Ark, Bruce Quinnell, Michael McClary, Cheryl Hagel, Tom Watkins, and Juan Suberville. I'd also like to thank Anthony Antonini for sharing his recollections of the Antonini family. Other family acquaintances I spoke with asked not to be identified.

I could not possibly have written this book without a generous leave of absence from the *Wall Street Journal*, for which I would like to thank Paul Steiger and the editors at the *Journal*. I'm also indebted to Carolyn Phillips for her help. Reporters Tina Duff and Teri Agins were particularly generous in sharing sources, leads, and suggestions. I'd also like to thank Robert Berner, Alecia Swasy, and Louise Lee for their help.

I'm grateful to my editor at Random House, Jonathan Karp, who was patient, supportive, tough, and a pleasure to work with. I'd also particularly like to thank my agent, Andrew Blauner, who convinced me to do the book in the first place.

While I was doing research in Arkansas, Diane Stull, of Eureka Springs, cheerfully shared her spare bedroom and beer, for which I remain grateful. I likewise relied on the hospitality of Irene Cavanaugh Ruth and Susan Ruth Gasca in Mesa, Arizona, my brother Dan in Oakland, California, and my mother, Ann, sister,

Nancy, and brother-in-law, Joel Wells, in Kansas City. Other members of the Ruth and Ortega families helped greatly with their suggestions and support, for which I thank you all.

Finally, I can't possibly express how deeply indebted I am to my wife for her unselfish and rock-steady support, for her willingness to listen to my gripes, for prodding me when necessary, for helping in a thousand ways big and small, and for inspiring me every step of the way. Thank you.

Notes

Chapter 1

1. This account is based on interviews with Royce Beall, one of Walton's hunting companions on that trip, and with Dr. Jorge Quesada, and in part on an account given by Vance Trimble in his *Sam Walton: The Inside Story of America's Richest Man* (New York: Dutton, 1990). Trimble's account varies from Beall's in saying that Walton was trying to climb into his own trailer and includes the detail of the dog whistle, which Beall didn't remember, but which Quesada said Walton had mentioned. Walter Schiel declined to be interviewed, under, he said, orders from Jim Walton.
2. Sam Walton with John Huey, *Sam Walton, Made in America: My Story* (New York: Doubleday, 1992), p. 258.
3. Walton with Huey, p. 6.
4. Larry W. Gibbs, "What Can We Learn from Sam and Helen Walton?" *Trusts & Estates,* August 1995, p. 60–62.
5. Walton with Huey, p. 6.
6. Walton with Huey, p. 71.
7. Peter Annin, "The Reluctant Chairman," *Newsweek,* May 25, 1992, p. 67.
8. Repeated in *Wal-Mart: A History of Sam Walton's Retail Phenomenon,* by Sandra S. Vance and Roy V. Scott (New York: Twayne Publishers, 1994), p. 98, among others.
9. Jeannette M. Reddish, "People of the Financial World," *Financial World,* Aug. 15, 1976, pp. 28–29.

Chapter 2

1. *Kingfisher Times*, Sept. 5, 1901, as quoted in *Sam Walton: The Inside Story of America's Richest Man* by Vance Trimble (New York: Dutton, 1990), p. 14.
2. Sam Walton with John Huey, *Sam Walton, Made in America: My Story* (New York: Doubleday, 1992), p. 3.
3. Walton with Huey, pp. 4–5.
4. Walton with Huey, p. 11.
5. Walton with Huey, p. 68.
6. "Sam Walton: Bargain Billionaire": on Arts & Entertainment's television program *Biography,* Dec. 2, 1997.
7. "Sam Walton: Bargain Billionaire."
8. Walton with Huey, p. 17.
9. This account comes from Trimble, pp. 41–43.
10. "Sam Walton: Bargain Billionaire."
11. Trimble, p. 43.
12. Walton with Huey, p. 27.
13. Walton with Huey, p. 29.
14. Trimble, p. 50.
15. "Sam Walton: Bargain Billionaire."
16. Walton with Huey, p. 35.
17. Sandra S. Vance and Roy V. Scott, *Wal-Mart: A History of Sam Walton's Retail Phenomenon* (New York: Twayne Publishers, 1994), p. 12.

Chapter 3

1. Alfred D. Chandler Jr., *The Visible Hand* (Cambridge, Mass.: Belknap Press, 1977), p. 213.
2. Richard S. Tedlow, *New and Improved: The Story of Mass Marketing in America* (New York: Basic Books, 1990), p. 272.
3. Cited in Chandler, p. 232, and Tedlow, p. 276.
4. Gordon L. Weil, *Sears, Roebuck, USA* (Briarcliff Manor, N.Y.: Stein & Day, 1977), p. 64.
5. Robert E. Wood, *Mail Order Retailing: Pioneered in Chicago* (New York: Newcomen Society, 1948), p. 9, as cited in Tedlow, p. 297.
6. Frank Farrington, *Meeting Chain Store Competition* (Chicago: Byxbee Publishing, 1922), as cited in Tedlow, p. 217.
7. Quoted in Tedlow, p. 219.
8. As quoted in Tedlow, p. 383.
9. Tedlow, p. 384.
10. Walton with Huey, p. 42.

Chapter 4

1. Vance H. Trimble, *Sam Walton: The Inside Story of America's Richest Man* (New York: Dutton, 1990), p. 100.
2. Sandra S. Vance and Roy V. Scott, *Wal-Mart: A History of Sam Walton's Retail Phenomenon* (New York: Twayne Publishers, 1994), p. 45.
3. Trimble, p. 104–105.
4. Trimble, p. 106.
5. Sam Walton with John Huey, *Sam Walton, Made in America: My Story* (New York: Doubleday, 1992), pp. 50–51.
6. Walton with Huey, p. 50.
7. Trimble, p. 104.
8. Mary Ellen Kelly, "DIY Distribution Set Stage for Growth," *Discount Store News,* Dec. 18, 1989, p. 199.
9. Walton with Huey, p. 48.
10. Walton with Huey, p. 91.
11. Walton with Huey, p. 95.

Chapter 5

1. Sam Walton with John Huey, *Sam Walton, Made in America: My Story* (New York: Doubleday, 1992), p. 110.
2. Walton with Huey, p. 110.
3. Vance Trimble, *Sam Walton: The Inside Story of America's Richest Man* (New York: Dutton, 1990), p. 180.
4. Walton with Huey, p. 149.
5. Walton with Huey, p. 158.
6. Wal-Mart Stores Inc., *1975 Annual Report*, p. 1.
7. *1975 Annual Report*, p. 2.
8. Walton with Huey, pp. 150–151.
9. "Wal-Mart Stores Chief Resigns, Is Succeeded by Company's Founder," *Wall Street Journal,* June 29, 1976, p. 15.
10. Walton with Huey, p. 153.

Chapter 6

1. Harold Seneker, "A Day in the Life of Sam Walton," *Forbes,* December 1, 1977, p. 45.
2. Walton with Huey, p. 127.
3. Walton with Huey, p. 128.
4. Walton with Huey, p. 129.
5. Walton with Huey, p. 120.
6. Austin Teutsch, *The Sam Walton Story: The Retailing of Middle America* (Austin, Texas: Golden Touch Press, 1991), pp. 33–34.

7. Kristy Ely, " 'One of the Good Ones'—Miss Jackie Recalls Early Days," *Wal-Mart World,* May 1990, p. 5.

8. Shewmaker declined to be interviewed. The account of his hiring comes from "Two Wal-Mart Officials Vie for Top Post," by Hank Gilman and Karen Blumenthal, *Wall Street Journal,* July 23, 1986, and also from Trimble, pp. 190–91, and was confirmed by other retired executives at the company.

9. Rhonda Owen, "Wal-Mart Employees Seek Teamsters Union," *Arkansas Democrat,* Oct. 11, 1981.

Chapter 7

1. "Teamsters Make Bid at Local Wal-Mart," *Searcy Daily Citizen,* Oct. 11, 1981, p. 1.

2. Sandra S. Vance and Roy V. Scott, *Wal-Mart: A History of Sam Walton's Retail Phenomenon* (New York: Twayne Publishers, 1994), pp. 30–31.

3. "Kmart 1962–1992: A Historical Overview," *Discount Store News,* Feb. 17, 1992. The account of the Sturges report comes from the same article.

4. David Halberstam, *The Reckoning* (New York: William Morrow & Co., 1986), p. 68.

5. James Howard Kunstler, *The Geography of Nowhere* (New York: Simon & Schuster, 1993), p. 191.

6. Sam Walton with John Huey, *Sam Walton, Made in America: My Story* (New York: Doubleday, 1992), pp. 81, 190.

7. Walton with Huey, p. viii.

8. Charles W. Stevens, "Kmart Stores Try New Look to Invite More Spending," *Wall Street Journal,* Nov. 26, 1980, p. 29.

Chapter 8

1. Sam Walton with John Huey, *Sam Walton, Made in America: My Story* (New York: Doubleday, 1992), p. 214.

2. Walton with Huey, p. 213.

3. Stephen Taub, "Gold Winner, Sam M. Walton of Wal-Mart Stores Takes the Top Prize," *Financial World,* April 15, 1986, p. 31.

4. Hank Gilman and Karen Blumenthal, "Two Wal-Mart Officials Vie for Top Post," *Wall Street Journal,* July 23, 1986.

Chapter 9

1. Sam Walton with John Huey, *Sam Walton, Made in America: My Story* (New York: Doubleday, 1992), p. 80.

2. Cathryn Jakobson, "They Get It for You Wholesale," *New York Times,* Dec. 4, 1988, Sec. VI, p. 24.

3. Jakobson, p. 54.
4. Jakobson, p. 54.
5. Walton with Huey, p. 201.
6. Margaret A. Gilliam, "Wal-Mart Stores Inc.," *Equity Research Report*, First Boston, March 14, 1988, p. 13.

Chapter 10

1. Isadore Barmash, "Kmart's Heir Apparent: Joseph E. Antonini, A Discounter Who Counts on Consumer Research," *New York Times*, Dec. 21, 1986, p. 6F.
2. Barmash, p. 6F.
3. Donald R. Katz, *The Big Store: Inside the Crisis and Revolution at Sears* (New York: Viking, 1987), p. 478.
4. Debra Hazel, "Kmart Launches American Fare," *Chain Store Age Executive* with *Shopping Center Age,* March 1, 1989, p. 16.
5. Tony Lisanti, "Antonini Ushers in a New Era of Risk-taking, Trendsetting," *Discount Store News,* Dec. 17, 1990, p. 51.

Chapter 11

1. Marly Heintz, "City Says No to Wal-Mart," *Donaldsonville Chief,* June 12, 1980, p. 1.
2. "Bonds Voted Down but Wal-Mart Still Coming," Capitol News Service, Feb. 2, 1983.
3. David Halberstam, *The Reckoning* (New York: William Morrow & Co., 1986), p. 680.
4. Joanna Dodder, "City Accuses Wal-Mart of Harassment," *Steamboat Pilot,* March 5, 1987, p. 1A.
5. George Lurie, "Image Is the Issue in Steamboat Springs, Colo.: Town Debates Whether Wal-Mart Fits," *USA Today,* May 26, 1987, p. 5A.
6. Karen Blumenthal, "Arrival of Discounter Tears the Civic Fabric of Small-Town Life," *Wall Street Journal,* April 14, 1987, p. 1.
7. Joanna Dodder, "Taj-Mahal of Wal-Marts Approved," *Steamboat Pilot,* Oct. 20, 1988, p. 1A.
8. "Wal-Mart Avoids Steamboat Springs Fight," Scripps-Howard News Service, April 19, 1989.
9. Sam Walton with John Huey, *Sam Walton, Made in America: My Story* (New York: Doubleday, 1992), p. 182.
10. Thomas Keon, Edward Robb, and Lori Franz, "Effect of Wal-Mart Stores on the Economic Environment of Rural Communities," Business and Public Administration Research Center and College of Business and Public Administration, University of Missouri, 1989, p. 1.

11. Bruce Buursma, "Wal-Mart's Area Debut No Cliché," *Chicago Tribune*, April 2, 1990, p. C1.

Chapter 12

1. Sam Walton with John Huey, *Sam Walton, Made in America: My Story* (New York: Doubleday, 1992), p. 158.
2. Walton with Huey, p. 163.
3. J. B. Ricketson, "6,000 Wal-Mart Faithful Gather," *Arkansas Democrat*, June 6, 1987, p. 1D.
4. Phil Moss, "What It's Like to Work for Wal-Mart," *Business Week Careers*, February 1987, p. 26.
5. Richard Behar, "They Gave Too Much," *Forbes*, Oct. 1, 1984, p. 65.
6. Walton with Huey, p. 240.
7. Mindy Fetterman, "Walton Starting Own Firm," *USA Today*, July 5, 1988, p. 2B.
8. See, e.g., "The Caribbean Clothing Industry: The U.S. and Far East Connections," by Peter Steele (Special Report 1147, *The Economist Intelligence Unit*, October 1988); "The Maquila Revolution in Guatemala," by Kurt Petersen (Orville H. Schell Jr. Center for International Human Rights at Yale Law School, 1992); "Child Labor in the Export Manufacturing Sectors of Central America and Mexico," by Kenneth L. Klothen (TADD International, May 1994); and "By the Sweat and Toil of Children: The Use of Child Labor in American Imports," (U.S. Department of Labor, Report to the Committees on Appropriations, 1994).
9. "Wal-Mart Sells 'Buy American,' Proudly Converts $16M in Textiles," *HFD, The Weekly Home Furnishings Newspaper,* June 30, 1986, p. 10.
10. Michael Barrier, "Walton's Mountain," *Nation's Business*, April 1988.
11. Walton with Huey, p. 241.
12. Marcia Ming, "Retailers Honor Wal-Mart Founder," Gannett News Service, Jan. 1, 1988.

Chapter 13

1. Tim Crane, "Travelin' with Sam!" *Wal-Mart World,* May 1989, p. 38.
2. "Exceeding Our Customer's Expectations," *Wal-Mart World,* August 1989, p. 3.
3. *Wal-Mart Associate Handbook,* July 1991, p. 1.
4. Phil Moss, "What It's Like to Work for Wal-Mart," *Business Week Careers*, Feb. 1987, p. 26.
5. As it turned out, she didn't nail his ass. See *Partners in Power: The Clintons and Their America* by Roger Morris (New York: Henry Holt, 1996), p. 143.
6. The account of the Sears case, along with the quote, are drawn from *Backlash: The Undeclared War Against American Women* by Susan Faludi (New York: Crown, 1991), pp. 378–388.

7. *Wal-Mart World,* June 1989, cited in *Sam Walton: The Inside Story of America's Richest Man* by Vance H. Trimble (New York: Dutton, 1990), p. 153.
8. Catherine A. Dold, "Muddle at the Market," *Audubon,* Sept.-Oct. 1990, p. 120.
9. This account comes from *First in His Class,* by David Maraniss (New York: Simon & Schuster, 1995), pp. 459–460.
10. Les Gilbert, "Wal-Mart Scores and Soars," *HFD, The Weekly Home Furnishings Newspaper,* June 18, 1990, p. 1.

Chapter 14

1. Sam Walton, "Keeping Our Partnership Strong," Message to Associates, *Wal-Mart World,* October 1989, p. 3.
2. Barlow's account and quotes come from "The Ties That Blind?" by Benjamin Weiser, *Washington Post,* Aug. 6, 1995, p. H1.
3. Millfeld Trading Co. Form 10-K, May 10, 1991, as cited in the Independent Shareholders' Proxy Solicitation for the 1992 Annual Meeting of Shareholders of Wal-Mart Stores Inc., May 15, 1992, p. 9.
4. Michelle Dalton, "Puttin' on the Ritz," *Dealerscope Merchandising,* July 1992, p. 1.
5. Janell Blount, "Wal-Mart Firmly Rebuffs Forced-Labor Resolution," *Arkansas Democrat-Gazette,* June 6, 1992, p. 1D.

Chapter 15

1. Charles P. Wallace, "Doing Business: New Shots Fired in Indonesia Wage War," *Los Angeles Times,* Sept. 22, 1992, p. C2.
2. Nena Baker, "The Hidden Hand of Nike," *Portland Oregonian,* Aug. 9, 1992, p. A1.
3. Many of these are detailed in studies published by Human Rights Watch/Americas, such as *Human Rights in Guatemala During President De Leon Carpio's First Year,* June 1994.

Chapter 16

1. "Head Office Systems: Primarily Mainframe-based, but Changing," *Chain Store Age Executive,* June 1993, p. 19A.
2. "Exploring New Worlds," *Discount Store News,* Feb. 17, 1992, p. 99.
3. Karen Blumenthal, "Shopping Clubs Ready for Battle in Texas Market," *Wall Street Journal,* Oct. 24, 1991, p. B1.
4. "Wal-Mart Hits Target Stores' Rebuttal Ads," *Women's Wear Daily,* March 30, 1993, p. 2.
5. Subrata N. Chakravarty, "The Best Laid Plans," *Forbes,* Jan. 3, 1994, p. 44.

6. George White, "Kmart Gets Red Light on Specialty Stock Plan," *Los Angeles Times,* June 4, 1994, p. D1.

7. Christina Duff, "Kmart Weighs Its Options After Defeat by Shareholders of Stock-Sale Proposal," *Wall Street Journal,* June 6, 1994, p. A2.

8. "The Antonini Transcript," *Discount Store News,* April 17, 1995, p. 12, reprinting a March 23, 1995, interview by Bill Bonds on *Bonds Tonight* on WJBK TV, Detroit.

Chapter 17

1. Jacqueline Walsh, "Anti–Wal-Mart Group Mobilizes," *Union-News,* Aug. 20, 1993, p. 1.

2. Constance E. Beaumont, *How Superstore Sprawl Can Harm Communities,* (National Trust for Historic Preservation, 1994), p. 53, quoting "Retailer Calls for Opinion," by Kathleen Cordiero (*Westford Eagle,* July 15, 1993), p. 1.

3. Ken Willis, "Anti–Wal-Mart Group Mulls Westford Pullout," *The Recorder* (Greenfield), Sept. 20, 1993; and "Feisty Yankees Resist Wal-Mart's Drive To Set Up Shop in New England Towns," by Suzanne Alexander (*Wall Street Journal,* Sept. 16, 1993), p. B1.

4. Deposition of Thomas Patrick Seay, Feb. 7, 1996, *Forrest Drive Associates v. Wal-Mart Stores Inc.,* 94 CVS 765.

5. Sophronia Scott Gregory, "They're Up against the Wal," *Time,* Nov. 1, 1993, p. 56.

6. Don E. Shinkle, "PR Measurement is the Answer," *Public Relations Quarterly,* Fall 1994, p. 16.

7. John Stauber and Sheldon Rampton, *Toxic Sludge Is Good for You: Lies, Damn Lies, and the Public Relations Industry* (Monroe, Maine: Common Courage Press, 1995), p. 91.

8. Stauber and Rampton, pp. 91–92. Ms. Whitney didn't respond to repeated requests for an interview.

Chapter 18

1. Genesis 26:15–18, cited in a discussion of the Amish faith in *Amish Society,* John A. Hostetler (Baltimore, Md.: Johns Hopkins University Press, 1980), p. 78.

2. Hostetler, p. 381.

3. From *60 Minutes,* April 30, 1995.

4. Karen Putt, "Donaldsonville, La., One Town's Tale of Wal-Mart," *Elizabethtown Chronicle,* Jan. 5, 1995.

Chapter 19

1. Writer Leah Rosen, in *New York Woman,* as quoted in *1994 Current Biography Yearbook*, p. 211.

2. Kathie Lee Gifford with Jim Jerome, *I Can't Believe I Said That!* (New York: Pocket Books, 1992), p. 45.

3. Gifford with Jerome, p. 73.

4. Gifford with Jerome, p. 103.

5. Gifford with Jerome, p. 123.

6. Gifford with Jerome, p. 124.

7. Gifford with Jerome, p. 181.

8. Bob Herbert, "Sweatshop Beneficiaries," *New York Times,* July 24, 1995, p. 13.

9. As quoted in "A Sweatshop Victory," by Bob Herbert, *New York Times*, Dec. 22, 1995, p. 15.

10. Peter Johnson, "Gifford Decries Allegation Linking Her to Child Labor," *USA Today,* May 2, 1996, p. 3D.

11. Jim Dwyer, "Kathie Lee'll Mend City Sweatshop Ways," *New York Daily News,* May 23, 1996, p. 3.

12. Barry Bearak, "Kathie Lee and the Sweatshop Crusade," *Los Angeles Times,* June 14, 1996, p. A1.

13. "Gifford Speaks Out against Sweatshops," Associated Press, June 1, 1996.

14. Beth J. Harpaz, "Celebrities Trust That Companies Won't Abuse Garment Workers," Associated Press, June 13, 1996.

15. Joyce Barrett and Joanna Ramey, "Sweatshop-Buster Charles Kernaghan: Fashion Hits Its Nader," *Women's Wear Daily,* June 6, 1996, p. 1. The Triangle Shirtwaist Factory fire, in 1911, in New York, killed 146 workers, mostly young girls. Public outrage sparked a series of substantial labor and safety reforms.

16. Charles Kernaghan, "Why I Picked On Kathie Lee & Co.," *New York Daily News,* June 21, 1996, p. 17.

17. Glenn Garvin, "View from the Garment Factory: We *Need* These Jobs," *Miami Herald,* Nov. 30, 1997, p. 1F.

18. Verena Dobnik, "New Gifford Sweatshop Link," Associated Press, Dec. 6, 1997.

19. "Perspiration-Free," (editorial), *Wall Street Journal,* April 16, 1997, p. A18.

Chapter 20

1. The account of Regalado's treatment by Wal-Mart and the Hinsdale store managers is drawn from interviews with Regalado, Clifford, and NLRB investigators, as well as from a complaint filed for Regalado with the NLRB and an NLRB petition filed on her behalf in U.S. district court in New Hampshire. Wal-Mart denied most details of this account, but offered Regalado a settlement to end the matter.

2. Rebecca Blumenstein and Louise Lee, "The Changing Lot of the Hourly Worker," *Wall Street Journal,* Aug. 28, 1997, p. B1.

3. "Federal Minimum Wage Increases to $5.15 an Hour," Associated Press, Sept. 2, 1997. The poverty level figure is for 1995, the latest year available.

4. The accounts of Michael Quinn and Randy Rients are taken from "Sold on the Job—Retailing Chains Offer a Lot of Opportunity, Young Managers Find" by Kevin Helliker (*Wall Street Journal,* Aug. 25, 1995), p. A1.

5. Helliker, p. A10.

6. This anecdote and the figures cited are drawn from "Lots of Trouble: Courts Begin to Award Damages to Victims of Parking-Area Crime" by Louise Lee (*Wall Street Journal,* April 23, 1997), p. A1.

7. Sam Walton with John Huey, *Sam Walton, Made in America: My Story* (New York: Doubleday, 1992), p. viii.

Conclusion

1. William Leach, *Land of Desire* (New York: Vintage Books, 1994), p. xiii.

2. Richard Reeves, "We Are What We Buy," *Travel & Leisure,* Aug. 1990, p. 19.

Bibliography

During the course of my research for this book, I reviewed thousands of articles and transcripts from all manner of publications—far too many to cite here. Individual articles from which quotes or significant material was drawn are cited in the notes. More generally, publications that proved particularly useful included the *Arkansas Democrat, Business Week, Chain Store Age Executive, Discount Store News, Forbes, Fortune,* the *Los Angeles Times,* the *New York Times, Time,* the *Wall Street Journal,* and *Women's Wear Daily.* Other important sources included *Wal-Mart World,* the company's internal newsletter, annual reports, proxy statements, Securities and Exchange Commission filings, and employee manuals and other documents from Wal-Mart, Kmart, Dayton-Hudson, Sears, and other companies. The following books were particularly useful:

Beaumont, Constance E. *How Superstore Sprawl Can Harm Communities.* Washington, D.C.: National Trust for Historic Preservation, 1994.

Benson, Susan Porter. *Counter Cultures—Saleswomen, Managers and Customers in American Department Stores, 1890-1940.* Chicago: University of Illinois Press, 1986.

Blasi, Joseph Raphael, and Douglas Lynn Kruse. *The New Owners.* New York: HarperBusiness, 1991.

Brill, Steven. *The Teamsters.* New York: Simon & Schuster, 1978.

Chandler, Alfred D. Jr. *The Visible Hand—The Managerial Revolution in American Business.* Cambridge, Mass.: Belknap Press, 1977.

Department of Labor. *By the Sweat and Toil of Children: The Use of Child Labor in American Imports.* Washington, D.C.: Bureau of International Labor Affairs, 1994.

The Apparel Industry and Codes of Conduct. Washington, D.C.: Bureau of International Labor Affairs, 1996.

Faludi, Susan. *Backlash: The Undeclared War Against American Women.* New York: Crown, 1991.

Gifford, Kathie Lee, with Jim Jerome. *I Can't Believe I Said That.* New York: Pocket Books, 1992.

Halberstam, David. *The Reckoning.* New York: William Morrow, 1986.

Hood, John. *The Heroic Enterprise.* New York: Free Press, 1996.

Hostetler, John A. *Amish Society.* Baltimore, Md.: Johns Hopkins University Press, 1980.

Human Rights Watch/Americas. *Human Rights in Guatemala During President De Leon Carpio's First Year.* New York: Human Rights Watch, 1994.

Hylton, Thomas. *Save Our Land, Save Our Towns.* Harrisburg, Pa.: Seitz and Seitz, 1995.

Katz, Donald R. *The Big Store.* New York: Viking Penguin, 1987.

Kowinski, William Severini. *The Malling of America: An Inside Look at the Great Consumer Paradise.* New York: William Morrow, 1985.

Kunstler, James Howard. *The Geography of Nowhere.* New York: Simon & Schuster, 1993.

Leach, William. *Land of Desire: Merchants, Power, and the Rise of a New American Culture.* New York: Vintage, 1994.

Mander, Jerry. *In the Absence of the Sacred.* San Francisco: Sierra Club Books, 1991.

Maraniss, David. *First In His Class.* New York: Simon & Schuster, 1995.

Morris, Roger. *Partners in Power: The Clintons and Their America.* New York: Henry Holt, 1996.

Nocera, Joseph. *A Piece of the Action: How the Middle Class Joined the Money Class.* New York: Simon & Schuster, 1994.

Petersen, Kurt. *The Maquiladora Revolution in Guatemala.* New Haven, Conn.: Orville H. Schell Jr. Center for International Human Rights at Yale Law School.

Shils, Edward B. *The Shils Report: Measuring the Economic and Sociological Impact of the Mega-Retail Discount Chains on Small Enterprises in Urban, Suburban and Rural Communities.* Philadelphia: Wharton School, 1997.

Shorris, Earl. *A Nation of Salesmen—The Tyranny of the Market and the Subversion of Culture.* New York: W.W. Norton, 1994.

Stauber, John, and Sheldon Rampton. *Toxic Sludge Is Good for You: Lies, Damn Lies and the Public Relations Industry.* Monroe, Me.: Common Courage Press, 1995.

Strasser, Susan. *Satisfaction Guaranteed: The Making of the American Mass Market.* New York: Pantheon, 1989.

Swasy, Alecia. *Soap Opera: The Inside Story of Procter & Gamble.* New York: Touchstone, 1993.

Tedlow, Richard S. *New and Improved: The Story of Mass Marketing in America.* New York: Basic Books Inc., 1990.

Teutsch, Austin. *The Sam Walton Story.* Austin, Tex.: Golden Touch Press, 1991.

Trimble, Vance H. *Sam Walton: The Inside Story of America's Richest Man.* New York: Dutton, 1990.

Vance, Sandra, and Roy V. Scott. *Wal-Mart: A History of Sam Walton's Retail Phenomenon.* New York: Twayne Publishers, 1994.

Walton, Sam, with John Huey. *Sam Walton, Made in America: My Story.* New York: Doubleday, 1992.

Weil, Gordon L. *Sears, Roebuck, U.S.A.: The Great American Catalog Store and How It Grew.* Briarcliff Manor, N.Y.: Stein and Day, 1977.

Index

ABOUT THE AUTHOR

BOB ORTEGA is a staff writer at the *Wall Street Journal*. He covered Wal-Mart and the retail industry for several years prior to writing this book. He has previously worked as a reporter at the *Seattle Times*, the *Anchorage Times*, and as managing editor of the *Homer* (Alaska) *News*. He has also worked as a television and radio reporter. This is his first book. He lives in Boulder, Colorado, with his wife, Dalyn Ruth.